PASSWORDS TO PARADISE

PASSWORDS TO PARADISE

How Languages Have Re-invented World Religions

NICHOLAS OSTLER

BLOOMSBURY PRESS

NEW YORK · LONDON · OXFORD · NEW DELHI · SYDNEY

Bloomsbury Press
An imprint of Bloomsbury Publishing Plc

1385 Broadway   50 Bedford Square
New York   London
NY 10018   WC1B 3DP
USA   UK

www.bloomsbury.com

BLOOMSBURY and the Diana logo are trademarks of Bloomsbury Publishing Plc

First published 2016
© Nicholas Ostler 2016

        ISBN: HB: 978-1-62040-515-4
               ePub: 978-1-62040-517-8

LIBRARY OF CONGRESS CATALOGING-IN-PUBLICATION DATA
HAS BEEN APPLIED FOR.

2 4 6 8 10 9 7 5 3 1

Typeset by RefineCatch Limited, Bungay, Suffolk
Printed and bound in the U.S.A. by Berryville Graphics Inc., Berryville, Virginia

To find out more about our authors and books visit www.bloomsbury.com. Here you will find extracts, author interviews, details of forthcoming events and the option to sign up for our newsletters.

Bloomsbury books may be purchased for business or promotional use. For information on bulk purchases please contact Macmillan Corporate and Premium Sales Department at specialmarkets@macmillan.com.

For my daughter,

Sophia,

true to her name

Tikaychiyqa

Ñuqaqchá ninkichis kay qhilqasqayta,
mana ñuqaqchu, amawtakunaqmi;
paykuna ari wanq'uyru jina
misk'ichirqanku.

Kay misk'itaqa tikayachirqanku
jamutayninwan wanq'uyrukuna;
qullanan t'ikanmantari chhumqaspa
tikayachirqan.

Ñuqapis ari misk'inta chhumqaspa
qankunaqta ari mikuchillaykis;
maymantaraqmi ñuqa yachakuyman
tikayachiyta?

Kay tikayachiyqa amawtakunaqmi,
mana rikrayqa chhikata phawanchu.
T'ikankunata pallanallaypaq
ch'uspillan kani.

Mikhullaychik ari, yachakuqkuna,
misk'isuptiykiqa yupaychallankis.
Ñuqallapaqqa puchullawanmi
yachakunalla.

Honeycomb

He wrote all this, I hear you say.
No way. The learned scribes,
like bees, have made
the honey in it.

This honey that you taste was wrought
by bees with expertise;
discerning flowers
they brought their harvest.

I forage too, and honey-fed
I try to bring you food.
Were it not so,
What could I offer?

Such honey by the wise alone
is made. I'd never fly
So high; I'm more
a buzzing midget.

If you have thirst, then drink your fill;
these sweets can power your mind.
But just for me
they're too abundant.

Juan de Figueredo[1]

Contents ·

Foreword

For one who grew up in the mid-twentieth century, the attractive power of revealed religions in the present era has come as an utter surprise.

I should make my standpoint clear: I received a Christian education in the Church of England, with thorough attention to the clearer parts of the Bible and occasional access to the ecstatic during Billy Graham's London crusades. At school, without choice, I attended a formal service of worship every day. But ultimately, I was not converted. The spiritual crisis of my mid-teens receded like a fever overcome, and I relapsed, like most of Europe and northern Asia, into nonspirituality. If anything, I found Christianity's spiritual claims both incoherent, and rather arrogant. A little later, I found out that my father—who had sent all his children for a good Christian upbringing—himself lacked faith. Later still, through an inspired birthday present from my wife, I discovered a closer kind of spirit in poetry, myth, and ancient cults of nature. But in the secular society of the West, as much in U.S. universities as European ones, I found that God was no longer a serious issue. Devotion to a creed and regular worship were things of the past. Yet what a past they had given to us Europeans!

Today, however, religions are experiencing a fresh influx of energy and growth in every continent but Europe. The big winners are Buddhism, Christianity, and Islam, precisely the missionary faiths that I discuss in this book. The yearning to belong to a largescale holy community has trumped all other sense—and sensibility.

This curious demographic success of religion makes it clear that its basis is not practical, scientific, or philosophical. Something else is drawing people in, showing that people have other motives for adopting a faith. But if religion is to be taken seriously regardless of reason, and even of ethics, it becomes doubly hard to refute the cults of shame and murder that have recently come to the fore in extreme sects within the ancient missionary faiths. If we must accept respectfully that some find their truth in scriptures, who is to distinguish between texts that are clear, beneficent, and fruitful, and others that are misleading, even disastrous, if taken seriously?

Missionary religion, consciously preached in order to gain converts, is nothing new in the civilized world: it is at least two and a half millennia old and seems to have the means to renew itself, even in a generation when science based on evidence has revealed an almost unimaginable depth in the world's past, and the basis of all terrestrial life in genetic codes. Despite the profundity of these new discoveries, the creeds that missionaries put across are, in many cases, older than the languages that are now used to expound, spread, and celebrate them. (Language change is thus revealed as a faster process than religious change.)

But where do those competing and ever so serious creeds come from?

We cannot study the origin of any religious creed directly. But it occurred to me that a new path to understanding the development of faiths and religious communities might be found in examining how a religion is affected when spread from one language group to another. This is a requirement for any missionary religion that aspires to global status; and all of them do. Each, after all, proposes a universal truth of value to all humanity. Somehow, a faith must retain its charisma as it is recast in the languages of new communities, with no natural limit to this process, as it crosses one linguistic boundary after another.

This book is the result of that investigation. Writing it has not been easy, and it is hard for me to say why. A kind of structure did soon emerge to characterize the various kinds of effects to look for as faiths were converted to new languages. But the faiths themselves resist classification or outlining, each having a very different central message. To this, new doctrines may be added, but each faith refuses any admission that its essence has changed. While the past histories of converted populations, mediated through their linguistic memories, do color their new reality as parts of a global church, it is easier to see the social effects on the community than to be sure of lasting influence on the faith itself.

Still, while humanity holds to a bewildering variety of mother tongues, we can look for those tongues' different resonances in the realm of the spirit. This is, after all, an aspect of human life not constrained by our day-to-day views of the physical and social world. The linguist Benjamin Lee Whorf contended that language conditions thought. If it is true anywhere, it should be true in our spiritual world.

At the same time, spiritual truths are felt to be more profound than anything else we know. And so when expresssing religious claims, diversity comes up against unity: diversity of expression in language reflects the insights derived from people's previous adventures before being converted, while unity of revelation—inevitably delivered by a prophet in a single given language, whether it be Pali, Aramaic, or Arabic—is the fundamental raison d'être of each of the great missionary faiths.

How have missionary faiths solved the paradox in order to present a single, universal truth, yet in so doing, persuade peoples so diverse in their thoughts? Could they, in some cases, have supplemented the unitary original with extra ideas favored by their new congregations? The reader will have to judge.

❦

I owe many debts of gratitude for aid received in this quest over at least five years. The first germ of the idea came from my colleague in the Foundation for Endangered Languages, the computational linguist Steven Krauwer. Since the early days when the project was known as *Swords of Faith*, it has been discussed first with my agent, Natasha Fairweather, and later with publisher George Gibson, and has certainly benefited from their tempering fire and formative hammering, not to mention the occasional dousing in cold water. The steady, encouraging faith of my wife, Jane, and of my daughter, Sophia, have also sustained me, as the chapters took shape and the swords were drawn from the stone.

My eager, but far from comprehensive, learning on the far-flung domains of Maharaja, Pope, Patriarch, Tsar, Caliph, and Catholic King have come to me from many teachers at Tonbridge, Oxford, and in Cambridge, Massachusetts: they are too many to recall, but the gratitude is real. I name a few whose generosity has directly helped the text presented here: Michael L. Gordin and Jack Tannous on Greek and Aramaic, Frank Salomon and Sabine Hyland on Spanish, Stella González de Pérez and Facundo Saravia on Chibcha, Lenka Zajícová and Marcos Gunzu on Guaraní, José Bessa and Eduardo de Almeida Navarro on Tupi, Sabine Dedenbach on Quechua, Frauke Sachse on Mayan, and the Very Reverend Dr. Ian Bradley on the Celtic missions.

I also thank Martín Prechtel and Daniel Everett for sharing the insights they gained from living with the Tzutujil and Pirahã peoples and in their languages. They have shown the enlightenment, and indeed fulfilment, that is to be found when indigenous peoples' experiences are given the kind of respect long demanded by the missionary for his own faith. As the movie gangster Brother Orchid discovered, these guys have real class.

Introduction
The Great Bonds of Humanity—Languages and Faiths

Denn, was man auch von der Unzugänglichkeit des Übersetzens sagen mag, so ist und bleibt es doch eine der wichtigsten und würdigsten Geschäfte in dem allgemeinen Weltwesen.

For whatever one may say of the (ultimate) unattainability of Translation, it is and remains nonetheless one of the weightiest and worthiest occupations in the overall Being of the World (i.e., for humanity).

Goethe to Thomas Carlyle, July 20, 1820[1]

SPEECH AND WORSHIP ARE universal activities of people, with unbroken traditions that extend to the very beginnings of our prehistory. As long as there have been men and women, we have talked to one another in symbolic codes of language, and have sought to make our peace with beings not easily seen, but envisioned as powerful agents for our well-being and happiness—or, if they choose, for our ruin.

Languages and cults began as characteristic to small human communities, on a scale of tribes and villages, rather than nations and cities. Tongues and religions were at first, and for many, many millennia, local, not separable from the texture of each particular community's social life—something that was itself self-sufficient, and not dependent on regular and systematic contact with that of others. These communities were at first organized around hunting and gathering, but then were transformed by the inventions of farming and herding, which increased human power and security.

As a result, the scale of human organization grew—agricultural and pastoral but then military and economic: by the last millennium B.C., all around the southern rim of Eurasia, from China to the Mediterranean sea, there had grown up empires of continental scale, a succession of large multilingual and multiethnic states, each one lasting several centuries: Assyria and Babylon, Han China, Maurya India, Achaemenid Persia, the Greek *oikumenē* of Alexander, and as a late—but particularly long-lasting—arrival, the *imperium* of Rome. Though centered far to the west in a European peninsula, Rome established control for a full millennium over western Asia and Egypt.

And beside the military power that they wielded, all these empires were also linked into a network of trade. It was the first—halting and incomplete—globalization.

In this age—identified as "Axial" by the philosopher Karl Jaspers, and lasting approximately from 800 to 200 B.C.—the large scale of political and commercial organization seems to have inspired a higher level of religious aspiration. All over, prophets and wise men arose, each claiming a new and better religious or ethical vision, one that was not just addressed to the ruling class, or the empire's founding races, but one that was truly universal, giving a spiritual guideline for the whole world.

In previous millennia, the great Amon-Ra had been the light of Egypt; the lord Marduk had been a warrior god for Babylon. Now in Persia Zarathushtra saw the whole universe as a struggle between Ahura Mazda and Ahriman, Good and Evil, with an imperative for everyone to choose sides. Confucius in China discerned general principles of ethical behavior that should govern every level from the royal court to the humblest household. Yet these paths of righteousness never succeeded in spreading far outside the culture-zones of Iran and China.

In the fifth century B.C., however, in the Himalayan foothills and plains of the Ganges, the sage Gautama achieved an enlightenment, as *Buddha*, "the awoken one," which offered the potential to lead all people everywhere out of suffering. Perhaps because empires in this area proved so unstable, Buddhism was never associated with any political loyalty. Carried largely by merchants, this road to virtue would spread its charm far beyond north India, to become the principal light of Asia in all directions, especially strong in Afghanistan, China, Tibet, Mongolia, Sri Lanka, Burma, and Japan.

Rather later, in the first century A.D., and out from among a host of different cults sprouting in the rich city-states of the eastern Mediterranean, arose the worship of the living Christ. This proposed a profoundly ethical path to salvation for all humanity, claiming that the Jewish messiah had arrived, and that he was none other than the Son of God. In the teeth of bitter opposition from the political power, the Roman Empire, Christianity succeeded in spreading itself far beyond the Jewish diaspora from which it started. Three centuries later it succeeded in winning a place as the established faith of the empire itself—the seeds of ultimate triumph throughout Europe. But there was a price to pay in chances for its success in the East—where Roman associations were less appreciated.

There were later competitors to Christianity, some partly inspired by it. Manichaeism was at its strongest between the third and seventh centuries, combining some of the themes of Zoroastrianism and Buddhism and attracting acolytes across the Old World from Britain, through North Africa and Persia to China. Ultimately it died out everywhere. Despite its widespread popularity, it had nowhere to put down political roots (except briefly among the Turkic Uyghurs in Central Asia, from 763 to 840).

By contrast Islam, which is traced to the inspired words of the prophet Muḥammad (given to him by God to consummate the prior revelations of Moses and Christ), had an assured political position from the very beginning, and owed its initial meteoric spread to the military and political expansion of the Arabs in the seventh and eighth centuries. That was enough to make it—almost instantly—the faith of princes and warlords from Central Asia to North Africa and Spain. But it spread later for other reasons: to Turks as they infiltrated and subdued these first Muslim states, and then to Indians as Turks conquered them; and also to sub-Saharan Africa, and later Southeast Asia, through the prestige of the Arab and Persian merchants.

These new inspired faiths laid the foundation for the missionary religions that will be the focus of this book. Buddhism, Christianity, and Islam are still thriving today, and each is still actively endeavoring to convert the rest of the world to accept the truth of its revelation, and so become part of it. In this they are unlike many of the other major faiths in our world, such as Judaism or Hinduism, or the religions of the Sikhs, Parsis, or Jains in India, or of the Druze, Yazidis, Mandaeans, or Baha'i in the Middle East: in all these faiths in historical times, belonging has come about not through persuasion and personal choice, but willy-nilly through right of birth.

Practice of a religion presupposes use of a language. Religion as understood in this book requires that there be worship, namely a ritual of conformity to the will of a spirit (not necessarily one with a personal identity—remembering Buddhism). There must also be some element of creed, a set of specific beliefs to which a member of the congregation must subscribe. Each of these requires assent, and possibly repetition, of some propositions that can only be made explicit through use of a language.

Any particular religious practice, then, must be formulated in some language. This applies to the earlier animist religions characteristic of hunter-gatherers and pastoralists, to the large state religions of the early empires that came later, and to the missionary religions that began to be formulated in the Axial Age and afterward.

Any religion will begin life in a particular language. An animist cult of a small community will naturally use the local language, a state religion may use the official language of state or empire (probably the local language of the group who set it up), and a missionary faith will probably adopt the language of its founding prophet—though Christianity, as we shall see, was a major exception to this presumption. So the Mayan cult of Santiago Atitlán in Guatemala uses Tzutujil; the hymns of Zarathushtra are written in the ancient form of Persian known as Avestan; and the revelation and prayers of Islam are written in Arabic.

Religious language, once established, tends to be extremely conservative (though once again, recent Christian practice, especially for evangelical purposes, is exceptionally modern in its form). As a result, it may get out of line with modern usage, and a "holy" form of the language get separately defined. This process has gone very far in Theravāda Buddhism, where Pāli—its ancestral vernacular—is a language in which no one is still fluent. The reverence that is shown to the Vulgate Latin Bible and to the King James version of the English Bible further illustrate this religious conservatism, which has no firm basis in theology, since both of these ancient texts are translations made several centuries after the texts' originals were written down, in Hebrew, Aramaic, and Greek.

If a religion relates to a small community, or indeed a large state that is not seeking converts to it, it may remain unchanged, and content with its expression in the original language. If, however, it is a faith deemed universal, this situation cannot rest: there is a duty on at least some believers—perhaps priests, perhaps just those who volunteer as missionaries, perhaps every believer—to enable access to the faith for those who are outside the current community of the faithful. Ultimately, there is a duty to enable access for anyone in the world—which seems to imply that its linguistic expression, or at least some part of it, must be translated into other languages.*

---

* The implication is only prima facie, because a missionary religion can still have a doctrinal objection to translation of its scriptures. As we shall see in chapter 15, this is the case for Islam, and the Qur'ān in its original Arabic. We shall there explore the status of translations in such a religion. But translations do remain necessary, and have in fact been provided.

The main value of a missionary religion, for those who embrace it, is that it provides a route map for its believers that will lead them to Paradise, a state—or more exactly, a place[2]—of perfect fulfillment or contentment, in this life or some future life. This is something that all missionary religions have in common, regardless of their spiritual basis.

Buddhism shows how a person with dedication, by becoming an *arhat* (literally, "a worthy one"), can achieve *nirvāna* or blissful extinction; in Mahāyāna versions, it also shows how bodhisattvas are actively seeking the salvation of others, and how it is possible for lesser adepts—their dedication expressed through almsgiving, or even verbal formulae—to live long with the enlightened in various *buddha-kṣetrāṇi* "buddha-fields," which are places of bliss. Christianity promises salvation, including resurrection from death and access to God in Paradise.[3] Islam too holds out the reward of the Gardens of Eden (*jannātu ʕadnin*) to the faithful, designating their highest level as *firdaws*, an Arabic transcription of *paradise*, probably in its Akkadian form.[4]

But how to get there? The faithful—or for Buddhism, the enlightened— must listen to the true gospel, have faith in it, read the scriptures to deepen their knowledge and understanding, and, in many cases, utter correct formulae in prayer or meditation, which encapsulate what they believe. All these, whether learning, studying, meditating, or worshipping, involve the use of language. But when the faith is being transmitted beyond its home- land, and its home speech community—as missionary faiths must be—this must be performed in new languages. In a phrase, new Passwords to Paradise must be devised.

This book inquires into whether and how the new languages transformed the original faiths. What happened to the Buddhist dharma when people cultivated it in the languages spoken to the north—Gandhari, Sanskrit, or indeed Chinese? How did the concept of Christ change as he was worshipped by churches that spoke Latin, Aramaic, Coptic, or Armenian? Was special pleading needed to introduce him to the illiterate, rustic nations of Europe, who, speaking Gaelic, Germanic, or Slavic languages, had no experience of Roman urban life? When Spanish friars—in a world first for linguistic science—solved the grammars of the principal languages of the Americas, how did they use their new facility to promote the Christian faith? How could they bridge the vast chasm of unshared history dividing them from these alien peoples' religious concepts, and the words that expressed them?

Finally we look at two more subtle situations: these did not involve converting the faith to new languages, but required believers to come to terms with truth as it was, even couched in languages alien to them. The faithful would need to separate the word of God, expressed with full authority, from what they could directly understand.

First, we examine what happened in the European Reformation: the close connection of religious concept with language medium was sundered. On the one hand, theological research must go to the obscure sources (in Hebrew and Greek), bypassing familiar languages (even Latin itself); on the other, the content of scripture must be thrown open, through translation, into any vernacular. This would not deform the faith but strengthen its roots. (The challenge to Rome, though, and to the Church of the Latin Rite, became permanent.)

Second, we ask how a faith that eschewed translation of its scriptures could yet spread to gain believers in the farthest corners of Asia. Did the faith change despite its linguistic purity? And anyway, why was translation prohibited?

In this book, the interest is all on the influence of language difference, and multiligualism, on these would-be unitary faiths. How has language affected the world's missionary religions?

The reverse influence of religions on languages is not our subject, except occasionally in passing. This story is an easier—and more superficial—tale to tell. In fact, the effect of religions on major lingua francas of the world is easily seen, often conveyed by the names of resulting languages: Buddhist Hybrid Sanskrit, New Testament (and later Patristic) Greek, Syriac Aramaic, Church (or Ecclesiastical) Latin, Old Church Slavonic, Pastoral Quechua, *Maya reducido, Guaraní reducido*[5] are all terms that have some currency, and denote varieties of the languages that were conditioned for religious use. They are endowed with the technical terms they need to represent a faith that may originally have been alien; and they are usually dialects that are kept relatively simple in their use of formal rules, since they were much used by non-native speakers—whether by missionaries learning them in order to preach, or by uneducated converts who were taught the basics of a language in order to pray.

Aspects of a Language

But any language is a vast thing, with many aspects. To examine the influence of a new language on the propagation of a faith, we need a way of pinning these aspects down, and talking about them separately. This classification will be essential to making sense of developments, in missionary situations all over the world. There are five that must be considered.

1. Most obviously, each language—whether of preacher, or of convert—had a **vocabulary**, a set of words, some of them having a technical sense in the religion that might have no equivalent among the converts' language. This is what needed to be directly translated in the context of a conversion.

2. Then, there are the relational elements of languages—lumped together as "**grammar**." Usually, these latter map invisibly from the original language to that of converts; but occasionally there are grammatical incompatibilities, where—at a highly abstract level— there seems to be a mismatch between the categories of the old and new systems. This can be a subtle obstacle to translation.

3. Besides this, since missionary faiths are universally associated with literacy, the receiving languages all had—or they gained—a **written form**, which was used to create some form of (accessible) **scripture**.

4. All languages of converts had a background in old liturgy, and possibly in stated creeds, as they had been before conversion to the new faith. This might be no more than a special phraseology for "deep" ideas; but it might also include reference to spiritual beings and places, which could be carried over somehow as what might be called **heirlooms** in the new faith.

5. Above all, every language gives a sense of solidarity to its speakers. Using the language is the audible and visible token of a language **community**, and in the context of a conversion, this community will need to be reconciled with, and at best integrated into, the community of those faithful to the religion.

These different aspects create a conceptual landscape, the places where use of the new language can create a divergence in the content of the new faith, as it might be embraced by people with perhaps unperceived conceptual baggage from their prior languages.

Words

It is a classic thesis of translation theory that a translator has just three options, when faced with a word where there is no exact equivalence between the source and the target language.[6] The word can simply be borrowed into the new language: this has the advantage of exactness, but the disadvantage that the words may be totally opaque to the target audience. The word can be translated with a calque, a loan translation that explains its meaning, but may seem clumsy and unidiomatic to the audience. Or the word may be replaced with the closest apparent synonym, a "loan-meaning": the result is apparent sense, but the particular sense of the original word is left vague, and the translator can only hope that the context, and further discussion, will make the new sense clearer. If it does not, then the old senses of the word may come to color the concept, and some part of the religion will be affected.

Consider, for example, the concept of "blessing." This idea, expressed in Hebrew by *bārak* (which seems originally to have meant "bend the knee"), was expressed in Greek as a loan-meaning *eulogía* ("well-speaking"), which classically had meant "praise." This was taken up into Latin as a loan translation, *benedictiō* (also "well-speaking"). However, its sense was also conveyed by an unexpected synonym (i.e., a loan-meaning), *signātiō* ("signing"), since concretely, one made the sign of the cross to achieve the effect of blessing.

Across northern Europe, this idea was then conveyed by all the possible routes. In Germany, a borrowing of one of the Latin words, *signāre* (in its verbal form) was turned into German *segnen*, whereas in the British Isles the other Latin word, *benedictio*, was chosen for borrowing, becoming Welsh *bendithion*, Gaelic *beannacht*. In English, a loan-meaning *blédsian* (originally, an old term associated with sacrifice, meaning "to spatter with blood") was pressed into service, because it had become associated with *bliss* (the abstract noun from *blithe*) and hence seemed to mean "to make happy." Meanwhile in the east, the loan-translation approach was adopted (either from Latin or from Greek), giving Slavonic *blago-slovenie* ("well-speaking" again).

Arguably, all of them have come to have the same meaning—e.g., as in Genesis 2:3 "And God blessed the seventh day." But it is clear that many routes have been followed, each with a trail of different nuances. In the event, they all found their way to the same semantic goal. But each could have involved a wrong turn.

Rules and Structures

Whether the grammar of a language can condition the form of a religion has been a matter of some controversy. For this to work, languages must have some parts of their grammatical systems that do not correspond to each other: a religion formulated and pursued in one of these languages is then preached and transmitted to people who speak the other.

It is not enough for one language to have comparable categories that happen to apply differently—for example, one language where tense-marking for past and future is on verbs (as in most European languages), but another where it is on nouns. In such a case, as in the Tupi and Guaraní languages in South America for example, equivalent sentences will be able to be translated into each other. There will be differences, e.g., a different way of talking about planning and frustration—as matters of the will interact with past and future—but this is not beyond the capacity of the less exotic Spanish and Portuguese to translate, if obliquely. As a result, some sophisticated ideas in Christology may even become simpler to express concisely, e.g., *aba-cue-rã* "he who was not to have been a man and then was" and *omano-bae-ran-gue* "he who was to die, but did not." The Tupi- and Guaraní-speaking colonies were run by Jesuits who appreciated these subtleties. But neither colony ever achieved sufficient prestige as Catholic communities for their concepts to flow back into the faith in which their speakers were indoctrinated.

A more radical way in which grammars might differ—which, if it occurs, could be disastrous for religious transmission, and hence relevant to this book—is for a language totally to lack some grammatical category that permeates another language. An example of this has been proposed recently by the American linguist—and former missionary—Daniel Everett.[7] Everett proposes that the Pirahã people (and language) of the Amazonian rain forest lack the power of recursion in their grammar, which means that they do not have subordinate clauses, such as relatives (e.g., *the thing that I keep forgetting is my fishing spear*) or complements (e.g., *she told me that it wasn't important*), and sentences cannot be open-ended in their structure (*here is the great, gray, green, greasy ... river*). But this does not seem to have cognitive consequences. Indeed, he maintains that Pirahã, in a sequence of short sentences, interpreted by their context in discourse, can actually express anything that recursive structures do in English or Portuguese.

However, he also claims—on the strength of twenty years shared experience—that Pirahã people are disinclined to accept stories of a past for which there are no living witnesses. This he calls the "immediacy of experience" principle, and it makes them pretty immune to religious preaching such as is offered by missionaries of world faiths.

It is at least possible that the absence of subordinate structures, which would enable anyone to speak directly about what he or she does or does not believe, would make the point of a creed—a set of propositions that it is virtuous to affirm—difficult to understand. Arguably the relation of people to particular beliefs is fundamental to a faith. Although Everett does not discuss the content of faith, he does say he has learned skepticism about truth itself from his Pirahã friends, preferring as they do simply to think about what works for them.

Conceivably, then, grammatical structures might impose a sort of minimum standard of complexity before a religion can be embraced. Could grammatical properties of a language also impose a constraint on the possible content of a faith? Sometimes the claim is made, for religions outside the major missionary traditions.

Martín Prechtel, an American who lived as a young man for more than two decades after 1970 in the Guatemalan village of Santiago Atitlán, learned the Mayan language Tzutujil as an apprentice and then official shaman [xmēn], rising to the position of *Najb'eey Mam*, "first grandchild," in charge of initiating youth. He recalls:

> One of the secrets of my ability to survive and thrive in Santiago Atitlán was that the Tzutujil language too has no verb *to be*. Tzutujil is a language of carrying and belonging, not a language of being. Without *to be* there is no sense that something is absolutely this or that . . . their lives are not based on absolute states or permanence . . . "Belonging to" is as close to being as the Tzutujil languages gets . . . one cannot say "He is a shaman." One says "The way of tracking belongs to him." . . . In a culture with the verb *to be*, one is always concerned with identity. To determine who you are, you must also determine who you are not. In a culture based on belonging, however, you must bond with others. You are defined by where you stand and whom you stand with. The verb *to be* also reduces a language, taking away its adornment and beauty . . .[8]

There seem to be a number of properties here that Prechtel has experienced as interrelated. The basic property is a grammatical one. In none of the Mayan languages is it possible to use a verb to make copulative statements like "I am your father," "You are a small man," "I am the shaman of this town." Instead, a weak pronominal ending will be added to the noun. In Yucatec Maya, these are, with the pronouns underlined:

A taataj-<u>en</u>	(your father-<u>I</u>),
Chan máak-<u>ech</u>	(small man-<u>you</u>),
U jmeen-il-<u>en</u> le kaaj-a'	(its shaman-who-<u>I</u> the town-here)[9]

In this respect the Mayan languages are like many languages the world over: noun-phrases in copulative sentences can act like predicates, with no explicit verb. (As it happens, both ancient Hebrew and modern Russian are languages totally unrelated—to Mayan, and to each other—that happen to share this property.) But the absence of a verb in these sentences means that they are clumsy and blunt: you cannot, for example, make the same statement in another tense, or easily negate it, without looking for a verb, which will inevitably add something, and change the bluntness of the bare assertion.

This, then, is one property of Mayan languages. They also have a stylistic preference to define people's roles in terms of actions instead of identity statements. In Yucatec, in identifying someone as a doctor, it is more natural to say

Teech ts'ak-ik máak	You the one who cures people

than (the still grammatically correct)

Teech le ts'kyaj-o'	You the doctor.[10]

And another example of this is the example given by Prechtel, where a shaman is identified by what he belongs to.

Thirdly, there is a problem with direct negation. This was hinted at by Prechtel, in claiming: "To determine who you are, you must also determine who you are not." In fact, direct negation is not routine in discourse, and is even impossible with a demonstrative element (meaning *this, that, here,* or *there*), so that when the negative *má'* is prefixed to a sentence that contains such a word, it becomes a strong positive, by some form of irony:

má' hé' kubin-o'	Of course, there she goes!
	(Literally, "There she doesn't go!")[11]

Furthermore, there is no simple way to ask existential questions, or make existential claims, in Mayan languages. Tzeltal, for example, has adopted the extreme solution of borrowing the Spanish verb *hay*, pronounced [ai], which supplies the meaning "there is/are."[12]

ay ha'	There is water.
ay k'in	There is a fiesta under way.
m–ay–uk	There is none.

These gaps in Maya grammar must have posed some problems in getting a straightforward understanding of the missionaries' Catholic catechism, which begins with questions and answers like:

"Tell me, is there a God?"
"Yes, there is."

and

"Are these three persons three gods?"
"No, they are three persons and one God."

Discomfort with explicit statements of existence, and identity, would make Mayan languages unlikely sites for the kind of theology that flourished in the early years of Christianity.* Rather than querying the existence and status of particular named spirits, Mayan thinkers would be more inclined to accept them as characters—defined, if definition be necessary, by what they do, and the bundles they carry, not what they are—and respond to the stories in which they play their parts.

This brings us to Prechtel's last point that "the verb *to be* reduces a language, taking away its adornment and beauty." The explicit equivalences and evaluations that this verb enables us to assert or deny lead the faithful to look for a literal, downright truth, rather than the kind of inspiration that might flow from following a poetic conceit. By contrast, he says, "[The] Holy understands metaphor ... Metaphor is images without the verb *to be*. When you do not have a verb *to be* you can't talk unless you use metaphor."[13]

Writings

Considering the spread of a missionary faith, a significant problem is always how to give the population of converts access to the religion's scriptures.

---

* See especially chapter 5 on Christology as practiced in the east of the Mediterranean.

Although initial approaches must have been based on bilingual explanation—most likely given by preachers, but also perhaps by aspiring converts—sooner or later the new population, if it is being offered equality with the original congregation, would have had to gain access to the documents that are the foundation of the religion.

The proviso that equality be offered is a serious constraint, because it was not always fulfilled, even in propagating religions that claimed to offer a love of God available to all on equal terms. In the propagation of the Christian faith to the Slavs, the decision to put the church service into vernacular Slavic, apparently egalitarian though it was, undercut the motive to translate scripture as a whole.

In some circumstances—notably those of the arrival of European colonists in the Americas—subject populations were denied not only equality, but even any promise or prospect of it. This was mitigated, in theory at least, by the duty placed on Europeans—in the Catholic empires of Spain and Portugal—to bring the conquered peoples to Christian salvation.* But this was a curiously one-sided deal, from an ethical point of view. The Iberian colonists had an obligation to preach (often rather scantily fulfilled). But the colonized had no option to reject the preaching, on any terms at all.

This one-sidedness may be one of the reasons why the kind of written materials offered to the converts by the Spanish and Portuguese were not the Scriptures that were available to the preachers, namely the Holy Bible itself. Instead, "Indians" were presented with *Doctrina* by Spanish and Portuguese in the form of special books, essentially beginners' guides written to explain the faith to new converts. These pedagogical works, written in widely used American vernaculars, did at least contain the minimum "passwords" required for personal salvation—as judged by the church in the Spanish and Portuguese empires. But they were not sufficient to lay down a foundation on which to build an indigenous priesthood.

And yet these cut-down primers remained the only religious manuals that would be translated into the local vernaculars. Indian converts were not allowed even the full texts of the Gospels, let alone the rest of the New

---

* The evangelism of imported slaves was not made a similar obligation for the Spanish and Portuguese states in their colonies. It might have been thought a natural implication of Christianity itself, but until the nineteenth century these slaves were largely considered to have the status of infidel Moors, of long standing in the Middle Ages, who had no right or obligation to receive Christian enlightenment.

Testament, or the Old Testament.* Arguably, this was not a tactic deliberately and specifically to keep the American Indians subordinate: after all, within Catholic Christendom before the eighteenth century, only those educated in Latin—and in receipt of the mature church guidance on how to interpret it—were supposed to have access to the full majesty of the Biblical text. But it played easily into the hands of the European supremacists, sadly both in the laity and the church, who wanted to keep Indians (including mestizos) in their place. The indigenous population were never allowed to join the clergy until well after the abolition of the empires.

But even where equality is allowed, there may be a separate constraint on the development of a new, vernacular scripture. Some faiths—even among the missionary religions—place a prohibition on the translation of the holy text. Islam has been one such. This may act as an effective guard on possible deformation of its content. But it leaves unexplained how those who do not know the original language can yet become converts to the faith.

But in the more usual case, where there is no effective constraint on attempts to reproduce a body of scripture in the vernacular language of the converted population, we can consider how far this new body of scripture might diverge in its message from the original. This divergence was certainly significant when Buddhism was taken north into Central Asia and China. And something like it might have happened in Northern Europe too without the continuing dominance of Latin as the primary language of the faith. As it was, this neutralized in the long term the importance of new scriptural texts written in Germanic languages.

A final threat to scripture, even long after the original conversion, is the possibility that its traditional form may be judged wanting by new generations seeking to deepen their faith. This is what happened to the Latin Bible, known as the Vulgate, when standards of scholarship began to rise in the western Europe of the Reformation, so that a higher source of authority (Hebrew and Greek texts) came to replace it as a criterion for Christian truth. This was, paradoxically, rolled up with a movement to allow greater scriptural access to the public at large, who naturally needed a fresh generation of translations into the vernacular. Thus was the Vulgate simultaneously condemned as both too elitist (for the congregation) and not elite enough (for serious scholars).

---

* The only exception to this was what happened—principally in Franciscan institutions—in the first generation after the Spanish conquest of their American colonies, when some of the Indian students were given instruction in Latin.

Heirlooms

It is widely believed that many Buddhist bodhisattvas—in Mahayana theology, potential Buddhas who are waiting compassionately for the rest of the world to catch up—are, by origin, pagan deities of Greece, Persia, or India in disguise, once upon a time re-dressed in order to reconcile simple converts by allowing them to hang on to their old protectors. Likewise, the ranks of the Christian saints—who may intercede for mere mortals through their special status in heaven after death—are swelled by pre-Christian demigods of the Mediterranean and Europe, and latterly even of the Americas. (The female figures Gwan-yin and the Virgin Mary are often seen as particularly liable to this kind of latter-day recasting.)

If these parts of the old linguistic world persist—imaginary characters that the newly converted do not want to lose—they will inevitably add something to the priorities of the faith that takes them in. Avalokiteśvara had been a particularly compassionate guardian spirit, but a male, as were all the original characters in the Buddhist story (except for the Buddha's mother, Mayā, and wife, Yaśodharā). When he was identified with Gwan-yin, his perceived sex changed, and with it the general presumptions about what it took to be a bodhisattva.

Likewise, when the Virgin Mary of Guadalupe was recognized as a patron saint in Mexico, the Virgin gained new attributes: most immediately her name Guadalupe (originally the Arabic name of a valley in Spain) was reanalyzed to make sense in Nahuatl: *coatla-xopeuh* "serpent crusher." This same personage had—at earlier points in her career—attracted the Greek name *theótokos* "God-bearer" familiar from the cult of the goddess Isis (thus revolutionizing Christology in the Near East); and had been attended in childbirth by the Irish saint and ex-goddess Saint Brigid. (This was perhaps because of her skill with domestic animals, who were present in the stable.) In gratitude for this, Mary had awarded Brigid a saint's day immediately before her own.

Saint Thomas was a historical figure who, we believe, spread the Christian faith quite literally into Central Asia and South India, dying many thousand miles away from Palestine. But he is also identified with a Tupi cultural hero Sumé, who is supposed to have brought the arts of civilization to Brazil. In the *Hêliand*, the Saxon retelling of the Gospels, he is represented as a warlike disciple, who called on his comrade apostles to follow Christ loyally into battle. New Christians need their links with proud moments in their past.

These characters stand out as linking the spiritual comfort that was available to people before and after their conversion to the new globalized missionary religion. Less vivid carryovers can also be found, such as the repertoire of saint's days in the Catholic church that partly reproduced the festivals of Ancient Rome.

And most naturally of all, adopting a new faith may not involve giving up on the phrases in the language that describe heroism. We can isolate phrases in the Mayan creed written in K'iche', describing the passion of Christ, that have a direct resonance in poetry that had recounted the adventures of the Mayan cultural heroes who—like Christ—cheated the Lords of Death of their prey.

All these retained heirlooms serve to color the new faith with details from the old, comforting the faithful and building bridges, without actually denying the new truths. They may, however, have an effect to decorate, extend, or even alter it.

The Speakers as a Group

The strongest feature, present in every language and in every religion, is a sense of community. Both languages and religions are social phenomena, bringing companies of human beings together and forging them as groups. According to the common saw, the family that prays together, stays together. It is equally widely believed—especially in the political discourse of the monolingual—that folk who can talk together are more likely able to live, or at least work, together.* It is certainly true that membership of a faith group, and of a speech community, gives each member an identity, which is re-inforced (usually unconsciously) by every act of worship, every conversation shared, every document successfully read.

Religious communities differ from linguistic ones in that they are more consciously exclusive: it is apostasy—at least in the religions of the Semitic origin—to profess more than one religion, but it is if anything a virtue to boast competence in more than one language. (Buddhists, in general, find it easier to share their practitioners with other faiths.) Nevertheless, it turns out to be a singular, and important, achievement to bring a language group successfully into membership of a faith community.

This is because the members of the group being converted will have to

---

* Though this is not the only social consequence. The goddess Iyatiku of the Acoma people in New Mexico is said to have divided their languages, so that one group would not so easily quarrel with another.

accustom themselves to viewing their own community differently. It was a jolt for the Nahuatl speakers of Mexico, thinking of themselves as defeated Aztecs and still only partially understanding the Spaniards, to start seeing their group identity as compatible with being Christians. Yet it happened, bringing Nahuatl- and Spanish-speaking Mexicans powerfully together in enthusiasm for Mary, both as *Tonantzin* and as *Madre de Dios*, provoked by the publication of tracts in both languages. But time has to pass for identities to change. The change occurred more than a century after the Spanish conquest, although the apparition of the Virgin was then projected back onto an era when the conquest had still been recent.

In an earlier era, the third century A.D., power structures had changed in the Roman Catholic Church when Latin came in from the cold: Latin, the local language of Italy, replaced Greek, first as its working language within the hierarchy, and then as the language used in worship and even theology. This had happened a good ten generations after Paul had first preached the Gospel as an alien creed on the streets of Rome, but no more than a generation before Constantine and Theodosius would convert Christianity into Rome's official faith. Ordinary Romans came to see themselves as Christians; and for this, the faith needed to speak their language.

The Christian faith community had by then spread into the East, changing vernaculars as it went, into Coptic, Ethiopic, Syriac, Armenian, Georgian, even Persian. But rather than resulting in a single church, most of the new churches came to be associated with, even defined by, their vernaculars. Inevitably this process ran ahead of the production of new versions of the Scriptures, but ultimately, they all created canonical texts in their own languages. (It is notable that in Persia, which always contented itself with the Scriptures in Syriac, the church did not ultimately survive.) The new churches remained conscious of their own languages, despite the differences among them. The diversity not only was good for spreading popular understanding, but reinforced a sense of national identity: the kingdoms that accepted the faith (Armenia in 301, Georgia in 317, Ethiopia in 330) were likewise conscious of their linguistic identity, as were the then Roman provinces of Syria and Egypt, not least because Christianity reinvigorated their literate traditions as separate from Greek.*

---

* Coptic, Armenian, and Georgian all owed their writing systems—hence literacy itself in these languages—to Christianity, as did the Goths and Slavs farther west.

And curiously, the linguistic boundaries came to be theological ones, as new ecumenical councils kept redefining the faith—and especially the nature of Christ—in ways that one church or another could not accept.

Radical evangelism (such as was needed to spread the faith in sixth-century Europe, beyond the Mediterranean area) required some ability for preachers to contact pagans in their own languages, since Gaels, Germans, Nords, and Slavs were largely monolingual. The preachers often responded by providing new alphabets and teaching people to read; the use of these alphabets gave the languages a manifest identity that was quite new. One result was that linguistic identity became bound up with religious identity, since the ones who knew what their language was were the newly literate, Christian, populations.

Goths and Slavs, who owed their Christianity ultimately to Greek evangelists from Constantinople, never ceased to associate their linguistic and religious identities, effectively creating new churches, which went on to have quite different fortunes.

But the rest of Europe had been converted by Catholics of the Latin rite, who insisted that the language had greater holiness because it was (parochially) seen as inseparable from Christianity. As a result, any recognition of a linguistic identity for their churches was delayed for a millennium. But with the Reformation of the sixteenth century, individual access to the Scriptures came to be seen as a priority—a right that implied that it must be possible for all to worship, and to study their Bible, in the vernacular. Translations followed, but somehow, this time, the new Protestant churches managed to transcend the identities that might have been given them by the particular languages of their founders. Protestant creeds were not united, and created many different communities; but their divisions, by and large, do not correspond to language: Lutherans do not, in general, speak German, nor Calvinists French.

Outside Christianity, the missionary religions insisted on their social identities—if anything—even more. Buddhism recognized the *sangha*—the community of Buddhist monks—as one of the three jewels of the faith (*triratna*) comparable in importance with the Buddha and the dharma, the founder and the teachings themselves. The *sangha* as such has never been seen as divided formally by region or language, although it is arguable that there is far more diversity in schools of Buddhism than among the profusion of churches of Christianity.

In the ancient region of Gandhara (just south of modern Afghanistan) Buddhists released from the adherence to the Buddha's own language developed a reputation as being close to the merchant community, not least because their monasteries—owing their endowment to rich merchants—were able in return to develop a banking service. It is not just a poetic metaphor that associates Buddhism with "jewels," since the high-value items to which the Buddhists referred in many of their scriptural texts were the stock in trade of their community.

In China, the productive program of translations over several centuries meant that a corpus of religious texts was built up that was in some ways fuller than the Pali (and Sanskrit) originals. This in turn gave Chinese Buddhists the increasing sense that the faith was a religion of their own: with their own set of Buddhist classics in Chinese, they no longer needed to seek enlightenment in India after the heroic exploits of scholars like Xuánzàng. Linguistic achievements therefore gave the Chinese, in particular, a new sense of their identity as Buddhists.

Islam is no exception to the rule that religions deliberately create communities. It insists on the importance of the *ummah*, the community of Muslim faithful. This term, however, has been subject to some ambiguity, since it originally referred to the Arab nation, the whole company of people on earth who speak Arabic. Islam has had the problems of success, in that its faith—which it proclaims to be of universal value—has far outrun the community of Arabs, even though it insists that its revelation, the Qur'ān, is only truly available to those who understand the Arabic language.

It has succeeded in making this paradoxical requirement a reality—to the extent that the *ummah* has now become the community of those who have studied Arabic in order to read the Qur'ān, whether or not they actually speak it; and the differences that do split the *ummah*—as notoriously between Sunni and Shia—are not reducible to differences between language communities, but intersect them all.* This is one of many ways in which Islam is exceptional as a missionary religion.

⊙≻≺⊙

Our viewpoint is that all these languages—and, by extension, the descriptions of religion that they supported—were reconceived as Passwords, proposed for access to spiritual Paradise. The rest of the book explores these languages' historical effects, one by one.

---

* This is true, even if most of the Shia congregation is found in countries where Persian is a familiar language.

CHAPTER I

❦

Scattered Jades
A Mexican Virgin Mary

In chalchuitl, nocamacpa no cōtequi no conchaiaoaia, in niquitoaia in iectlō
cuicatli. Ca amo çā ie isqch ī monemac y, tlaçopille christianoe, ī tipiltzi
S. Iglesia: ca oc oalca in molhuil, in momaceoal . . . intla uel
ticmonemiliztiz in christianoiutl.

The precious jades that I also shape with my lips, that I also have
scattered, that I have uttered, are a fitting song. Not only are all these a
gift for you, beloved son and Christian, you who are a son of the holy
Church; even more are your due . . . if you follow Christianity well as a
way of life . . .

Bernardino de Sahagún: *Psalmodia Christiana*[1]

THE STORY IS ONE of the best known in the early years of Christian
America: how the poor self-effacing Mexican Juan Diego was called by
a mysterious lady to visit the newly appointed bishop of his town, and so
persuaded him to dedicate a chapel to her worship. It is a tale of humble
piety, reinforced through astounding miracles. It also involves a healing, and
so it is as if designed according to the rules of the Roman Catholic Church
to ensure the canonization of poor Juan Diego—which indeed, though much
delayed, came about in 2002.

It is told, in perfect Nahuatl of literary quality, in a tract entitled *Huei tlama-*
huiçoltica "By a Great Miracle," published in 1649, a century after the events
that it recounts ("Ten years after the City of Mexico was conquered, with the
arrows and shields put aside, when there was peace in all the towns . . . the year
1531 . . ."). Although there are—of course—secular doubts as to its historical
truth, there are none as to its sincerity, or its significance in the story of how
Mexico came to accept the Catholic faith from conquistadores.

I

Nican mopohua, motecpana, in quenin yancuican huey tlamahuizoltica monexiti in cenquizca ichpochtli Sancta Maria Dios Inantzin tocihuapillatocatzin, in oncan Tepeyacac, motenehua Guadalupe . . .*

Here is told, is set down in order, how a short time ago the Perfect Virgin *Sancta Maria* Mother of *Dios*, our Queen, miraculously appeared out at Tepeyac, widely known as Guadalupe.

First she caused herself to be seen by a native named Juan Diego, poor but worthy of respect; and then her Precious Image appeared before the recently named *Obispo* Don Fray Juan de Zumárraga.

Juan Diego keeps seeing the Virgin, who gives him a message for the bishop:

"Because I am truly your compassionate mother, yours and of all the people who live together in this land, and of all the other people of different ancestries, my lovers, those who cry to me, those who seek me, those who trust in me . . . Go to the residence of the Bishop of Mexico . . . I very much want him to build me a house here, to erect my temple for me on the plain . . . You will deserve very much the way that I reward your fatigue, your service . . . Now, my dearest son, you have heard my breath, my word: go . . ."

He twice visits the bishop, to endeavor to persuade him of her commands, though he doubts he is the man for the job.

"My dear little Mistress, Lady Queen, my littlest daughter, my dear little girl, . . . I am really a man from the country, I am a rope, I am a backframe, a tail, a wing, a man of no importance; I myself need to be led, to be carried on someone's back . . ."

As he expects, his words do not convince the bishop: he is told he needs to bring a sign.

He said that not simply because of his word would his petition be carried out, would what he asked for happen; that some other sign was

---

* This is Luis Laso de la Vega's original Nahuatl, but having made the point that this is nothing like Spanish, we shall continue with a bare English translation.

very necessary if he was to believe how the Queen of Heaven in person was sending him.

Then his uncle is taken ill. Juan Diego tries to avoid a fourth visit to the Virgin, since he is now under his family's orders to summon a priest to hear his uncle's confession. But she intercepts him.

"What's happening, youngest and dearest of all my sons? Where are you going, where are you headed?"

He remembers his manners, but pleads his family responsibility.

He prostrated himself before her, he greeted her, he said to her: "My little maiden, my youngest daughter, my girl, I hope you are happy; how are you this morning? Does your beloved body feel well, my lady, my girl? Although it grieves me, I will cause your face and your heart anguish: I must tell you, my little girl, that one of your servants, my uncle, is very ill."

The Virgin reassures him that his uncle is already cured. Instead, she directs him to a clump of flowers, blooming at the top of the desolate hill where he had met her first. These he gathers at her behest. He has some difficulty getting past the bishop's doormen with his sign, but when he does (with some miraculous help) and tells his tale, the bishop is immediately convinced: not least because the image of the Virgin is now wondrously inscribed on Juan Diego's garment.

The indigenous words of this story are touching, even in translation: in a few lines of dialogue they characterize Juan's diffidence and the Virgin's motherly kindness. And, as should already be clear even from the translation into English, they are not in the usual style of miracle tales: they feature affectionate backchat between saint and Virgin, all those metaphors and diminutives. They were applied to popularize and propagate the gospel brought by foreigners, to provide a direct example of what Christianity became on the lips, and in the hearts, of Nahuatl speakers.

As such, it goes straight to the heart of conversion in its most central sense. What happens to a faith when it is spread in a new language? How can a language, a medium of thought and communication formed for one way of life, for one worldview, be pressed into service for another, and what does it do to the character of its new message? A universal faith, proffered in new lands to new peoples, must by its nature, and its aspiration, be open to all: but unless it splits, and so fails to grow as a single church, it must somehow bridge the gap between the converts' old ideas and its new synthesis of truth. The converts' language will have to grow—that is clear—to embody the new concepts and ideas that come with the religion of the preachers; but so will the religion, as it absorbs the lifeways of its new believers, hitherto inseparable from their old language.

Catholic Concepts in Nahuatl

The narrative of the *Huei tlamahuiçoltica* makes reference to many Catholic concepts, which needed to find expression in Nahuatl words. By and large, the writer was sparing in his use of vocabulary borrowed directly from Spanish: we only find *lunes* "Monday," *obispo* "bishop," *Dios* "God," *Santa Maria de Guadalupe*, and *Iglesia Mayor* "Main Church." And of these, only the first three are used as straight technical terms. The others are here more like proper names, to designate the new object of veneration, and to specify the particular building that was chosen by the bishop to preserve her image. And the Spanish words are often directly reinforced by a phrase in Nahuatl, producing the parallelism so typical of the language's style: *Teotl Dios* "God-God" (in Nahuatl and Spanish), *teopixca-tlatoani obispo* "priest-ruler bishop." Even here, the ecclesiastical hierarchy is being modified to fit the Nahuatl concept of authority, incorporating the term for leader, *tlatoani* (more literally "speaker"), which had once dignified the last Aztec ruler, Montezuma himself.

Far more, the *Huei tlamahuiçoltica* expresses Catholic concepts by conversion into Nahuatl equivalents, the process often called calquing, or loan translation. So the whole course of events is described as *tlamahuiçolli* "that which is marvelled at" (a miracle). The Virgin keeps requesting a *teo-cal-tzin*, a "chapel" or literally a "god-house-little." She herself is given various titles: *Ilhuica-c Cihua-pilli* "in-sky woman-noble" (i.e., Queen of Heaven), *Teotl Dios Itlazo-nantzin* "God's beloved-Mother Dear" (i.e., Mother of God), *Cenquizca Mahuiz-Ichpochtli* "perfect wondrous maiden" (i.e., Immaculate Virgin Full of Grace).

This last may disguise some tacit reinterpretation of Nahuatl, however. *Ichpochtli* is the word for a nubile but unmarried girl, but the precise sense of sexual inexperience is nowhere seen in texts that show the preconquest use of the word. Luis Laso de la Vega, the named author of this text and a Spaniard himself, certainly worked hard, in his later commentary on the narrative, to establish this nuance. Of Juan Diego, he wrote:

> He was a widower. Two years before the Immaculate Virgin appeared to him his wife died. She was named María Lucía. They both lived in purity, they kept themselves [so]. She died a virgin. He also lived as a boy. He never knew a woman.

This is all quite orthodox by the contemporary standards of Spanish Catholicism. But more was to come: the Virgin was in fact more generally known as *To-nantzin* "Our Mother Dear," taking the precise title for an Aztec goddess, who had previously been worshipped, and received sacrifices, on this same hill, once known as Tepeyac but now rebaptized as Guadalupe.* This was a step too far for Fray Bernardino de Sahagún, the great documenter of Aztec civilization. He wrote, in 1576:

> Whence the foundation of this *Tonantzin* has come is not certainly known; but this we do known for sure, that the word has signified from its first imposition the ancient *Tonantzin*, something that should be remedied because the proper name of the Mother of God, Saint Mary, is not *Tonantzin* but *Dios inantzin* (literally, "God's Mother Dear").[2]

Lurking here, *Tonantzin* reminds converts subliminally of the Nahuatl worldview, and perhaps shows what Fray Bernardino was so worried about. Little is known of Tonantzin's cult, but it is no stretch to associate her with flowers. Fray Bernardino identifies her[3] with the goddess *Cihuacoatl* "woman-serpent," but another of her identities was *Xochi-quetzal* "flower quetzal-bird," whose cult had involved flower offerings. It was highly

---

* This name Guadalupe comes from a river in Spain already famed for its previous link with miracles of the Virgin, here better known as Nuestra Señora de Extremadura. Since "Guadalupe" is not, phonetically, a possible word in Nahuatl, it is sometimes interpreted as a divinely inspired mishearing of *coatla-xopeuh* "serpent crushing": though this is not actually attested as a title for the original Tonantzin, it is eminently suitable for a saint who offers protection from the Devil.

suggestive then that her miracle placed flowers at the center. In the Juan Diego story, the Virgin tells him:

> "My youngest and dearest son, these diverse flowers are the proof, the sign that you will take to the bishop. You will tell him from me that he is to see in them my desire, and that therefore he is to carry out my wish, my will."

Nepapan xochitl "diverse flowers" is a familiar phrase in Nahuatl, which had been used for example as a symbol of the value of culture. The poet-king of Texcoco, Nezahualcoyotl, writing a generation before the Spanish conquest and rhetorically addressing himself, had summed up his contribution as *xochitl tic ya mana, in nepapan xochitli* . . . "you offer flowers, diverse flowers . . ."

The phrase now recurs in this narrative, and once includes a loan adjective, *Caxtillan*:

> "And she ordered me to the top of the hill where I had seen her before, to cut different Castilian flowers up there."

This involves a return from the Nahuatl to the Spanish worldview, for these "Castilian flowers" are conventionally identified as roses, flora of the Old World previously unknown in Mexico. These, of course, would be an ideal symbol to represent a conversion of Mexico through a strange new beauty, and one sourced from Spain.

Since Nahuatl would naturally not have had a word for this novel bloom, perhaps this is the closest it could get to saying they were roses. In Molina's 1571 dictionary, *rosa de castilla* is translated into Nahuatl as *Caxtillan xuchitl* (although Simeón's Nahuatl dictionary, published in 1885, says that *castillan xochitl* means "a clavellina", i.e., "a pink").

The Nahuatl-speaking world had a curious ambivalence of attitude toward people seen as important: essentially, it had little difference between expressing respect and expressing affection, public as against personal regard. Formally, the suffix *-tzin* (also extended as *-tzintli*) was reverential, and could be either an honorific or an endearment: thus *Tonantzin* can be translated "Our Mother Dear," although might just as well have been given as "Our Reverend Mother." This ambivalence gives the curiously intimate feeling to dialogue between Juan Diego and the Virgin Mary, even if she is his Heavenly Queen.

Implicit in this formal suffix on nouns, the ambivalence recurs in saluta-
tions Juan Diego naturally utters when he is confronted by the Virgin, even
unexpectedly:

"No-chpoch-tzin-é, no-xocoyohu-é, cihuapill-é, ma xi-mo-paquilti-tié,
quen otimixtonalti? Cuix ticmohuelmachitia in mo-tlazo-nacayo-tzin,
No-tecuiyo-é, No-pil-tzinzin-é?"

"My little maiden, my youngest daughter, lady, please to be happy;
how are you this morning? Does your beloved body feel well, my
patron, my most noble one?"

Here three of the nouns have the *-tzin* suffix (or even redoubled *-tzinzin*):
no-chpoch- "my maiden," *mo-tlazo-nacayo-* "your beloved body" and *no-pil-*
"my noble." One might assume that Juan Diego really means it honorifically,
but he intersperses another word that can only be endearing: *no-xocoyo-* "my
youngest." And he uses quite an intimate word to enquire how she slept:
ixtonaltia "to blush" (like the dawn), recalling the Spanish morning greeting
"¿Cómo amaneciste?", literally, "How did you dawn?"*

Commingling of reverence with intimacy may have been a good fit with a
Catholic ideal of holy devotion; but it meant that Nahuatl Christianity was
very much in the tradition of Aztec power relations. In this world children
would call their fathers "dear little brother" and their mothers "dear baby."
And citizens called their ruler "child," "grandchild," and "nephew."[4]

Another innovation would be the inclusion in Christian discourse of
Nahuatl rhetorical style, with its balanced couplets of synonymous phrases.
There is little of this in the *Huei tlamahuiçoltica* itself, although Juan Diego's
piling up of different appellations for the Virgin are very much in the spirit,
and likewise the Virgin refers to her instructions to him as "my breath, my
words" (*in ni-iyo, in no-tlatol*), and the bishop is to carry out for her "my
wish, my will" (*in no-tlanequiliz, in no-cializ*).

These are all good examples of heirlooms from Nahuatl present in
the Guadalupe cult. As Nahuatl liturgy for Christianity developed, it would
take over much of this style, a development that could lead to theological

---

* This kind of inversion is still common in modern Spanish, where it is quite natural for a
son to address his mother affectionately as *Mijita* "my little daughter"—though perhaps
not quite so naturally with the Virgin Mary.

anomalies. Sometimes, the conventional epithets were applied so directly that there was danger of simply re-creating the prayers offered to pre-Christian gods.

So in the sixteenth-century *Tratado y Manual de Doctrina Cristiana*, there is the following exchange:

> [A Franciscan friar and a native called Francisco greet each other.]
>
> Francisco: I welcome thee, I greet thee, O my beloved Father. <u>How is the health of thy honorable person?</u> Does the *Lord of the Near, of the Nigh, he by whom we live*, our Lord God, stir up his wrath, his castigation, his punishment? And does he cast upon thee the pointed stick, the broad nettle, the dewy reed, that corrects one, reprimands one?

This is a rather implausible opening exchange in a conversation, though the opening greeting (underlined) is very similar to how Juan Diego addressed the Virgin when she accosted him on the road. But even so, the native who is here so apparently intoxicated with his own verbosity seems to be forgetting that the content of the questions is all reminiscent not so much of the Christian God (explicitly *Dios*) as of the Aztecs' own omnipotent god of rulers, sorcerers, and warriors, incredibly named "Smoking Mirror," Tezcatlipoca, who was well known as the "Lord of the Near and the Nigh" (*in tloque nahuaque*) and "He by Whom We Live" (*i-pal nemoa-ni* "where-by living-cause").[5]

Dramatizing Catholicism

Contemporary drama, the art form known as *Auto*, or "Act," is another source of insight on Nahuatl Catholicism. Its aims were to bring to life the great stories and issues of the faith, and its scenes may be no more taken from life than the *Treatise* was. But since they were designed not so much to communicate language and ideas as to use Nahuatl to channel the audience's emotions, they can be viewed as more psychologically telling. The tradition, which grew up in adaptation of works for the Spanish stage, did require active, and creative, work by native Nahuatl speakers.

As it happens the earliest such drama that has come down to us, entitled *Holy Wednesday*, enacts many of the events of the last week before the Passion, and contains a scene of confrontation between Jesus and Mary: he needs to warn her of his impending suffering and death. We can compare the scene in Nahuatl with its Spanish original.[6]

Whereas the Spanish-language Christ asks his mother for permission to submit himself to the foreseen life-and-death struggle, his Nahuatl equivalent is content to foretell in some detail what is to come, admitting that it is all by his own will. He is also more reluctant to part from her, with extra speeches of mutual regret, blessing, and encouragement. Unlike the Spanish Christ who denies his mother's natural hopes, to save him, or at least to spare herself the grief by dying first, the Nahuatl Christ engages in an exchange of beautiful oratory, what the Aztecs had called "fine jades, fine turquoise, fine reeds, well rounded" (*uel chalchiuhtic, uel teuxiuhtic, uel acatic, uel ololiuhqui*).[7] In the Aztec way, he persuades through eloquence, not point-for-point argument.

In ti-tlateochihual cenquizca ichpochtli	You are a blessed and perfect maiden,
in ti-cihuapilla tohuani	you a noblewoman and sovereign,
in ti-no-tlaço-nan-tzin	you who are my precious mother,
in oticmitalhui c̄ica nelli melahuac	what you have said is very true and correct
in ca nelli ixquich no-huelitzin	It is true that I have total power.
ca mochi huel mochihuaz	Everything can be done,
in tlein nicnonequiltiz	whatever I may wish,
inic ni-teotl ni-tlatohuani	since I am the divinity, I am the sovereign.
Auh ça ye ma xicmomachilti,	But first may you know
ca hatle yc ni-tlacueppaz	that in no way will I turn things around.
ca nelli ni-cneltiliz	It is true that I will cause to come true
in oc achtopa itotiyaque in prophetas . . .	That which the prophets left foretold . . .

This to represent a Spanish original:

Virgen sagrada muger	Sacred Virgin woman
ò madre, que es escusado,	oh Mother, it is forgiven.
que cierto a mi parecer	Certain is in my opinion
lo que està profetizado,	what is prophesied,
no puede dexar de ser.	it cannot fail to be.

On this evidence, Nahuatl-speaking Christianity had an inbuilt tendency to reform ideas of relations among the holy family on a more traditionally Mexican basis, more fatalistic and accepting, less individualistic and argumentative. This was another way in which Nahuatl made it possible, and indeed natural, to channel Catholicism into a more familiar Mexican worldview.

◊≼≽◊

The scriptures of the Catholic church were to be routinely augmented in the New World by translated catechisms, confessionals, and collections of prayers, all printed in the languages of conversion. These served the day-to-day purposes of religious instruction, worship, and personal confession and were the first works to be published in the New World (before anything in Spanish). Indeed for Nahuatl, the earliest exemplars[8] came out in 1539 and 1540, a decade after the date of the supposed time of Juan Diego's miracle on Guadalupe, and more than a century before Laso de la Vega would publish his account of it.

But in producing the *Huei tlamahuiçoltica*, Laso de la Vega was consciously adding to holy literature. He was, after all, compiling a hagiography of the miracle of Guadalupe that amounts to a Christian witness in print. The fact that it is in Nahuatl, not Spanish, loomed very large for him. He mentioned it (*nahuatlàtolcopa*) explicitly four times in his two-page preface, and compared it with the fact that the commoner Juan Diego was called by the Virgin in his own "commoner language" (*maçehual-làtolli*), noting that it has been written so that other commoners might learn of the Virgin's charitable acts in their own language (*in-tlàtoltica*). He quoted Saint Bonaventure (an Italian theologian of the thirteenth century)[9] "that the great exalted miracles of our Lord God are to be written in a variety of languages (*nepapan tlàtoltica*)," even comparing this with the placard on Christ's cross

> in three different languages so that different peoples in different languages would see and marvel at his altogether great and lofty, marvellous love by which he redeemed the world . . .

De la Vega ended by mentioning the gift of tongues that had come to the disciples from the Holy Spirit in the description of the miracle of Pentecost, and he prayed for similar "reverend tongues of fiery coals" (*i-tlexoch-nenepil-tzin*) to trace this miracle too.

❈❈❈

In addition to the effects on the word, thought, and scripture of Catholic Christianity, which came about when the miracle of Guadalupe was set down in Nahuatl, there was a social development too, as there always is when a language group comes to accept another religion. The Spanish Crown early decided that Nahuatl, as the "general language of the Indians," would be used in preference to Spanish "for the explanation and teaching of the Christian doctrine, and for curates and priests to administer the sacraments to them." This integrated its speakers into a new, extended community of the Catholic church and resulted in something like a national revival. A booklet in Nahuatl, made at the midpoint of the seventeenth century, and combined with a Spanish account of the miracle that had been published just one year earlier (Miguel Sánchez, *Imagen de la Virgen María, Madre de Dios de Guadalupe*, 1648), led off a boom in devotion to the Virgin Mary. The works had come out one hundred years after the events that they purported to describe, but it seemed to be just the right moment for the success of the cult of the Virgin in Mexico.

For the next century and a half, there was a surge in images, chapels, and Nahuatl-language references to this apparition, first in central Mexico but later taken up across the empire.[10] In 1737 the Virgin of Guadalupe was proclaimed patroness of Mexico City, and in 1746 her patronage was accepted throughout the kingdom of New Spain, from California in the north to Guatemala in the south.

This phenomenon became the first fully regional, and later, national cult: in fact, devotion was strongest in the parts of the country more dominated by families of Spanish origin, especially the capital.[11] There was a clear parallel with an earlier cult based at Guadalupe in Spain, where the Virgin had appeared, and followed almost the same narrative. This reinforced the Hispanic, almost metropolitan, significance of this cult for the dominant criollo class in Mexico; yet the impeccably Nahuatl credentials of the *Huei tlamahuiçoltica*, containing explicit instructions—in Nahuatl—from the Virgin herself, nullified any sense of an intrinsically Spanish revelation.

In its ultimately national scope, this cult of the Virgin was quite exceptional. But her association with a particular location—in this case the hill of Tepeyacac so close to the capital—was typical of saints as they figured in the Nahuatl acceptance of Catholic Christianity. Just like the gods of the preconquest religion, saints were most importantly seen as local beings, symbolizing the *altepetl* "city-state" to which they were attached, and as such inspiring local loyalties. Accordingly, the Virgin's first, and most persistent, request to Juan Diego, and through him to the bishop, was for *no-teocal* "my church," a chapel that she could call her own.

Whether an Aztec temple, or a Christian church, it was still—in Nahuatl—a *teocalli* "god house" or *teopantli* "god place," a focus for local patriotism and personal devotion that had somehow survived the Spanish conquest and invasion. As the Nahua transmuted their loyalties, and committed themselves to serve their new patrons the Christian saints, the Catholic church too developed with a vastly expanded, but socially and racially split, congregation.

A Divided Congregation

The Nahuatl word for Christian, *quirixtiano*, is clearly a loan from Spanish *cristiano*, and in speech (as legal documents show) tended to be interpreted racially, simply to mean a Spaniard,* even if de jure all were on a par before God. The word (spelled *Christiano*) figures prominently in the Confessional expositions of the faith for the study of natives.[12] In fact, of course, there was no practical option as to whether one was a Christian or not: the issue for all was to make themselves *good* Christians (*qualtin Christianos*).

Nonetheless, indigenous Nahua, as well as their mixed-race brethren the mestizos, were formally banned from ordination as priests (and thence bishops). Legally, this was only for a very short period (1555–85), but in practice they were excluded for very much longer. This was justified, if at all, in terms of their social unacceptability to congregations.[13] But inevitably, as *teopan-tlaca* "church people" and members of *cofradias*, volunteer societies who organized religious rituals and festivals in Mexico much as analogous societies did in Spain, the Nahua played many essential roles in the actual operation of churches.[14]

---

* There was an irony in that the usual word for their own (common) people, *macehualtin*, also had, in its etymology, a religious sense: "those made deserving" *macehualli* (implicitly by "divine sacrifice" *macehua*). Like so much in Nahuatl, this survived the conversion to Christian religion. The Nahua never accepted the Spaniards' favorite word for them, Columbus's famous misnomer, *indios*.

The presence of the Nahuatl language itself, and its continued use, was symbolic of the new extent of the faith. This was registered for Catholicism as a whole at the Council of Trento in 1546, which explicitly required the teaching of the Gospels in natives' languages. The Spanish Crown in the person of Philip II had early decided that Nahuatl, as the "general language of the Indians," would be used in preference to Spanish "for the explanation and teaching of the Christian doctrine, and for curates and priests to administer the sacraments to them."

This was how Christianity remained in Mexico for the next two centuries, essentially a bilingual faith, with practical emphasis on Nahuatl, until the arrival from Madrid in 1769 of Archbishop Francisco Antonio de Lorenzana y Buitrón, who was steadfastly opposed to use of any language but Spanish. Lorenzana was the twenty-third successor of Juan de Zumárraga, the bishop who had in the end listened to Juan Diego's message from the Virgin of Guadalupe. Lorenzana's reasoned reluctance to do as twenty-two archbishops had done before him, and learn the language of his new see, chimed with the contemporary spirit of the Enlightenment (known in Spanish as *la Ilustración*). Furthermore, he had the ear of the King (Carlos III), who was prevailed upon to deliver his *Real Cédula* (royal decree) of 1770,

> that at once may be achieved the extinction of the different languages used in the said domains, and the sole use of Castilian be spoken . . .*

Such a death sentence may have been an overreaction. But it was comprehensive: the death knell sounded for Nahuatl in Catholic worship was applied to indigenous languages throughout the Spanish empire. Spanish— and indeed Latin—would survive as liturgical languages. But Nahuatl, along with all its "Indian" cousins, from the Philippines to Tierra del Fuego, was unceremoniously dropped.

❖

This quick look through the language, the worldview, the texts, and the social impact of the *Huei tlamahuiçoltica*, Luis Laso de la Vega's miraculous

---

* "*Para que de una vez se llegue a conseguir el que se extingan los diferentes idiomas de que se usa en los mismos Dominios, y sólo se hable el Castellano . . .*" quoted in Triana y Antorveza 1987, p. 511.

narrative in Nahuatl, has given a first, and I hope enticing, glimpse of the different ways that a language can have an effect on religion. It is an object lesson in how much more a language is than a clear channel of communication.

A language is like a tissue, a woven texture, of associations. It enables and facilitates thought and emotion, but it also channels and colors these mental acts. Natural languages, being the heirs to long traditions of actual thought by real human beings, contain pathways, which are popular, even if they support arguments that are not, strictly, valid.

CHAPTER 2

On Ass's Lip, and a Great Conveyance
The Buddha Taken North

During the seventh week, the Thus-Gone [*Tathāgata*] dwelt at the foot of the fig tree (under which he had found enlightenment) . . .

Then two brothers from the north-land (*Uttarāpatha*), skilled and shrewd merchants, named Trapuṣa and Bhallika, having acquired great wealth, and bringing various kinds of goods, were on their way from the south to the north-land, accompanied by a great caravan and five hundred full wagons . . .

As soon as the travelers saw the Thus-Gone shining like fire, well endowed with the thirty-two signs of a great man, resplendent with the majesty of the rising sun, they said, struck with amazement: "Who is this then? Is it Brahma come down to us here below, or Indra (Śakra) the lord of the gods? Is it Kubera (Vaiśravaṇa)? Is it the Sun or the Moon? Is it a mountain god, or a river god?" . . .

Having taken the honey and the precious vessel, going to the foot of the master's fig tree, they said: "Take this dish; accept this food offered in good heart and eat it!" . . .

In benevolence to the two brothers and knowing their ancient intention, the all-knowing teacher accepted, ate, and threw the vessel in the air . . .

And so the Thus-Gone delighted the merchants Trapuṣa and Bhallika, saying: "May the blessing of the gods which renders places favorable and brings success to business be with you! May all your affairs turn out promptly as you will them . . ."

From the *Lalita Vistara*, chapter 24 (third century A.D.)

SIDDHARTHA GAUTAMA, THE questing sage who became the Buddha, lived and taught in the fifth or fourth century B.C. in the towns and villages around Pāṭaliputra, what is now the Patna area of Bihar in north-eastern India. In the course of his life, his fame traveled farther, perhaps aided by Pāṭaliputra's status as an imperial capital; and so the disciples he attracted spoke in a range of dialects, though, as in north India today, the majority of them would have been clearly related, and in those days not far removed from the common Aryan speech now known as Prakrit—"natural"—but usually polished up as Sanskrit—"composed."

Some of the disciples were concerned about this disorderly hubbub, fearing perhaps that the crucial, or at least the full, detail of the sage's teaching might be lost, and proposed rendering it into Sanskrit verse, in dignified *chandas* form. The Buddha, however, forbade it, adding:

Anujānāmi bhikkhave sakāya niruttiyā buddhavacanaṃ pariyāpunituṃ.

I require, monks, mastery of the enlightened word in one's own expression.[1]

Whose own (*sakāya*) interpretation he meant has remained a matter of dispute, but it was clearly not to be in Sanskrit metrical form. His insistence may have arisen because that form was then primarily associated with canon-ical Brahmanical religion: the classic Sanskrit grammarian Pāṇinī, who may have been a contemporary of the Buddha, also uses *chandas* to mean the meters used in the Vedas.*

Regardless of these fourth-century vagaries, the founder of Buddhism is on record as voicing concern about innovation in the language in which his teaching was to be expressed, perhaps on his guard against the linguistic effects and transformations that are the focus of this book. As a result, those concerned about this saying of his kept the expression of his law in the language that became accepted as the Buddha's own, *Pāli*. This particular form of Prakrit has been in use to express Theravada Buddhism (*Theravāda* in Pali meaning "elders' doctrine") for more than two millennia, a period of

---

* The word for "expression," *nirutti*, was also a bit ambiguous. It was not the usual word for "language" or "dialect" (*bhāsā*, literally, "speaking"). In fact, it is a term for the discipline of "linguistic analysis," a recognized "limb of the Vedas" (*vedanga*), and derived from Sanskrit *nir-uk-ti* "out-speech-ness," with the same prefix seen in *nibbāna* (Sanskrit *nir-vā-na*) "out-blow-ing" i.e., extinguishing).

stability in spelling and structure exceeding those of Latin from Lucretius
to Sir Isaac Newton. This durability has done justice to the Buddhist
word for law, *dhamma*, which etymologically means nothing other than
"holding firm."

Buddhism spread out all over India in the following centuries, and as it
pervaded the center and south of the subcontinent, it largely maintained the
Theravada doctrine, along with use of the Pali language. It highlights the
four noble truths (Pali *cattāri ariyasaccāni*): the truths of suffering (*dukkha*);
of its cause (*samudaya*), in craving (*taṇhā*) induced by ignorance (*avijjā*); of its
possible cessation (*nirodha*); and the means of the eightfold path (*aṭṭhangiko*
maggo)—the essence of virtue, intellectual and practical—that will ultimately
lead to the goal of "being blown out" or nirvana (Pali *nibbāna*). This creed
remains as the core of Buddhism.

As it moved north, however, there was less linguistic fidelity. Doctrinal
works, known as sutras, came to be written in Sanskrit itself, while Sanskrit
was felt less and less to connote Brahmanical Hinduism, more as a general
medium for serious writing. Pali, therefore, no longer had a monopoly
on Buddhist scriptures, and it is clear that, orally too, doctrine was being
preached in Prakrit languages rather than Pali.

Most notably it was preached in the Prakrit centered on Gandhara (approximately southern Afghanistan and northern Pakistan in modern geography).
We have its version of the Dhammapada (Pali "Word of the Law"), a primer
in Buddhism produced very soon after the Buddha's death, which runs to
395 verses in Pali, and which seems to have been popular everywhere. The
manuscript itself turned up in fragments in Khotan and Kashgar, cities on
the opposite side of the Pamirs from Gandhara. This "Gandhari" became the
version of spoken Aryan used as a lingua franca across much of Central Asia
from the third century B.C. to the seventh A.D.* It has since developed into
the modern Indo-Aryan languages of the region, of the Dardic, Lahnda, and
Sindhi groups. There are many, the largest being Kashmiri and Sindhi. But
two thousand years ago Gandhari was a dialect very closely related to Pali.

---

* "Gandhari" is in fact a recent name for the language, suggested by Harold Bailey in 1946,
and since adopted with acclaim. Previously it was generally known to scholars as "North-
West Prakrit," but including the "Niya Prakrit" or "Kroraina Prakrit" northeast of the
Pamirs on the road to China. A likely term its speakers might have used for their speech is
Udīcya "northern."

Buddhist Terms in Aryan languages

ENGLISH	PALI	SANSKRIT	GANDHARI*
Buddha, awoken	*buddho*	*buddhaḥ*	*budha*
dharma, law	*dhamma*	*dharmaḥ*	*dhama*
the four noble truths	*cattāri ariya-saccāni*	*catvāri ārya-satyāni*	*catvari ariya-sacaṇa*
suffering	*dukkha*	*duḥkham*	*dukha*
causation	*samudaya*	*samudayaḥ*	*samudaya*
craving, desire	*taṇhā*	*tṛṣṇā*	*taṣa*
ignorance	*avijjā*	*avidyā*	*avija*
cessation	*nirodha*	*nirodhaḥ*	*nirosa*
eightfold path	*aṭṭhangiko maggo*	*aṣṭhangika-mārgaḥ**	*aṭhaṃgiga mago*
arhat, adept	*arahanta*	*arhan*	*arahadi*
nirvana, blowing out	*nibbāna*	*nirvāṇam*	*nivaṇa*
impermanence	*aniccatā*	*anityatā*	*anicada*

A chart of these and other Buddhist technical terms, which define the principal doctrine of the *dharma* in these three languages, shows how close Gandhari is to both Pali and Sanskrit (above).

Any changes in the Buddhist creed as it spread across the vast Gandhari-speaking zone cannot be plausibly put down to a mismatch of terminology in translation. Switching from Pali to Gandhari was more like changing dialect than changing language: all the same words were available, even if in slightly unfamiliar disguise.

Yet despite this terminological equivalence, Gandhari was to become—socially and historically—a distinct language, put into a different cultural context from Pali (and indeed Sanskrit) by the political situation of Gandhara.

Gandhara had been a satrapy of the Achaemenid Empire centered on Susa in faraway Persia: it was under Persian rule from the mid-sixth century until the mid-fourth B.C. Even then, as Persian control crumbled, it did not revert to India, as its linguistic links might have suggested, but was

---

* In this chapter, our romanized spelling follows usual Sanskrit usage: the symbol c represents English ch, ṣ represents sh, while ś represents a more forward sound, like the h in "human." The letters ṭ, ḍ, and ṇ represent retroflex t, d, and n and ḥ is h with a short murmured vowel following.

suddenly taken by Alexander the Great in 334–326 B.C. The Macedonians were attempting to digest his conquests as part of a wider Greek *oikoumenē*, when just a generation later, it was reconquered—fairly briefly, as it turned out—for the Indian cultural world by Chandragupta Maurya in 305 B.C.

After four or five generations within the Mauryan Empire, it was taken by expanding Indo-Greek dynasties, beginning with Demetrius I of Bactria in 185 B.C. and culminating with Menander, who reigned until 130 B.C., seems to have controlled the Punjab as well as Gandhara and Bactria, and campaigned as far afield as Pāṭaliputra. After three or four more generations, Greek control yielded to Scythian (Śaka), and then Parthian, invasions; finally, the region was added to the empire of the Tocharians, which dominated the whole of Central Asia and northern India for three centuries, well into the third century A.D.

To sum up, for these nine centuries (sixth B.C. to third A.D.) Gandhara had provided a perfect example of what Buddhism had always seen as the essence of life—*anicada*, impermanence.

The earliest of these periods, under the Persians, saw the invention and spread of the quite distinctive script *Kharoṣṭhi*, in which all Gandhari documents (and virtually no others—except a few marginal Sanskrit ones) were written until the third century A.D. Kharosthi, the name of which means "ass-lipped" in Sanskrit,[3] looks rather like the Aramaic script used throughout the Persian empire for well over a millennium, beginning with its conquest of the Near East in 700 B.C.; and many of the letters have similar forms. It is also like Aramaic, and unlike all other Indian scripts, in being written from right to left. This would certainly have been enough to dignify Gandhari to the public as a language in its own right.

Chandragupta had an equally great grandson, Aśoka. He was moved to set up monumental Buddhist edicts all over the Maurya domain, an empire that extended as far south as modern Mysore. The vast majority were inscribed in his home court language of Magadhi Prakrit in Brāhmī script (conveniently, for a Buddhist, very similar to Pali); but significantly, he chose to make the inscriptions in the Gandhara region, unlike all the others, multilingual. At Kandahar close to the border, he wrote in Greek and Aramaic, representing the Greek and Persian minorities who must still have been significant there. There are more Aramaic inscriptions in Laghman (a town not far from Jalalabad). Farther to the east, in Mansehra and Shābazgarhi, he used Gandhari written in Kharosthi.

The records of inscriptions, coinage, and surviving documents show that Gandhari in Kharosthi was by no means the only literate language in use in the wider area that centered on Gandhara: besides Greek and Aramaic, there was Bactrian (called by its users "Aryan"—αριαο, and written in Greek script with a single extra letter Þ, pronounced "šo"), and more than one tradition of writing Śaka.[4] But the new script for Gandhari turned out to be crucial for Buddhism. The faith continued to be preached and practiced orally in an Aryan Prakrit, the Gandhari still so very similar to Pali; but when written down, Gandhari writings would, for a time, constitute a new and separate body of scriptures, what might have been—but never was—characterized as a *Tripiḍaǵa*, to stand apart from the Pali *Tipiṭaka* "three baskets" of authentic texts.[5]

Beyond Pali

And sure enough, changes did come about in this process of language transfer; within this period (ca. 200 B.C. to A.D. 200) and over this area (northern India and Central Asia) the distinctive doctrines of the Mahayana were added to the Buddhist faith. Their first medium of communication was Gandhari, and second Sanskrit itself: but the doctrines' origins—especially as to worldview and identity—may have come from farther back and farther west, from the long generations of Gandhari speakers who would have been bilingual in Pahlavi, Aramaic, and Greek.

The dharma had been—as it remains in the Theravada's Pali Tipitaka—a doctrine for adepts, exposing the moral and causal constitution of the world, and showing how, by following the Buddha's example, this knowledge could lead to escape from the constant round of suffering and rebirth.

But in the Mahayana, it was now generalized into a program for humanity, where anyone could set out on the path of the bodhisattva,* with an aim not just to find personal nirvana, but to bring all beings to deliverance. The historical Buddha known as Gautama, far from being unique, was now seen as just the latest in a long series of teachers, of which at least twenty-eight were on record. (The number continued to increase during the following

---

* This crucial term is not usually translated, but it has two possible analyses in Sanskrit: either it is a compound of two abstract nouns meaning "having enlightenment as essence"; or a gerundive verb-phrase "one whose enlightenment is yet to be." The latter seems more likely, since the Buddha too describes himself as a bodhisattva (in Pali) when recalling his previous existences ("I, too, monks, before my Awakening, when I was an *unawakened bodhisattva* [*anabhisambuddho bodhisattova*], being subject myself to birth, sought what was likewise subject to birth." (*Majjhima Nikāya* 26 PTS: M i 160: *Ariyapariyesana Sutta* 15).

centuries, though the chronology remained vague.) Many of the bodhisatt-vas, like him, expressed their boundless compassion by acting as supernatural (*lokottara*) helpers. Since nirvana was a long way off, one of the better stages in a long career of successive births was to be reborn into one of the paradises (*buddha-kṣetrāṇi*, "Buddha-fields") over which they presided. This was more likely as one accumulated merit (*puṇya*) from various good deeds, including worship of some deities and bodhisattvas. Besides good deeds as such, "skillful means" (*upāya-kauśalya*) might—on purely pragmatic grounds—be recognized as positive for one's progress. The world was more abstract than it appeared, being in reality a void (*śūnyatā*), just as the individual soul was an illusion. Underlying all was the Buddha-nature (*buddha-dhātu*, also known as *tathāgata-garbha* "womb of the Thus-Gone"), the quality that pervades all beings, and through which they can obtain release.*

These doctrines became fundamental to Buddhism as it was later spread through China, Japan, Tibet, and Mongolia. There is consensus—though little documentary evidence—that the first scriptures to expound these addi-tional doctrines are not as old as Buddhism itself, but began to arise in the four centuries from 200 B.C. to A.D. 200. Buddhist scriptures are usually known as sutras, and are seldom easy to date.† In this case, the time limits are given by the reign of Aśoka, the Buddha-preaching emperor, fixing the beginning, and the known years when the sutras began to be translated into Chinese, fixing the end.

In this period, a new metaphor was established for Buddhist faith itself. The Buddha had characterized it as *maggo* (Sanskrit *mārgaḥ*), "a road"; but now it was seen as a *yānam*, "a conveyance."

It has recently been suggested that this may have been due to faulty understanding: the Great Knowledge (*mahājñānam*—Gandhari *mahañana*) being misheard as the Great Cart (*mahāyānam*—Gandhari *mahayana*). The words could easily have been confused by poor scholars; and simple converts were primed to make this mistake, since the Lotus Sutra,[6] many people's

---

* The Indian terms in this paragraph are all in Sanskrit, not Pali.

† The spatchcocking of Sanskrit into the tradition is responsible for the invention of *sūtra* as a word for a Buddhist scripture. In Pali, the word had been *sutta*—which could represent either *sūktam* (from *su-uktam* "well-spoken") "wise saying" or *sūtram* "thread" (which in classical Sanskrit was metaphorically interpreted as "rule, maxim"). The Buddhist Hybrid Sanskrit tradition picked the latter, even though all the *suttas* traditionally begin in Pali: *Evam me sutam*, "Thus I have heard." And analogously, Sanskrit sutras would begin: *Evaṃ mayā śrutam*, though no one ever heard this from Gautama.

main access to Buddhism, contains a memorable parable for the difficulty of preaching, where a loving father (the Buddha) has to entice his children out of a burning house by promising them rides on special carts, but then delivers them a carriage better than they could ever have hoped for.[7]

This meant that Buddhism came more and more to be seen as something that, if accepted, would carry one, rather than a direction to be taken exclusively through personal effort. It became usual to distinguish this new (and self-acclaimed) *mahā-yānam* ("Great Vehicle") from the classic doctrine, from the *śrāvaka-yānam* ("the disciples' vehicle"). Soon the innovators were deriding the old way as *hīna-yānam*, where the prefix (the past participle of *hā* "to desert") is definitely derogatory: not so much a "lesser vehicle" as an "abandoned, failed, clapped out, vehicle." As the Lotus Sutra itself puts it rather combatively, in chapter 15:

ekam hi yānaṃ dvitīyam na vidyate: tṛtīyam naivāsti kadāci loke

there is but one vehicle; a second is not known;
neither is there a third anywhere in the world.

The empire under which these new Mahayana doctrines first flourished was the Kuṣāṇa realm, which united Bactria, Gandhara, northern India, and much of Central Asia north of the Himalayas for more than three centuries, starting ca. 30 A.D.

The founders of this empire were called Tocharians by major Greek authors Strabo and Ptolemy in their accounts of the fall of the Indo-Greeks,[8] but were better known in Chinese as *Yuè-zhī*.* They were moving westward around the central plateau of Qinghai and Tibet after being displaced from the borders of China by Huns. After the Tocharian takeover in the first century B.C., Bactria (the province of the city of Bactra, modern Balkh) came to be known for some six centuries as Tokharistan, Persian for "place of the

---

* *Yuè-zhī* is a modern Mandarin pronunciation of unchanging Chinese characters, 月氏 or 月支, where the first represents "moon" and the second "kin" or "branch." These were the "moon folk." Beckwith 2009, pp. 380–2, gives a bravura demonstration of language changes that together mean that 月, which was clearly pronounced as *ngwat* in Middle Chinese, would have had a dialectal pronunciation **tokwar*, and so is a plausible Chinese phonetic proxy for Bactrian Τοχοαρ, i.e., Tokhwar, "Tocharian." QED.

Tocharians."* One of the five tribes of the Yue-zhi, the Guishuang, assumed the leadership under one Kujūla Kadphises (mid-first century A.D.) and proceeded to set up an empire, generally known by their Sanskritized name Kuṣāṇa, which spread from Bactria down to the mouth of the Indus and central India. A subsequent great king, Kaniṣka (mid-second century A.D.), took its borders as far south as Patna and Ujjain in India, and into the Tarim basin round the Taklamakan Desert on the borders of China. The empire kept its coherence until the middle of the third century A.D.

Like the Indo-Greeks and the Śaka and Parthians, the Kuṣāṇa demonstrated their official multilingualism on their coinage: it is inscribed in Greek on the front and Gandhari (in Kharosthi script) on the back. Furthermore, in the second century A.D. the emperor Kaniṣka held an influential Buddhist synod, probably in Kashmir, and appointed the noted Sanskrit poet Aśvaghoṣa (believed to be a converted Brahman[9]) to compile its official *vibhāṣā* or proceedings: this marks the point at which official approval was given for the use of Sanskrit for Buddhist sutras.[†] Subsequent Mahayana works are written not in Gandhari, but in Sanskrit—or rather, its less grammatically exact approximation, now known to scholars as Buddhist Hybrid Sanskrit.[10]

Since this "fourth synod" is the stuff of legend rather than documented fact, it is difficult to be sure of Kaniṣka's motives in calling it. However, they may have been analogous to the Roman emperor Constantine's wishes for the Council of Nicaea (in 325 A.D.), which was an attempt to standardize and unify the most influential faith in the empire. Constantine was especially motivated by the frictions from the influential heresy of Arianism. Buddhism, too, had divided since the time of the Buddha into major sects, divisions probably aggravated by the onset of Mahayana ideas: the appeal

---

* There are grounds for believing that these Tocharians derive from the same population who spoke the Tocharian language around the Tarim Basin (attested from documents of the sixth to eighth centuries A.D.) and were called *twyri* by their neighbors the Uyghurs, but no remnant of this language has been discovered in "Tocharistan." It appears that the marauding Tocharians were content to adopt the language of their subject peoples in Bactria and Gandhara. (See Beckwith 2009 again, p. 383, for a rousing marshaling of the arguments.)

† There was always a tendency for languages to get associated with particular doctrinal schools within Buddhist theory: in this context, Sanskrit was especially favored by the realists of the Sarvāstivādin school. (*Sarva-asti-vāda*, literally the "all-is" theory.) However, such theoretical divisions about what really is there have little to do with paths to paradise or nirvana.

to associate Buddhist scriptural authority with the established authority of Sanskrit (quite against the stated preference of the Buddha himself) has the ring of a bureaucratic solution.

As to the choice of Sanskrit, there is also the fact that inscriptions quite generally, and not just Buddhist ones, begin to be written in Sanskrit, rather than the local Prakrit, from the mid-second century A.D. Since Sanskrit had originally been the Brahmans' special language, this has been taken by some as evidence of the increasing influence of Brahmans at royal courts. And on this ground it has been conjectured that Buddhists "needed to defend their interests at the royal courts in Sanskrit. They had to use Sanskrit in the courts because Brahmans had been able to secure themselves a central place at the courts, by way of their indispensable skills . . ."[11]

Aside from this possible political charge to the use of Sanskrit, there has been some speculation as to why it was thought desirable to "Sanskritize" Buddhist texts as well. It has been suggested that there was an element of "keeping up with the Joneses," an attempt to show that Buddhists were just as educated as the Brahman elite,[12] a motive consistent with the theory of Brahman political influence at court.*

For the crucial period of the third century B.C. to the third century A.D., then, the principal literate languages in the very widepread Indo-Greek and Kuṣāṇa domains were Aramaic, Greek, and, above all, Gandhari early on, and latterly—especially for written records of religion—Sanskrit. All of these must have derived their original prestige in the empire from their inherited traditions, since they were not tongues native to the Kuṣāṇa ruling elite.

---

* More cosmically, there is the view that the adoption of Sanskrit marked the beginning of a kind of intellectual outflanking by Brahmanism. Brahmans, on this view, would— through the use of Sanskrit—have been able to "set the terms" for debate with Buddhism, and so (ultimately) marginalize it. (Bronkhorst 2011, pp. 153–69.)

But this trend needs to be kept in proportion. The Buddha's distinctive approach to *dhamma* did undeniably get reframed by Brahmans in India, with the Buddha reconceived, and put in his place, as (no more than) an avatar of the Hindu god Vishnu. But this was not to happen for another six hundred years after Kaniṣka's Buddhist synod.

This development is better seen as one result of the geopolitical restructuring, whereby Buddhism in India was cut off from regions beyond the Hindu Kush. Conquests by Sassanid Persians (232–350) and the Hephthalite "White Huns" (350–550) detached these northern regions, and so the center of cultural gravity for Buddhism moved south, where it was more exposed to the Brahman worldview (cf Elverskog 2010, pp. 27–30). These conquests came a century too late to explain Sanskrit's encroachment on Buddhism under the Kuṣāṇas.

And whatever the ultimate decline of Mahayana Buddhism in India, once its Sanskrit-speaking home, it would go on to a magnificent career (in other languages) across East Asia.

As to why it was Gandhari, among the various vernaculars, that spread so far with Kuṣāṇa power, there is no evidence. The three usual stimuli for lingua francas—army, trade, and religion—are all possibilities, but the presumption must be that literate Aryans from Gandhara, who wrote in the Kharosthi script, rather than Greeks, played a major role in Kuṣāṇa administration.[13]

Owing to the activities of the Greek kingdoms and the Kuṣāṇa empire that followed them, Gandhara was the central zone of a literate administration. Its main medium and lingua franca was Gandhari; but to be effective, this language must have interacted with a number of quite different literate languages to the north: Greek, Bactrian, Śaka, and Parthian. There must have been effective bilinguals in Gandhari and all these. When Buddhism was committed to writing in Gandhari, it became accessible to speakers of those other languages too. No Buddhist texts are found in them, however; we must infer that, under Kuṣāṇa rule, Buddhism remained a faith whose documents, the sutras, were expressed exclusively in an Aryan dialect—Pali, Gandhari, or Sanskrit.[14]

The edicts of Aśoka (from the third century B.C.) are an apparent exception to this language policy for Buddhism. Almost all are indeed in an Aryan language (Magadhi Prakrit, which is closely related to Pali). One exemplar, however, set up in Kandahar on the outermost border of his empire, is in Greek and Aramaic. This bilingual text contains little specifically Buddhist content beyond ethical exhortations, especially to vegetarianism and filial piety, and it is short on use of the great technical terms (or their equivalents), though *dharma* is mentioned.[15]

In one place (Bairat, near Jaipur) Aśoka even recommends some spiritual reading. This is his only use of the word *ārya*, written as *aliya*, part of the name of a sutra title (otherwise unknown): *aliyavasani* "the lineage (or dwellings?) of the noble." *Brāhmana* figures in other edicts: Girnar, where *brāhmaṇa* are linked with *śramana* (presumably "monk") as a class deserving of respect; and Mansehra ("even among the Kambojas, Yavanas, and Gandharas, the Rāshtrika-paitranikas and other peoples dwelling about the western borders of my dominions") where they are linked with "the ruling class."

Consistently, the word for "nobility" that characterizes the best behavior is always *ārya* (Pali/Gandhari *ariya*); furthermore, in texts such as the Dhammapada, *brahmana* (supposedly a term for the highest, and most spiritually attuned, caste in Indian, viz Aryan, society) is reinterpreted to mean someone who attains enlightenment—i.e., an *arhat*.*

---

* This not itself a related word, being derived from the verb *arh*-: so, literally, "deserving."

It might appear, then, that early Buddhists had no reserve about associating the spiritual heights with being of the best race and the best family, and possibly even the best language. But in fact, they were attempting to separate the traditional social meaning of the words from their sense as indexes of quality.

This is the moral of the story of Bindumatī, a courtesan who shows Aśoka her transcendent power, in an "act of truth," to roll back the waters of the Ganges. The source of her power, she reveals, is just her taxi-cab morality: she treats all her clients equally, sensitive to the color of their money, but not their caste. "When I see he is a noble (khattiyo-*kṣatriya*) I make no distinction in his favor. If I know him to be a slave (suddo-*śūdra*) I despise him not. Free alike from fawning and from dislike I do service to him who has bought me." This indifference to class was what made for real quality.[16] Likewise, in the Tipiṭaka, the Buddha himself pointed to Yona and Kamboja (Greek and Iranian) society as having just two classes (noble ayyo-*ārya*, and serf dāso-*dāsa*), being so far from inborn that people could move between them.[17]

It would be an exaggeration to characterize all the changes that came over Buddhism in the Mahayana movement as due to working in a new language. But clearly, the production of new versions of the sutras in Gandhari, then—apparently by royal decree—in Sanskrit, gave a license to expand, and in so doing reinterpret, the canon of Buddhist scripture. Translation inevitably requires some level of active understanding to construct a meaningful text in a new language, and so gives an opportunity to recast it—or even misunderstand it. By contrast, established texts—whether learned by heart or copied faithfully in writing—are necessarily conservative.

⊗⃟⃟⊗

In this cosmopolitan, and multilingual, world of the Kuṣāṇa empire, the Buddhist faith underwent many fundamental changes. All but one of them may be seen as linguistic effects, derived from reinvention of Buddhist *dhamma* in a new language, and for members of a new—extended—language community. Overall, their varied nature still makes sense, and validates dynamic framework for religious change set out in the introduction to this work. And the remaining one, while it does not fit as a linguistically motivated change, still shows how a new realm of religious concepts may be derived from a new environment and its vocabulary.

These major changes were: First, a new, reverential attitude to written *scripture*. As new works were added to the canon, not now handed down by tradition, but written down in languages other than Pali, a radically new attitude was conceived, of respect to the physical existence of written works.

Second, a change in iconography, derivable from the traditions of a new linguistic *community* being inducted into Buddhism. Henceforth the Buddha would be represented artistically as a perfect man. These were the Greeks of Bactria, with their cultural self-confidence, but relative openness to new deities.

Third, a new philosophy that conceived abstract ideas as beings in their own right—essentially, drawing on a conception of *grammar* that interpreted abstract nouns as necessarily referring to things.

And fourth, a number of different concepts and personages derivable from the past folklore, legend, and cultures of these language communities, a whole population of imagined and remembered spirits and places inherited as *heirlooms* from a past spirit world.

Finally, because of the interpenetration of the communities of Buddhist monks and merchant *upāsaka*, ("sitters-by," i.e. lay followers) united through use of the Gandhari language, the highest-value goods of the caravan trade were reimagined as spiritual goods, jewels and treasure that could symbolize the ideals which Buddhists were seeking.

◈◈◈

Respect for the Written

The presence of the different language traditions nevertheless made its impact on the content of the faith. One was on the reverence for scriptures in written form. India's tradition was against this, but the new Mahayana attitude was almost fetishistic in its respect for texts.

Both Greece and Persia had long and strong written traditions. The Aramaic-script tradition in particular had its successor in the Kharoṣṭhi script used for Gandhari, but there were in fact many competitors known in India. This is noted in the Lalita Vistara (of the third century A.D.), in which the schoolboy Gautama, on his first day at school, asks his overwhelmed teacher which of the sixty-four scripts he is to be taught.[18] (He never did get an answer.) Indian tradition, even at the highest level of grammar, was resistant to written language, hence its established sayings:

Pustakasthā tu yā vidyā parahastagatam dhanam.

Knowledge in a book: money in another's hand.

(Cānakya-nītī 16–20, of the early third century B.C.)

Vedavikrayiṇaç cāiva vedānāṃ cāiva dūṣakaḥ
vedānāṃ lekhakaçcāiva te vāi nirayagāminaḥ.

Sellers of the Vedas, misreaders of the Vedas,
writers of the Vedas, all alike on the path to hell.

(Mahābhārata, of the early first millennium A.D.)

The *sangha*, the community of the Buddha's disciples, originated within this common Indian tradition. It had preserved its founding doctrines and stories for the first few generations purely orally. A learned monk was *bahussuta*, one who had "heard much." In fact, to judge from the Tipitaka, in the Buddha's era there may have been as yet no knowledge even of writing, and when it did arise, it was a secular medium, not one for religious matters.

The Questions of Milinda is the only Theravada text contemporary with the earliest Mahayana sutras to mention it, listing book learning as just one of seventeen ways of recall:

> [Memory springs up through . . .] reference to a book, as when kings calling to mind a previous regulation, say: "bring the book here," and remind themselves out of that . . . [#16]

But it contrasts it with proper scriptural knowledge:

> Learning by heart, as the repeaters of the scriptures by their skill in learning by heart recollect so much . . . [#14][19]

Yet in Mahayana, quite a different attitude to written texts was to prevail. The *Prajñā-pāramitā* ("Perfection of Wisdom") sutra, one of the earliest and most authoritative, sets up its own written words for worship, and, in images, is constantly depicted as a volume embraced by Manjusri, Tara, and other goddesses who represent the knowledge it imparts. In a typically flowery passage, the Lotus Sutra sings its own praises as a physical book:

> Should there be one who receives and upholds, reads and recites, explains and teaches, or copies out The [Lotus] Sutra, be it even a single verse, looking upon the Sutra text with reverence as he would the Buddha himself, making various kinds of offerings of flowers, incense, beads, powdered incense, paste incense, burning incense, silk canopies, banners, clothing and music, or who even join his palms in reverence, O Medicine King, you should know that such a person has in the past already made offerings to tens of myriads of millions of Buddhas, in the presence of those Buddhas, accomplishing great vows . . .[20]

A quotation from a sutra might be written out as a *dhāraṇī*, a kind of magic charm, and "it is implicitly stated that depositing the dhāraṇī from our text in a stupa [the characteristic Buddhist monument, built in conical form] generates more merit than is generated by depositing any of the four kinds of relics."[21] The faithful acted on this. A text of the Saṃghāta sutra, with traces of sandalwood paste, vermilion, and saffron on its binding, was found deposited in a stupa, making it a votive object comparable to a relic; and clay tablets with devout maxims were often similarly buried, even at the Nālandā university site: evidently fluent literacy was no bar to this kind of magical reverence for written texts. Xuanzang, an intellectual Chinese visiting India in the seventh century, remarks on a particularly widespread variant of this practice:

> Jayasena . . . was exceedingy simple-minded and moderate. He amused himself amid the forests and hills, dwelling in a sort of fairy-land, while his mind wandered amid the limits of truth . . . It is a custom in India to make little stupas of powdered scent made into a paste . . . they place inside them some written extract from a sutra; this they call a *dharma-śarīra* [literally "dharma body"] . . . When the number of these has become large, they build a great stupa, and collect all the others within it, and continually offer to it religious offerings. This then was the occupation of Jayasena . . . Thus he acquired the highest and most excellent religious merit.[22]

And such clay stupas, made of miniature stupas, and signed with the classic *dhāraṇī* that was almost the Buddhist creed, have indeed been found. The text reads:

*Ye dhammā hetuppabhavā tesāṃ hetuṃ tathāgato
āha tesāñca yo nirodho evamvādi mahāsamano 'ti.*

Those dharmas arisen from a cause, the Thus-Gone their cause
has said; and what is their cessation also the great ascetic has spoken.

and has been found in Bodh Gaya and Rajgir in Bihar, Paharpur and
Mainamati in Bengal, Harwan in Kashmir, and Ghazni and Gilgit in the
northwest. The couplet is known as the *pratītya-samutpāda* "dependent
arising" formula, and is the dharma in a nutshell. As such, it could be identified with the *dharmakāya*, the "dharma-body," again the essence of the
Buddha himself. This was a high status to give to a concrete written text,
which could, of course, be copied at will.

Although this tradition of worship for written sutras began in Kharoṣṭhi,[23]
it was to be carried on in many other Indian scripts (all of them, as it
happened, descended instead from the Brahmi used by Aśoka).

It led to a new interpretation of the Pali term *cetiya* (Sanskrit *caitya*),
which had meant a massive burial mound or stupa (both words—*cetiya* and
stupa—meaning literally a "pile"), but came to mean any image of or monument to the Buddha. *Cetiya* had been stupas, carved footprints, parasols,
the bodhi tree, or the eight-spoked wheel. Now that it was accepted that the
body of the Buddha was the dharma itself, the *tathāgata-caitya*, "a symbol of
the Thus-Gone," might even be an image of the Buddha himself: it was this
tradition—later taken up by all Buddhists—that the Greeks seem to have
founded, although the evidence is physical, rather than declarative.

Influence from the Greeks

Archaeological remains show that, under the Indo-Greeks and the Kuṣāṇa,
Buddhist influences percolated society.* According to the Mahāvaṃsa
chronicle (a Theravada document in Pali written in Śri Lanka around the
sixth century A.D.), Gandhara and "Yona" (that is, the Ionians, the Greeks)
had received their own mission sent by Aśoka, while another Greek was
sufficiently firm to be sent to minister on the western frontier, and make

---

* This evident fact contradicts a widespread prejudice, seen in Indian texts at least until the
second century A.D., that the northern barbarians—Pahlava (Parthian), Yavana (Greek),
Śaka (Scyth), and even Kuṣāṇa alike—were violently *dharmadveṣin* "hating the Buddhist
law," *tīrthika* "heretical," and *anārya/anārja* "un-Indian." (Cf Nattier 1991, pp. 154–57.)

converts. This took place in the partitioning of missionary zones after the Third Buddhist Synod, which would have taken place around the 230s B.C.[24]

Greek culture stood out for the elegance and realism of its art, and it is widely believed that the representations of the Buddha that became so famous, with curly hair and topknot (*uṣṇīṣa*, a word that had previously meant "turban" in Sanskrit), and flowing robes, and above all the contrapposto stance with weight more on one leg than the other, was a Greek innovation in Buddhism.[25]

These tantalizing images, showing the Greek intelligence applied to Buddhism, provide the best evidence for widespread Greek attention to Buddhism in India. It is frustrating that there is no surviving document in Greek that attests to Buddhist faith; there are no Greek-language dedicatory inscriptions on shrines, much less sutras. When there is such a dedication (as by the provincial governor Theodoros in Swat*), it is in Gandhari. Perhaps this absence of Buddhism expressed in Greek is not indicative of anything but the ultimate extinction of the Greek language in India, and hence the loss of any manuscript tradition in it. How convinced Buddhists addressed their faith in Greek is unknown, whereas we do know that Greek intellectuals describing Indian religion would interpret all foreign deities as their own in a foreign disguise. This phenomenon is generally known—in Latin—as *interpretatio graeca*. So for example, Megasthenes, Greek envoy from the Seleucids to the Maurya court of Chandragupta in the late fourth century B.C., represented Śiva's exploits as local beliefs about Dionysus and Herakles.

On "Indian philosophers" he was more objective, using borrowed terms for the two types, βραχμᾶναι and σαρμάναι (i.e., Brāhmaṇa and Śrāmaṇa), presumably Hindu sages and Buddhist ascetics. And there is a very occasional invocation of Indian deities in Greek script, for example in a manuscript in Bactrian of the fifth century A.D.: ναμωο σαοκομανο βοδδο ... ναμωο λωγοασφαροραζο ... ναμωο ραδανοκωταμο βοδδο ... ναμωο σανδαροβανο βοδδο "homage to Lokeśvararāja buddha ... homage to Ratnakottama Buddha ... homage to Chandrabhānu Buddha."[26]

However, the outstanding Indo-Greek king Menander (mid-second century B.C.) placed an eight-spoked wheel on the reverse of his coins: this most likely represented the wheel of dharma (a symbol of the eightfold path). Many rulers, Greek, Scythian, and Kuṣāṇa, would symbolize their

---

* *Theudorena meridarkhena pratithavida ime sarira sakamunisa bhagavato bahu-jana-stitiye:* "The meridarch Theodoros has enshrined here relics of Lord Shakyamuni, for the welfare of the mass of the people." This was written on a vase buried inside a stupa. (Konow 1929, 1–4, plate 1.1; *Corpus Inscriptionum Indicarum* 2.1.4.)

adherence to Buddhism with a *tathāgata-caitya*, such as this wheel, the tree under which the Buddha achieved enlightenment, or a roaring lion. Menander is reputed, too, to have set up a stupa in Paṭaliputra (Patna), then the dominant city of northern India, when he took it at the end of his campaign.[27] He and other Indo-Greek kings, such as his successor Strato, appear on their coinage with the Greek title ΔΙΚΑΙΟΥ (*dikaiou* "the just"); but since its Gandhari equivalent on the reverse side is *dhramikasa* "of dharma," this may be an appropriately "interpretative" Greek code for a Buddhist.*

In fact, the only direct account we have of Greek encounter with Buddhist belief is in Pali. It is enshrined in the work *The Questions of Milinda*, in which King Milinda (this a novel transliteration of Menander's name) raises finer points of philosophy with the sage Nāgasena. The most likely language for the original of this work is Gandhari, since both the extant versions, a Pali *Milindapañha* and a Chinese manuscript known as *Nāgasena-bhikṣu-sūtra* ("Text of the Monk Nāgasena") seem to be translations.[28]

Kaniṣka, three centuries later, has the Buddha on a coin (pictured, and named as ΒΟΔΔΟ); and on other coins one finds Buddha Śākyamuni, the reverential title for the historic Gautama Buddha (ΣΑΚΑΜΑΝΟ ΒΟΥΔΟ) and the buddha of the future, Maitreya (ΜΗΤΡΑΥΟ ΒΟΥΔΟ).[29] There is still no clear-cut evidence of Mahayana, since all these had featured in earlier Buddhism.[30] However, there are also a wide variety of other Greek, Iranian, and Hindu gods pictured on Kuṣāṇa coins, showing that these religions were all current in the empire; even for Kaniṣka, host of the Fourth Buddhist Synod, Buddhist representations make up a tiny minority of extant coins. Nevertheless, it is argued that they effectively place the buddhas on a par with divinities, a significant move toward Mahayana.

But Buddhism was affected by this cosmopolitan mixture of Greek and Kuṣāṇa culture, emanating from Bactria and Gandhara. It seems that this mixed pantheon was present not just in different communities making up the empire, but also in individual worshippers' minds. An extreme example of mixed traditions from Gandhara shows the Buddha supported by the Greek god Herakles and the Iranian goddess Harītī.

Herakles, with his usual curly hair and beard, carries a stylized thunderbolt (*vajra*) rather than his traditional club, showing that he is replacing

---

* ΔΙΚΗ *dikē*, literally "justice," seems a reasonable equivalent for dharma. But as mentioned, it had not been Aśoka's term, when he talked about Buddhism in Greek: ΕΥΣΕΒΕΙΑ *eusebeia* is more theological, closer to "reverence."

the usual attendant bodhisattva Vajrapāṇi (whose name means "thunderbolt-hand"). Harītī is often identified with Greek Tyche, and represents good fortune, for she carries a cornucopia, symbolizing all the blessings of the world. Herakles, a personification of passionate strength, and Tyche, of arbitrary outcomes, may seem strange companions for one whose power comes from enlightenment and total understanding of the universe's working. But for the *Tathāgata*, the "Thus-Gone," nothing is alien.

Grammatical Thinking and the Mahayana

The fact that a new set of doctrines flourished—as did its authorization as *buddhavacana* "Buddha's words/enlightened discourse"—remains to be explained somehow, whatever the mechanism. Scholars of the Mahayana are driven to find a way in which the dharma tradition was "off stage" for a time, to allow changes to occur in doctrine while maintaining the apparent authority of a traditional origin. Thus A. K. Warder speculates that changes took place somewhere in southern India, rationalizing the Buddhist legend that the tradition was for a time carried on among Nāga dragons.[31]

Paul Williams has pointed out that the change in the Buddha's status itself made it easier to expand approved doctrine, the *buddhavacana*. The Buddha had been reconceived, as not (just) a self-perfected man of the past, but as a perfect being who exists in multiple worlds, and is in fact only one representative of such perfection. This widens radically the process of validation for *buddhavacana*.

As Śāntideva wrote in his eighth-century *Śikṣāsamuccaya* ("Compendium of Instruction"): whatever is *subhāṣita* "well-spoken" enhances understanding of the *buddhabhāṣita* "Buddha-spoken"; meanwhile, the Buddha (and his coequal buddhas) continue to exist throughout many worlds, hearing all that is good from whatever source, and approving it.[32]

Philosophically, the fundamental ground of Mahāyāna is *śūnyatā* "emptiness," the apparently positive correlate to *an-ātman* "non-self," which is originally the denial of the absolute existence of any self or soul (*ātman*). An important characteristic of this empty world is *tathatā* "thusness," which focuses on any properties with which it may present. These things may all be identified with *tathāgata-garbha* ("Thus-Gone's womb") also known as the *buddha-dhātu* ("Buddha root"), which are dynamic properties that constitute the transformative Buddha-nature in everything.

From a grammatical point of view, it is notable that these words in Sanskrit (or indeed Pali) are all "names."[33] Now according to standard grammar, names are *sattva-pradhāna* "entity-prevalent" and *sattva-abhidhāyaka* "entity-denoting": that is to say, they denote entities, whereas verbs denote action, being, or becoming. There is a grammatical bias, therefore, to reify what these terms stand for. Mahayana Buddhism did not resist this tendency in any way. Abstract entities began to multiply, and then be given animate characters.

In Mahayana theology, the Buddha, far beyond being a single, exceptional man, came to be identified with the universe itself, and by the same token was equated with *śūnyatā* "emptiness," *an-ātman* "non-self," *tathatā* "thusness," and *tathāgata-garbha*, the "Buddha nature in things." This pantheistic view, identifying entities as different aspects of the same, rather than relating or articulating them, was highly compatible with Hindu philosophy influential in India, such as *tat tvam asi* "that thou art," the doctrine of the Chandogya Upaniṣad (pre-third century B.C.) that identified every being as a microcosm of the world as a whole. An interesting twist was that on the Hindu view (known as *Vedānta* "the Vedas' end") the universal Brahman was identified with *ātman* "self," rather than its denial *an-ātman*. Nonetheless, it can be seen as an aspect of the worldview that came along with the use of the Sanskrit language (just as Gautama might well have feared!).

Heirlooms from the Past

The Buddha, properly understood, was everything. In the world of metaphysics (known in Sanskrit as *abhidharma* "the out-and-out dharma") a theory of the Buddha was nothing less than a theory of the whole universe, void (*śūnyam*) as that might be in the final analysis. Specifically, although Gautama had famously registered a firm "no comment" on matters of speculative theology (*mayā avyākataṃ* in Pali, literally, "by me undeclared"),* there was room for at least three classes of apparently divine—or *lokuttara* "world-transcending"—beings:

---

* E.g., "Therefore Malunkhyaputta, hold the undeclared as undeclared. Malunkhyaputta, what are the not-declared? The world is eternal, is not declared by me. The world is not eternal, is limited, is not declared. The soul and body are the same; the soul is different from the body; the Thus-Gone One is, after death; the Thus-Gone One is not after death; the Thus-Gone One is and is not after death; the Thus-Gone One neither is, nor is not after death: all are not declared by me." *Majjhima Nikāya* II.2.3 (63) Advice to Venerable Malunkhyaputta. (By "the Thus-Gone One" the Buddha is of course referring to himself.)

in increasing rank, the *deva* (or traditional deity), the *bodhisattva* (a superior being who was dedicated beyond the cycle of births to work for mankind's enlightenment), and the *buddha* (already in a state of enlightenment, but still providing refuge in a *buddha-kṣetra* heaven for some imperfect beings). The existence of these different statuses is justified through *abhidharma*, but their actual characters, as Mahayana Buddhists identified them, seem to owe more to worldviews that come from other (very wide) religions.

Deva was the ordinary Sanskrit word for a god.* For Buddhists, these were not eternal, nor in any way superior to human beings in matters of karma and the unending vicious cycle of rebirth (*saṃsāra*), though they might, of course, be much more long-lived and powerful; yet their privileged status laid them open to the danger of being "corrupted through play."[34]

The *devas* represented by Mahayana Buddhists were largely a selection of Hindu deities, including Indra as a general god of sky and weather, presiding over a court of thirty-three divinities on Mount Sumeru, and Yāma as lord of the underworld. Another *deva* is Kubera, the god of wealth, who is king over the *yakṣa* (rustic spirits); he is also identified with Pañcika, consort of Harītī, who presides over childbirth and children.† Some of the important supporters in Buddhist iconography have this lesser status of *yakṣa*, such as Vajrapāṇi, the Buddha's bodyguard. *Gandharva* are musicians, retained for divine entertainment, while less exalted still are *asura* and *rākṣasa*, demons largely concerned with fighting and hostility. Among them must figure Māra, the force of temptation, analogous to Christ's Satan, who did his best to distract the Buddha from the dharma and this path to enlightenment.[35]

The known bodhisattvas, on the other hand, are largely non-Indian, hence are heirlooms that —if not based on real people— go back to Parthian, Greek, or Scythian deities. In principle, anyone who makes progress toward enlightenment, but holds back in order to help others, can be a bodhisattva. By the end of time, if the prophecies are true, all beings must sooner or later become bodhisattvas. But there is a fixed number of famous bodhisattvas, who are available to those who turn to them in prayer, and are thus like guardian deities (or saints) in their role in Buddhism. Since they persist,

---

* As such it has cognates all over the Indo-European world, including Iranian *daeva*, Latin *deus*, Greek *Zeus*, Irish *Dia*, Anglo-Saxon *Tiw* (as in "Tuesday"), Norse *tívar*, Lithuanian *diēvas*, and even Hittite *sius*.) Its root meaning seems to be "shining" or "brilliant," which shows up in many words meaning day, e.g., Latin *diēs*, Slavic *dĭnĭ*, and Sanskrit *divasa-, dina-*.

† We saw, in the opening passage from the Lalita Vistara, that the Buddha was first mistaken—by the two worldly merchants from Bactria—for Indra or Kubera.

quasi-eternally, between lives, and are aways accessible, they must have some properties in common with *devas* rather than regular people.

Avalokiteśvara (*avalokitā-īśvara* the "Lord Who Looks Down") is the most popular bodhisattva. He is said to have originated as a beam from the eye of a buddha, specifically Amitābha, and retains his link with him, bearing this buddha's symbol in his headdress. He is often seen as a second member of a trinity, with Amitāyus ("Measureless Age") above and Mahāsthamaprāpta ("Great Strength Achieved") below.* But more generally he is a comforter, compassion incarnate, definitely motherly in style, and thus later reconceived in the Far East as a merciful goddess, Gwan-yin in China, or Kannon in Japan. As such the name is also interpreted as *avalokita-svara* "he of the cry that is noticed."

There are many more bodhisattvas with famous names and images. All were available to be invoked as refuges for the ordinary Buddhist, and many went on to have significant careers under Chinese, Japanese, or Mongolian names. Mañjuśrī ("Lovely Glory") symbolizes the embodiment of *prajñā* ("transcendent wisdom") and is usually depicted riding on a lion. This is interpreted as showing his ability to subdue the fearsome beast that is the mind. Analogously, Samantabhadra ("Universal Worthy") rides an elephant and embodies the virtues obtained through meditation. Together with Mañjuśrī and Śākyamuni Buddha himself, he forms another Buddhist triad.

Ākāśagarbha ("Sky Womb") and Kṣitigarbha ("Earth Womb") are two bodhisattvas, sometimes seen as twins, representing the riches of the elements sky above and earth below. Kṣitigarbha, though assumed like most bodhisattvas to be male, is reputed to have begun as a Brahman maiden who devoted her piety to saving her mother from hell. This accomplishment led to a particular concern for children and the fate of all beings undergoing torment in hell. Vasudhāra ("Stream of Gems") is an unambiguously female bodhisattva, and like the Hindu goddess Lakṣmī, whom she closely resembles, is noted as a dispenser of wealth to those devoted to her.

The latest bodhisattva in time, but first in inspiration, is Maitreya (who—being of early conception within Buddhism—also has a Pali name, Metteya). He is a Buddha to be, but as such is held as a bodhisattva, dwelling until his descent to earth in the *Tuṣita* ("Contented") heaven. The name appears to be derived from the abstract name *maitrī* "kindness" derived from the familiar

---

* There is an Iranian trinity, Zurvān "Time" with Ahura Mazda the spiritual principle and Ahriman the force of matter, which could be compared.

term *mitra* "friend" in Sanskrit, but which means "contract, bond" in the Avestan language of Iran. Maitreya holds our appointment with destiny in a perfect future.

Overall, the concept of a bodhisattva itself evokes a new possibility in Buddhism, the chance of spiritual aid, whereby one being can, through acquiring merit but then sharing it, effectively rescue others. This is the idea of a savior or redeemer, which, although originally alien to Buddhism, is right at the heart of various religions originating in the West. These include the Saoshyant in Zoroastrianism (Avestan "who sets about benefiting"), a figure who appears at the end of each millennium to save the world; and the Messiah (*mašíḥ* "anointed one") long promised to Israel.* It is notable that Greek kings (especially the Ptolemys in Egypt, but also those in the Indo-Greek dynasties) also liked to style themselves *sōtér* ("savior"—*tratara* in Gandhari), making a similar claim on the loyalties of their people, and in fact evoking the term not as it would be used for Jesus Christ—centuries later—but for Zeus: Zeus the Savior was honored in countless temples in ports, as the god who would bring sailors home safe from a voyage.

Above all, the Buddhas tended to multiply over time. First the seven Buddhas of the past were recognized, with Gautama as the seventh. Then twenty-eight names were recorded in the Mahayana canon. Ultimately, as many as a thousand Buddhas were assigned to each *kalpa,* or aeon, of the many that make up history past and future.

They are coordinated as a system by the *tri-kāya* ("three-body") doctrine. By this, the historic manifestations on earth of the Buddha (Siddhartha Gautama, or Śākyamuni, and his predecessors) form merely the *nirmāṇa-kāya* or "manifestation-body." The truest body of the Buddha, which is the dharma itself, is the *dharma-kāya* or "law-body": this is the essence of the Buddha as truth itself, known and worshipped as Mahā-Vairocana. Besides these two, there are a number of buddhas, representing the *sambhoga-kāya* ("enjoyment-body" or "reward-body"), bodhisattvas who have already achieved buddha-hood (though apparently without the extinction that is nirvana) and exist each in their own *buddha-kṣetra* or paradise. They are, strictly speaking, manifestations of the law-body, and have accumulated so much merit from previous lives as bodhisattvas that they have become a copious source of it for the less fortunate.

---

* The Jews had even seen Cyrus, King of Persia, as a *mašíḥ,* when he authorized the rebuilding of the Temple in Jerusalem. Isaiah 45:1: "This is what Yahweh says to his anointed [*l-mšíḥ-u*], to Cyrus . . ."

The best known *sambhoga-kāya* is Amitābha Buddha, who dwells in *Sukhāvatī* ("Blissful") and has promised rebirth there—the best life Buddhism can offer—to all those who call his name.* But another such is Bhaiṣajya-guru, "Medical Teacher," the Buddha of healing, particularly popular in Gandhara, who has two bodhisattvas in attendance, Sūryaprabhā and Candraprabhā ("Sunlight" and "Moonlight").

These additions to the cast and scene-setting of the Buddhist world, accepted and integrated into Mahayana, are plausibly analyzed as borrowings from pre-Buddhist worldviews, which had possessed their own gods and spiritual concepts.

Merchants' Wares as Buddhist Treasure

Gandhari, as we have seen, although formed in the mountainous northwest of South Asia, had become the lingua franca of the Kuṣāṇa empire, giving access to widespread networks that held this multinational community together, all over northern India, in what was known at the time as the *Uttarapatha*, literally, "the northern path." The military and administrative sides to the organization of this dominion are largely unknown to us, for lack of documentary evidence. But the commercial side is clearer, involving the movement of large caravans of pack animals. Recall Trapuṣa and Bhallika, whose encounter with the Buddha led off this chapter: they were merchants, involved on that fateful day in leading a caravan northward in Bihar, along the Phalgu River to the then Maurya capital, Rajgir (or *rājagṛham* "King-home"). They became the first two lay Buddhists and dignified the new role of *upāsakaḥ* "sitter-by," as opposed to the ordained monks who were known as *bhikṣuḥ* "beggar" from their frank reliance on alms for survival.

Buddhism was a faith well adapted to a society organized on a large scale, beyond the village and the city.[36] The fifth to third centuries B.C.—at some point during which the Buddha lived—witnessed the rise and consolidation of the Mauryan Empire. This presupposed the establishment of a military hierarchy (under *cakravartin* "wheel-turner" kings) and large-scale bureaucracies, at the expense of more traditional village communities.

---

* This is none other than the Amida-Butsu of the Jōdo "Pure Land" cult in Japan, promising paradise to all who chant the *nembutsu* phrase in Japanized Sanskrit: *namu Amida Butsu.* (Cf the Sanskrit original: *Namo Amitābhāya.*)

This was one net result of the advent of the Iron Age, which had begun early in the first millennium B.C., but which achieved the finest quality of steel around 300 B.C.:* besides better weapons (Indians were already famous in Greece for their iron-tipped arrows in the early fifth century[37]), this introduced iron plowshares, which would have enabled bigger agricultural surpluses.[38] At the same time, the widespread use of metal currency (the first punch-marked coins dating from the mid-fourth century) facilitated the accumulation of wealth in cash, as well as active trading in high-value goods.

The bureaucracy to be maintained by the royal state is theorized in Kauṭilya's *Arthaśāstra* ("Theory of Wealth"), which may have been written as early as the fourth century B.C. and certainly dates no later than the first century A.D. It clearly sees merchants' activity as essential. It requires the king to promote commerce by setting up trade routes by land and by water and market towns along such routes to be kept free of harassment and from being damaged by herds of cattle; frontier officers to be responsible for the safety of merchandise on the roads and to make good what is lost; and merchants, if authorized to sell crown commodities at prices set by the chief controller of state trading, to compensate the government for consequent lessening of direct revenues.[39]

Such trade was facilitated throughout North India and Central Asia by the widespread lingua franca Gandhari. And a kind of synergy developed in this area between traders and the Buddhist *sangha*, largely organized as it was into monasteries. Had not the Buddha himself blessed Trapuṣa and Bhallika? In a telling exchange of respect, the Buddha was often referred to as *mahā-sārtha-vāha*, "great caravan leader." Although the mendicant monk (*bhikṣu*), through study and meditation toward enlightenment as an *arhat*, had to eschew material gain, he would still require support from the working world of agriculture and commerce.

Agriculture was wrong for a monk, since plowing fields and reaping harvests disrupted the natural world, and so did violence to some lesser beings, even if only insects and worms. But monks could provide safekeeping for items of value left with them, and so a kind of banking service. And

---

* Within this millennium, the Sanskrit word *ayas-* changed its meaning from "copper" to "iron"; as did the synonym *loha-* (which seems originally to have meant just "red," as *hiranya-* "gold" had meant "yellow"). According to a Roman historian, in 326 B.C. the defeated Indian king Pōrus (Sanskrit *Paurava*) made Alexander a gift of one hundred talents (2,600 kilograms) of steel ("white iron"—*ferri candidi talenta C*). This was Quintus Curtius Rufus ix.8, writing in first century A.D.

especially with the new Mahayana doctrines, the enlightened Buddhist community could do much to bless lay "sitters-by" (*upāsaka*) who gave alms—in quantities commensurate to their own wealth—to the *sangha*. They could transfer merit (*puṇya*) built up by their own exertions to those less well placed to acquire it, and they could show their lay brothers (and—though with some handicap—sisters) how to progress toward rebirth in a paradise. In Buddhism, no further ceremony was required, beyond material contributions, to convince the monastery of a donor's devotion. There was no Buddhist baptism, or ceremony of initiation, for an *upāsaka*.

Records of such Buddhist contributions are very common among the inscriptions from this era. They typically record the dedication of stupa structures or reliquaries and other portable objects.[40] Where the donors are merchants,

> the most common . . . designation . . . is *śreṣṭhin* [or Prakrit equivalents] . . . "a banker or merchant or the foreman of a guild. Other merchant titles . . . include *sārthavāha* . . . (perhaps denoting a merchant involved in long-distance trade in inscriptions), *vanij* . . . (probably traders in basic goods), *negama* (members of guilds of traders or artisans), *hairaṇyaka* . . . (goldsmiths or treasurers), *gandhika* (roadly meaning merchants and shopkeepers) and *vyāvahārika* (a general term for businessman).[41]

The availability of Buddhist enlightenment through Gandhari discourse and written texts, making new use of a preexisting lingua franca, therefore enlarged the community of the faith, fulfilling too the predicted social dimension of language transfer. Buddhism would embrace all users of this language, potentially the whole population of the Uttarapatha. Any language in use creates an implicit community among its speakers, and theorists of religious conversion have long noted that the process goes fastest among those who already know and trust one another.[42]

While the administrative use of Gandhari was no doubt a major factor favoring the use of Gandhari as a long-term lingua franca for Buddhist religion in Central Asia,[43] its use in trade was probably even more important. The transmission of Buddhism through Gandhari-speaking merchants effectively made it a more "mercantile" religion, with a greater use for material goods.

Long-distance merchants in every age have a special fondness for low-volume, high-value goods. Costs of transport are kept to a minimum, while the potential for profit per unit transported is high. For Europeans trading across the Indian Ocean in the seventeenth and eighteenth centuries, these goods were spices—pepper, nutmeg, ginger, cloves, and many more. For the Indians traveling the Silk Routes in the early centuries A.D., there were, above all, the Seven Treasures, *sapta-ratna*. Such goods even assumed a special spiritual role within Buddhism.

Evidently seven was an auspicious number, independently of what was counted. For example, Kauṭilya had identified *saptānga*, the seven limbs of a good government organization, in his Arthaśāstra. But applied to treasures (*ratna*) the fixed list of seven treasures first appears in the Mahāvastu ("The Big Thing"). This was compiled over a long period, possibly the five centuries from the second century B.C., so that dating individual passages is hard. At its first mention,[44] the *sapta-ratna* is used ambiguously, between assets of government (not the same set as Kauṭilya's) and luxuries to build into a palace:

> At that time there was a bodhisattva, who was a universal king [*cakra-vartin*], ruling over the four continents, who was triumphant, possessing the seven treasures [*sapta-ratna-samanvāgato*], who was righteous [*dharmiko*], a king of righteousness [*dharma-rājā*], pursuing the path of the ten skilful actions [*daśa-kuśalakarma-patha-samādāya-vartī*]. These seven treasures [*imāni sapta ratnāni*] are the wheel, the elephant, the horse, the precious stone, the woman, the householder and the counsellor [*cakra-ratnam, hasti-, aśva-, maṇi-, strī-, gṛhapati-, pariṇāyaka-ratnam*] . . . This universal king supplied the perfect Buddha Samitāvin and his company of disciples with all the requisites, with robe, alms-bowl, bed, seat and medicines for use in sickness. He had a palace built of the seven treasures [*sapta-ratna-mayam prasādam*], gold, silver, pearls, lapis lazuli, crystal, white coral (or agate), and ruby [*suvarṇa, rūpya, muktā, vaiḍūrya, sphāṭika, musāragalvā, lohitikā*] . . .

This list is fixed in the Mahāvastu, where it occurs in eight different contexts. But later there was some equivocation about the tail end of this list, with occasional substitution of red pearl (*rohita-mukti*) and/or *aśma-garbha* (literally "rock-womb," i.e., emerald, though amber, coral, and diamond are also proposed).[45]

These evidently achieved a religious significance since they are found as offerings in stupas, with collections of gold and silver sheets and disks, quartz, crystal beads, pearls, and precious stones in green, red, and blue varieties. But the stones are not always anything better than colored glass of the right colors. Even if not always genuine, it seems that—as we might have predicted from their interest to Buddhist merchants—these goods were exported with no fuss to China. This is why the Chinese word for transparent glass 玻璃 *bōlí* (pronounced in Early Middle Chinese *phaliə*) reflects *phalika*, a Prakrit version of *sphāṭika*, i.e., "quartz"), while that for opaque glass 琉璃 *liúlí* (EMC *luwliə*) comes from Prakrit *velūrya* "lapis lazuli." This loan vocabulary represents what were (at least originally) exotic imports from India, even if all that the Chinese actually received was cheap substitutes for the good stuff.[46]

Likewise, the high-value goods coming in the opposite direction were given a holy use by the devout merchants. Silk was the Chinese product par excellence (hence the very term "Silk Road" for the trade route). Silk was highly prized as an adjunct to worship in the same Mahāvastu—though naturally, given the Indian climate, it tends not to survive in stupas or *caityas*:[47]

> He who has placed a festoon of fine silk (*paṭṭa-dāmam*) on a monument of the savior of the world (*lokanāthasya cetiye*) prospers in all his aims, both among gods and among men, avoids base families and is not reborn among them.[48]

As the monasteries made use of some of the entrusted funds and treasures to beautify their buildings and parks, the results provided an ideal, profoundly ethical showcase for the treasures of society, and reinforced the impression of providing a path to paradise for all.

It all seemed a remarkably virtuous and self-sustaining system, even if the king's government nonetheless might—with engaging cynicism—keep up its guard against rascalry, from monks and merchants alike:

> *Evaṃ corān acorākhyān vāṇik-kāru-kuśīlavān*
> *bhikṣukān kuhukāṃś-ca anyān vārayet deśapīḍanāt*

> So as for those who act as merchants but are undercover thieves, like mendicants and other rogues, [the king] should stop them from ruining the country.

> (Arthaśāstra 4.1.65)

CHAPTER 3

"Fine Words Are Not Trusty"

Aryan Vehicle on Road into Chinese

At first I objected against the wording [of this translation] as being unrefined. Vighna replied: "As to the words of the Buddha, we are concerned with their meaning, and do not need to adorn them; the grasping of the doctrine they [contain] is not effected by adding embellishment. Those who transmit the scriptures [in another language] must make them easy to understand, and the meaning must not be lost—[only] then is the work well done."

All those present quoted the words of Laozi:

信言不美，美言不信。 *xìn yán bù měi, měi yán bù xìn.*

Trusty words are not fine, fine words are not trusty.

> Preface to the *Dhammapada* in Chinese, mid-third century
> A.D., probably by the Kuṣāṇa translator Zhī Qiān 支謙*[1]

B Y   T H E   S E C O N D   A N D   T H I R D   C E N T U R I E S   A.D., Buddhist believers, whether *bhīkṣu* or *upāsaka*, were—thanks to the Kuṣāṇa empire, and its trading networks—free to travel not only throughout the plains and mountains of North India and Central Asia, but also into neighboring states, Parthia to the west, Sogd to the north, and China to the east. In this era the sutras, the texts that served as authorities for their faith, were available only in a family of closely related cousin languages, notably Pali, Gandhari, and Sanskrit. Though believers were careful to distinguish themselves from the more traditional Indians who stuck by Brahman-dominated Hinduism,

---

* The Laozi slogan is from the eighty-first and last chapter of the *Dào Dé Jīng*, Taoism's authoritative text (known more familiarly as *Tao Te Ching* or *Dao De Jing*).

the rest of the world, and particularly the Chinese, knew this speech as "Brahman talk."*

Although this language was then the lingua franca of merchants around the Kuṣāṇa empire, and current from Bactria to Mathura and Khotan, it seems to have been quite impenetrable to any Chinese who may have heard it. The Chinese of this era, already denizens of a large self-regarding empire, were largely monolingual. Yet the Buddha's dharma was potentially a truth for all, as its reception by Greeks, Parthians, Scythians, and Tocharians had shown. To bring it to Chinese understanding, however, it would need to be interpreted in Chinese, and this is what happened from the middle of the first century A.D.

First we hear of two missionaries who took the Buddha's word to the Chinese capital, Luoyang, in 67 A.D. Although they are supposed to have been Indians, their names are given in Chinese as 迦葉摩騰 and 竺法蘭, names that would be sounded in modern Chinese as *Jiāshè Móténg* and *Zhú Fǎlán* (but a millennium ago would have been *Kiaɕiap Madəŋ* and *Truwk Puaplan*†). The former is transliterated into Sanskrit as Kāśyapa Mātanga, and the latter translated (via "law-treasure") as Dharmaratna.‡ Memorably accommodated in the 白馬寺 *Bái-mǎ-sì*—the "White Horse monastery"— they produced a Chinese work called the "Sutra in Forty-two Sections" (四十二章經). The Chinese word 經 *jīng* means either a Buddhist sutra or a Chinese "classic," and the text actually reads more like a classic: for example, each section begins with the two characters 佛言 "Buddha says," just as in the Analects of Confucius we find the two characters 子曰 "The Master says."

The work appears to have been drafted directly in Chinese: at any rate, no Indic original is known. Besides alluding to the four noble truths and eightfold path, and enumerating such issues as "twenty difficult things to attain in this world," it is mostly made up of similes. It compares the pleasures of the world to honey on a knife blade, clinging wives to tigers' jaws, evildoers to people who spit up at the sky. An earnest pilgrim is like a log in a river, inevitably progressing if he avoids entanglements; or a man cautiously

---

* 梵文 buamʰ ʔwən "Brahman text," 梵語 buamʰ ŋiɑʰ "Brahman talk." This is Early Middle Chinese (EMC) pronunciation (reconstructed for ca. 600 A.D.), rather than second-century A.D. Still, it shows the original far more clearly than modern Chinese (*fàn-wén, fàn-yù*) or Japanese (*bonbun, bongo*). These are still used in Chinese and Japanese as elegant names for Sanskrit.

† 竺 abbreviates 天竺 tʰɛntruwk, which weakly represents [Hinduka], i.e., Indian.

‡ A "transliteration" as Gobharana, presumably based on modern Mandarin, is also current.

carrying inflammable hay among fires; or an ox steadfastly carrying a burden through mud. Much attention (fully one seventh of the work) is devoted to the perils of lust:

佛言：愛欲莫甚於色，色之為欲，其大無外。 賴有一矣，若使二同，普天之人，無能為道者矣。

The Buddha said:
Of passions there is none like lust (色 *sik*, literally, "color"*); there is no desire so great as the sexual urge. Be sure that there is but one. For if there were two such, no one normal could follow the Way.

Since there was so little direct communication possible between "Brahman-talking" citizens of the Kuṣāṇa realm and Chinese subjects of the Han, one can only speculate what the motive was for these pioneering missionaries. The records of this era are tantalizing and fragmentary. There is a garbled report that in 2 B.C. a Kuṣāṇa prince gave instruction to a Chinese emissary on Buddhist sutras; and reports of a functioning Buddhist monastery in 65 A.D., as far east as Pengcheng (near Xuzhou, in modern Jiangsu province), evidently still functioning in 193 A.D. Here the King of Chu (a Chinese) had practiced Taoist "Huanglao"† arts, while fasting and "performing sacrifices to the Buddha." An edict from the Ming emperor in 65 returned a gift of silk to him, "to contribute to the lavish entertainment of *upāsakas* and *śramaṇas* [written as 伊蒲塞 *yipusai* and 桑門 *sangmen*]." This was evidently an exotic touch from the emperor's secretary, but Zhang Heng's anthology *Xijing Fu* 西京賦 "Western Capital Verses," from about 100 A.D., includes the claim that the court ladies of Chang'an "would captivate even a śramaṇa," suggesting that these holy foreigners already had proverbial status in Chinese.[2]

Buddhism, then, may have had a certain exotic Western charm for Chinese of the Han dynasty. What made it spread among them was "conversion by voluntary association," with Indian merchants trading into China.[3] There was no military or economic takeover of China by the Indian Buddhists, nor did

---

* *Rāga* in Sanskrit/Pali has the same ambiguity. Two of the fetters that bind to the wheel of rebirth are *kāma-rāga* "sensuality" and *rūpa-rāga* "the urge to assume some form through rebirth."

† Huang-Lao is a portmanteau word, referring to Huangdi (黃帝 "Yellow Emperor") and Laozi (老子 "Old Master," i.e., the originator of the Dao). It was the central Chinese doctrine in the Han dynasty, an amalgam of Taoism and Legalism.

the Chinese assimilate, since the spread of Buddhism was a phenomenon of a minority's influence expanding within a vast majority population of Chinese.[4]

The trade routes into China were viewed by the Chinese as the "Western Regions" 西域 *xiyü*, and there is an authoritative contemporary Chinese report on them: the 後漢書 *Hòu Hàn Shū* ("Records of the Later Han"—viz 25–221 A.D.) edited by Fan Ye 范曄. He was writing in the early fifth century, but he drew on reports from the Chinese general Ban Yong, who had been active in the regions over many years since his youth and submitted his report to the Chinese emperor close to 125 A.D. It has little to say about Buddhism in parts explicitly under Chinese control, but that "*Tiānzhu* is one name for *Shēndu* [viz Sindhu/India] . . . they practice the Buddha Way, no killing or war, as has become the custom."[5] This might suggest that Buddhism was fast becoming fashionable in China at the time.

But surviving information about Kuṣāṇa or other Indian merchant activities in China is scant. In general, the best-documented foreign merchant communities in China are associated with the Sogdians, themselves great producers of Buddhist translations. They were certainly active already on the Silk Road, since already in 29, 25, and 11 B.C. Chinese chronicles are commenting on a Sogdian presence at court in Chang'an: "Those who bring gifts . . . are all merchants and men of low origins"; "if we ask . . . why [Kang-zhu, viz Sogd] sends its sons to attend [at the Han court], we find that desiring to trade, they use a pretence couched in fine verbiage."[6] Two and a half centuries later in 227 A.D., at Liangzhou in the Gansu corridor through to China, Zhi Fu and Kang Zhi, ennobled leaders of the Kuṣāṇa and Sogdians, were in a deputation sent to receive the commander of a conquering army. In 313 Sogdian merchants sent a report home on the Huns' sack of the Chinese cities Yeh and Luoyang. They noted that "in Luoyang . . . the Indians and Sogdians there had all died of starvation" thus noting both their, and their Indian colleagues', desperate commercial presence in the Chinese capital of the day.[7]

Gradually, foreign merchants were establishing themselves as respected pillars of Chinese communities.[8] And the process continued, with a multitude of Sogdian foundations, especially in the seventh century. Their names bear evidence of their populations' identity: *Xinghu-cheng* "Sogdian Town,"* *Putao-*

---

* 興胡 *xīnghú* "prosperous foreigner," under the Tang government, was a title actually more like "licensed trader," with rights to move and transact business on the same terms as Chinese subjects. Most of the holders would no doubt have been Sogdians (cf Arakawa 2011, p. 39).

cheng "Grape Town" (the Sogdians being famous vintners); and *Xincheng* "New Town" was also known as *Nuzhi-cheng*, meaningless in Chinese, but showing the Sogdian adjective *nwc* [nōč], "new," in the feminine.[9]

Considerations of supply and demand suggest the main reasons for the uptake of Buddhism in China.

On the supply side, the second century A.D. was a prosperous time for the Kuṣāṇa Empire, whose merchants, increasing in number over time, brought an opportunity for higher living standards through exotic products, and introduced some interesting new ideas about a better life to be won through right effort, and especially almsgiving. Missionaries often traveled with the merchant caravans, anxious to spread knowledge of the saving dharma. And expertise in languages—often concentrated in particular individuals roaming far from their homes, such as Parthians and Sogdians—was used not just for trade negotiations, but also to support interfaith discussions and undertake translation of religious scripture.

On the demand side, China was going through an unstable period in the second century A.D., as the central government of the "Eastern Han," based in the northern cities of Luoyang and Chang'an, gradually lost its coercive authority. After 220, there was no single accepted capital, and the Three Kingdoms period began, ushering in three centuries of disputed leadership. Given the Chinese ideal of *tiān xià* 天下, "under heaven (a single government)," it was clear that the world was not as it should be. Culturally, there seems to have been no loss of the sense of common Chinese identity, but spiritually there was continuing tension between the Confucians, with their aspirations for social conservatism and hierarchical loyalty, and the Taoists, who emphasized oneness with nature.

China, then, was ready for a new source of inspiration, a new doctrine fit for unpredictable times, especially if it could be made to chime with a preexisting system of belief. The most immediate common feature was "the Way": the Buddhist *mārgaḥ* or eightfold path was crying out to be identified with the Taoist *dào* 道, each of them being fundamental to the good life. But Buddhism, at least as traditionally understood, would require a rather different approach than the Chinese way, a path that could only be followed through highly effortful concentration; by contrast, following the *dào* was more like going with the flow, an attitude of *wú wéi* 無為 "non-action."

Gradually, the curious documents translated by Buddhists traveling to China were received into Chinese intellectual currency; and gradually, through the establishment of monasteries in China, Chinese could also become monks (僧 *səŋ*, a loan from Sanskrit *sangha* "community") or indeed *upāsaka* ~ 優婆塞 *ʔuwbasək*.

Translations to Chinese

The first known translations into Chinese were undertaken not by Indians or Kuṣāṇa but by Parthians.* These must have been independent adventurers, since Buddhism in any form was never widely accepted in Parthia. The first, An Shigao, was a monk who reached Luoyang in 148 A.D., and translated more than a dozen Hīnayāna scriptures. The second, a merchant called An Xuan, was apparently working with a Chinese partner, Yan Fo Tiao. In 181 they produced a basic version of the Buddhist primer *Ugradattaparipṛccha* "The Questions of Ugradatta," known as the *Fǎ jìng jīng* 法鏡經, or "Law Mirror Sutra."

The next, highly prolific, translator was a Kuṣāṇa hailing from Gandhara, his name given in Chinese as 支婁迦讖, which having the phonetic reading in Early Middle Chinese as Zhī [ləwkatṣʰimʰ], probably represents the Sanskrit name *Lokakṣema* "world-welfare."† Born in 147, he appears to have moved to Luoyang in infancy and grown up there, doing his main translation work as a bilingual native speaker between 178 and 189. Lokakṣema translated the *Pratyutpanna Sūtra*, "The Sutra of the Present," the founding text for belief in the Amitābha Buddha and his Pure Land. In Chinese, he called it 般舟三昧經 (*Bān zhōu sānmèi jīng*, the "Boat-Like Samādhi Sutra"). He also pioneered in Chinese the Prajnā-paramita Sutra (the "Perfection of Wisdom") in its longer eight-thousand-line version. It is known in Chinese as 道行般若經 (*Dào xíng bānruò jīng*, the "Path-Practice Wisdom Sutra"). There is no more important text for the Mahayana. In addition, there is evidence that he also translated the *Śurangama-samādhi-sūtra*, the "Indestructible Concentration Sutra," which became in Chinese 首楞嚴三昧經 *Shǒu léng yán sānmèi jīng*. This was seminal for Chán (Japanese Zen) Buddhism.‡ None of the rest of his oeuvre (perhaps another ten works) has survived.

---

* The surname 安 An, used by Chinese for all Parthians, is a shortening of Ansik 安息, the Chinese name for Parthia, derived from their ruling dynasty the Arsacids.

† The surname 支 Zhī is the second syllable of 月支 *Yuè-zhī*. Chinese for Tocharian or Kuṣāṇa.

‡ It was translated at least twice afterward, and today is only known in Chinese translation.

Lokakṣema worked with an Indian, known in Chinese as Zhú Shuòfó,* who provided many of his original manuscripts. He is credited with having laid the foundation for Mahayana Buddhism in China, since he was the first to produce advanced-level texts that Chinese monks could read.

He also worked with three Chinese laymen, two of whom are identifiable as Taoist devotees. Indeed, the *Dào Dé Jīng* 道德經, the fundamental "Classic of the Way and Its Virtue," begins in words that could almost have been uttered by the Buddha himself.

道可道非常道。

> The Road that Can be Taken is not the eternal Road.

名可名非常名。

> The Name that can be Named is not the eternal Name.

dào kě dào fēi cháng dào
míng kě míng fēi cháng míng

無名天地之始。

> The Nameless is Heaven and Earth's beginning;

有名萬物之母。

> the Named is of ten thousand things the mother.

wú míng tiān dì zhī shǐ
yǒu míng wàn wù zhī mǔ

故常無欲以觀其妙。

> He ever without Desire sees its subtlety;

常有欲以觀其徼。

> he ever with Desire sees its outline.

gù cháng wú yù yǐ guān qí miào
cháng yǒu yù yǐ guān qí jiào

此兩者同出而異名

> These two are same in origin, distinct in name:

同謂之玄。

> calling them the same is dark.

cǐ liǎng zhě tóng chū ér yì míng
tóng wèi zhī xuán

---

* The surname Zhú 竺 is a shortening of 天竺 Tiānzhú, and denotes an Indian. This name, 竺朔佛, might represent a Sanskrit name such as Uttarabuddha, "Buddha of the North."

玄之又玄　　　　　　　　　　　　It is the dark of dark,
眾妙之門。　　　　　　　　　　　of all subtleties the gate.

xuán zhī yòu xuán
zhòng miào zhī mén

Buddhism was to be looked to as a source of light on this darkness, what Taoists would identify as the 玄学 *xuánxué*—the "Dark Learning." From the first, then, there was close sympathy between Dao and dharma, though naturally a distinctively Chinese spin was put on the Buddha's Law.

Indeed, the claim that the Buddha could have written the opening to the *Dao De Jing* needs some restriction: it takes no account of some fundamental linguistic differences between "Brahman talk"—in whatever Indian language—and Classical Chinese. For one thing, Chinese was a language that blithely overlooked time and mood, and the kind of precise relations—agent, patient, recipient, instrument—that are expressed curtly but obligatorily in the endings of Sanskrit or Gandhari verbs and nouns. Furthermore, equivalents needed to be found for all the technical terms of Buddhism—for the first time—in a wholly unrelated language.

As a result, the key concepts of Buddhism now assumed a very different guise from what had happened when they had been translated in Gandhara. Of these, just four, *buddha*, *duḥkha* (suffering), *arhat* (adept), and nirvana, are represented by phonetic transcriptions into Chinese characters, transcriptions so purely phonetic that they make nonsense if interpreted: 佛陀 *but-da* (viz *Buddha*) meant literally "great bank." No Chinese could have gathered from this that the term really meant "the awakened one." Likewise, interpreted literally as characters, 阿羅漢 *alaxan*[h] (viz *arhat*) meant "old-net-Chinese," and 豆佉 *dəwʰkʰa* (viz *duḥkha*) meant "bean-surname." For *nirvāṇa*, the rendition 泥洹 *nɛjwuan* was replaced after a couple of centuries of use (ca. 400 A.D.) by 涅槃 *nɛtban*, presumably to better match the Pali *nibbāna* instead of Sanskrit *nirvāṇa*.

Other new terms, very much in the majority, were attempts to map the Buddhist concepts into something more familiarly Chinese. An alternative, much clearer rendition of "suffering" was 苦 *kŭ*, which means precisely that; and for "craving, desire" we find 愛 *ài* (literally "love"), for "ignorance" 無明 *wú míng* (literally, "not bright" or "blindness").

Philosophical terms require the largest conceptual jumps: "causation" is represented by two terms that mean respectively gathering and awaking (集 *dzip*, 起 *kʰi'*), and the favorite word *ārya* "noble" is conceived as 聖 *ɕiajŋ*[h] "sage"—the same word that was ultimately to be adopted by Chinese Christians to mean "holy" or "saint." *Arhat*, the Buddhist adept who has achieved enlightenment, was also often translated for meaning rather than for sound: either literally as "deserving" 應供 *yìnggōng*, or else (following the popular etymology *ari-hat* = "enemy-slayer") as 殺賊 *shāzéi*.

But the highest levels of entity had the most tendentious—not to say, confusing—translations. 道 *daw*ʰ "Way" denoted the Buddhist eightfold path, just as much as its competitor, the Taoist Way. 法 *puap* "Law" was also chosen to express the Buddhist dharma, regardless of the fact that it was the central technical term of Han Fei Zi's "Legalist" philosophy. This was a no-nonsense political doctrine ("Obey the Law"), which had reached its peak of dominance in the Warring States period of the fifth to third centuries B.C. With such terminology as this, it would sometimes have been hard to distinguish Buddhist insights clearly from the intellectual or spiritual theories that had preceded it in China.

Among the technical terms distinctive to Mahāyāna, some taken from Chinese philosophies, and notably Taoism, are essential. *Śūnyatā*, the void that is the main substance of the world, is translated as 本無 *běnwú* "original non-being," a central term of Taoist *xuanxue* "Dark Learning." And the term that established itself as the equivalent of *māyā* "illusion" is the metaphorical *yěmǎ* "wild horses," in the sense of "shimmering air."[10] Curiously, it almost inverts the syllables of the Brahman-talk equivalent (*yěmǎ* : *māyā*). The metaphor goes back to the first chapter of Zhuangzi's great poetic work, which conjures the effects when a vast mythical bird takes flight:

野馬也，塵埃也，生物之以息相吹也。

It is wild horses, it is dust, it is ceaseless blowing-about of living creatures.

The contemporary scholar Cheng Xuanying (who flourished 632–650) comments on this: "In the spring time, the heat-haze shimmers. When you watch the middle of the swamp in the distance, it looks like running horses. Hence the name *Yema*."[11]

After Lokakṣema's generation, another team of foreigners were at work, two with the "Indian" surname Zhū, and a "Sogdian," Kāng Mèngxiáng 康孟詳,* and around 190 A.D., they produced the first life of the Buddha in Chinese, entitled

---

* Kāng 康 is an abbreviation of Kāngju 康居, the land equivalent to modern Uzbekistan and Tajikistan, and is a common Chinese surname for Sogdians, and possibly others—e.g., Tibetans—who seemed to originate from that northwesterly direction.

修行本起經 (*Xiūxíng běnqǐ jīng*) supposedly representing Sanskrit *Cārya-nidāna*, "The Origin of What Goes On." The title shows its proposed value, but the content would have been more of a narrative, a gospel of the Buddha in effect.

These early attempts at translation had established a basis for Chinese Buddhist practice, with an accepted terminology—quite a major step in mediating the transition between languages as different from each other as Sanskrit "Brahman talk" and Chinese "literary expression." But the best practice, as the Han dynasty gave way to the more uncertain times of the Three Kingdoms, was still far from full and thorough conversion.[12]

The great Buddhist translator Dharmarakṣa, also known as Zhú Fǎhù 竺法護, adopted this surname out of respect for his teacher. Yet he was not an Indian, but a member of a Kuṣāṇa family who had grown up on the borders of China in Dunhuang and, as a result of wide travel, supposedly read all the languages of Central Asia. He was working at the end of the third century A.D.[13]

At least relatively early in his career, when he produced his version of the Lotus Sutra, his knowledge of Brahman talk (whether translating the original from Sanskrit, Gandhari, or some other Prakrit) was imperfect. Yet he may have been the only Brahman-Chinese bilingual working in what was a fairly large team of scribes, critics, and potential commentators. This kind of multilingual milieu seems to have flourished in the Silk Road cities along the Tarim Basin around the Taklamakan Desert, and particularly in Kucha, a Tocharian city. The first colophon on the translation describes the situation in which the translation was accomplished, over about three weeks:

> On [September 15, 286 A.D.] the Yuezhi [i.e., Kuṣāṇa Tocharian] *bodhisattva śrāmaṇa* from Dunhuang, Dharmarakṣa, holding the foreign [hú胡] scriptures in his hand [so the specific language of the original is left vague], orally delivered and issued the 27 chapters of the *Zhēng Fǎ Huá Jīng*, conferring it upon the *upāsakas* [four Chinese named], who together took it down in writing. [Another seven scholars with Chinese names] "all took pleasure in encouraging and assisting" [though two of them have the surname Zhū, which suggests Indian origin] . . . The Indian *śrāmaṇa* Zhū Li, and Kuchean house-holder Bo Yuanxin both collated the translation . . . [A Chinese] of Chang'an [then the capital of China] copied it with simple glosses.[14]

Many of the errors are attributable to a lack of facility with the Indian sound-system (very different from Chinese).[15] So *bāla* "foolish" is confused with *bala* "strong," *pratipatti* "good conduct" with *pradīpa* "lamp," *ghaṇṭa* "bell" with *gandha* "perfume," *Druma*, a proper name, with *dharma* "law," *bho(n)ti* "is/are" with *bodhi* "awakening," *nātha* "lord" with *nāda* "roar," *pravadanti* "declare" with *prapatanti* "fall down," *kṣetra* "field" with *citta* "mind," *kāṇaka* "one-eyed" with *kanaka* "gold" and even *bhūta* "being" with *buddha* "buddha," and *jñāna* "knowledge" with *dhyāna* "concentration, zen" and *dāna* "donation."

Some words are constantly misunderstood, as if the lexical item was just unknown: for example, *dāruṇa* "cruel" is variously interpreted as forms of *dhar-* "receive or hold" or *dharma* "law."

The work also shows unfamiliarity with some basic features of Brahman talk's word structure: the present participle for Atmanepada voice, ending in *-māna* (or Prakrit *-mina*), is often confused with *manas* "mind"; and the Indians' much-beloved abstraction ending *-tva* is taken as a reduced form of *stūpa* "burial mound" : so *arhatva* is taken not as "arhat-hood" but as 無著塔 *wú zhuó tǎ* "the no-attachment-stūpa."

These are pretty basic errors that can make nonsense of a passage—although they are mitigated by Dharmarakṣa's spread-betting practice of doubly translating items where his vague grasp of Indian sounds makes them consciously ambiguous to him: so, for example, *lokavidu* "world knower" is translated as 世之聖父 "world's sage father," since it might just possibly have been *loka-pitu* "world-father." And the *tathāgata-pāṇi-marjita-mūrdhānai* "Thus-Gone hand-stroked heads" are rather excessively (and perhaps heretically) claimed to "seek the water of the Thus-Gone and aspire to be in the Buddha's palm" just in case that word *pāṇi* "hand" should really have been read as *pāṇiya* "water."

But the misunderstanding becomes serious, and crucial to theology, when the translator is unsure whether an arhat is being referred to as 緣覺 (*yuánjué*) *pratyaya-buddha* "one awoken through (external) cause" or as 獨覺 (*dújué*) *pratyeka-buddha* "one awoken on his own," and so combines them as 緣一覺 (*yuányījué*)* *pratyay-eka-buddha* "conditioned-single buddha." This is arguably just Dharmarakṣa's passing embarrassment, but it may have had a more general significance. In fact, it has been claimed[16] that the whole concept of the *pratyeka-buddha* arose from a mistaken back-translation of the Chinese for *pratyaya-buddha*—a case where a mistranslation can be claimed to have changed the creed itself, and permanently.*

---

* This is something that strikes most people as a major danger when the creed of a faith is translated. But in practice, it is a rare event in the annals of religious conversion.

The *Sangha* Becomes Chinese

The exotic new religion, now accessible—if tentatively—in Chinese garb, had a thitherto unsuspected value, as a force for unification under a foreign elite. It was unexpectedly adopted as official religion by new conquerors of Northern China. These were nomadic herdsmen from the steppes of Siberia across the Gobi Desert, known as the Tabgach (拓拔, now pronounced in Chinese as the Tuoba), who became assimilated to Chinese dynastic politics as the "Northern Wei" (北魏朝; *Běi Wèi Cháo*). They established themselves through battle and rapine in 386 A.D., but it took about a century for them to assert control of all the north. Once they did so, in 439, they would hold power for a century, until 534.

There were some hiccups in the establishment of the Buddhist faith, perhaps foreseeable when a quietist religion was enforced with a mailed fist. The first full emperor, Tuoba Tao, actually ordered the secularization of Buddhist priests in 438, and a full persecution of Buddhists in 446. However, he was deposed in 452, and his grandson, Tuoba Jun, then reversed the policy. Thereafter all the Wei were devout, and in fact proceeded to glorify the Buddhist *sangha* through a program of temple building, sculpture, and exquisite decoration. They also supported a translation program for Buddhist sutras.

This role in dynastic politics turned out to do Buddhism no harm at all. It pocketed its gains, making inroads into elite Chinese society on the strength of royal support. Moreover, it apparently suffered no adverse reaction a century later, when the Northern Wei dynasty fell from power.

Dynastic politics aside, the most important long-term effect on Buddhism of the translation of the sutras into Chinese was that it gradually enabled the Chinese to leave Sanskrit and the authority of Indian-generated traditions behind: to recenter Buddhism on Chinese texts, as interpreted by Chinese monks.

This can be seen as a major instance of the community effect of translation, whereby a foreign linguistic community is transformed into a self-reliant heartland of the faith, perhaps recognizing it in quite a different form. Arguably, this would have been impossible if no translation had been required to make Buddhism accessible to the Chinese.[17]

The process took several centuries, but it can be seen under way in the career of the cardinal sutra named *Vajra-cchedikā Prajñā-pāramitā* "Diamond-splitting Wisdom-Perfection,"[18] highly valued because being relatively short (in thirty-two chapters) it could be committed to memory and recited frequently, thus accumulating merit. This point is made in chapters 11–12:

> The Buddha told Subhūti, "Just so, if good men and good women accept and maintain even a four-line *gāthā* from within this *sūtra*, speaking it to others, then the merits of this surpass the former merits.
>
> "Moreover, Subhūti, if one speaks even a four-line *gāthā* from within this *sūtra*, you should understand that this place is like the shrine of a buddha."

It was first translated (and well translated) by the Kuchean master linguist Kumārajīva in 402, whose intellectual renown was such that he had been personally summoned to the capital, and afterward forcibly rescued from a warlord's kidnap, by the Northern Wei emperor Xianwu.

It was nevertheless retranslated five more times in the following three centuries, on almost a fifty-year cycle: three times by immigrant Indians— Bodhiruci in 509, by the Brahman Paramārtha in 562, and by Dharmagupta, from South India in 605, with commentary—then twice by Chinese pilgrims who visited India in the quest to improve their learning: Xuanzang in 648, and Yijing in 703. After 703 there were no translations of this text, although it remained central for the faith in China.[19]

This pattern, of a lessening of translation starting in the eighth century, was typical. Relations with Indian scholars were maintained, but translation projects largely ceased in the early ninth century; and although one large-scale translation program was undertaken much later (by the emperor Taizong of the Song dynasty, who reigned from 976 to 997)

> the newly translated texts . . . failed because they were rarely used by the contemporary Buddhist community. The growth of indigenous Buddhist schools, practices and scriptures in China diminished the need to study and disseminate new doctrines from India . . . they [the texts] had become totally irrelevant to the trajectory Chinese Buddhism had taken since the Tang period [618–906].[20]

Xuanzang and Yijing were traveling scholars, who had studied Sanskrit and come from China to India to acquire the most authentic knowledge about Buddhism from its source. They were not alone: indeed Yijing noted that there was an academic centre at Śrī Vijaya in Sarawak dedicated to giving the necessary training. But they came toward the end of a period when Buddhist authenticity could only be found in the dharma's heartland, and specifically at the college in Nālandā outside Paṭaliputra (Patna) in Bihar. They returned to the Tang capital of Luoyang and produced, in quantity, translations of classic sutras, but the effect was rather to sate demand for Indian learning, than to stimulate it.

Xuanzang overcame the doubts left by the Chinese texts he had known in his youth, and found a basis to ground the *Yogācāra* "Yoga-Practice" school of metaphysics, not least because he had studied for a decade with the master Śīlabhadra at Nālandā. Yet the result was not to create a common Indo-Chinese school; instead, he founded the Chinese *Fǎxiàng-zōng* (法相宗, "Dharma Characteristics school"), or as he would prefer the *Wéishí-zōng* (唯識宗, "Consciousness Only school"*), which went on to be developed separately by his disciple Kuījī. This was ranged against the *Sānlùn-zōng* (三論宗, "Three Treatise school"), which had been brought to China by Kumārajīva himself, a philosopher as well as a translator, and corresponded to the Indian Middle Way between Idealism and Realism. This was known as *Mādhyamika*, having been originally founded in India by Nāgārjuna in the early third century A.D.

These schools, largely dedicated to philosophical metaphysics, did not survive in the long term. But other Chinese schools, especially those with a more popular approach to devotion, turned out to be extremely long-lasting. Although they claimed roots in Sanskrit sutras, they had grown up independently of India. Among these was the *Tiāntāi zōng* 天台宗, founded by Zhìyǐ in the later sixth century, and named for the mountain "Sky Roof" on which he lived. The sect claimed inspiration from the Lotus Sutra (*Saddharma puṇḍarīkasūtra*, 正法華經 *Zhēng Fǎ Huá Jīng*) and attempted to classify and synthesize a range of Buddhist doctrines. Another was the *Huáyán-zōng* 華嚴宗, "Flower Garland school," which derived from the sutra of that name, called *Avataṃsaka* in Sanskrit. It started a little later than Tiantai, supposedly founded through the contributions of five different sages, among them most notably Fazang (643–712), and was supported by Empress Wu (who died in 705) in its early days. Philosophically, it emphasized the extreme

---

* In Sanskrit *Vijñaptimātra*. Conceptually, this Idealist theory fits neatly into a triad with the Realist *Sarvāsti-vāda* ("Everything Is" theory), and the intermediate *Mādhyamaka* school.

connectedness of things, and mutual causation, all being based in the four-fold *dharma-dhātu* 法界 *fǎ-jie* "law root."

Most popular of all was the Pure Land school *Jìngtǔ Zōng* 淨土宗, with its emphasis on how the lowly believer may be saved, and reach paradise through faith in the Buddha Amitābha. This is based on the *Pratyutpanna Sūtra*, or in Chinese "the Sutra of the Present" 般舟三昧經 (*Bān zhōu sānmèi jīng*—"the Boat-Like *Samādhi* Sutra").

In addition to all these, there was present in China the tradition known in Sanskrit as *dhyāna* "meditation" which—apparently with strong Taoist influences—developed into Chinese 禅 (dʐjan; later to be recognized as Japanese *Zen* and modern Mandarin *Chán*).* After the Song dynasty (960–1279), it tended to merge with the Pure Land school, adding the idea of an induced sudden revelation leading to enlightenment. And the word *samādhi*, literally "concentration, pulling together" (which appears in so many of the Chinese sutra titles as 三昧 *sānmèi*), refers to a state of intense contemplation that may be achieved through Zen.

The growing confidence of Chinese Buddhism—autonomous and proud of it—can be seen expressed surprisingly in an action of the brilliant pilgrim Xuanzang. After an epic journey across a closed Chinese border and through the principal states of Central Asia, in 630 he reached the borders of India.† He circulated aound the Himalaya foothills for the next seven years, no doubt becoming fluent in Brahman talk on the way, and reached Nalanda, the center of India's Buddhist academe, in 637. There he studied with the school's principal and entered into debates with all comers. He seems to have attracted as much admiration in India as he had done as a youthful prodigy of scholarship in China, and this must have filled him with self-confidence as a potential authority on the dharma, even in its own heartland.

He was much attached to a sutra known as 心經 *xīn jīng* "the Heart Sūtra," and recounted how he had received it in his youth from a diseased and destitute man whom he nursed back to health, and recited it to himself

---

* This must have involved, at some point, the invention of a new Chinese character, combining the "showing" radical 示 (implying a form of instruction) with the phonetic 單 dʐjan, which seems originally to have pictured a "cicada." (www.chineseetymology.org)

† As a Chinese he had known the country as *Tiānzhu*, but now preferred to call it 印度, then pronounced [ʔyindɔʰ], explicitly equating it with the Sanskrit word *induḥ* "moon." He makes no mention of the Greeks or Persians, or their names derived from the Sindhu river, *Indos* and *Hindu*.

at moments of extreme danger on his travels, more effective even than invocation of the bodhisattva Avalokiteśvara/Gwan-yin, renowned for the power of comfort.[21] He used it, then, less as a sutra reminding him of truth, and more as a *dharaṇī*, capable of warding off evil spirits.

The text is extremely short, a mere twenty-five lines of Sanskrit or some three hundred Chinese characters. It is unlike a sutra in that it does not begin with *Evaṃ mayā śrutam* "Thus I have heard," nor is it a reported speech of the Buddha, but rather—implicitly—some remarks of Avalokiteśvara. Also, it is strange in its ending, being not a report of the audience reaction, but rather a recommendation of a mantra:

gatē gatē pāragatē pārasaṃgatē bodhi svāha

gone gone gone-beyond gone-altogether-beyond awareness well-said

The content of the text, after the introduction associating it with Avalokiteśvara, is a disquisition of the universality of *śūnyatā* "emptiness," coexistent with *rūpam* "form," and so providing the ground for a bodhisattva to rely on the Prajna-paramita ("Perfection of Wisdom").

By origin it is a short excerpt from one of the longest sutras, the *Pañcaviṃśatisāhasrikā-Prajña-pāramitā-Sūtra* or "Perfection of Wisdom in 25,000 lines"; but although this section can be located, it is curiously different from the text of the Heart Sutra in Sanskrit, saying the same things, in the same order, but with different vocabulary and different phraseology. Even more curiously, this is not true of the Heart Sutra in Chinese, which matches almost word for word, and character for character, the passage in Kumārajīva's Chinese translation.*

Jan Nattier has persuasively answered this riddle[22] by supposing that the "Heart Sutra" is not a sutra after all, but a section cut from the Chinese translation of the Perfection of Wisdom, which has been topped and tailed with context (including a neat Sanskrit maxim), and then retranslated into Sanskrit, for added credibility. 心經 *xīn jing* could mean, in fact, not "Heart Sutra," but "a sutra to get by heart." She even adds spice to the theory by suggesting the author of this subterfuge might have been Xuanzang

---

* This is the intimidatingly entitled 摩訶般若波羅蜜経 (which, however, read phonetically as *moho-panjo-polomi-jing*, can be seen as a section of syllables from *Mahā-Pañcaviṃsatisāhasrikā-Prajña-pāramitā-Sūtra*, i.e., the "Great-5-Perfect."

himself.* (Perhaps disappointed to have been unable to find the "original" of his favorite *dharaṇī*, he may have simply used his skill in Sanskrit to reconstruct it.) The work thus seems like a paraphrase of the original, because it is a translation of its Chinese translation.

That a Chinese might have had the audacity to supplement the Buddhist canon in this way suggests that in the seventh century, as China's golden age of the Tang dynasty was just getting under way, Chinese intellectuals were beginning to participate as equals, and even leaders, in Buddhist thought. It has been a truism throughout history that the Chinese—despite going through some political and diplomatic hard times (as in the Three Kingdoms period of the third and fourth centuries, or the nineteenth and early twentieth centuries)—find it difficult to see themselves as followers rather than leaders, especially in their own central world "under heaven." The Tang dynasty, by which time the classic texts of Buddhism had largely been sensitively and knowledgeably translated into Chinese, was a time for Chinese Buddhists to become masters of their own house, as well as offering sage advice to neighboring smaller countries, such as Vietnam, Korea, and Japan.

Overall, the trend of Chinese translation was to slide toward the free. And this, naturally, gave more scope for Chinese to develop their own interpretations of Mahayana Buddhist faith—something for which there would not have been room if the Chinese monks had simply accepted the Tipitaka in the Pali, Gandhari, or Sanskrit in which they had found it, and got on with learning them as sacred languages.

* It must have been a Chinese-Sanskrit bilingual of his era or shortly after, since the oldest commentaries on the Sanskrit text are from the late eighth century. Yijing might be another suspect.

CHAPTER 4

"To Deep of Lip and Heavy of Tongue"
From Galilee to the Gentile

καὶ εἶπεν πρός με υἱὲ ἀνθρώπου βάδιζε εἴσελθε πρὸς τὸν οἶκον τοῦ ισραηλ
καὶ λάλησον τοὺς λόγους μου πρὸς αὐτούς

διότι οὐ πρὸς λαὸν βαθύχειλον καὶ βαρύγλωσσον σὺ ἐξαποστέλλῃ πρὸς τὸν
οἶκον τοῦ Ισραηλ, οὐδὲ πρὸς λαοὺς πολλοὺς ἀλλοφώνους ἢ ἀλλογλώσσους
οὐδὲ στιβαροὺς τῇ γλώσσῃ ὄντας

οὐδὲ πρὸς λαοὺς πολλοὺς ἀλλοφώνους ἢ ἀλλογλώσσους οὐδὲ στιβαροὺς τῇ
γλώσσῃ ὄντας ὧν οὐκ ἀκούσῃ τοὺς λόγους αὐτῶν καὶ εἰ πρὸς τοιούτους
ἐξαπέστειλά σε οὗτοι ἂν εἰσήκουσάν σου

He said to me: Son of Man, go to the house of Israel and speak my words
to them. For you are not sent to a people deep of lip and heavy of tongue,
but to the house of Israel. Nor to many peoples of different voice or
different tongue, nor to those of stiff of tongue whose words you will not
hear. Even if I had sent you to such people they would have listened to you.

Ezekiel 3:4–6 (Greek version)[1]

T**HE FIRST CENTURIES OF** Christianity can be seen as an extended
series of experiments conducted to display the effects of language
transfer on a great faith. And these transfers began in the very first generation of preaching after Christ's death.

Christianity, the cult of the charismatic prophet Jesus of Galilee recognized as savior, had begun as a reform movement within Judaism, centered
on its holy capital Jerusalem. Nonetheless, it was addressed to all of the faith,
including the many peripheral Jews outside Palestine.

Furthermore, there was a surprising degree of interest among non-
Jews, so that an early issue arose: would they need to be accepted as Jews

(and specifically circumcised) before they could be accepted as Christians, symbolically reborn through the rite of baptism? The church's earliest leader, Simon Peter, had at first thought that they should be circumcised, but he came to believe this was a mistake. And this openness to outsiders was the doctrine that prevailed, controversial though it was in the first generation. Acceptance into the Christian community should not be restricted to Jews. Instruction in Christianity, known as *catēchēsis* ("voicing over"), and acceptance into the community through *baptismos* ("dipping") should be available to all.

Linguistically, this implied that the most useful language in which to develop a Christian community would, surprisingly, not be vernacular Aramaic. This language had been spoken by Jesus and his original disciples. It was the predominant language of the Jews of Syria and Palestine, those still inhabiting their "promised land"; no parochial dialect, it was in practice the current replacement for the Jews' ancestral language Hebrew. It had no official status as a state language in this period. Nonetheless it was a literate, and literary, language, and the numbers speaking it were vast through much of the Roman east and beyond, into Mesopotamia and Persia. This resulted from its continuing use over the previous millennium under the Babylonian, Persian, and Greek empires. In practice, it still enjoyed great value as a lingua franca across western Asia.

Despite this, the language chosen for the propagation of Christ's doctrine was the lingua franca of the eastern Roman Empire, Greek, in its *koinē diálektos*, "common speech." This had been, historically, the speech of the city of Athens, spread since the fifth century B.C. by trade and cultural influence around the eastern Mediterranean. As a commercial medium, it also happened to be the primary language of Paul, and Paul became the church's first great international preacher. Paul is recognized as an authentic apostle (*apóstolos*, "envoy (of God)") though he remarked wryly of himself that he received his commission *hōsperei ektrōmati*, as if to a premature baby, since he had never seen Jesus in life, and should for that reason be considered the least of the apostles.[2] This was a singularly proud kind of modesty, since it put him, uniquely, on a comparable level with Jesus's own personal friends and disciples.

Peripheral Jews, his primary targets for conversion, are often termed *Hellēnes* "Greeks" in the New Testament letters; Greek was their language, both for secular business, and also for their religion, since the most widely used text of the scriptures at the time was not the Hebrew original, but a

Greek translation, which dated only from the third century B.C.* This term *Hellēn* was decidedly disrespectful as a name for a Jew, even if they did speak Greek. Its implication was that they were potentially lapsed, and it was also used as a term for arrant non-Jews in Palestine, for example the suppliant mother whom Jesus tried to turn away—on grounds of non-Jewishness—but who prevailed on him through her quick repartee (as perhaps one might expect from a "Greek").

> Now the woman was a Gentile [*Hellēnis*, literally, "Greek woman"], of the Syro-Phoenician race. And she kept asking him to cast the demon out of her daughter. "First let the children eat all they want," he told her, "for it is not right to take the children's bread and toss it to their dogs." "Yes, Lord," she replied, "but even the dogs under the table eat the children's crumbs." (Mark 7:26–28)

The mixed nature of the faith in its early years—something like "improved Judaism for Jews and others"—is expressed by the very title that believers adopted. *Khristianoi*—the very word is a jumble. The evangelist Luke tells us that the first to adopt this title (around 50 A.D.) were believers in Antioch, a Greek-speaking city on the edge of Syria. A Latin ending (-*iani*) has been added to the Greek word Χριστός *Khristós*, itself a literal translation of the Hebrew מָשִׁיחַ (*Māšiaḥ*), Aramaic *Meshiah*,, "the anointed one." Transliterated rather than translated, it comes out as *Messiah*—with a meaning that is rather more vivid in modern English.[3]

And so Christians bore their cosmopolitan faith on their sleeves. They are the ones dedicated to a Greek acceptance of the fulfillment of a Jewish promise: that Jesus of Nazareth was indeed the Christ, the anointed one who was to come to save Israel from its own iniquity. But what should Greeks or other non-Jews of the first century care for the fate of Israel? These Christians' commitment went beyond theology, and they were more than adherents of a doctrine. The Latin ending, as used at the time, shows that they were servants of a master. Just like *muli Mariani*, "Marius's mules"

---

* This text has been known (at least in Latin) since the time of Augustine (early fifth century A.D.) as the *Septuaginta*, deriving its name from the legendary seventy-two scholars who had prepared it in Alexandria on the orders of King Ptolemy II, himself a Greek presiding over the Greek-speaking government elite of Egypt. (Augustine, *Civitas Dei*, xviii.42: *ut septuaginta uocetur, iam obtinuit consuetudo*.)

(a satirical title for the standing army that had stood at the bidding of the ambitious Roman general Gaius Marius in 107 B.C.), *Christiani* were the Christ's men and women, charged to follow his orders.

Of course, not everyone took them at their own evaluation. To many Jews they were not to be dignified with the title of Messiah-followers, even in Greek (though *masīḥī* afterward became a common term for "Christian" in Arabic.) The Jews preferred to call them after Nazareth, the humble place of origin of their prophet. Hence the Jews called them (in Greek) *Nazōraioi* or *Nazarēnoi*, a term used later to refer to Christians who were also Jews. Among Christians themselves, this word was only taken up in the East Syrian tradition: in Iran, for example, Christians of the Syriac rite were known as *nāṣrāya*, while Greek-speaking westerners were *kristyānē*.[4] But its use had, as Matthew notes with pride, been predicted in prophecy.[5]

The non-Jews who, perhaps unexpectedly, were soon to become the majority of Christians were known from a traditionally Jewish viewpoint in Hebrew as *gōyīm*, literally "the nations," a term whose translation is also familiar in Greek as *ta ethnē* or in Latin as *gēntīlēs*. Unlike *Hellēn*, these words carried no pejorative tone. What is striking about them is the extreme ordinariness that they connote: these Gentiles are just "people," whereas the Jews are special.*

But even the Jews spoke many languages, by this period. Just how many is the point of the miracle at Pentecost, recounted in Acts 2.

> And when the day of Pentecost was fully come, they were all with one accord in one place. And suddenly there came a sound from heaven as of a rushing mighty wind, and it filled all the house where they were sitting. And there appeared unto them cloven tongues like as of fire, and it sat upon each of them. And they were all filled with the Holy Ghost, and began to speak with other tongues, as the Spirit gave them utterance. And there were dwelling at Jerusalem Jews, devout men, out of every nation under heaven. Now when this was noised abroad, the multitude came together, and were confounded, because that every man heard them speak in his own language.

---

* Curiously, the word used for these masses in Aramaic/Syriac (the vernacular at the time) is *Aramāye*, literally, "Aramaeans." This at least shows how little this language's name carried Jewish overtones in the era. A deformation of this, *Am'maya*, became the regular word for Gentiles in subsequent usage of Syriac.

The disciples gathered for the feast were simple Galileans (hence some kind of Aramaic speakers), but when the Holy Spirit came upon them, they found themselves able to preach to the holiday crowds in their home languages, reaching out to visitors whose homes ranged from the Black Sea coast to Arabia, and from Rome in the west to the Parthian empire in the east.

> And they were all amazed and marveled, saying one to another, "Behold, are not all these which speak Galileans? And how hear we every man in our own tongue, wherein we were born? Parthians, and Medes, and Elamites, and the dwellers in Mesopotamia, and in Judaea, and Cappadocia, in Pontus, and Asia, Phrygia, and Pamphylia, in Egypt, and in the parts of Libya about Cyrene, and strangers of Rome, Jews and proselytes, Cretans and Arabians, we do hear them speak in our tongues the wonderful works of God."

If those visitors were really hearing their own vernaculars, this must have included at least half a dozen languages besides Aramaic and Greek: Persian, Elamite, Latin, and Arabic are explicit but others are implied by the places mentioned.

This was billed as the miraculous route to cosmopolitan conversions, an extreme expedient that God might support on occasion. At the very least, it sketched the diversity of zones where Christianity would be preached. In practice, the faith of Jesus Christ would be put forth to far wider audiences, but through a succession of more pedestrian linguistic strategies, all of which played out over the new millennium. These strategies ultimately established Christian churches as far as Ireland in the west, Iceland in the north, Ethiopia and Kerala in the south, and Persia, Central Asia, and even briefly China in the east. As each new language barrier was crossed, the faith had to change—if only subtly—to accommodate the alien peoples being asked to see it as the answer to their problems, problems that as yet, perhaps, they had barely conceived.

In the first century, Paul was already wary of multilingualism, conscious that, even if impressive, it might be divisive within local churches. He wrote:

> For he that speaketh in an unknown tongue speaketh not unto men, but unto God: for no man understandeth him; howbeit in the spirit he speaketh mysteries. But he that prophesieth speaketh unto men to

edification, and exhortation, and comfort. He that speaketh in an
unknown tongue edifieth himself; but he that prophesieth edifieth
the church ... Therefore if I know not the meaning of the voice, I
shall be unto him that speaketh a barbarian, and he that speaketh
shall be a barbarian unto me.[6]

The Choice of Greek

Rather than attempting to reach each in his or her own language, the revealed
strategy of the early church (at least outside Syria and Palestine, where the
targets were local Jews) was to rely on the lingua franca of the eastern Roman
Empire, namely Greek. It attempted to grow the faith within a single
language community which was already large and far-flung, for this had
various implicit advantages.

First of all, it was accessible to large numbers of Jews, and not just those
of the diaspora who no longer lived in Syria or Palestine. The "Septuagint"
Greek translation of the Jewish scriptures was widely used throughout
Jewry. It alone is quoted in the books of the Greek New Testament, and
as such became the standard Christian authority for the "Old Testament,"
though often known to western converts through fragmentary translations
into Latin (the so-called "Vetus Latina") until Jerome produced a new Latin
version derived from the original Hebrew in the early fifth century A.D.
(This is known as the Vulgate, and has remained in use ever since.)

The use of Greek as the Christian lingua franca meant that missionary
work could be taken up in the various Greek-speaking cities of the eastern
Mediterranean. The most immediate evidence of this is the travels of the
apostle Paul, described in detail in the Acts of the Apostles, which took him
to Seleucia and Antioch in Syria; to Caesarea, Tyre, and Sidon in Judaea;
then to Issus, Adana, Tarsus, Iconium, and Antioch in Anatolia; and on to
Philippi, Apollonia, Thessalonica, Pella, Athens, and Corinth in Greece,
and Ephesus on the coast of Anatolia, before ending up in Jerusalem to be
arrested by the Roman authorities. In all these places, his command of Greek
allowed him to communicate directly with converts and pagans, and foster
the growing church as a single community. His writings also make it clear
that he was in touch with Greek speakers farther afield, notably Apollōs
in Alexandria, the capital of Egypt, and the couple Priscilla and Aquila, a
Jewish couple with strong Roman connections.

Greek was not Paul's only language.[7] He hailed from the Cilician city
of Tarsus, which had been highly hellenized since Alexander's conquest
(333 B.C.), so it may well have been his first language. But when Christ had
addressed him directly to reproach him for his persecutions, in the famous
vision on the road to Damascus, Christ had spoken *tēi hebraïdi dialektōi*,
literally "in the Hebrew dialect."[8] And Paul was also capable of addressing a
hostile Jerusalem crowd—to good effect—in this language.* His facility in
Greek would have been seen as a facet of his familiarity with Gentiles, and
evidently gave him a prima facie appearance as a lax Jew to this orthodox
audience. Paul replied, by attempting to show that he was as orthodox as
anyone, following the recommendations of the Jerusalem elders.[9] But it is
clear that in the mid-first century A.D., to broach Jewish religious matters
and propose reforms while communicating in Greek could come across to a
simple-minded Jewish crowd, at best, as inauthentic. There was a price, then,
that was paid for this language policy of the early church.

But a corresponding advantage of using Greek was the potential to preach
directly to actual Greeks, a highly influential public. These, of course, would
not be Jews, even lapsed ones; but some might be proselytes (προσηλυταί—
"approachers," something like "fellow travelers"), i.e., non-Jews who were
attracted by Jewish doctrines, who wished, as far as possible for outsiders,
to get close to them. Nonetheless, it was already clear to Paul that Greek
society and Greek education made them rather different from orthodox Jews
as prospects for conversion: "for the Jews require a sign, and the Greeks seek
after wisdom"—different mindsets, but neither well prepared (as Paul saw it)
to surmount the stumbling block and accept the epic folly of Christianity.[10]

Greek was also a language widely understood in the imperial capital
Rome, and this was Paul's declared destination.† He is said to have been
commanded explicitly in a dream to go there,[11] as a sequel to his visit to

---

* We can only presume that this actually refers to Aramaic, not Hebrew. The New Testament
never refers explicitly to Aramaic (nor Syriac), although this language was then current as
the vernacular of Palestine, as various verbatim quotations show. The use of the noun
diálektos may be enough to indicate that the spoken vernacular is intended, hence not the
Hebrew of the Scriptures.
† In the Jewish catacombs in Rome, 74 percent of the inscriptions are in Greek, as against 24
percent in Latin, and just 2 percent in Hebrew or Aramaic. (Finegan 1992, pp. 325–26.)
Greek, in fact, had a particular profile among Romans, spoken especially by the elite, as it
was the language of higher education. But it was also much used by courtesans, and also by
slaves, many of whom had lost their freedom in Rome's wars in the eastern Mediterranean.

Jerusalem, but had already stated this intent during his travels through Macedon and Greece;[12] and his companions during that journey had included Priscilla and Aquila, who had departed Rome as part of expulsions ordered by the emperor Claudius.[13]

The most likely rationale for this plan to go to Rome was to take the new religion to the political center of the world, whence it would have the best chance of propagation at large, whether to Hellenized Jews or to Gentiles: Paul and his fellows did not intend to hide their light under a bushel. But in practice, this may not have been the optimal strategy to spread the faith: a statistical analysis of the dates of foundation of churches in cities round the Empire[14] demonstrates that, with the exception of Rome itself, Christianity did better in its first two centuries in relation to proximity to Jerusalem than to Rome; indeed Romanization seems to have acted initially as a brake on the acceptance of the new faith.

At any rate, Paul fulfilled his ambition to reach Rome, though—from a secular point of view—not in the most promising of circumstances, since he was traveling in Roman custody, explicitly to face trial on his arrival. Yet in the end, he apparently enjoyed at least two years of freedom in which to propagate the gospel.[15] There is no contemporary account of his death, but he is usually presumed to have perished in the anti-Christian pogrom stimulated by Nero in retaliation for the Great Fire of Rome in 64 A.D. A pogrom under Nero is attested by Roman historians Tacitus and Suetonius, writing no more than two generations afterward.[16] Already a generation after the death of Christ (ca. 35 A.D.) the number, or more likely the notoriety, of Christians in Rome made them credible as a scapegoat community.

Besides its use in the imperial capital, and among Greeks and Hellenized Jews, Greek was also one medium of communication in many other cities of the empire in the west, notably such centers of trade as Massilia (Marseille), Karthago (Carthage), Gades (Cadiz), and Hispalis (Seville) on or near the Mediterranean coastline, and Lugdunum (Lyon), Augustodunum (Autun) and Corduba (Cordova), major cities farther inland. All of these hosted Christian churches (celebrated by bishoprics or martyrdom[17]) in the first three centuries A.D., somewhat later than the great cities of the east.

The acceptance of Greek as the first medium of the Christian message, and Christian fellowship, would have major effects on the development of the community.

Most directly, use of Greek was the sign of an eastern cult, of which there were many in contention in the Rome of the first century A.D. They included devotion to the Phrygian Great Mother Cybele, with her attendant lions and her self-castrated consort Attis; to the Egyptian mother goddess Isis, whose faithfulness enabled the rebirth of her son Osiris, related to the sacred bull cult of Apis, or jointly Serapis (representing original Egyptian pronunciation *wsejr ḥep*); to Sabazius, a Phrygian or Thracian deity identified with Jupiter, but with orgies like Dionysian revels, who might offer an afterlife to worshippers; and the bull-slaying Mithras, another Phrygian but with a Persian name, who was a great favorite with Roman soldiers. These gods all suffered in some way, and acolytes, in their worship, identified themselves with their trials.

Although referred by Romans as kinds of *externa superstitio* "foreign trance,"* these cults were all enacted in Greek, rather than the language of their origins. Hymns to Cybele and Isis were chanted in this language, and the Mithraic mysteries were ordered by membership of a hierarchy whose grades were all named in it.[18]

To Romans, then, this medium of Greek might at the outset have tended to convey the idea that Christianity was "just another eastern cult," an impression that would have been reinforced when they learned a little about its content: it was another creed of sacrifice, leading to the death and rebirth of the victim, associated with possible redemption in an afterlife. Outsiders might be confused (even willfully so) and use the presumed similarities to discredit the faith. So the early church father Origen, in a published dispute with the philosopher Celsus, has to insist that "neither do our prophets, nor the apostles of Jesus nor the Son of God Himself, repeat anything which they borrowed from the Persians or the Cabiri."[19]

It would have seemed distinctive perhaps, in its assertion that the founding god's passion had occurred so very recently, on a particular date (Nisan 14 in the eighteenth year of the emperor Tiberius—784 years since Rome's foundation) and in a determinate city (Jerusalem) under a known Roman governor (Pontius Pilatus). Both Tacitus and Suetonius, Romans with no known reason to love or loathe the Christians, said gratuitously

---

* The etymology of *superstitio* is dubious. Literally, it means "standing above": but how, and above what? The derived adjective *superstitiosus* primarily means "ecstatic," which might give the key. But the word could also mean "something superfluous, excessive." It is tempting to see it as a "survival, hang-over" (cf *superstes* "survivor"), but that is a modern way to characterize an ancient belief. Cicero (*On the Nature of the Gods*, ii, 28, 71–2) opposes the term to *religio* "proper religion," and offers a folk etymology: "who were praying all day long and making sacrifice in order that their children should survive them."

negative things about them. Tacitus: "whom the crowd, hating them for their vices, called 'Christians' . . . a disastrous superstition . . . they were convicted for their hatred of the human race"* (*Annales*, xv, 44); and Suetonius: "Christians, a race of people with a strange [literally, "new"] and wicked superstition"† (*Nero*, xvi, 2). Possibly these substantial writers were picking up on Christians' reputation for "atheism," viz the refusal to acknowledge the existence of any god but their own, and specifically not the Roman emperor, conventionally deified, obeisance to whom served throughout the empire as a necessary, convenient—and to most, harmless—sign of loyalty to Caesar.

Effects on the Creed

These attitudes from outsiders may have had little to do with the language in which Christianity was expounded and promoted. But the predominance of Greek would have other effects on the content of the Christian faith. We have already seen that Paul had noted that Greeks, unlike the Jews, looked for "wisdom" (*sophía*), by which he most likely meant clever analysis. Increasingly over the years and centuries, many with higher education in this language would take holy orders, and come to dominate theological discourse. Hence the kind of abstractions with which Greek philosophers were so much at ease—but which might have seemed quite nonsensical, or at least gratuitous flights of fancy, to those in other cultures—became the crucial issues on which all believers would have to take a stand.

Take, for cardinal instance, the relation of Jesus Christ to God the Father.

Origen (ca. 184–ca. 254), in a commentary on the second book of John, claimed that only the Father could be referred to as Ὁ ΘΕΟΣ (*ho theos*, literally, "the God") as a subject with definite article (as typical in Greek for personal names), whereas Jesus, although divine, must be ΘΕΟΣ (*theos*, "God") without the article, as if godhead is a quality predicated of him. This is using a grammatical property of Greek to make an abstract point about Christ. (Although both Hebrew and Aramaic have definite articles too, they are not used in this way, to single out personal names.) Likewise, Origen was happy to coin typically Greek compound nouns (impossible in

---

* *Quos per flagitia invisos vulgus Chrestianos appellabat . . . exitiabilis superstitio . . . odio humani generis convicti sunt.*

† *Christiani, genus hominum superstitionis novae ac maleficae.*

the original languages of Judaism) to clarify status: he is the ΘΕΑΝΘΡΩΠΟΣ (*the-anthrōpos* "God-man"), and his mother Mary was the ΘΕΟΤΟΚΟΣ (*theo-tokos*—"God-bearer").[20] This latter became a point of contention in a later era, especially at the Council of Ephesus in 431, when sects of the church who prayed and discoursed in languages other than Greek disputed whether Mary had borne God, or only the human Jesus.

Since the cardinal texts of Christianity, the Gospels, the Acts of the Apostles, and the letters of Peter and Paul had Greek originals, there was no issue of translation as such, which might—in principle—have led to innovations in Greek style when talking of Christian realities. These scriptures were authoritative in Greek, and the question of how to represent vernacular terms used by Jesus and his disciples did not become a matter for discussion. However, in some cases there was ambiguity about the sense of a Greek term, not unrelated to unease about what Jews had believed about the corresponding concept.

One such term was ΠΑΙΣ (*pais*), which was often used to designate Jesus's relation to God. In general, the word means "child" or "boy," but like the latter term in English at one time this could mean more specifically "slave, servant" on the one hand, or "son" on the other. In fact, from the viewpoint of Hebrew tradition, neither term had made a particularly strong claim, even of loyalty, when referred to God. The word is the usual translation in the Septuagint for Hebrew עבד (*'abd*, "slave" or "servant"), which has always been a happy word for a faithful believer: for example, the name Obadiah, which is nothing other than יהעבד (*'abdyah,* "slave of Yah[weh]), a tradition continued in such names as 'Abdu-llah, 'Abdu-l-rahīm, and 'Abdu-l-wāhid in Arabic, meaning "slave of God," "slave of the Merciful One," and "slave of the One." On the other hand, the God of Moses recognizes Israel as his first-born; even when faithless, his people are his sons and daughters.[21] In Acts 4:25, the apostles Peter and John refer to King David as the *pais* of the Lord, who spoke with a holy (*hagion*) breath/spirit, just two verses before calling Jesus himself God's holy (*hagios*) *pais*.

But the ambiguity seems fairly harmless, and not something that would have led to radical reinterpretation of Jesus's status, since there are two occasions in the New Testament narrative, his baptism and his transfiguration (both repeated in Matthew, Mark, and Luke[22]), where Jesus is explicitly recognized as "my beloved son, in whom I am well pleased." Here the term used is not *pais* but *huiós*, which is quite unambiguously the son of a parent. And this is reinforced even more clearly (though editorially, rather than in the reported speech of the Father) by the other evangelist, John, who characterizes Jesus four times as God's "only-begotten son" (*ho monogenēs huiós*).[23]

The evangelists, then, are determined to go beyond the anodyne sense of Jesus as "child of God" (as we all are, in some sense, and certainly all Jews are) to make him share in the godhead, to be of God's own personal lineage, and in this respect to be quite unique. Yet this seems to make him less like a charismatic rabbi, and more like what a Greek might envisage: compare Zeus's many children conceived (like Jesus) with mortal women, who shared in his divine nature to become heroes or demigods—though only one of them, Herakles (better known in Roman guise as Hercules), actually died and ascended to immortality in Olympus.

But the Christians were soon insisting that Jesus's conception, as a child to be born of a mortal woman, was by no mortal man at all. (This became a characteristic doctrine of the church everywhere, but is not mentioned in the works of Paul.) The motivation for this doctrine may have been linguistic: the Hebrew text of Isaiah's prophecy of Emmanuel (7:14), conventionally translated as "behold a 'virgin' shall conceive and bear a son," in fact contains a word *'almah* that means a young woman, whether virginal or not. The Septuagint version (cited by Matthew 1:23, emphatically as relevant to Jesus) rendered this as *parthénos*, which does tend to have the connotation "virgin," as when applied to the Maiden Goddess Athena, although this too is not strictly part of the word's meaning: it means unmarried rather than virginal.[24]

Although this issue appears to distract from the substantive point of Christ's incarnation—what, after all, is the problem if Jesus as a man was conceived like every other human being?—debates continued to rage about this doctrine. One such was the second-century dispute between the Christian apologist Justin and the Jew Trypho.*

In the context of a debate like this, it would be agreed between Justin and Trypho that Greek mythology was beyond the pale. But from the point of

---

* But curiously to us, the game is played on a purely Greek field, the difference centering not on the adequacy of the Septuagint translation to the Hebrew, but on a new Greek version by then current (due to Aquila, Symmachus, and Theodotion), which used *neânis* "young girl" instead of *parthénos*.

Trypho, a Hellenized Jew with a Greek education, also argued that the Christians' denial of Jesus's human conception, rather than enhancing his status, actually put him down on a par with the pagan Greek hero Perseus, born of the virgin Danaë by Zeus, who attended her as a shower of gold.

view of winning converts among those who lived and thought in Greek, such a mythic feature of Christian theology may once have been advantageous: and there are other aspects of Christ's nativity that echo Greek myths.

Notable here is the birth of Herakles. He was a human hero, begotten by Zeus, the supreme deity, on the mortal woman Alkmene, who already had a husband, Amphitryon. When Amphitryon became aware that Zeus had fathered a son on his wife (in fact causing Herakles to share her womb with his own son Iphikles) he—like Joseph—felt that he should have no further sexual relations with her, though in his case for fear of the high god's resentment. Herakles had in fact been born with a destiny, to save the Olympian gods from the Giants (and hence to redeem the world); when he had achieved this purpose, he died an agonizing death, and was received into full divinity in heaven.*

This was the popular, mythical side of the Greek spirit. One can trace the development of the word *mûthos* from "spoken word, speech, conversation" in Homer to "story" in later Greek, applicable to Aesop's fables, the plot of a play, legends of gods and heroes, or sacred narratives such as Plato might adopt to justify claims that he could not back with reason. *Mûthos esôthē*, literally "the story was saved," meant that it came to its appointed end, whereas the opposite, *mûthos apôleto*, "the story was lost," meant that it had either fallen on deaf ears, or it went on interminably: one way or the other, the audience or the teller had lost the plot. Greek myths were supposed to have a point.

But besides seeing the point of a good story, Greeks were notorious for their relentless logic and devotion to *sophía*, following not the *mûthos* but the *lógos*. John the Evangelist wrote the classic treatment of Christ as *lógos*, i.e., divine "word," beginning:

> *En arkhēi ēn ho lógos, kaì ho lógos en pròs tòn theón . . .*

In the beginning was the word, and the word was with God . . .[25]

But of all the Greek ways of saying "tale" or "word," this is notoriously the most ambiguous, with ten major senses: computation, proportion, explanation,

---

* The analogy of this and the nativity story was exploited in detail by the German humanist Johannes Burmeister (1576–1638) to create the play *Mater-Virgo*, an inversion of Plautus's *Amphitruo*. (Fontaine 2015.)

inward debate, narrative, utterance, saying, subject matter, wording, Wisdom (of God).[26]

The concept, however, does not need to be seen as a wholly Greek addition to Christian theory. The *lógos* had indeed been fundamental to Creation for some Greek philosophers from the beginning. For Heraclitus, who in the sixth to fifth centuries B.C. was first to develop a complete theory of the world, everything came about according to the *lógos*, which was equivalent both to fire, and to harmonious balance of things. There is no reason, however, to think he personified it—something that very clearly was done by the Jew Philo of Alexandria, who lived about a generation before Christ. Philo saw it as "the first-born of God," a *demiourgós* ("artisan," Plato's term for creator) that mediated between God and brute matter, thus transmitting God's creative power into the universe. Concurrently with this idea, in a Hellenistic form of mysticism known as Hermeticism, the Greek god Hermes was identified with the Egyptian creator god Thoth, himself the source of all wisdom (including written learning). And even in the Palestinian Targums (Aramaic paraphrases) of the Jewish rabbis, the Hebrew phrase that begins Genesis, בְּרֵאשִׁית *be-rashīt*, "in beginning," is interpreted as בְּמֵימְרָא *be-memrā* "in (or by) word," the same word that is often substituted in recital for the ultimate name of God יהוה YHWH.[27]

Even before John, then, there was a rich tradition, shared by the three principal civilizations of the eastern Mediterranean, that saw wisdom or reasoned understanding as the principle of creation: it was an Egyptian and a Hebrew, rather than a Greek, contribution to personify this wisdom, as John does quite explicitly in his first chapter. John adopts a similar phrase to that used by Heraclitus, but instead of saying that all has come about according to the *lógos* (*katà tòn lógon*), he says that all has come about through it (*di' autoû*): the *lógos* is now more a causal agent than a reference principle. He also identifies it with the light of mankind. Then he tells us that this *lógos* became flesh, and camped (*eskēnōsen*, from *skēnē* "tent") among us. This gave us the opportunity to see its *dóxa* (perhaps "glory," perhaps even "doctrine") "as the only-begotten from the Father, full of grace and truth."

Although this is rather a conceptualized, abstract way of looking at Christ as an agent in the world, we are now moving from abstraction to relations with persons. Those who take Christ have the power, or the authority (*exousía*), to become children of God (*tékna theoû*). So this is presented as the nature of Christian faith—the ability and the right to be part of God's own family.

This personalized theory is distinct from the rest of John's gospel (where, indeed, it never appears again); but making statements of this kind came to be central to Christian theology. Despite this, the philosophical relation between God and his son remained exceedingly controversial—and even when agreed, never straightforward. And when the duality of Father and Son was expanded to a trinity, by recognizing that the Holy Spirit too was God, the problem became so complex that no universally acceptable formula to reconcile the various ideas was ever found.

It is a legacy of philosophy in Greek, and its intellectual style, to presume that highly abstract, and ultimately unverifiable, states of affairs can find a single, correct representation in a form of words. But the obligation to get that answer right, on pain of damnation, was also given a deeper bitterness by the sense of human, personal relations with God that derive from the Hebrew-Aramaic side of the developing Christian background.

CHAPTER 5

"In This Sign You Will Conquer"

Chosen by Emperors

Commonitus est in quiete, ut caeleste signum Dei notaret in scutis atque ita proelium committeret. Facit ut iussus est et transversa X littera, summo capite circumflexo, Christum in scutis notat. Quo signo armatus exercitus capit ferrum.

[Constantine] was warned in sleep to mark the heavenly sign of God on his shields and so join battle. He does as ordered, and with the letter X sideways, the top of its head bent round, he marks Christ on the shields. Armed with this sign, his army wins the day.

Lactantius, *On the Deaths of the Persecutors,* xliv.5–6

NEXT COMES THE STORY of what happened when Christianity began to reach those who did not speak Greek.

The first such language community the Christians broached was Latin, the language that had originated with the city of Rome itself. The faith reached the city in its first generation, in the mid-first century A.D.*

Rome was not typical of the Roman Empire in the west, being a cosmopolitan city where a lot of Greek was spoken—not least among the acolytes of foreign cults. It is unlikely that Paul, for example, would have needed a Latin interpreter when preaching in Rome, since he could have relied on much ambient competence in Greek.

---

* Paul reached Rome, preached there, and died there ca. 65 A.D., though he was not the first to preach, since the emperor Claudius, who reigned from 41 to 54, had already found reason to expel Jews and some Christians from the city (including Priscilla and Aquila, who were to become Paul's friends). And Paul wrote a letter to Christians in Rome while traveling in Greece, ca. 59 A.D.

Thereafter, it was a fairly slow process of linguistic transplantation, which took three centuries, or ten generations, to complete. The first sacred texts were translated in the second century (including the "Vetus Latina," the ad-hoc translations that were used to supply a first, fragmentary Latin Bible), essential to support the understanding of local converts. Church correspondence moved to Latin in the middle of the third century, showing that the church had become a normalized feature of life in the west, staffed by locals. But the liturgy—the accepted language of collective prayer—was only adapted into Latin a full century later, under Pope Damasus in 360–382. From this point it could be identified as *Ecclesia Ritus Latini*—the Church of the Latin Rite. The circle was completed with the availability of Jerome's official Latin Vulgate text of the Bible at the end of the fourth century—and this already two generations after the emperor Constantine's acceptance of Christianity as a religion for the whole empire. His Edict of Milan (in Latin) in 313 had established the church's rights and immunity,[1] and the Council of Nicaea in 325 (largely conducted in Greek) attempted to provide a doctrinal basis for Christian unity throughout the empire. Then in 380 the emperor Theodosius, with his Edict of Thessalonica (written in Latin), had made Catholic Christianity—as defined at Nicaea—compulsory for "all peoples whom the restraint of our clemency governs." It prescribed an alternative for "those demented madmen who uphold the infamy of a heretical dogma": their assemblies were to be denied the name of churches (*ecclesiae*) and "to be requited first by God's vengeance, and then the emperor's own action, derived from judgement of heaven."[2]

In the Roman Empire, within eighty-seven years, profession of the Christian faith had gone from being a capital offense, to being a protected and favored option, and then to being an absolute obligation imposed by the emperor.

The first Christian church that was known to be functioning in Latin had actually been in North Africa. Tertullian, who lived in Carthage, in the fourth or fifth generation of Christians (160 to ca. 220), wrote eloquently in Latin. Apparently he was the first Christian to do so, but this new language was already causing some doctrinal difficulties. Consider the effects of trying to put into Latin Saint John's characterization of Christ's theological identity.

In Tertullian's Latin, the *lógos* is translated as the *sermo*, "discourse." This emphasizes the coherence of thought and understanding that *lógos* was intended to convey. However it focuses on the social, conversational side of language (Latin, for example, is often called *sermo Latinus*) rather than on the rational, explanatory side—namely to give an account. Arguably, a closer equivalent in Latin for *lógos* (as Heraclitus and Saint John meant it) would have been *ratio*. Tertullian tends to agree, as a matter of logic, but it seems that *sermo* had already established itself in Christian Latin:

> God had the *ratio* which he had in him, his own, that is. For God is rational, and *ratio* is in him first, and then from him comes everything: this *ratio* is his very understanding. This is what the Greeks call *lógos*, which we call *sermo*: and therefore our people are in the habit of saying for simplicity of interpretation that *sermo* was primordially with God, when it is more appropriate to say that *ratio* was held prior in time, because God was *sermonal* from the beginning but *rational* even before the beginning, and because *sermo* too, consisting of *ratio*, shows *ratio* to have priority as *sermo*'s substance.[3]

The other surviving great Christian writer of Tertullian's era, Cyprian, bishop of Carthage (ca. 200 to 258), did indeed use *sermo* as the equivalent of *lógos*.[4] However, Cyprian's great contemporary and opponent, Novatian (who was a Roman rather than a North African bishop), used both *sermo* and *verbum*. It is hard to claim that *verbum* is a better translation, meaning as it does a single word or verb (Greek *léxis* or *rhēma*); but it did seem to have the virtue of minimality. Why would God waste words in verbiage? And furthermore Christ was clearly his only-begotten son, better represented by a single word.[5] *Verbum* thereafter dominated in the literature until Augustine (354–430), who noted that there are two traditions for translating *lógos*, and in fact used both. Then, without further ado—or explanation—Jerome, writing in about 382–390, canonized *verbum* in the Vulgate, to be officially accepted thereafter. One might summarize: *verbum sapienti* "a word to the wise," and end of story.*

Tertullian is also famously the first attested user of many of the key terms in Christian Latin, terms that would set theology alight in the next three

---

* Except that it is not, Latin being a rather special language in European history. Jerome's judgment is queried, and *sermo* reinstated, eleven centuries later by Erasmus, who was himself (ca. 1512) attempting a translation of the Gospels from the Greek into Latin. He would have preferred *oratio*, "speech," as a translation for *lógos*, but was stymied by its inconvenient feminine gender (Boyle 1977, pp. 163–64). Languages are full of such disobliging technical details if their grammar is theologically interpreted.

centuries and that have echoed down to the present: *persona, substantia, unio, distinctio, trinitas.* And he was already being compelled to tread carefully in articulating doctrine:

> So in these few words the distinction of the Trinity is clearly expounded: for the one who pronounces is the Spirit, and the Father the one to whom he pronounces, and Son the one of whom he pronounces. And so on, what now are pronounced by the Father to the Son, or now by the Son of the Father or to the Father, now by the Spirit, constitute each severally a person in their own distinct nature . . .
>
> Who, if he himself is God according to John—God was the Word—you have two of them, one saying it should be made, the other making it. But they are other, as I just claimed you should take them, as person not as substance, to make a distinction not a division.[6]

This logic-chopping began with Tertullian, before Latin was even established as a liturgical language of Christianity, but echoed on for more than a millennium: it gives a first taste of the danger of attempting to reproduce the kind of theology that the Greeks loved, but in a new language. Not that it could not be done; but the linguistic nuances of words in a new language would inevitably complicate the statement of arguments that were already fraught in Greek.

Reasons for Latin

Christianity, presented in Latin, had a number of advantages within the western Roman Empire, advantages that it could not match if it stayed restricted within its Greek original.

The most obvious of these was the opportunity it gave for many more people to worship in the vernacular. This was good personally for a vast mass of Italian, African, and other Western converts, actual and potential, in the second to fourth centuries. As a Latin commentary of the late fourth century put it:

> It is evident that our heart is ignorant, if it speaks in a language it doesn't know, just as Latin people often sing in Greek, enjoying the sound of the words but not knowing what they mean. The spirit given

in baptism knows what the heart is praying, when it speaks, or mouths off in a language unknown to itself; but the mind, which is the heart, is without fruit. What fruit can it have, if it does not know what it is saying?[7]

Use of the vernacular also profited the church community, by building solidarity. Paul had thought it better for worshippers to speak the language of the congregation as a whole, no doubt with Greek in mind; but his argument turns on the public benefit ("He that prophesies edifies the church"— 1 Corinthians 4:3), so it remained valid even when that public was more at ease, or only at ease at all, in Latin. The fact that in these early centuries it was as yet a totally Gentile language, the very medium of their pagan Roman oppressors, was testing, but irrelevant.

Contemporary opinion also saw the use of the vernacular as a fine example of openness and plain speaking—tending no doubt to allay the popular rumors of the early days that Christianity was a dark business of secrets and necromancy. That commentary goes on:

> The simple man understands him and is understood, hearing him praise God and hearing Christ worshipped, and sees clearly that the religion is true and to be venerated: in it he can see that nothing is done in obscurity as the pagans do, for their eyes are kept blindfolded in case they should see the things they call holy, and so realize that they are being cheated by gaudy vanities. For every imposture seeks the darkness, and shows falsehoods as if truths: therefore in our case nothing is done slyly, or under wraps, but quite simply the one God is praised.[8]

But besides this clarity of language, which would support solidarity in the church, Christianity presented in Latin would have a social benefit: far more than Greek, at least in Italy and the western provinces of the empire, it could reach all classes. The move into Latin Christianity can be seen as a step toward the gentrification of the faith.

Knowledge of the Greek language had originally had a skewed, and indeed bimodal, distribution in the west. Higher education for the Roman elite had been in Greek, from the mid-second century B.C. until the end of the second century A.D.; and Greek immigrants were consistently reputed for their greater skills, expertise, and often learning than even the Roman elite. But Greek was also the argot of slaves and prostitutes. In the language of Plautus, the comic playwright of the third-to-second centuries B.C., Greek borrowings were common, but predominantly on the lips of slaves.

This complex reputation went back to the second century B.C., when Rome had conquered the principal Greek-speaking powers of the eastern Mediterranean, taking vast numbers of prisoners to fill her slave markets, and hence ultimately as domestic and works staff, but also opening up her own cities to Greek enterprise: Italy, and above all Rome, was filled with Greek tutors, professors, and experts, putting their education at the service of well-heeled Romans, in return for some disposable income.

Saint Paul himself, whose experience of Christianity outside Jerusalem had been primarily as a Greek-speaking religion, had written to the Corinthians:

> For you see the results of your preaching, brothers and sisters: not many hear the call who are wise in the ways of the world, not many who are in power, not many who come of noble families.[9]

This suggests a profile of Christian believers in his day as predominantly poor, down-trodden, and lower-class, and so perhaps they were at the beginning. The story of Ananias and Sapphira (Acts 5:1–5) suggests as much. It is an object lesson in how the pooling of property was rigorously enforced: if the wealthy tried to get around it, they would be embarrassed and exposed without mercy. But modern historians and sociologists tend to doubt that this milieu would have been the likely cradle of an innovative cult like Christianity.[10] And if it ever had been true, it had emphatically ceased to be so in the fourth century A.D. By that time, the emperor himself had chosen to declare that he had won the empire through the support of the Christian God (Constantine, having defeated his opponent Maxentius in 312). And sixty years later, the high-ranking son of a Roman *praefectus praetorio* (i.e. governor-general of western Europe from Britain to Spain) would opt to become a bishop (Ambrose, bishop of Milan 374–397).

Converting the Romans

Before these spectacular developments could come about, it was necessary that Christianity should gain a following more generally among the influential. This process is difficult to track. We have very little surviving literature that represents the inducements for comfortable Romans—indeed for any Romans—to turn to Christ: most of what has been passed down from those crucial first four centuries A.D. is doctrinal argumentation, pastoral care, or devotional prayers and hymns—all for the benefit of those already converted.

Nevertheless, there is one text, the *Octavius*, written by a highly polished orator Marcus Minucius Felix, just about the same time as Tertullian (first to second centuries), which goes to the trouble of actually marshaling arguments for Christian conversion.

The text is in the form of a dialogue between a reasonable but misinformed pagan, Caecilius Natalis, and an even more reasonable Christian, Octavius Januarius, as they relax with the author on the beach at Ostia, the port of Rome. The instance for the argument is Caecilius' reflex action in blowing a kiss to an image of the Egyptian god Serapis, a private gesture that Octavius nonetheless feels demeans him; and Caecilius' reaction that this is an implicit assault on his presumed ignorance.

The debate begins with an onslaught by Caecilius against Christianity, largely for Christians' doubtful reputation (including association with Jewry) and poor status, contrasting Rome's religious traditions, especially the cult of auspices and oracles, which had stood it in very good stead. Some damaging rumors are added—for example, that Christians worship an ass's head and the genitals of their priests, and feast on babies' blood. They are said to hold their rites in secret, suggesting something to hide, and indeed are without permanent images or temples. Their pretense of universal fraternity appears to be a cover for licentious practices.

It is clear from these charges that Christianity was being discredited by association with other Greek-speaking *superstitiones*.

Octavius retorts in detail to each of these charges as ill-aimed, claiming that many are true of others, but none about the Christians. The Romans' traditional observances have not benefited them, by and large, whereas these rumors about the Christians are baseless. Furthermore, various features of the natural world suggest that the Christian emphasis on resurrection is indeed the way of the universe. There will be justice for all, believers or not, and the Christians are if anything to be commended for living so modestly.

Caecilius is convinced, and all three end up agreeing that Octavius (and the Christians) are in the right—the best conclusion, if they are all to remain firm friends.

This shows a little of the faith—perhaps a bit optimistically—as it was being taken up by Latin speakers in the third century A.D. But to win Roman converts with a modicum of education, Christianity needed to modulate its tone, appealing to the popular Stoic virtues of justice and temperance, rather than to the fulfillment of Jewish prophecy, extreme pacifism, or abstract philosophy. It would also need to accept wealthy converts, encouraging them to become donors to the poor, and to the church itself—rather than condemning them if they held anything back.

The greater availability of Latin for Christianity co-occurred with a gradual and general abandonment of Greek by Romans. Roman gentry had for most of the four centuries 200 B.C. to 200 A.D. acquired Greek as a necessary part of their education, reflecting the superior development and sophistication of Greek knowledge to what was available in Latin alone. The Greeks' continuous tradition of written learning went back to the fifth century B.C., but technical advance had not stopped. The satirist Juvenal still found the Greeks newsworthy in the mid-second century A.D.: "Schoolmaster, lecturer, geometer, painter, trainer, fortune-teller, tightrope-walker, doctor, magician, a hungry Greek knows every trade: tell him to go to the sky and he will."[11] A late fruit, for example, of Greek culture—long after their painstaking and influential analysis of how to speak effectively—was the development of a full grammatical analysis of their language: the rules of word structure were comprehensively stated by Dionysius the Thracian in *Tekhnē Grammatikē* "The Scholarly Art" (ca. 100 B.C.), but were supplemented as to syntax by Apollonius Dyscolus only in the second century A.D.

Meanwhile, the most advanced of Roman scholars were continuously concerned to catch up. Throughout this period, they were translating, adapting, and reproducing Greek works in their own terms. Most notable among them was Cicero himself, who largely succeeded, in a few brief years at the end of his political career, in providing a Latin guide to the whole existing corpus of Greek philosophy. Greek-style grammatical analysis was applied to Latin almost as soon as Greek, through the independent labors of Terentius Varro (116–127 B.C.) and Remmius Palaemon (in the first century A.D.), but summed up by Aelius Donatus in the fourth century.

Latin poets, historians, satirists, and even novelists proceeded apace, producing work that at its best was more original than that of their Greek contemporaries, and building up a body of classics that was capable of comparison with the Greek literary canon. As a result of this paralleling of Greek texts and Greek ideas, Romans were less drawn to study through it, or even to learn it: a cheaper alternative—in money and effort—was becoming available for Latin speakers in their own vernacular. Learning Greek came to seem like an unnecessary luxury, even a burden. In 326 Constantine—having legitimized Christianity in 313—went on to establish a separate Greek capital of the empire at Byzantium. Thereafter, the western provinces came to see themselves as separate, with an identity expressed exclusively in Latin.

The vernacularization of western Christianity, specifically through the use of Latin, fitted snugly into this trend. But its own literary traditions were, at the outset, something of a barrier to solidarity between Christians and traditional Romans, even if they all spoke Latin in the street. Written Latin was, by habit and conscious rule, just too formalized. The strict grammar traditionally required in writing and public speaking (itself a carryover from Greek as used in literature, rather than the familiar colloquial *koinē*) had seemed like a burdensome distraction, even a weapon of class warfare.

So Arnobius, a rhetorician from Africa who became a Christian at the beginning of the fourth century, felt the need to write: "When the point is something serious, beyond showing off, we need to consider *what* is being said, not how elegantly; not what soothes the ears, but what brings benefits to the hearers."[12] A century later, Saint Augustine himself—though personally well educated in Latin—felt the need to buttress Christians' self-confidence, even when they were speaking spontaneously:

> For what is called a solecism is nothing other than putting words together on a different rule from that followed by our authoritative predecessors . . . And likewise, what is a barbarism but pronouncing a word differently from those who spoke Latin before us? . . . [It] is indifferent to the man who is praying to God, with whatever words he can, to pardon his sins. What is correctness of diction beyond sustaining usages that happen to be hallowed by the authority of former speakers?[13]

Conscious linguistic egalitarianism was part of early Latin Christianity. And this temporary mixing of the classes in what had been a highly stratified society may have played an early part in the changes that would transform Latin into Romance—a language with fixed word order, simpler syntax, and, much later, radically less inflexion in nouns and verbs—the common ancestor of most of the dialects of western Europe. But written Latin, buttressed by an unchanging school curriculum, ultimately dismissed the challenge. After a century or two of turmoil, Latin did manage to sustain much of its outward show, and preserve it for another millennium of active use. But as we find it written, it has become discernibly—from a modern perspective—easier to read.

Christianity Goes Roman

The major effect of latinization was to assimilate Christianity to the Roman Empire in the west. The empire's established religion became Christianity, and Christianity's primary language—from a Western perspective—became Latin. A few developments indicate how deeply this Latin-speaking church came to adjust to the Roman heritage of its new center, incorporating a variety of pagan heirlooms into the Roman church.

First, although clerics did not adopt secular titles (beyond the general-purpose *vicarius*, which means deputy, and is the origin of "vicar"), they did accept pre-Christian terms for the priesthood: *sacerdos* "priest," *pontifex* "high priest." They called a larger church building a *basilica*, since such buildings resembled the traditional style of Roman public buildings, with colonnades.* Construction of these enjoyed a major boom after the Edict of Milan.

Second, some Roman festivals were reinterpreted with a Christian meaning. The whole year had been partitioned in a sequence of dated festivals from time immemorial, some of them honoring the birthdays (*natales*) of gods; now, a specifically Christian calendar would come to be organized around a new set of heroes, the martyrs, the first to be recognized in an unending parade of saints deemed triumphant after their deaths.

The clearest case of a specific Roman festival equated with a subsequent Christian feast is Saturnalia, the midwinter feast, which began on December 17 and culminated on December 25 with the birth of *Sol Invictus*, the "invincible sun." This day had in fact only been instituted as part of a cult for soldiers by the emperor Aurelian in 274 A.D. Still, this could be reinterpreted as a celebration of Christ's birth, and the gold, incense, and myrrh that the magi from the east had brought to honor the newborn Christ (according

---

* The word itself is originally Greek, meaning "royal," since the Romans had themselves borrowed this style from Greek public architecture. Notably, there had been a *stoa basilikē* "royal colonnade" in Athens.

to Matthew 2:1, 11) could now be now taken as a sanction for the ancient Roman custom of gift-giving in this season.*

The custom of singing carols too may well also be derived from Roman tradition, and some of the earliest have come down to us. A few verses by Bishop Ambrose himself show the style and kind of message they contained:

Veni, redemptor gentium,	Come, redeemer of the world
ostende partum Virginis;	show how the Virgin gives birth;
miretur omne saeculum:	let every age wonder:
talis decet partus Deum.	such a birth is worthy of God.
Non ex virili semine,	Not from man's seed
sed mystico spiramine	but by a mystic breath
Verbum Dei factum est caro	the Word of God is made flesh
fructusque ventris floruit.	and the fruit of the belly flowered.
Alvus tumescit Virginis,	The Virgin's belly swells,
claustrum pudoris permanet,	the seal of her modesty stays fast,
vexilla virtutum micant,	the banners of her virtues shine,
versatur in templo Deus.	God dwells in his temple.

Christianity's first great poet in Latin, Prudentius (348–ca. 413), echoed Ambrose:

O beatus ortus ille,	O blessed that birth,
virgo cum puerpera	the Virgin with her childbirth
Edidit nostram salutem,	Produced our salvation
feta Sancto Spiritu,	pregnant by the Holy Spirit,
Et puer redemptor orbis	And the boy redeemer of the world
os sacratum protulit.	showed his sacred face.
Sæculorum sæculis.	To the ages of ages.

---

* This all makes good sense, even if the assignation of Christ's birth to December 25 is, in fact, overdetermined. Since the date of Christ's crucifixion was conventionally assigned to March 25, corresponding to Nisan 14 of Passover, it was proposed by the theologian Hippolytus of Rome (170–235)—assuming that Christ's life, because perfect, must have lasted a whole number of years—that his conception be assigned to the same calendar date; hence his likely birthday nine months later would fall on December 25.

Psallat altitudo caeli,	Let the height of heaven play harp,
psallite omnes angeli,	Play, all you angels,
Quidquid est virtutis usquam	Whatever virtue there is anywhere
psallat in laudem Dei,	Let it play in praise of God,
Nulla linguarum silescat,	let no tongue fall silent,
vox et omnis consonet.	and let every voice sing in harmony.
Sæculorum sæculis.	To the ages of ages.

Elsewhere equation of the Roman and Christian calendars becomes vaguer. The varied feasts in late February that endorsed family love and respect (especially the *Caristia* or *Cara Cognatio* on the twenty-second) were identified with the feast of Saint Peter and Saint Paul. But although this is the story as represented on the *Laterculus* (calendar) of Polemius Silvius, a work of about 448 that attempts to correlate Roman with Christian dates, in later Christian practice this date marked the enthronement of Peter in Antioch, while the feast of Peter and Paul was celebrated on June 29. A little earlier in February was the (to Christians) scandalous Lupercalia, where young men ran around and ritually flicked girls and young women with strips of hide from sacrificial goats, notionally to enhance their fertility. This is sometimes associated with a later feast of Saint Valentine on February 14, but the early history of this saint's day is obscure. Ambarvalia (meaning "around the fields") at the end of May was the major rite of agricultural fertility, involving a circuit of the field boundaries and a sacrifice of pig, sheep, and bull (the *suovetaurilia*). It was supplanted by the Christian feasts of *Rogatio* ("prayer") and *Ascensio* ("ascent to heaven"), occurring forty days after Easter.

Whatever the story on particular dates, the Christians seem also to have followed the Romans in a particular approach to the arithmetic of festival dates, since some feasts were movable (*conceptivae*). This policy of indirect calculation, rather than a fixed date, was adopted by the Christians for Easter and its dependent feasts, and formalized in 325 at the Council of Nicaea, which also determined the (Nicene) Creed. Although there was a date for the Crucifixion accepted traditionally (March 25),* the date for the celebration of Easter would be (and still is) determined by the *computus*, a computation.

---

* This corresponds to Nisan 14—the Friday (literally, "preparation day") of Jewish Passover, which John 19:14 specifies (ἦν δε παρασκευη του πασχα).

Christians also happily took up soldiers' slang. The empire had always looked to the military for leadership and engineering skills, and soldiers were at work wherever state action was needed, as in building public works or roads. But the Christians decried all participation in violence, military or otherwise. Furthermore, until Constantine's measures to habilitate the church in 313, the army had not even been a possible career for Christians, requiring as it did the routine swearing of loyalty to the cult of the emperor, something sacrilegious for Christians or Jews. But the military was somehow hallowed by Constantine's victory at the Pons Milvius in 312 explicitly under the *labarum*, the *chi-rho* symbol of the Christian god. In fact, Christian soldiering did not really pick up until a good fifty years later, with lower ranks joining later than officers.[14] After that, some words characteristic of Christian Latin clearly show the soldiers' viewpoint: *pagani* "villagers, civilians" became the favorite word for nonbelievers; *sacramentum*, which had meant the soldiers' loyalty oath, was repurposed as a word for Christian ritual.

But metaphorical soldiering—focused on the effort, loyalty, and pains of military service—had never been a problem for Christians. Paul was already urging Timothy to be a "fine soldier of Jesus Christ" (2 Timothy 2:3). Tertullian too adopted the military metaphor, especially martyrs, two centuries before it was a practical possibility: "We were called to serve in the militia of the living God when we responded to the words of the *sacramentum*" (*Ad Martyres* iii.1). "Serving under this *sacramentum*, I am challenged by the enemy. I am equal to them, if I do not surrender to them. Defending this I hold my position, I am wounded, I am stricken, I am killed" (*Scorpiace* iv.5). But he expressed severe reservations, amounting to denial, about any Christian's suitability for actual military service (*De Corona Militis* xi.4–6), talking of *fides pagana*, "one's duty as a civilian," and he quipped that for Christ, a soldier is no less bound to his duty as a civilian than a civilian is to be a faithful soldier of Christ. (*Apud hunc tam miles est paganus fidelis quam paganus est miles fidelis.*)*

But Latin was not just another language. Latin was still symbolic par excellence of the world's greatest power, in a Greco-Roman world that knew, and could conceive, of little beyond its own borders. In the very long term,

---

* It is interesting that in this era, the second century A.D., *paganus* had as yet no sense of "pagan."

this adoption of Latin was key to the imperial bearing that the Latin Rite, or, as it preferred to style itself, *Ecclesia Catholica*, came to assume. Some would claim that the church early identified with Rome's traditional attributes as a capital, *caput orbis terrarum* "capital of the world."

Partly, it was a matter of habit. Military command came easily to some Romans, who may strike us as unlikely Christians but several of whom played an important role in the early days of the officialized church. Ambrose, bishop of Milan and later saint, had first followed his father's footsteps and distinguished himself as a general, becoming consular prefect of Liguria and Aemilia in north Italy. But after being made a bishop—rather suddenly and unexpectedly—he aggressively defended Nicene Christianity against all comers in assertion of orthodoxy. Even Theodosius I, the very emperor who had made this creed compulsory for all his subjects, could not stand up to Ambrose when Ambrose found him too tolerant. The story was also recorded of another bishop (Saint Germanus of Auxerre) visiting Britain for pastoral reasons in 429, indeed to preach against the remnants of the Pelagian heresy. But he found time—perhaps harking back to a previous career—to train up a local militia against Pictish and Saxon marauders, teaching them to cry *Alleluia* as they went into battle.[15]

Certainly the church adopted a system of administration based on that of the Roman Empire. After Diocletian's reforms in 293, the four major units of the empire, the prefectures, were divided into *dioceses* (from Greek διοικήσεις *dioikēseis*, literally, "managements"). This term was later adopted for episcopal sees, a usage that has lasted until the present day in all churches that recognize bishops.* This paralleling of civil and ecclesiastical organization was not confined to the Latin-speaking Roman world, however. In the east, the bishops' sees were termed ἐπαρχίαι *eparkhiai*, precisely the same word used there for imperial provinces. Over time, as bishoprics multiplied, the scale of both *dioceses* and *eparkhiai* became smaller; and ultimately the civil references of these concepts died away, leaving the Christian church—both

---

* The constituent parts of an imperial diocese were provinces (so, for example, the diocese of *Britanniae* "the Britains" was divided into five provinces); but the parts of an episcopal diocese came to be called the parishes, *parochiae*, which ought to mean "provisionings" but is in fact a deformation of the Greek *paroikíai*. This word is deliberately ambiguous between "neighborhoods" and "communities of sojourners," so reminding Christians that their earthly life was a mere temporary abode. (Saint Peter had remarked: "Pass the time of your sojourning here in fear." 1 Peter 1:17.)

in the Latin west and the Greek east—as the sole inheritor of the imperial system.

The Roman Catholic Church as it developed is unthinkable without the precedent of the (western) Roman Empire. At the time of Constantine's legitimizing of the Christian faith (313) and Theodosius's imposition of it (380), the church in the basin of the Mediterranean sea was undivided, just as was the empire itself. Across its whole extent it embraced both the (Greek) titles *katholikē* "universal" and *orthodoxos* "of correct doctrine"—as it did so many other technical terms: *anathema, angelus, apostolus, baptizo, charisma, diabolus, diaconus, ecclesia, episcopus, presbyter, propheta*, and many more.

However, the unity of Christianity could not withstand the increasing separation of the eastern and western halves of the empire, a difference that was marked above all by the contrast of their lingua francas, Greek versus Latin. The Roman elite, traditionally bilingual, was beginning to separate into monolingual streams.

In the fourth century, the first of official Christianity among the Romans, Greek began to lose its value as the apex of a Roman's education. Augustine, for example, was able to dominate the intellectual life of his era (354–430) without ever becoming competent in Greek.[16] Meanwhile, Jerome (his friend and colleague the Bible translator, ca. 331–420) wrote to him from Palestine: "We suffer a great poverty of the Latin language in this province."[17] Greeks, who had always largely disdained Latin, were now finding themselves at a disadvantage in trying to make headway in imperial careers in the west, where they could no longer get by ignoring Latin. Libanius (ca. 314–392), a rhetorician who had specialized in teaching Greek, wrote wistfully of how the traffic in his age was all of Greeks wishing to acquire Latin for career reasons, less and less the converse.[18]

For a time, Greeks who had a good command of Latin were in special demand, even for government work in the east, their value driven up by their rarity. Ammianus Marcellinus (330–395), a Greek who himself wrote his noted histories in Latin, mentioned two high officials in the east appointed primarily for their competence in Latin—which must mean it was seen as exceptional.[19] However, two centuries later, John the Lydian (490 to ca. 560) noted with foreboding how the courts were no longer using Latin, and so must soon fall foul of the prophecy of Romulus that Fortune would abandon the Romans if they should forget their paternal language.[20] And the emperor Justinian (who reigned 527–565), despite his own preference for "the paternal voice" (Latin), was compelled to issue in Greek much of the law code for which he is famous, in order to ensure it could be applied across the whole empire.[21]

The linguistic division of the empire—where, increasingly, neither Greek nor Latin could be relied on as a universal language—was soon mirrored politically in the different fates of east and west. The east would retain its core territories, Greece and Anatolia, for most of the next millennium and went on speaking Greek there until immersed in Turkish settlers after the Battle of Manzikert in 1071. But the west saw its German borders overrun on the last day of 406 by Vandals, who would then proceed, within twenty-five years, to establish themselves in North Africa. Other Germanic speakers deprived Rome of its imperium in Spain (418, Visigoths and Suevi), in Gaul (425, Franks), in Britain (450, Angles and Saxons) and even in North Italy (410, Lombards and Ostrogoths). To put a cap on it, in Rome itself, the legitimate emperor was deposed by a Goth in 476.

One result of this was a failure of solidarity between the Christians who lived in the Latin and Greek parts of the empire, a rift that would never be healed. Although Justinian in the east would make a partly successful effort to reclaim the west's Mediterranean territories in the name of the empire of the Romans—in effect the empire in the east—this would not come for a century. And in this time the western Christians had made certain accommodations to their sadly reduced situation—accommodations that emphasized the difference between the Latin and Greek rites and compensated for the diminished temporal power of the western empire with overweening claims of the centrality and superiority of Rome in the church.

Augustine, having become bishop of Hippo in North Africa, had needed in particular to explain away the coincidence of unprecedented failure in Rome's border defenses with the empire's recent acceptance of Christianity: surely it must be a clear requital for Christian Rome's desertion of Jupiter and all its ancestral gods? In his great work the *Civitas Dei*, his answer was to distinguish between a City of Man, which might indeed be defeated, and a City of God, which would triumph ultimately but was not of this world. This meant distinguishing between the empire and all its works—shown to be fallible, and indeed to have feet of clay[22]—and the church, which was based on imperishable values. Hence from the contemporary difficulty of the barbarian invasions, and the clear failure of the empire in strategy, albeit declared Christian, Augustine drew conclusions that enhanced the long-term authority of the church over the secular power. The empire had been beaten at its own game, namely the struggle for military victory and political control, he argued: how much more important it was to give one's loyalty to the source of all true glory, the Holy Mother Church, and so become a citizen of God, rather than of Man.

The ubiquity of the Latin language gave a new focus to the community of Christians in the west. In accord with folk wisdom, the peoples that "prayed together stayed together"; and although the political result of the fractured empire in the west was a collection of independent states, detached from the temporal authority of Rome, the fact that they all prayed and worshipped in Latin gave them a sense of joint identity as western and central Europeans in the coming centuries. As it always had, the Latin language—through its literature, its shared history, and its domain of common understanding— defined a worldview, and one that was centered on Rome.[23]

For a couple of centuries, one foreign body had posed a threat to the unity of this western, Latinate, Christian community. This was the loyalty of the invading Goths and Vandals to the Arian church—a faith acquired before their career of conquest in western Europe, and tellingly delivered in Gothic language to its faithful. But for military and diplomatic reasons (the west-ward thrust of the Eastern Empire in the Mediterranean, and the internal politics of the new Germanic-led states), the Gothic church was doomed, being stamped out, or dying out, everywhere—in North Africa, in Burgundy, in Spain, and in Lombardy—over the course of the sixth and seventh centu-ries. For those deprived of their Arian traditions in this period, and brought, forcibly if necessary, within the Catholic church of Rome, a striking feature would have been its universal use of the language of Rome, Latin.

The Latin language, then, by the middle of the first millennium, came to be associated not so much with the vanquished Roman Empire, and the Roman aristocracy that had led it, as with the newly preponderant Roman Catholic Church, with a community that prayed in Latin, even if it used a variety of other languages at home and at work.

CHAPTER 6

"Every Man Heard . . . His Own Language"
One Christ, Many Tongues?

And when the day of Pentecost was fully come, they were all with one accord in one place. And suddenly there came a sound from heaven as of a rushing mighty wind, and it filled all the house where they were sitting. And there appeared unto them cloven tongues like as of fire, and it sat upon each of them. And they were all filled with the Holy Ghost, and began to speak with other tongues, as the Spirit gave them utterance . . . Now when this was noised abroad, the multitude came together, and were confounded, because that every man heard them speak in his own language . . . And they were all amazed, and were in doubt, saying one to another, What meaneth this?

Acts 2:1–4, 6, 12

I N THIS EARLY CHRISTIAN text, the apostles are seen witnessing for Christ, telling his truth as they knew it, without linguistic barriers, and through the miraculous aid of the Holy Spirit. Explicitly, we are told that each person in the crowd who gathered to hear the apostles heard the message not in a lingua franca—such as Aramaic or Greek, or even Latin— but "each in his own language."

Yet if we look at early sources of this story, Luke's text in Greek from the sixties A.D., and even at an Aramaic equivalent, presumably translated from it (though a few believe it is the original)[1] and appearing in the text of the Bible known as the Peshitta, we soon notice differences.

One appears trivial, namely the difference between the day, or the days, of Pentecost. The Greek seems to suggest the events occurred at the end of the feast day itself, while the Aramaic says rather that it happened just on the feast day, after the fifty days (from Passover) were completed.

But other differences allow for the interpretation to begin to change. In Greek, the apostles were gathered *homothymadon* "with common intent," while this sense is missing from the Aramaic (though *ʾakḥədā* "together" could correspond to the word). Much more pertinent is the reaction attributed to the crowd. In Greek, they wonder *ti an theloi touto einai* "What would this mean [literally, "wish to be"]?" But in Aramaic they seem to have doubts more focused on the source of the miracle: *dəmānā (hy) hādē ṣəḇūṭā* "What, or how, is this affair?" In a world full of spirits, it is not obvious that a miracle produced by strangers will be benign.

But the authors of these accounts were in no doubt: they saw it as due to *pneumatos hagiou* = *bərūḥā dəqūḏšā*, i.e., the Holy Wind. These are the original expressions for the Holy Spirit, and the only way of expressing the concept in Greek or Aramaic.[2] (Latin *spīritus* too is derived from *spīrāre* "blow.") This was directly, or subliminally, reinforced by the fact that, in both Greek and Aramaic, the divine force that comes among the apostles is in the form of a roaring wind. The metaphor is reinforced by a natural phenomenon.

And this metaphor in revelation is reinforced by another. The apostles are crowned with *diamerizomenai glōssai hōsei pyros . . . ʾ leššānē dəmetpalgīn (h)waw ʾayk nūrā* "divided tongues as of fire" and immediately find that they have the gift of expression *heterais glossais . . . bəleššān leššan* "in various tongues"—with content that they no doubt saw as fiery in its power to set men's hearts ablaze.

These fiery words may have been available in principle in every tongue, but every tongue defined a community, a company of people who thought in it and lived in it. The body of Christians was in fact many such companies, people who could associate together in Aramaic, or in Greek, or in the other languages of the eastern Mediterranean where Christianity had originated, and first grew. The medium of its early growth was through networks of friends and acquaintances, and though Aramaic and Greek were both extremely widespread languages within that area, they would naturally form and give access to different, if overlapping, communities.

The early growth of the church in Greek—a language of importance in the Roman Empire in the first century A.D.—facilitated the spread of the religion to the west, closer to the traditional centers of Roman power, and ultimately into communities in Italy and Africa whose vernacular was Latin.

The Church Spreads in Aramaic

Meanwhile, the church was also spreading through Aramaic. Use of this language would not have restricted the faith to ethnic Jews, even if a Syro-Greek such as the evangelist Luke might have thought of it as "Hebrew dialect." Aramaic was the dominant vernacular in Roman Judaea of the first century A.D., but this same language had spread with the Babylonian and Persian empires over most of the first millennium B.C.; now, even under the successor empires of the first century A.D., Parthia and Rome, it was widely understood all over Egypt, Palestine, Mesopotamia, and Persia, as well as in its homeland Syria. Like Greek, Aramaic was to become a major language of Christian evangelism.

Christianity began as a religion of the streets, and its early centers were in cities: Jerusalem and Caesarea in Palestine, Antioch and Damascus in Syria, Alexandria in Egypt. All of these had established churches before 100 A.D., within two generations of the death of Christ. Geographically, then, early Christianity had a big potential audience in Aramaic, quite comparable to the faith as it spread—concurrently—to cities where Greek dominated: in Asia Minor (Pergamum, Sardis, Smyrna, Ephesus), mainland Greece (Athens, Corinth), and of course Rome, which likewise all had churches in the first century A.D.[3]

Which of these linguistic communities could claim greater legitimacy? In the early days the fact that Aramaic did not need to be converted in order to be understood by authentic Jews did tell in its favor. This is shown by Paul's impromptu display of eloquence in the "Hebrew dialect" in which he said he had also received his vision from Christ.[4] It is explicitly noted that the language impressed his Jewish audience:

> And when they heard that he was addressing them in the Hebrew dialect, they kept the more silence . . . (Acts 22:2)

Despite the description as Hebrew, we must infer that the decision of westward-bound Christians to build communities in Greek was a matter of convenience, not a symbolic act. No specific association connected Aramaic with Jews, and Greek with Gentiles.* Paul, in the context of the controversy

---

* In fact, as we have already seen, in the Aramaic language "Aramaean" came to have the nuance of non-Jewish, i.e., Gentile.

over the necessity of circumcision for non-Jewish Christians, had claimed (in Greek) that "There is no longer Jew and Greek, circumcision and foreskin, barbarian, Scythian, slave, free; but Christ is everything, and in all" (Colossians 3:11). Although there was some friction over this face-to-face between Paul and Peter, recounted by Paul in Galatians 2, the Synod of Jerusalem soon afterward would settle this matter as he had argued: there would be no requirement for Greek Christians to accept laws that were specifically Jewish, much less any mention of a different regime between Greek and Aramaic speakers.

By the same argument of practice, Christians on the eastern shores of the Mediterranean maintained their vernacular Aramaic, with little temptation to switch to Greek or any other language that might allow better access to fresh target congregations. There is a tradition in the Syrian Orthodox Church of Antioch that the establishment of Christianity in Antioch was arranged in two stages by Saint Peter, one for Jews and a later one for Gentiles, and that the first bishops, Ignatius and Evodius, had at first ministered to the Jews and the Gentiles respectively. But after the death of Evodius, Ignatius took charge of a unitary diocese of Antioch,[5] and indeed inaugurated the term *catholic* (meaning "universal") *church* (ἡ καθολικὴ ἐκκλησία) in a letter he wrote—in Greek—to the Christians of Smyrna around 110 A.D.[6]

The city of Antioch (Ἀντιόχεια—modern Antakya) in northern Syria had had a Greek-speaking elite since its foundation—and appointment as capital—in the last decade of the fourth century B.C., by Alexander's general Seleucus I Nicator.* As such, it had become the most important city in Syria. Later, after Pompey's conquest in 67 B.C., it was made capital of the new Roman province of Syria, and the headquarters of the Roman power in the east, a choice that—given the virtual absence of Latin east of the Balkans— would also have promoted its use of Greek. Nevertheless, its church there always maintained Aramaic, the predominant language of the townsfolk, as it was of the city's Syrian hinterland.† By repute, the words of the Eucharist

---

* It was named in memory of his father, Antiochus, another Macedonian general.

† Libanius, a Greek rhetorician and lifelong resident of Antioch in the fourth century A.D., mentions the existence of Aramaic just once: "One such as he was more of a disgrace to the Senate than all those who cry out in the language of Syrians (τῇ φωνῇ τῇ Σύρων) for customers looking to get their wooden bowls mended." (*Orationes* xlii.32). A curious view-point. Yet for all this, "Greek-speaking Antioch was an island in a sea of Syriac" (i.e., Aramaic, Mango 1994, p. 22). Libanius was never one for gritty realism: ever the Hellene, he wrote his sixty-four speeches as if there were no Christianity in his world (and this late in the century when Theodosius had imposed it as the empire's only permitted religion).

that has continued in use until today in the Syrian Orthodox Church were composed by Saint James, brother of Christ.[7]

Christianity spread from its homeland in Roman Syria to create centers in a number of neighboring cities. One that was to be particularly influential was the town of Edessa, about 220 miles to the northeast of Antioch. This ancient city, refounded in 304 B.C. (again by Seleucus) and named nostalgically for the capital of Macedon, was the capital of a state known in Syriac as *Orhay* (Greek *Osrhoēnē*).* In the borderlands between the empires of the west (Greek or Roman) and the east (Persian, Parthian, or Sassanian)—and, importantly for its merchants, on the trade route that linked them—it had kings (all named Abgar) who changed alliances several times. Whatever its politics, its language remained steadily Aramaic; and it was in fact that dialect of this city that became the model for Syriac, the form of Aramaic[8] that was to go around the Old World in Christian text and liturgy, ultimately reaching Mongolia, Beijing, and the southern coasts of India. Christianity came to Edessa early, and supposedly the first church was destroyed by a flood in 201, making it the first historically verified house of Christian worship.

Within the same tradition, and likewise apparently in the second century A.D., there were church foundations too in Nisibis (modern Turkish Nusaybin), Arbela (modern Kurdish Erbil), and crucially Seleucia-Ctesiphon (21 miles south of modern Baghdad). This was another of Seleucus's refoundations, but had gone on to become the capital of the Parthian and later Sassanian empires—the actual capital of latter-day Persia until the Muslim conquest. As it turned out, for much of that time it also hosted the patriarchate of the Church of the East, the Christian communion dismissed in the west as "Nestorian," but which would spread for many centuries even farther east, to China and Mongolia.

Each center was some 150 to 220 miles east of the last, although Ctesiphon is more like 250 miles south of Erbil. These are all sites of preaching attributed to Mar Mari, the legendary *catholicos* of the church ca. 87–120: such stories may be rather precocious about the spread of the faith, but are certainly correct in siting its early centers in western Asia.

At the same time, Christianity was spreading to take up the other dimensions of the known world. Most immediately, it appeared in Egypt, whose leading city in this era was Alexandria, yet another city founded within

---

* Today it is known as Şanlı-Urfa, in which *şanlı* is Turkish for "renowned," a title dating to 1984.

Alexander's spreading empire from four centuries earlier. The faith was supposedly brought, in the first flush of Christian evangelism, around 43 to 48, by Saint Mark the evangelist, who was later martyred in the same city in 62 or 68. Apollōs, a disciple contemporary of Saint Paul's, is mentioned as a Jew from Alexandria, although his appointed ministry (after 52–53) seems to have been in Greece. But historically, the first known bishop of Alexandria was Saint Demetrius, who held the post from 189 to 232. Christianity had first been seeded among the Jewish community in the city, but after harsh Roman measures to extirpate Jewish revolts (in 41, 66, 73 and 116–17), it was largely left to Greeks. Despite the lively Aramaic and Syriac churches then growing in Asia, and the long history of Aramaic speech in Egypt over the two centuries when it had been part of the Persian empire (522–332 B.C.), Aramaic-language Christianity in Egypt seems to have been confined to monasteries.

The Greek Christians here became famous for an intellectual approach known as *gnōsis* "knowing," which led to Gnosticism, a rich source of heresy, but also for its main opposition to it, *katēkhēsis* "oral instruction." Later, ethnic Egyptians themselves began to assume leadership, but the process by which they ascended is obscure. The first texts in the Egyptians' indigenous language as written in the Greek alphabet, known as Coptic, are Christian, but they are not known before the turn of the third/fourth centuries A.D. These are the works of Abba Anthony, an early desert father, and are the first fruits of a lively Christian literature that developed in this language.*

North and northwest of Syria was Asia Minor, the Aegean Sea and Greece. This was precisely the area that Saint Paul had targeted for his evangelism, as can be seen from a map of his travels and (to a less inclusive extent) the addressees of his surviving letters: the churches of the Corinthians and Thessalonians were in Greece, of the Galatians, Ephesians, Philippians, and Colossians in Asia Minor. In his day, this whole area was mostly Greek-speaking. Like Egypt, Asia Minor had experienced Aramaic-language administration—or, at least, centralized communications in Aramaic—under Persia for up to two centuries until 330 B.C. But the sudden conquest by Alexander and his Macedonians that then occurred had led to almost

---

* This stream was checked, and began to be choked off, with the Arab (and Muslim) conquest of Egypt in the 640s, although original work continued to be produced for a few more centuries. And in the liturgy of the Coptic church, the use of Coptic language continues to this day.

total Hellenization, working its way inland from the coasts.* Cities from this area were also notable among the early gains of Christianity: Athens and Corinth in mainland Greece, Pergamum, Sardis, Smyrna, and Ephesus in Asia Minor.

A new star was about to be added to their firmament, however: the city of Constantinople itself. Byzantium had been nothing more than a strategically located port before the emperor Constantine refounded it in 324, and consecrated it in 330: it was to be nothing less than a second Rome.

His concerns were primarily strategic, moving the empire's center of gravity closer to the chronic threats, and wealthy territories, such as Egypt and Asia Minor. But Constantine held that he had achieved his victory over his contender for empire, Maxentius, *instinctu divinitatis* ("at God's prompting")†, and the strategic keynote of his whole reign was alliance with the Christian church. To honor this, he ensured that his foundation of a new capital city would be dignified with two unique temples, one dedicated to the Holy Peace (Ναός της Ἁγίας Εἰρήνης), and—as a pièce de résistance that would set the seal on his reign—a second dedicated to the Holy Apostles (Ναός των Ἁγίων Ἀποστόλων). He wished to be buried here, amid the relics of all twelve that he hoped to gather.§

New buildings were going up in Rome to dignify its new place of honor in the empire, and its bishop—currently Sylvester I—was not about to accept any diminution of his paramount status among the patriarchs, as the supreme leaders of the apostolic sees (Rome, Antioch, Alexandria, Jerusalem) were known.[9] But the rank of the new foundation was guaranteed: the see of Constantinople had just recently been made independent of the neighboring diocese of Heraclia (a small city on the Bosphorus), but now it would rank as apostolic. In time it would be assigned authority over the whole world where Greek was established as mother tongue: Greece, Thrace (in the Balkans), and Asia Minor, including its Black Sea coastal province of Pontus.

---

* It seems that some ancient languages of Asia Minor (notably the Phrygian once spoken by King Midas, but perhaps also Lydian, Sidetic, and Pisidian) may have lived on in rural pockets until the fifth—or even the seventh—century A.D. (Brixhe 2004, p. 780.)

† As advertised on the Arch of Constantine in Rome.

§ He was indeed buried here, by his son Constantius II. But unfortunately it proved beyond his power to gather relics of more than one apostle: he did however locate and rebury here Saint Andrew. Saint Luke and Saint Timothy were also added later.

Other Language Communions

But other Christian churches were being founded in this period, each on a different periphery of the eastern Roman Empire. Since these outer territories did not have Greek, nor Aramaic, as a widely spoken language, access to the faith, and thus the church itself, was—at the outset—restricted to an educated elite. But after translations of scripture and liturgy were made, it percolated more widely in these linguistic communities, and it effectively turned them into congregations, Christian communities with a degree of cohesion.

The closest to the eastern public at large was the Gothic church. The bishop who had baptized Constantine on his deathbed in 337 was Eusebius of Nicomedia. He went on to consecrate another famous bishop, Wulfila ("Wolfie"—a Gothic name also greco-latinized as *Ulfilas*) in 341, who thereby at the age of thirty assumed spiritual responsibility for his countrymen the Goths. In the course of his duty he designed an alphabet for Gothic—the first ever for a Germanic language—and used it to translate the Bible as a whole, starting with the Gospels. His community was settled north of the Danube in the Balkans, outside the northern limit of the empire; but in 348, seeking refuge from their pagan kinsmen, they were granted leave by the emperor Constantius II to move south of the river into Roman Moesia (modern Bulgaria). This was the nucleus of the Gothic church, which was reinforced a generation later, in 376, by a further immigration of Goths under another Christian, Fritigern (by name a yearner after peace[10]).

Edessa makes the claim to have been the first Christian principality in the world, on the presumption that their king Abgar VIII (177–212) was indeed a Christian. This is still an era of legend, but the first historic king to have been undeniably a Christian was king Tiridates III (natively *Trdat*) of Armenia, who was converted some time in the first two decades of the fourth century (officially in 301). Tiridates was the son of a king of Armenia, Khosrov II, who had been assassinated in a Parthian-inspired coup in 252. Parthians took control of Armenia, while the young prince (a toddler of two at the time) was spirited away to Rome for safety, where he subsequently received an elite education: he returned in 287 on the crest of a Roman advance that was pressing back the eastern power (the Parthians had been unseated by Sassanians meanwhile), and succeeded in putting him back on the throne, as Tiridates III.

The family of the man who had assassinated Khosrov, Tiridates' father, now had only one surviving member: this was Gregory, who had been just five in 252; had grown up in Caesarea, Cappadocia (modern Kayserí), part of the Roman Empire, with the Christian Holy Father Phirmilianos; and had developed into an exceedingly devout Christian. Nevertheless, he married and had two children, before retiring to a monastic life, and then returned to Armenia to atone somehow for his father's great wrong.

Tiridates was at this period of his reign (like his Roman patron, the emperor Diocletian) a great persecutor of Christians, and he had Gregory thrown into an underground dungeon, at a place now known as Khor Virap, and kept there for thirteen years. However, when Gregory was at last released from prison, he succeeded in converting Tiridates to Christianity, and gained a commitment to make Armenia itself a Christian kingdom, with himself as the first *catholicos*. He become known thereafter (in Greek) as *Phōstēr* ("the Illuminator"). In 318 he appointed as his successor his second son, Aristaces.*

Armenia has continued as a Christian kingdom ever since, but lacking literacy, the first two or three generations of Armenian Christians had to content themselves with ad-hoc oral translations of the scriptures. The full conversion of the population probably awaited the activities of Mesrop Mashtots (362–440), who did for Armenian much of what Wulfila had done for Gothic: namely, to provide its first alphabet, and organize the translation of the Bible into it. At least for the New Testament, the originals from which his team worked were in Syriac, and the results were then revised in the light of Greek texts brought specially from Constantinople.[11]

North of Armenia, the Georgian church traditionally names Saint Andrew and Simon the Zealot (or the Canaanite) as its evangelists, but there is no historical basis for any preaching by them in the Caucasus. More substantial is the story of King Mirian III's conversion (ca. 337), apparently through the influence of a Cappadocian woman named Nino. Hereafter there was an official representation of Christianity at court, in the royal city of Mc'xet'a (Mtskheta) in K'art'li. The central state of K'art'li (Iberia) dominated the westerly state of Laz (Colchis) in Georgia, but since it was not a highly urbanized society (unlike many other Christian societies), the episcopate was less centralized, bishops tending to reside in aristocratic estates. At this point the Georgian church still looked to Antioch as its patriarchate, far, far away on the Mediterranean; but most of the prelates of the church were foreigners.[12]

---

* This conversion may have been less of a radical innovation than a gradual advance of the Christian tide. It seems that Gregory was supported by Meruzanes (a bishop) and other notable Christians of the province of Armenia Minor. This was separate from Armenia proper, in the east, the Arshakuni kingdom over which Tiridates ruled. (Nersessian 2007, p. 25.)

Literacy came to Georgia in the form of the (now ancient) *Asomtavruli* script at about the same time as in Armenia, viz the turn of the fourth and fifth centuries. Another alphabet was designed at the same time, used for the Caucasian Albanians of the northeast, now the territory of Azerbaijan and Daghestan. The actual genesis of the systems is contested. At any rate, whether or not they are due to the Armenian sage Mesrop Mashtots, mutual influence between Armenia and Georgia must be presumed, and that influence is likely to have been predominantly one-way: the Armenian state was considerably larger and more powerful. *Asomtavruli* was applied in the fifth century to translate scripture and commentaries, and by the end of the century, original Georgian literature began to appear.

Ethiopia is the last of the five outliers from this early period of expansion of the Christian church directly from its foundation sites. Despite a few references to *Aithiopia* "Burnt-face land" in the New Testament, including to a eunuch servant of the Meroitic queen Candace, instructed by the apostle Philip in Acts 8:26–40, the substantive history of the Ethiopic church begins with a shipwreck. Around 333, two young native Christians from Tyre in Phoenicia (Syro-Phoenician Greeks) were the only survivors of a massacre of a ship's crew on the Red Sea coast. They were called Frumentius and Aedesius, and the latter apparently provided an eyewitness account to the historian Rufinus. They were inducted as slaves into the Ethiopian court (Kingdom of Axum) and engaged to teach the young heir Ezana, who would be the first Christian king of Ethiopia. They contributed to the creation of a Christian community in Ethiopia, enlisting merchants among others.

Later Aedesius returned to Tyre, where he was ordained as a priest. Frumentius went with him as far as Alexandria and petitioned for a bishop and some priests to go and organize a church properly in Ethiopia. He was sent himself by the patriarch Athanasius, who would afterward become a leading figure in Christological controversy. Thus the Ethiopian church was founded, and the tradition was initiated whereby all the bishops of Ethiopia would be appointed by the Coptic patriarch of Alexandria.

At first, however, based on texts received in Greek, the faith was an elite affair. Only six or seven generations later, in the early sixth century, did the scriptures begin to be translated into the then vernacular language of Ethiopia, Ge'ez. Supposedly a group of holy men arrived "from Rome," the "Nine Saints," who would in fact have come from the eastern Roman Empire, Constantinople, Syria, Cilicia, Caesarea. Though they could hardly have provided bilingual abilities to found the translation process, they may well have brought the expertise to know what texts needed translating; the net effect of these vernacular scriptures seems—as usual—to have been the spread of the faith to the masses.

By 200, then, there were nascent churches worshipping in vernacular Aramaic (or Syriac) across the Fertile Crescent, from Antioch in Syria to Seleucia-Ctesiphon in Mesopotamia. At that point, the church in Alexandria (in Egypt) was still worshipping in Greek, a language long used by the Egyptian elite, but within a century (to 300) it would be changing language to its own vernacular, Coptic. Meanwhile, all across Greece and Asia Minor, Greek-speaking churches were springing up over the second and third centuries, though not yet organized hierarchically, except informally by the rank of apostle or disciple who was held to have founded them.

But there was an emerging sense of regional division of responsibility, as a result of diocesan organization modeled on the empire. Hence, we read as Canon II of the Synod of Constantinople (381):

> The bishops are not to go beyond their dioceses to churches lying outside of their bounds, nor bring confusion on the churches; but let the Bishop of Alexandria, according to the canons, alone administer the affairs of Egypt; and let the bishops of the East manage the East alone, the privileges of the Church in Antioch, which are mentioned in the canons of Nicaea [325], being preserved; and let the bishops of the Asian Diocese administer the Asian affairs only; and the Pontic bishops only Pontic matters; and the Thracian bishops only Thracian affairs . . .

And the metropolitan, i.e., bishop of a *mētropolis* ("mother-city"), the principal city of a province (in Greek, *eparkhía*), would come to be seen as representing all the bishops and dioceses within that province. The administrative structuring of the church was creating the divisions on which it would be possible for the church to fragment.

This distinctness of *metropolis*, *eparchy*, and *diocese* was inevitably reinforced by the regional community marked by a language. The diocese of Alexandria in Egypt naturally developed into "the Coptic church"; that of Constantinople was identified with "Greek Orthodoxy," and that of Rome with "the Latin rite." This linguistic identification of churches was even easier with the newer, farther flung, but geographically concentrated establishments in Armenia, Georgia, and Ethiopia. By contrast, the Gothic church, officially identified as "Christians in Gothia," was officially localized in Caffa (modern Feodosia) in the Crimea, but was very much on the move, dispersing throughout the empire (especially Italy, Spain, and North Africa) during the period of its existence from the fourth to the seventh century. Nevertheless, there was an archdiocese from the fifth century, within the patriarchate of Constantinople: at the Gothic church there, a Gothic priesthood read, preached, and sang in Gothic.[13]

A Series of Synods

The differences among these "national" churches began to surface when the church—initially at the invitation of the emperor—began to hold ecumenical synods—the Greek for "world meetings," when οἰκουμένη meant "the inhabited world." These were funded by the emperor as opportunities to find a basis for unity in the church, which was now accepted as an institution of the Roman Empire. As such, they never accepted delegates from the Church of the East, based in Seleucia-Ctesiphon; rather, they played a role in expelling deviant churches beyond the Roman limits.

And as a means to create unity, they had a curious effect. They did succeed in reaching agreement on matters of considerable subtlety among the intellectual leaders of the different communions, even though—as shown—the participant bishops were largely expressing these doctrines in different languages. But conversely, each new synod found reason why one or more of the remaining churches could no longer continue in communion with the Catholic and Orthodox creed to which they all aspired. One by one, the dioceses foreign to Rome and Constantinople were supplanted. Rather than finding and asserting a central core of truth that would unify the churches, the ecumenical synod became an exquisite engine of schism.

The language communities, then, were to develop into different churches, but the ecumenical synods—and their leaders' reactions to the theories propounded there—gave them reasons to believe themselves significantly different.

Nicaea

The first ecumenical synod was called to Nicaea in northwestern Asia Minor (modern Iznik) by the emperor Constantine himself. The emperor thought it essential to unify the faith that he had licensed throughout the empire, and to this end he offered to defray the travel costs of all invited to attend—a substantial outlay, since all secular dioceses of the empire (except for Britain) sent one or more representatives. The synod was held in 325. Its main doctrinal focus was to reach a common position on the doctrines promoted by Arius,* a north African presbyter, who believed that as son of the Father, Jesus Christ could not have been coeternal—or equal—with him. He was at most ὁμοιούσιος "of similar being" with the Father, and since he must have had an origin at some time (unlike the eternal past existence of the Father), ἦν ποτε ὅτε οὐκ ἦν (ēn pote hote ouk ēn): this slogan meant "[there] was a time when [he] was not."

This was the first glimmer of a debate that would echo down the next half-millennium: what was the true nature of Christ, so that he could be equally God (hence eternal, with all that implied) and Man (hence mortal, in time and capable of suffering)? Nuanced in various ways, the issue, and the various answers proposed to it, served to divide all the churches of Asia and Egypt (though not Greek Orthodox from Roman Catholic): curiously, the permanent fault lines that stood revealed by it were mainly among language communities.

The Arian approach, which emphasized the distinctness of Son from Father, was a widely held doctrine in the church of the fourth century, and indeed twenty-two of the bishops at Nicaea came in its defense, led by Eusebius of Nicomedia. Yet the doctrine was proscribed, the Son declared ὁμοούσιος ("of same being") with the Father (proverbially, there was "one iota of difference between the two doctrines"), and Arius and some of his followers were exiled. The formal text of the Nicene Creed approved there includes the word ὁμοούσιος, and concludes:

> And whosoever shall say that there was a time when the Son of God was not, or that before he was begotten he was not, or that he was made of things that were not, or that he is of a different substance or essence or that he is a creature, or subject to change or conversion—all that so say, the Catholic and Apostolic Church anathematizes them.

The decision soon seemed like a dead letter, however. After a few years, Arius was quietly recalled from exile, and in 336 he was restored to

---

* Perhaps significantly his Greek name, Ἄρειος, gave him a connection with Ares, god of war: certainly he was to prove the source of much dissension.

communion by the Synod of Jerusalem. Constantine was baptized on his deathbed (in 337) by none other than Eusebius, and the following emperor, Constantius II (who reigned from 337 to 361), was himself an Arian sympathizer. His successor, Julian the Apostate (reigned 361–363), tried unsuccessfully to restore paganism); but his successor was Valens (reigned 364–378), yet another Arian. Not until the next emperor, Theodosius I (reigned 379–395), called another ecumenical synod, to Constantinople in 381, was Arianism effectively purged. The Constantinople synod reiterated the Nicene Creed with added corroborative detail.*

In the meantime, in about 341, Eusebius of Nicomedia had elevated the young Goth—and evident Arian sympathizer—Wulfila to a bishopric and charged him to see to the conversion of his people. This he did with great success over the next forty years. The tenor of the emperors (Constantius II, Valens) was still in sympathy with Arianism, and it seems to have penetrated deep into Gothic Christianity. Hence, the Gothic church grew in Arianism on the periphery of the Roman domain, initially in Moesia and neighboring parts of the Balkans, even in the persistent knowledge that its faith was—by the lights of Nicaea and Constantinople—heretical.

This—together with scriptures and a church rite observed in Gothic language—gave a distinctive character to their Christianity as it spread around the empire with Gothic (and Vandal) conquests in the fifth century—conquests that would make Ostrogoths dominant in north Italy and Burgundy, Visigoths in Spain, and Vandals in North Africa. The Gothic church was never restored to communion with the Roman Catholics before these several strands had come to their ends—largely through military defeats. The Vandals were put down in 534 by Constantinople's general Belisarius, the Burgundians in the same year yielded to the (Roman Catholic) Franks, the Ostrogoths in 563 fell to another—though this time short-lived—onslaught from Byzantium. Twenty years later the Visigoths in Spain were converted peaceably to Catholic orthodoxy, and the Lombards in northern Italy (who had quickly supplanted the Byzantine victors in north Italy) succumbed to a Roman takeover among their own ranks in the seventh century.

---

* "And [we believe] in the Holy Spirit, the Lord and Giver-of-Life, who proceeds from the Father, who with the Father and the Son together is worshipped and glorified, who spoke by the prophets. And [we believe] in one, holy, Catholic and Apostolic Church. We acknowledge one Baptism for the remission of sins, [and] we look for the resurrection of the dead and the life of the world to come. Amen."

Arianism for three centuries had been distinguished linguistically, and by descent, as a Gothic, Germanic congregation, with its own service and scriptures. But as the Goths and Vandals ceased to rule, and so ceased to maintain a separate political identity, the faith melted away. It was as if Christ had lost his separate substance from the Father, as his Gothic believers had stopped insisting on it.

Ephesus

The third ecumenical synod, held at Ephesus (modern Efes) in 431, addressed the question that became known as Nestorianism, and with it the separate identity of the Syriac-speaking church in the east. The issue again was one of Christology, the status of Christ with respect to God, but perhaps a more subtle aspect of it.

The nub of the Arian issue had been the οὐσία (*ousia*, the abstract noun derived from the present participle of the Greek verb "to be," so literally, the *being*) of Christ, and its relation to the being of God.* But if the Son and the Father were of the same being or substance, what was the difference between them? Crucially, the Son alone was the man Jesus, and had been born of the Virgin Mary, suffered in the world, died, and had risen again. But how could he have done all this, and still been God? In what respects did Christ share his substance with God the Father, and in what respects was he distinct?

The issue was brought to a head in a dispute about the legitimacy of terming the Virgin Mary θεότοκος, i.e., "God-bearer." Clearly Mary had given birth to the man Jesus, and Jesus Christ was God. But could she, as a woman in the world, have given birth to God himself, as the Holy Word? Was not God immune to the indignities of suffering in the world? Thinking this way, Syriac-language Christians† resisted this term "God-bearer" (or its Syriac equivalent), even though it remained a favorite of the Greek-language

---

* The point was expressed in Latin by the somewhat different term *substantia*, derived from *substare* "to stand under, hence support," since the verb "to be" in Latin had neither a present participle, nor an abstract noun. The received translation for Greek *homoousios* was therefore Latin *consubstantialis*, literally "sharing substance," a well-formed, if cumbersome, word in Latin, although this might obscure the crucial iota of difference with *homoiousios*, for which there was no recognized Latin equivalent.

† They liked to distinguish Theodore of Mopsuestia (died 428) as their founding bishop. As it happened, he had been the teacher of Nestorius in Antioch.

church. The term seemed to give a borrowed divinity by association to Mary, and so had enabled a smooth transition to Christianity from the Greek-language cults of Isis-Horus, a similar mother-son relation popular especially in the east of the Roman Empire, which had made Isis accepted as "Queen of Heaven."

To analyze the nature and status of entities philosophically, other terms had been used in Greek, at least since the time of Aristotle (eight centuries before): φύσις, ὑπόστασις, πρόσωπον—approximately in order of decreasing abstractness, and increasing referential exactness. They are usually translated into English as *nature, hypostasis*, and *person. Nature* defines the kind of thing something is, *hypostasis* the material basis (literally, "support": *hypostasis* is in fact the Greek for "under+standing," the precise etymological equivalent of *substantia*), and *person* defines the specific identity. These could be thought of as answers to three questions: Of what kind is X? What is X? and Who is X?

A strong line was hammered home at the Synod of Ephesus—by Cyril Archbishop of Alexandria, and in determined opposition to Nestorius, then patriarch of Constantinople: on this line, Christ had two natures, divine and human, but both natures had the same, single hypostasis. There was, in fact, a "hypostatic union," which was then represented in a single person, God the Son. Therefore it is perfectly acceptable, even obligatory, to call Mary "bearer of God."

This was not a position that Nestorius could accept. He had found it impossible that distinct natures could be supported by a single hypostasis. He maintained that the union occurred at the level of person, so that the Son was a single person whose double nature was supported by two distinct hypostases. This was anathema to Cyril, who decried Nestorius as a believer in "Two Sons": for Cyril, two hypostases logically implied two persons, whereas for Nestorius, conversely, two natures implied two hypostases—or at least two *qnōmē*, to express the term in Aramaic.

It is not known what language was Nestorius's mother tongue, though he must certainly have been fully conversant with Aramaic and Greek. His known works (only two of which have survived, a *Liturgy* and the so-called *Bazaar of Heracleides*, which is an apologia for his life's work) were apparently written in Greek, but translated into Aramaic.[14] His family hailed from Mesopotamia, he had grown up in southern Anatolia, and he had received his higher training in Antioch.[15]

Nestorius's position makes sense if he was reasoning in Aramaic, where the received equivalents for the three aspects, φύσις, ὑπόστασις, πρόσωπον (*physis* nature, hypostasis, and *prosōpon* person) were *kyānā*, *qnōmā*, and *parṣōpā*. The third of these is just a borrowing of the corresponding Greek term (but also, like the Greek word, has the sense of face, appearance, or a character in a drama). *Kyānā* is used as a translation for Greek οὐσία *ousia* as well as φύσις, while, in Aramaic, *qnōmā* is, basically, the word for "self"—for example, as in washing oneself rather than washing another: it means the object of any reflexive activity.[16] So in Aramaic, Cyril's analysis of Christ amounted to saying he had two natures (or substances), but a single self in a single person—a claim that the natures (human and divine), while different, were here made identical. This, from an Aramaic viewpoint, was a contradiction in terms: for, in Syriac terms, they could only both be present if one person had two identities. A nature was an abstract quality, and could only be present in reality if supported by a self, an identity, a *qnōmā*. Nothing prevented a person from having two identities, but it was nonsense to suppose that one identity could simultaneously have two (defining) natures.

A contemporary way of expressing the contradiction appears in a homily of the Syriac theologian Narsai, from the late fifth century (two generations after Ephesus), commenting on the famous words of John's gospel, 1:14, "the word became flesh, and camped in/among us..." Narsai writes: "It is possible for one to [come to rest] in another in perfect love, but how is it possible for one to [come to rest] in himself [i.e., in his *qnōmā*]."[17] The idea was that the person of Christ had put on flesh, and taken up a temporary dwelling in humanity: i.e., he had taken on, temporarily, the quality of being a man. For this he needed to have a *qnōmā* as a man; otherwise, he would be dwelling temporarily but still in his natural *qnōmā* as God, which would achieve nothing out of the ordinary. The "camping" in human nature would be either quite vacuous, since his identity would remain divine; or worse still, a mixture of divine and human.

There seems to be an explicit claim of two *qnōmē* in an apparently sixth-century document (a hymn attributed to this same Narsai):[18]

> Two *kyānē* (natures) and two *qnōmē* (selves) is our Lord, in one *parṣōpā* (person) of the divinity and the humanity.

As Nestorius himself summed up the consequence (and so solving the initial problem of the Virgin Mary):

I confess in One Christ two natures without mixing. In his divinity he was brought forth by the Father, in his humanity by the Holy Virgin.[19]

This doctrine, unacceptable to Greek or Latin theology after Ephesus in 431, would nonetheless become standard in the sixth century for Syriac-language churches, both for the bishops of Antioch (who by mischance had arrived late for the synod, and had attempted in vain to undo its decision) and in the wider world of Christianity ruled from Seleucia-Ctesiphon, the Church of the East. More than a dozen bishops from Antioch were deposed at the same time as Nestorius, and there was afterward a significant move of Syriac-speaking clergy eastward toward, and into, Persia. Since Edessa became known as a hotbed of this "Nestorian" doctrine, the emperor Zeno closed its school in 489: the result was that yet more of those who took this line moved eastward, into Nisibis, and into Persia beyond the grasp of Roman Christianity.

In the end, Nestorius himself played only an instrumental role, by articulating and drawing attention to the issue. He never joined the Church of the East himself, but his name came to be used in the West as a byword—intended as a slur—for the despised, so-called "Nestorian," Church of the East. He was stripped of his Constantinople patriarchate by the synod—chaired and directed by Cyril, without the participation of the Antiochene bishops. After four years in a monastery, he was exiled to Egypt, where he spent the rest of his life. He died about twenty years after the synod, around 451—by legend, a day before he could be invited to the Synod of Chalcedon, in which the pendulum of accepted orthodoxy was to swing very much in his direction.

His own works were generally ordered burned by the emperor Theodosius, as part of an extreme attempt to erase his views deemed so pernicious: even children who bore his name were rebaptized.[20] As a result, his detailed views were only known in the (misrepresented) form of Cyril's attacks on him for the next 1,450 years. But in the 1880s a Syriac translation turned up, of his chief work—and self-justification. Its title is curiously mistranslated as the "Bazaar of Heracleides."[21] It shows that he did not, as Cyril had claimed, believe in Christ as two persons, one divine and the other human.

Chalcedon

The next major division among the Christian churches came as a result of the Synod of Chalcedon, convened by the emperor Marcian on

October 8, 451. Some five hundred prelates attended, but none from the Church of the East in Seleucia-Ctesiphon. Its aim, as ever, was to ensure unity; but its effect, as ever, was to finalize splits: in this case, to split the Latin and Greek churches in the Roman Empire from all the others, including the remaining churches on the periphery of Roman power.

The synod was held in Chalcedon, a small town on the Asian coast of the Bosphorus, very close to Constantinople: the original choice, Nicaea, historically resonant from the first synod of 325, had to be withdrawn at the last moment for security reasons—namely the imminent threat of Hun attack.

There had been considerable ferment since Ephesus, culminating in a second synod there in 449. This synod had been dominated by the Coptic pope Dioscorus of Alexandria, successor to Cyril, who had died in 444. The business of the meeting had been focused on endorsing the decisions of Cyril at Ephesus, but also aimed to rehabilitate one Eutyches (Greek for "lucky"), an archimandrite (monk) who had emphasized the greatness of the divine nature of Christ to the point where he believed it must engulf any human remnant ("as the ocean consumes a drop of vinegar"). The result was a view of the distinctive substance of Christ that—through its overwhelming divinity—could not be said to be consubstantial with humanity. The thinking of the church in Alexandria was coming close to the Monophysite position, namely that Christ's nature was single and divine. Cyril himself had already taught that "There is only one *physis*, since it is the Incarnation, of God the Word." The danger was that this position seemed to trivialize Christ's human life and his suffering on the cross, and to question whether his was a real human death at all. If so, what was the resurrection?

This proceeding had been dismissed by Pope Leo I in Rome as a *latrocinium* ("coven of robbers"): not only had it denied a hearing to his own *ex cathedra* communiqué (famously known as the *Tomus* "the book"), but it had even descended into violence through Dioscorus's inviting a mob into the assembly. The resulting scuffle had caused the death of Flavian, archbishop of Constantinople. There had been a stalemate while emperor Theodosius II had been alive, since he had summoned the second Ephesus synod and stood by its outcome. Pope Leo was able to take advantage of Theodosius's death in a riding accident in 450 to prevail on the new emperor, Marcian, to try again.

The outcome of the Synod of Chalcedon was very different from Ephesus II, indeed almost the converse. Its doctrine of Christology, derived from the Pope's *Tomus*, is worth stating in toto:

One and the same Christ, Son, Lord, only begotten, to be acknowledged **in two natures, inconfusedly, unchangeably, indivisibly,
inseparably;**

ἐν δύο φύσεσιν ἀσυγχύτως, ἀτρέπτως, ἀδιαιρέτως, ἀχωρίστως
in duabus naturis inconfuse, immutabiliter, indivise, inseparabiliter

the distinction of natures being by no means taken away by the
union, but rather the property of each nature being preserved,
and concurring in one Person (πρόσωπον) and one Subsistence
(ὑπόστασις), not parted or divided into two persons, but one and
the same Son, and only begotten God (μονογενῆ Θεόν), the Word,
the Lord Jesus Christ;

This became, quite literally, the last word on the subject. It is the state-
ment of the dyophysitism (Two-Naturedness) that is endorsed by the Roman
Catholic Church (and all its Protestant heirs) as well as the Greek Orthodox
Church, together with its communicating churches in Bulgaria, Romania,
Serbia and Russia.* It succeeded in unifying Europe, then; but it was less
successful elsewhere.

With the exception of Georgian, none of the churches that worshipped
in languages other than Greek and Latin was able to accept this formula.
They saw the outright acceptance of the two natures, however articulated
with hypostases and *prosōpa*, as verging on Nestorianism (as they had been
persuaded to call a view of Christ as having two persons). Instead, they held
to Cyril's view.

There was not an immediate schism. Although the Coptic church—heartland of Cyril—immediately broke off, the Roman Empire avoided pressing
the issue for at least ninety years. In fact, thirty years after Chalcedon, in
482, the emperor Zeno actually proposed a *Henōticon* (ἑνωτικόν "unifier"),
a dogmatic formulation that tolerated the one-nature view within the
empire.[22] This was an executive act, passed without any further consultation
of bishops, although the text was actually prepared by Acacius, patriarch

---

* Father John Meyendorff holds that the orthodox churches also remain open to Cyril's
converse formulation (one nature of the Word of God, incarnate), to give a two-sided
picture of Christ.

of Constantinople. But the situation was unstable, especially as a dual administration began to develop within the Syriac-speaking church in Antioch. A separate wing established itself, more in sympathy with the emperor's view (much later to be known as Melkite, derived from Syriac *malkoyo* "royal"). Then between 535 and 548 the emperor Justinian invited a delegation of five monks, led by the Coptic priest Abraham of Farshut, to a meeting at Constantinople, where he gave them an ultimatum. As was to be expected, they remained true to their creed, and Christian unity was the loser.

The non-Chalcedonian churches term themselves Miaphysite* (Greek for "one nature") and they are known collectively (in English) as the Oriental Orthodox Churches, or (in most other European languages) as some equivalent of "Ancient Oriental Churches." Nowadays, there are six of them: the Coptic, Ethiopian, Eritrean, Western Syriac, Malankara Syrian (of Kerala, in South India), and Armenian Apostolic churches. Although originally, in the mid-sixth century, there were Greek speakers on all sides, the Miaphysite communion stabilized into just those churches that (outside Persia) spoke Coptic, Ge'ez, Syriac, and Armenian.

It was painfully clear that membership of different language communities correlated with religious loyalty;[23] large speech communities on a national scale, even within a faith that has a worldwide aspiration, fall over time into distinct churches. Undeniably, the links of person-to-person communication in a language community, reinforced by frequent contact, build a solidarity far more effectively than the leadership of emperors, or perhaps even bishops. Once the language community is established, however, it can be characterized and strengthened by giving it a cause, or a title, that is derived from a theoretical argument. Thus, for example, the Ethiopian church is officially the Ethiopian Orthodox *Tewahedo* Church, where [*tæwahədo*] ተዋሕዶ is a Ge'ez word (cf the Arabic equivalent *tauḥid*) meaning "unified": so the title makes a direct reference to the status of Christ in Miaphysite theology.†

Nowadays it is rather difficult to appreciate what all the fuss was about in the Chalcedon settlement, and why it proved totally impossible to reconcile

---

* For no linguistic reason, they prefer this to "Monophysite" (which is an exact synonym in Greek "for a single nature"). However, they believe this term to be a slur cast by the non-Miaphysite world.

† It is in fact the only fully Ethiopian word in the title: the church is usually now called (in modern Amharic) *Yäityop'ya ortodoks täwahedo bétäkrestyan*, where every other word has its root in Greek.

the parties. About the central mysteries of Christianity, such as the Trinity and its members, God's Incarnation as the man Jesus, and his atonement for human sin through his undeserved death, they were all in agreement: but they chose to emphasize different aspects of this faith through a philosophical dispute over technical terms regarding Christ's dual status, during his earthly life, as God and man. Did he have one nature or two?

Fault Lines Revealed by Languages

There may have been something intrinsically Greek in this kind of dispute: Gregory of Nyssa, who attended the first synod of Constantinople in 381, described the enthusiasm he met with in the streets:

> The whole city is full of it, the squares, the market places, the crossroads, the alleyways; old-clothes men, money changers, food sellers: they are all busy arguing. If you ask someone to give you change, he philosophizes about the Begotten and the Unbegotten; if you inquire about the price of a loaf, the answer is that the Father is greater and the Son inferior; if you ask "Is my bath ready?" the attendant will have laid down the law that the Son came to be from nothing. I don't know what to call this plague, inflammation of the brain or madness, or why this should be so widespread, causing such derangement in people's thinking.[24]

But the concern went far beyond a besetting madness of the Greeks. When bishops returned from Chalcedon to Jerusalem in Palestine and even Antioch in Syria—all Aramaic-speaking communities and supposed centers of the "Antiochene" theology associated with Nestorius—they found rising opposition from their congregations, incensed that they had acquiesced in Pope Leo's Roman formulation of this evidently sensitive area of their faith. Juvenalis, bishop of Jerusalem, withdrew at first to Constantinople to take counsel, but returned with an imperial force that soon caused significant casualties among the monks of Neapolis (modern Nablus), north of Jerusalem.[25] Outbreaks were far worse in the streets of Egypt, which had long been the home of the so-called "Alexandrian" school of thought, most famously defended by Cyril at the Synod of Ephesus. The Egyptian bishops had warned "We shall be killed!" when they were asked to sign the Chalcedon creed. And sure enough, when their leader Dioscorus was deposed, and replaced by his more complaisant deputy Proterius, he could only rule through high-handed actions. The result was a bloody mess: Romans and Egyptians armed themselves on the streets of Alexandria, and ultimately Proterius was assassinated.[26]

All in all,

> countless numbers fell victim to slaughter, and the mass of corpses filled not only the land but now even the air as well[27]

in the surprisingly intemperate words of the *Henōticon* itself, issued though it was a generation later, in a vain attempt to soothe and reframe the resulting divisions.

Farther afield, there was less immediate hubbub.

In Ethiopia, the close relation of the church with the Copts in Alexandria seems to have determined the outcome, so that there was little controversy in opting for Miaphysitism, which was even incorporated into the name of the church, *Tewahedo*.

In Armenia no mention of Chalcedon in the fifth century has survived.[28] Later, in 506 the first of a series of Armenian synods at Dvin endorsed the *Henōticon* and condemned Nestorianism, seen as the doctrine of two natures in Christ, and specifically as a doctrine of the Persian Church of the East. This decision was also seen as deliberate rejection of Chalcedon.[29] A second synod of Dvin in 555 opted officially for a Miaphysite approach.[30]

In Georgia, political relations with the Roman and Persian empires appear to have had more influence on the outcome, with the church wavering throughout the sixth century. Roman orthodoxy favored the *Henōticon*, then Chalcedon again, while Persia—being host to the Church of the East—was in general for their even older Dyophysite position. Only the historic link with Armenia promoted the Miaphysite view. At length, at the third synod of Dvin in 608–609 the Armenian church, which had previously claimed seniority, and some degree of supervision of the Georgian church, excommunicated the *catholicos* of Georgia for acceptance of Chalcedon. Then, in 629, the Roman emperor Heraclius decisively defeated Persia in battle, using his victory symbolically to return the True Cross to Jerusalem. This set the seal on Georgia's allegiance to Constantinople, and thence to its acceptance of Chalcedon.[31] The age-old unity of the Armenian and Georgian churches was thereafter sundered.

In the thirty years 632–661, however, the whole political framework was suddenly, fundamentally, and irreversibly transformed. Militant Islam, an unforeseen power that spoke an unknown language, Arabic, and propagated a faith unknown to either the Roman or Persian empires—though it could have been seen by Christians as a new extreme form of Arianism, since it demoted Christ to the rank of prophet—emerged from the Arabian desert. Thenceforth all the Miaphysite churches were permanently cut off from any further political connection with Constantinople or Ctesiphon, the political hegemonies of Rome and Persia that had been assumed for the previous seven hundred years.

Armenia and Georgia too lost these political links, although the Muslims' control of these regions would remain insecure.

The ultimate distribution of opinions among the various churches on the nature(s) and person of Christ (and how they might be related) was assigned, as we have seen, according to language community. But this simply shows where the boundaries between religious communities would fall. It does not imply anything about which language group would get which creed. The pattern of Christian belief in the East, from Egypt to Persia and beyond, is not an artifact of the senses of particular words in the local language, or mistakes in translation.[32]

The indifference of language to the outcome of this theological issue is reinforced by what happened in the Church of the East (resolutely Dyophysite, ever since Nestorius) as against in the Jacobite church, the Oriental Orthodox church of the West Syrians, centerd in Antioch (which became Miaphysite in reaction to the Roman Empire's attempt to enforce the doctrine of Chalcedon). Both churches—despite their differences of the number of *qnomē* (hypostases—or perhaps "selves") possessed by Christ—went on worshipping, praying, preaching, and disputing for 1,500 years in the same Syriac dialect of Aramaic.

Misunderstood differences, then, in the full senses of words that are deemed translation equivalents, or the absence of a theologically important distinction in some language's traditional discourse, seem seldom—at least in the long term—to indicate the content of differences that actually do arise between the forms of a religion observed in different language communities. People will not be misled by the terminology of their own language to embrace a heresy or misunderstand the creed. They are much more likely to do these things if they are in contact—and especially, in a speech community—with others who, for whatever reason, are minded to take a path in the faith different from the majority, or from the self-presuming authority.

Language-Inspired Differences

But this does not mean that a language will have no intrinsic effect on the content of creed. People may well understand what others are saying in a different speech community, and yet choose—perhaps unconsciously—to innovate, using ideas familiar in their own cultural traditions to illustrate and animate the key facts in the new creed.

For example, there is a view of Christ, specifically in the Church of the East—but not in other language traditions—that sees him as a hostage sent into the world by God.[33] (The word used, *hmayrā*, is a borrowing from Greek *homēros*, though Christ is never *homēros* in the Greek conception.) Hostages in the ancient world were not taken by force (as they are today) to disarm an opponent, but rather given, as a long-term pledge by the giver, usually the weaker power in a negotiation, to enhance their credibility. "See: I trust you with my son and heir: respect our agreement."*

A classic example was Theoderic, who as an Ostrogothic prince was held from age eight to eighteen at Constantinople (462–480): later he assumed kingship of the Goths, and later still, originally at the behest of the Roman emperor Zeno, he took control of Italy, with considerable sympathy for the Roman way (493–526). In the other direction, Saurmag II, king of Kartli-Georgia from 361 to 363, gave his son as a hostage to the Persians, limiting his freedom of action with the Romans too.[34] Hostage giving and taking between Rome and Persia was always exceptional, since neither power would accept the other as its superior; nevertheless, exchanges of hostages did occur.[35]

This status of Christ as a *hmayrā* fit well within Nestorian thinking, emphasizing as it did the importance of God's incarnation as a human being, as well as a presumed sacred requital. But note that the direction of giving is from Man to God, just as it was the inferior powers who would give a member of their families to the dominant superpower, Rome or Persia. He is the *hmayrā d-men gensan* "the hostage from our race." It is not the Son who is offered as a temporary human being—even a live sacrifice—to show God's

---

* There was also an element of acculturation, reminiscent of modern graduate schools in rich countries: educate the elite youth of your enemy, and in the next generation, their people will be your friends. Thus, whether he was called a hostage or not, the situation of a prince whose faction had been deposed at home—such as Tiridates III in Armenia—was not very different in what the Romans might hope to get out of the arrangement.

intent to save fallen and intellectually fallible Man, but the body of a mortal man that has been offered as a temporary abode for God, with long-term good consequences. Here are two passages from the *ḥudra*, the East Syrian liturgy, which recur often.[36]

> "O Lord, . . . who in your compassion lowered yourself to your flock, and who, out of your love, took from our race a hostage of peace [*ḥmayrā d-šaynā*] and made him a choice abode for yourself for the purpose of your economy."
>
> "Blessed is the Good One . . . [who] came from heaven for our salvation and too from our mortal race a hostage for his glory, and he granted him to become leader and head."

This way of seeing Christ's incarnation is a metaphor, one may say, distinctive of the Syriac imagination. Such hostages may be sacrificed (as, for Ephrem the Syrian, the children massacred by Herod were "slain hostages, clothed in symbols of the killing of the Slain King"), or they might be chosen to survive (as the poet Narsai says that Enoch was taken by the Lord of the Universe as a peace hostage and preserved in life to proclaim to the members of his race). It is a Syriac believer's way to express a particular quality seen in these actions: the giving of a human being as a hostage to God shows conversely that there is a pledge (*rahbōnā*) given by God to humanity.

And this word—together with its borrowed version ἀρραβών *arrhabōn* in Greek—is precisely how Paul characterizes the promise of the Holy Spirit, that which gives us a clear claim on our inheritance (in Ephesians 1:13–14).[37]

So although the "hostage" metaphor itself is distinctive, and might be thought a theological innovation due to a Syriac tradition, it leads the doctrine back to Pauline orthodoxy.

Another such favorite metaphor—which creates a viewpoint on the faith, without actually changing it—is the Syriac fixation with vestments. The crucial turning points of sacred history—from Adam's and Eve's fall in the Garden of Eden to the Incarnation, the institution of baptism— are all seen as the putting on or the taking off of clothing. Adam and Eve lost their robes of glory when they knew they were naked. Christ put on Adam, a human body, in the Incarnation; he deposited his own robe of glory in the River Jordan in his baptism, which is why it is available to wear afresh, to all those baptized after him.

The drama is told concisely in a stanza of Ephrem the Syrian:

> All these changes did the Merciful One make, stripping off and putting on; for He had devised a way to reclothe Adam in that glory which Adam had stripped off. He was wrapped with swaddling clothes, corresponding to Adam's leaves, He put on clothes instead of Adam's skins; he was baptized for Adam's sin, he was embalmed for Adam's death, he rose and raised up Adam in his glory. Blessed is he who descended, put Adam on and ascended.[38]

Ephrem seems to be building a conceit, in which Adam owes his salvation in Christ to the fact that he could be taken off and put on like a garment.* Curiously, this seems to derive from the converse metaphor in Paul's letter (Romans 13:14 and Galatians 3:27) where the Christian "puts on Christ."[39] It is characteristic of Syriac theology, expressed as it often is in poetry rather than dialectic, to play with these metaphorical concepts and reapply them. This is something that Syriac does, when Greek did not, and so "puts new raiment" on thought about Christ's mighty achievement.

Given an independent situation, it is possible for a self-confident language tradition to develop a religion in this way. A language tradition, given enough time and some freedom of expression, will change the style of a faith. The Church of the East, and the Miaphysite churches, had a fair amount of such independence after the east was shut off from Greco-Roman influence by the Arab conquests. It simply ceased to be an issue—as it had been at Chalcedon—what the Syrians, Armenians, Egyptians, or Georgians were going to believe.

But language diversity would strike closer to home. The Greek and the Latin rites themselves, which seemed to have achieved a modicum of unity at Chalcedon, were going to find their differences progressively harder to bear.

---

* Something of the general familiarity of this metaphor, and the analogy of flesh with clothing, is shown by the fact that in Syriac, "putting on" a woman like a garment is a euphemism for sexual intercourse. (See *Comprehensive Aramaic Lexicon* http://cal1.cn.huc. edu/, under the word *lbš*.)

The same metaphor is used in Arabic in the Qur'ān 2:187: "The night of the fast will be (the time) for you to have intercourse with your wives. For they are a garment for you, and you are a garment for them . . ."

Schism of Greek and Latin

The moment of formal sundering between the church in its Latin and Greek rites—what came to be seen familiarly as the Roman Catholics and the Greek Orthodox—came in 1054, when each church formally excommunicated the patriarch of the other, Pope Leo IX and Michael Kērularios. Although this mutual act was not withdrawn until 1965, there was in practice no enforcement of a standstill in relations between the two Christian domains—such as there had been, by contrast, in 553 after Justinian's final imposition of the judgment of the (century-old) Synod of Chalcedon, when the Miaphysite churches were cut adrift. But the situation was not quite unprecedented in the Greco-Roman church: there had, in fact, been a previous formal schism, when in 867 the Orthodox patriarch Photius had excommunicated Pope Nicholas I, only to be condemned himself, and so deposed and his acts annulled, by an ecumenical council, in Constantinople just two years later in 869–70.

There continued to be attempts at major collaborations between the two churches, often military ones: for example, after the (Byzantine) Roman emperor's defeat by Turks at Manzikert in 1071 and subsequent losses in Anatolia, Pope Gregory VII called for the *milites Christi* ("soldiers of Christ") to go to the aid of these eastern Christians. A little later, a practical alliance between Frankish crusaders and Byzantine forces in the First Crusade expelled Turks from Nicaea in 1097 and pressed on (largely without Byzantine help) to the war in Syria and Palestine.

But relations continued to deteriorate over the following decades and centuries. A notable low point was the sack of Constantinople itself—simply for the loot it contained—by western Christian forces in 1204 (as part of the supposed Fourth Crusade); and when the last Roman emperor (tellingly named Constantine) had appealed for Christendom's aid in its final hour of need in 1453, there was no effective alliance to resist the onset of Mehmet II and the Ottoman Empire. This last event—among much else—disestablished Orthodox Christianity as the imperial faith in the eastern Mediterranean, and so put it at a considerable political disadvanatage in comparison with the Church of Rome, whose authority was largely acknowledged by all the states of western Europe.

There are many differences over faith that divided the two churches, which had grown up since their moment of unity at Chalcedon in 451, among them variances in canonical practice as to whether parish priests could be married men (as was universal in the east), and whether communion bread could be unleavened (as it largely was in the west, making loss of holy crumbs less of a problem).

The theology of the Trinity was differently viewed. Did the Holy Spirit proceed solely from the Father (as the Synods of Nicaea 325 and Constantinople 381 had opined)? Or did the Spirit proceed from the Father **and the Son** (*filioque*)?—a phrase the Roman Catholic Church had officially inserted, without consultation of the Greek Orthodox, in 1014.* In fact, the Greek Orthodox Church still maintains that the Synod of Ephesus in 431 explicitly forbade any such modification of the Nicene Creed.

Above all, there were questions of precedence among the churches. Did the bishop of Rome retain a superiority inherited from Saint Peter, over Christianity as a whole? Was deference due, perhaps even equal deference, to the so-called Pentarchy, the five centers of the early church, in Jerusalem, Antioch, Alexandria, Rome, with Constantinople inserted late in the day?

None of these issues, of course, is a linguistic difference. Yet the watershed between the churches at dispute was a linguistic one: both at the liturgical level, between the Latin rite of the Catholics and the originally Greek rites of the Eastern Orthodox, and more generally, between western and eastern European languages that are the spoken vernaculars of the two religious communities.

Both the Latin-using and Greek-using halves of Romania, the lands that were once included in the Roman Empire, were heirs to the Greek philosophical tradition, the foundation for the kind of theological analysis that was the stuff of churchmen's disputes, and perhaps the bedrock of their faith, too, in the first millennium A.D. The shared enthusiasm for these theological disputes provided some issues, admittedly arbitrary, but viewed as important, on which to hang a sense of community differences, even though the real difference was not in points of abstract faith, but social and cultural, as between members of societies that had increasingly little to do with each other, and buttressed about by growing public ignorance of each other's languages.

---

* The history of this addition is quite involved, but seems to go back to a supplement to the Nicene Creed introduced in Spain in the seventh century, as an implicit rejection of Arian doctrine. It spread through western Europe informally, and was finally inserted in the Roman creed in 1014, at the request of the German king Heinrich II, who had come to Rome to be crowned emperor.

Some of the theologians saw the language barrier as crucial. But the reason might be subtler than ignorance: differences might have stemmed from attempts at translation between Greek and Latin that were too literal, attempts that went against the mode of expression. Maximus the Confessor, writing in Greek in the seventh century, thought that the *filioque* dispute (already agonizing ecumenical relations) could be resolved if only the Romans could clarify what they meant by the procession of the Holy Spirit. "I have . . . asked the Romans to translate what is peculiar to them [i.e., the *filioque*] in such a way that any misleading implications can be avoided." But he was not sure they would succeed: "I doubt whether in fact they may comply . . . especially since you cannot make exact an idea in a language and words that are foreign to oneself as one can in one's mother-tongue, just as we cannot in our own. But anyway this problem will dawn on them from the abuse they will find they receive."[40]

Constantine's transfer of the empire's capital to the east (established in 330) had laid the basis for a system in which the role of Greek would be extended from everyday speech into every function, although for some centuries, the government went on making the attempt to maintain Latin in law, administration, and the military. Yet by the era of the emperor Heraclius (610–641)—who styled himself not *imperator*, not Caesar or Augustus, but βασιλεύς *basileus*—the exclusive use of Greek in the East was fully established. This was paralleled by the universal official use of Latin in the West, even though it was divided into a greater variety of kingdoms than the East. The political domains that the emperors had defined initially for administrative convenience turned into speech communities with quite separate lingua francas, Greek and Latin.[41]

It is difficult to assess which was the driving force, differences of creed and practice derived from a different social order, or difference of language that made it unnecessary to intercommunicate. But the fact was that, in the second half of the first millennium A.D., Greek and Roman Christendom had become separate communities, and from the inherited and growing difference in linguistic media, developing this became all the easier.

In the West, abandoned as the center of imperial power, and no longer even united after barbarian invasions had created a network of independent kingdoms, the influence, dominance, and indeed power of the bishop of Rome came to seem the one uniting force. In the East, meanwhile, the church was seen, almost from its outset in the reign of Constantine, as an aspect of the central government, looking to the emperor as its head and protector.

Eusebius, the first church historian, had characterized Constantine (on his thirtieth anniversary) as chancellor (ὕπαρχος *hyparkhos*) of God the ultimate king, ruling the world according to his word (λόγος *lógos*) and this theory of the Eastern Roman emperor persisted for the next millennium, in fact until the final destruction of the empire itself.[42]

A Faith Beyond Languages?

We can reflect now on Christianity's degree of success in trying to establish a multilingual faith that was yet doctrinally united, as the miracle at Pentecost had suggested should be the church's aim.

Looking back on the first millennium, one has to admit that—despite their acknowledgment of largely common scriptures (read in a variety of local translations),[43] the church (as a whole) did not, in the long run, succeed in creating faith communities larger than the speech communities of the individual languages. Syriac, Greek, Latin, Gothic, Coptic, Armenian, Georgian, and Ethiopian each had their own faith; and in the case of Syriac, there were at least two—the Oriental Orthodox based on Antioch, and the Church of the East based in Seleucia-Ctesiphon.

Attempts (through a series of ecumenical synods) at agreeing on a unified creed resulted only in clearly defining the doctrinal differences among the various language communities, differences that it has proved impossible to undo, even after the Arab conquests, which totally transformed the vernacular language situation in the region.

The differences have had little evidently to do with the languages in which they are expressed but have nonetheless been sufficient to keep apart—through religious loyalties—the communities who speak, or once spoke, those languages.

CHAPTER 7

❦❧❦❧

"Proclaiming the Good News"
With Christ into Northern Europe

And Jesus came and spoke unto them, saying, "All power is given unto me in heaven and in earth. Go ye therefore, and teach all nations, baptizing them in the name of the Father, and of the Son, and of the Holy Ghost: Teaching them to observe all things whatsoever I have commanded you . . ."

Matthew 28:17–19

BY THEIR NAME, THE Christians of the Roman Empire were the ones dedicated to a Greek acceptance of the fulfillment of a Jewish promise, the anointed, the Messiah. But the Roman Empire itself was not a creature of that oriental world, even if it aspired to dominate many who were. Even in the first century A.D., its provinces to the north and west put it in contact with peoples of quite alien traditions and identities. When the faith began to cross its borders, it reached tribes whose ethics stemmed from fear of being shamed in public, rather than any inward sense of sin from acknowledged failings, and who saw glory as arising directly from simple strength and victory, rather than more subtly (or perversely) from compassion and martyrdom. Disputes on the number, or human nature, of the divine were a closed book to them, since they could not read. The heroic cults of the Aryan gods—represented in Europe by the Celts, the Germans, and the Slavs— would now face the aggressive standards of the Living God. And yet the accommodation that they would reach, in ceding the Lordship of the World to him, would not be wholly one-sided.

At the close of the New Testament Gospels, Jesus expresses to his disciples the Great Commission, namely to take his message of salvation "to all the nations"—in Greek πάντα τὰ ἔθνη, using the same word *ethnē* that is used as the standard word for Gentiles, the non-Jewish peoples of the world.[1]

This duty of the faithful to present the good news actively, in order to persuade others to be baptized and be received into the church, was conveyed in various words of Greek and Latin. But surprisingly many of the terms we now use are fairly recent coinages in English, reflecting terms that were new in late Latin—*proselytize* (1679), *mission* (1622), *propagation* (1623)—so that they have only been applied to the missionary activity that accompanied modern European empire-building. Rather than use these, the basic pattern of the early church is well summed up in Acts 14:21–23:

21. After they had **proclaimed the good news** to that city and had **made** many **disciples**, they returned to Lystra, then on to Iconium and Antioch.	εὐαγγελισαμενοι τε την πολιν ἐκεινην και **μαθητευσαντες** ἱκανους ὑπεστρεψαν εἰς την Λυστραν και Ἰκονιον και Ἀντιοχειαν	Cumque **evangelizassent** civitati illi et **docuissent** multos, reversi sunt Lystram et Iconium et Antiochiam,
22. There they **strengthened** the souls of the disciples and **encouraged** them to continue in the faith, saying, "It is through many persecutions that we must enter the kingdom of God."	**ἐπιστηριζοντες** τας ψυχας των μαθητων **παρακαλουντες** ἐμμενειν τη πιστει και ὁτι δια πολλων θλιψεων δει ἡμας εἰσελθειν εἰς την βασιλειαν του Θεου	**confirmantes** animas discipulorum, **exhortantes**, ut permanerent in fide, et quoniam per multas tribulationes oportet nos intrare in regnum Dei.
23. And after they had appointed **elders** for them in each **church**, with prayer and fasting they **entrusted** them to the Lord in whom they had come to believe.	χειροτονησαντες δε αὐτοις **πρεσβυτερους** κατ᾽ **ἐκκλησιαν** προσευξαμενοι μετα νηστειων **παρεθεντο** αὐτους τω κυριω εἰς ὁν πεπιστευκεισαν	Et cum ordinassent illis per singulas **ecclesias presbyteros** et orassent cum ieiunationibus, **commendaverunt** eos Domino, in quem crediderant.

So the process was to give out the good news generally (*evangelizare*), followed by instruction of actual converts (*docere*). Thereafter, confirmation and encouragement (*confirmare, exhortari*) were offered to the recent converts, and a basic church hierarchy of elders (*presbyteri, ecclesia*) was set up. The converts were then formally entrusted to the Lord (*commendare*).

At some point in this process, presumably at the point of *commendatio*, baptism too must have been given, since this mark of entry to the church goes right back to the beginning, and was explicitly in Christ's commission.[2]

In general, Christ's disciples are urged to "proclaim" the Gospel, using the verbs (κηρύσσειν, *praedicare*) that are characteristic of a public herald or town crier. This would be the regime expected of an apostle (ἀπόστολος, literally, "emissary, one dispatched") or a martyr (μάρτυς, a "witness"). But given the prevalence of persecution in the history of the early church, it is usually believed now that the main channel of new conversions was not the conscious seeking-out of converts, which would have endangered both preacher and proselyte, but a process of conversion by association through networks of friends and relations.[3]

In whatever way the Gospel, and the faith it inspired, were transmitted across the western empire, it had evidently made the journey to the outermost limits well before the ending of Christian persecution. In 177, the first martyr-doms in Gaul had been recorded, in Lyon.[4] In 314, the year immediately after Constantine's Edict of Christian Toleration was pronounced at Milan in 313, the emperor called a council to Arelate (Arles on the Mediterranean coast) and summoned more than thirty western bishops to it. This represented a quasi-official list of significant bishoprics: ten or so cities in Gaul (including Lyon, Vienne, and Autun in the center and Rouen in the north), three in Britain (including London and York), and at least one on the German border (at Trier, which also represented Cologne and Tongeren to its north).*

In the early fourth century, then, before any official authorization of the Christian movement, there were churches throughout Gaul and Britain, and also on the borders of Germany. This is precisely the period of the earliest Christian mosaic found in Britain, at Hinton St. Mary, in Dorset, which demonstrates that Christianity was already beginning to be adopted by some wealthy provincials there. In this century, however, there was little likelihood that the faith was being propagated in any language other than Greek or Latin.

The first known teaching of Christianity in an indigenous language of the north was the mission of Wulfila, to his own people, the Goths of Crimea, part of the eastern spread of the church. The resulting Gothic church persisted for four centuries, its worship holding firm to its own Germanic language, and practised in many parts of Italy, Spain, and North

---

* The contemporary names (spelled as per the manuscript in Corbie Monastery in Picardy, France, were: Lugdunum, Vienna, Augustudunum, Rotomagus; Londinium, Eboracum, Colonia Londinensium; Triveri, Agripenensis, Tungri. It is assumed that "Londinensium" is a mistake for something else: perhaps Lindensium (Lincoln) or Legionensium (Caerleon-on-Usk).

Africa. As often in the history of religious sects, this linguistic and scriptural loyalty proved essential to preserving its identity: when the last active notes of Gothic liturgy and scripture died away in the seventh century, so did the separate existence of the Goths as a people.

Use of the Gothic language, then, became a marker of belief in Arian Christianity. But it is difficult to identify any causal link between the Goths' language and specific qualities of their faith, beyond a historic maintenance of loyalty to Wulfila, the original apostle to their people, or to Valens, the emperor who had authorized their crossing of the Danube into the Roman Empire in 376.[5]

Curiously, though, there were features of Gothic-language Christianity, revealed in their practices of translation, that do show a special attitude. When compared with the faith of the contemporary Greeks and Romans, and indeed of their northerly Germanic cousins who would be converted three centuries later, Gothic faith stands out for its mild-mannered pacifism.

This is particularly strange, since the Goths themselves were known mostly to Romans, in this period, as a persistent warlike threat, which through force of arms would come to dominate and humiliate the Roman Empire, sacking Rome itself no fewer than three times in a century and a half: in 410 (by the Visigoths under Alaric); in 455 (by the Vandals under Geiseric); and in 546 (by the Ostrogoths under Totila). These were the deeds of the Arian-inspired warriors.

The creation of specific vocabulary for Christianity in Gothic goes back to Wulfila's translation of the (Septuagint) Bible and liturgy in the mid-fourth century. The pacific intent of his translation—and his creation of Gothic scriptures—can be seen from his refusal to include the two books of Kings. According to an ancient source, he translated "all the books of Scripture with the exception of the Books of Kings, which he omitted because they are a mere narrative of military exploits, and the Gothic tribes were especially fond of war, and were in more need of restraints to check their military passions than of spurs to urge them on to deeds of war."[6]

Wulfila's determination to turn away from martial sentiment can also be seen in contrasting his choice of Gothic technical terms with those made later by other translators of closely related languages. His word for "Lord" (Greek *kýrios*) as, above all, the Lord God, or the Lord Jesus, was *fráuja*, the lord of a household, and unrelated to words for leadership in war, the translations favored in other Germanic languages. For "holy" or "sacred" (Greek *hágios*) he adopts *weihs*, a term associated with pre-Christian magical powers, and not *hailags*, which was to be the choice of Anglo-Saxon and High German and which had long been associated with the glory of victory in battle.* Gothic converts were reached individually, through the appeal of the Christian message as witnessed by the Gospels, and not through convincing the tribes (and above all their military leaders) that Christ's leading advantage lay in the granting of military victory.[7]

But it was in his term for "pagan," "unbeliever," that Wulfila was to be most influential for later Germanic languages and translators. He was the first to write down the Germanic term *heathen*, or rather its Gothic original *haiþnō*. He applied it as a translation of *Hellēnis* (literally, "Hellenic woman," i.e., Gentile), introducing the Syro-Phoenician who gives an effective repartee to Jesus (Mark 7:26–28).[8]

The word has traditionally been taken as a Germanic sense-translation of Latin *paganus*, with Gothic *haiþi* "field, rough country" standing in for *pagus* "country district." However, it is not clear that *paganus* had developed its sense of "traditional unbeliever" by the fourth century (though the origin for this in Roman soldier slang, its meaning "civilian," certainly goes back to the first century A.D.). Another possible origin for the term is via Armenian, since that language (possibly familiar to Wulfila through his family connections wth Cappadocia) had borrowed the original Greek for Gentile, *ethnos* "tribe," in fact the single of *ethnē*. This turned up (with a breathy Armenian accent) as հեթանոս *het'anos*, which does indeed appear in the Armenian translation of this same passage. This might give a Gothic version *haiþans*, whose feminine would be *haiþnō*.[9]

The term Wulfila used for the Gentiles more generally is *þai þiudô* "those of peoples" (Matthew 7:7) or *þiudôs* "peoples" (Matthew 7:32). This is close to a literal translation of Greek ἐθνικοί *ethnikoí*, or τὰ ἔθνη *ta ethnē*. But unlike the Greeks' "ethnic" word, this is the very term that Germanic nations came to use of themselves par excellence. In mediaeval Latin, *lingua thiudisca* meant "German language," and this word has survived to the present day as *deutsch* itself.

Heathen and its cognates became the standard word for unbelievers in the Germanic-speaking world: we see Old High German *heidan*, Anglo-Saxon *hǣðen*, Old Norse *heiðinn*, just as all of these languages have a word like

---

* This association was gratuitously reinforced seventeen centuries later with the German Nazis' reemphasis of *Sieg Heil* as a militarist chant.

heath that means "rough country." But more widely in northern Europe, as they were converted to Christianity, there was a need to express the concept, and no presumption that German was the background language. Celtic languages, in the British Isles, adopted the Latin words: so Irish speaks of *genti* or *pāgān*, Welsh and Breton *pagan*. At the other end of Europe, Slavic languages did likewise: Bohemian (Czech) has *pohan* and Croatian *poganin*, and farther east Church Slavonic calls the "*Hellēnis*" who confronted Jesus (Mark 7:26) *poganyni*, feminine of *poganinŭ*.

But eastern Slavic has another word of its own, more comparable to *heathen* in Germanic: this is seen in Church Slavonic *języci* "the nations," which may have arisen as a direct equivalent of Greek *ethnē*; but literally this means "the tongues" or "the languages." A single pagan is called *języčĭnikŭ*, "tongue-ster," still in use in modern Russian язычник *yazyčnik*, where there is a collective term for heathendom, really "language-dom": язычество *yazyčestvo*.*

This Slavonic metaphor for random foreigners makes sense in the mid-first millennium A.D. Diversity of language was then a salient character of the tumultuous masses outside the urban civilization of Rome or Constantinople; north Europeans would inevitably have seen those ancient and literary, apparently monolingual, cultures as the source of the Christian faith. By contrast, only the Greeks and Romans themselves, as insiders to the empire and its values, may have had the more nuanced sense of Christianity as something originally alien to their traditions, a gift from the simpler, less materialistic life in the rebellious, impoverished province of Judaea.†

---

* While the general word for "language", and hence "nation", acquired a distinct pagan overtone in Slavic, its converse, the word for Christian believer, moved its sense in the opposite direction. This was крⷭ҇тїӕнїнⷤ *krĭstĭjaninŭ* in Church Slavonic, but the association with the cross крⷭ҇т *krĭst* (Russian крест *krest*) became overwhelming so it came into Russian as крестїянин *krestĭjanin*. With the full-scale conversion of the Russians from the tenth century, this word came to connote just a decent person. (Cf the old use of English "godfearing" to mean decent and normal: e.g., T. B. Macaulay, *History of England,* vol. 3, p. 87. London: Longman, 1855: "Those honest, diligent, and godfearing yeomen and artisans, who are the true strength of a nation.") After the fourteenth century it was particularly used to refer to lowly people working on the land, and in modern Russian the word simply means "peasant," "farmworker." Meanwhile "Christian" has been reintroduced into Russian close to its original form: христианин *xristianin*.

† It seems the word *pogan-* went down in the world once in competition with *yazyčnik*, coming to mean just plain "bad." (De Vincenz 1988–1989, p. 263.)

CHAPTER 8

"Adze-Headed Across the Sea"
White Martyrdom

So Saint Brendan instructed his brothers in the name of Father, Son, and
Holy Ghost to get on board. And when he alone was standing on the
shore and blessing the harbor, lo! three brothers had come over from their
monastery after him. They fell at the feet of the holy father, saying:
"Father, release us to go with you where you are to go; else we shall die
in this place of hunger and thirst. For we have decided to travel abroad
[*peregrīnārī*] all the days of our life."

Navigatio Sancti Brendani Abbatis, iv. (ca. 988)

S CANNING THE HORIZON FROM west to east reveals how different
northern peoples made linguistic sense of the Christianity that was
increasingly coming out to meet them.

The faith does not seem to have crossed the Roman limits into Ireland
(*Hibernia* "winter-land") until the fourth or fifth century A.D.: but the
advent of Palladius, the first bishop in Ireland, sent from Rome, is precisely
dated to 431.[1] Some have inferred from this that an established Christian
community must have already been in place, and according to Irish tradition
this would have been in the south. By contrast the first amply documented
churchman was Patrick, who was active to the north, in Meath, Connaught,
and Ulster, probably toward the end of the fifth century.[2] (His name was
Patrīcius in his native Latin, or *Cothriche* as this was originally transcribed
into Irish.) The other great apostle, Columba (in Irish *Colum Cille* "dove of
the church"), was active a century later (521–597) and took the faith farther
north, from Donegal and his island monastery on Iona into the kingdom of
Dál Ríata, which extended from Ulster as far as the Scottish Highlands. A
generation afterward, in 634, the Irishman Saint Aidan led a mission from

Iona to Lindisfarne on the coast of the North Sea, and this became a base for the evangelization of northern England.

There is no evidence that any of these movements, or Irish Christianity as it developed more generally on its home territory, founded any tradition of worship in their vernacular Gaelic. The first Irish Christians were all monks, full-time specialists who—often in remote and isolated colonies and cells—would have devoted themselves to understanding the new faith in its full rigor. This included the rigor of a foreign language, Latin, which was particularly strange for them, in that it provided their first encounter with a written language.* It also provided—almost immediately—the spur to start writing Irish in the Latin alphabet.

The original advent of Christianity to Ireland is evoked with typical terse wit in an Irish verse, suggesting the early missionaries were seen as forbidding-looking aliens. ("Adze-headed" is a reference to the curious Celtic tonsure, which shaved the front half of the head.)

Ticfa tailcend	There-will-come adze-headed
tar muir meircenn	across the sea crazy-headed
a bratt tollcend	his cloak hole-headed
a chrand cromchend	his branch crooked-headed
*a **mias** i n-airthiur a tigi*	his **mass** to the east of the house
*fris[c]erat a **muinter** huili:*	there-will-answer his **people** all
Amen	Amen.
Ticfat tailcind	There came adze-headed
*conutsat **ruama***	There were seen **Romans** [clerics]
*noifit **cella***	There-were-built **cells** [churches],
*ceoltigi **bendacha***	music-houses [bell towers] **blessed**,
ben[n]chopuir ili	**copper**-peaks [steeples] all,
*fla[i]th him **bachla**.*	By the prince of the **staff**.

These verses were preserved as a quote in a book from the late ninth century written in a medley of Irish and Latin, the *Vita tripartita Sancti*

---

* Admittedly, the Ogham alphabet must have been invented no later than in this era. But this is not known for any use besides the engraving of names (sometimes with titles) on monumental stones. Although it looks like the notches carved on a tally stick, it is credibly analyzed as being invented by persons with knowledge of Latin letters (McManus 1997, pp. 23–31).

Patricii ("Life of Saint Patrick, in Three Parts"). Although the verse itself is evidently a piece of secular literature, the penetration of Latin borrowings is clear, with Irish versions of seven Latin words (originally, *missa, monasterium, Romani, cella, benedicta, cuprum,* and *baculum*) in twelve lines.

Latin posed no risk, in the short or long term, to the Irish language, but the priests in Ireland persisted with it, and so Christianity—both the creed and the liturgy—was interpreted by bilingual priests to monolingual congregations. It took a long time, however, for ordinary Irish men and women to be converted, and to a very large extent, early Irish Christianity was a monastic, rather than a parochial, religion.

The Latin terms, when they were borrowed into Irish, show clearly the origins of the first missions from the Roman world. Irish Gaelic words like

> *Trindōid, pōg, purgadōir, sagarbaig, sagairt, orōid, altōir, nōdlaig, eglais, Laiden*

derived from Latin

> *Trinitātem, pācem, purgatōrium, sacrificium, sacerdotem, orātiō, altāre, nātālicia, ecclēsia, Latīna* (with meanings: Trinity, kiss [sign of peace], purgatory, sacrifice, priest, prayer, altar, Christmas, church, Latin)

exhibit ō where Latin had ā, and have voiced consonants (b, d, g) where Latin had unvoiced (p, t, c) or (f, th, ch) between vowels: these recall the sound system of Wales, Cornwall, and Brittany. We know this both from the spelling variation in manuscripts from before the year 1,000: these in turn reflect pronunciations that may go back to the sixth century,[3] and from what had happened to Latin words on their way to modern Welsh. Welsh *egwyddor* "element, alphabet" is from Latin *[ab]ēcēdārium, trindod* from *trīnitātem, nadolig* from *nātālicia,* all showing an ō where Latin had a stressed ā. By contrast, in contemporary Gaul (the other potential source of Christian influence) no such changes had taken, or would take, place.

On this evidence, these missionaries came not from Gaul but from Britain, and most likely from Wales. The incoming priests had grown up speaking British (the ancestor of modern Welsh) but they preached in Latin. We have no sign of how the language barrier was overcome between Briton and Gael, since their peoples would not naturally have understood one another.

There must have been bilinguals plying across the Irish Sea, presumably for reasons of trade, or slave-kidnap, or even adventure. But some of them—like their spiritual brothers in trade, a world away on the Silk Road—had holy business too in mind. At all events, for both preachers and converts, Christ was soon being worshipped in Ireland in a learned lingua franca that was a mother tongue to neither preachers nor converts. And the Christianity that was implanted—for no translation to another vernacular was involved—was largely unchanged in its vocabulary and its global view of God's community, the church. The new Irish converts were brought up to be good Roman Catholics.

Some seem to have doubted that this identity was much to the point:

Téicht do-Róim	To go to Rome,
mór saido becc torbaí	much labor, little profit:
In-Rí chondaigi hifoss	the King you seek there,
ma-nim-bera latt nífogbái	unless you bring him with you, you will not find.
Mór báis mór baile	Much folly, much frenzy,
mór coll ceille mór mire	much loss of sense, much madness,
olais airchenn teicht do écaib	since going to death is certain,
beith fo étoil Maíc Maire	to be under the displeasure of Mary's Son.[4]

The Pilgrim as Martyr

Christians of the Latin rite they were, but changing some ways of the Celtic soul in these converts turned out to be a harder thing: some of the practices had particular appeal, and were given an Irish stamp that came to be identified, in the history of the church, with "Celtic Christianity." These included a fondness for hearing the life stories of those heroes of the early church, the saints, especially where they could be identified with local shrines in Ireland and in Britain. And the Irish church in its founding centuries was a church on the move: *peregrīnātiō*—foreign travel or (to use its derivate in English) pilgrimage—remained important. It had many purposes: to visit holy shrines out of personal piety, to establish new monasteries and churches, to propagate the faith among the pagan, or simply to voyage abroad through God's great creation.

Strangely in Irish—unlike all other European languages—there is no directly borrowed form of the word: a pilgrim is an *ailithir* and pilgrimage is *ailithre.* These are home-grown terms, from *aile* "other" and *tír* "land." But a pilgrim would also be recognized as one who has taken up his staff—*gaibid bachall* or *trost*, both of which have roots in Latin (*baculum* "stick," *transtrum* "beam"). Curiously, but showing how seriously pilgrimage was taken as a kind of religious devotion, *ailithre* and *gaibid bachall* also mean to retire to a monastery.[5]

Ireland was a land where tales of valor and violence were extreme, as witness this exchange between warriors at an ancient Irish feast:

> "It is quite proper," said Conall, "that you should challenge me! I accept your challenge to single combat, Cet," said Conall. "I swear what my tribe swears, that since I took a spear in my hand I have not often slept without the head of a Connaughtman under my head, and without having wounded a man every single day and every single night." "It is true," said Cet. "You are a better hero than I am. If Anlúan were in the house he would offer you yet another contest. It is a pity for us that he is not in the house." "He is though," said Conall, taking the head of Anlúan from his belt, and throwing it at Cet's breast with such force that a gush of blood burst over his lips.[6]

This joy in literary savagery may serve to cover up a guilty little secret of the church in Ireland: the early Irish had not one martyr to their name.[7] Perhaps it was the lack of towns or cities in sixth-century Ireland, or the peaceable spirit of Irish druids, but disconcertingly for militant Christians seeking a martyr's crown, there seem to have been no intolerant authorities to put up a brutal and bloody resistance to Christianity. Tertullian had declared the blood of the martyrs was the seed of the church: and certainly, where would Greek or Roman Christianity have been without heartless magistrates and organized persecutions? But in Ireland there were none. Propagators of the faith would need to look elsewhere for the glory of victorious suffering.

They did it through a redefinition of martyrdom. The earliest surviving prose text in Irish is the Cambrai Homily (so called from its home in northern France), dating from the turn of the seventh to eighth centuries. It is a sermon on the text Matthew 16:24:

> Then Jesus said unto his disciples: If any man will come after me, let him deny himself, and take up his cross, and follow me.

In it, a triad of types of martyrdom are distinguished by color:

> Every affliction in the three kinds of martyrdom is accounted a cross.
> It is so accounted if one receives *baan martre* [white martyrdom],
> or *glas martre* [gray/blue/green martyrdom]* or *derc martre* [red
> martyrdom]. *Banmartre* to a person is, when he parts for God's sake
> with everything which he loves; though the afflictions of poverty may
> reach him. *Glas martre* is, when one parts with his passions in sorrow
> and advances to penance and repentance. *Derc martre* to him is to
> suffer crucifixion and slaying for Christ's sake . . . (§§21–28)[8]

Glasmartre required self-mortification, most directly through fasting. It has
been suggested that this latter color may have been chosen for the hue that
the body goes, when so mortified.[9] Meanwhile, *banmartre* was associated
with loneliness and the travails of pilgrimage: in white martyrdom, the crown
is being offered to the Irish pilgrim, suffering spiritual deprivation through
loss of the delights of home.

No doubt Irish pilgrims did suffer, from homesickness and much else:
but it is clear that there was a more life-affirming side to the travels of these
"white martyrs."

A luxuriant feature of Irish literature in Latin (and in Old Irish) is the
Vita Sancti (in Irish, *Bethu*), which dwells on miraculous deeds and local
associations of a saint's life, a feature that has stayed with Irish Catholicism
throughout its 1,500-year history. Early on, there are also tales of voyages
(Irish *immrama*—literally "rowings around"—suggesting the limited class of
maritime craft that dwelt in the Celtic imagination). These stories formed a
genre of Old Irish literature, recounting the adventures (*eachtrai*) of legendary
heroes, such as Bran, who set off on a quest (ultimately successful) for the
Tír nan mBan ("Land of Women"), but stayed an eon there, so could never
return to his home—on pain of disintegration if he touched shore.

Such tales had a sacred continuation, notably in the *Navigatio Sancti
Brendani Abbatis* "The Voyage of Abbot Saint Brendan," which built on the
adventurous side of a saint's travels to spread the Gospel, and cast them
across the Atlantic. But the tone of the fantasy is poised between the *One*

---

* This color is hard to match in English. The *Dictionary of the Irish Language* (DIL) says:
"descriptive of various shades of light green and blue, passing from grass-green to grey,
opposed on the one hand to *uaine* green and on the other to *gorm* blue."

Thousand and One Nights and Dante's *Inferno*: the mariners—like Sinbad the Sailor—make a fire on an island that turns out to be a basking whale; but they also encounter Judas, on his days off from torment in hell.

The real Saint Brendan lived in the sixth century, around 484 to 577, and is accounted one of the twelve (nonmythical) apostles of Ireland.* It is difficult to relate his actual life to the events of the voyage. But the *Navigatio* was a bestseller as a narrative: it survives in some 120 Latin manuscripts, ranging between the tenth and fifteenth centuries. The book became a kind of metaphorical, spiritual classic, at least on the continent of Europe: for there were no translations into Welsh or Irish until the late fifteenth century.[10]

Another famous Celt of this era—a theologian focused on the nature of free will, who would travel the empire and cross quills in scholarly debate with Saint Augustine of Hippo—was named Pelagius. He lived from about 354 to 418. It is unknown whether he was British, Breton, or Irish, but his unique name bears witness to Irish aspiration: it is a learned Latin word derived from Greek *pélagos*, and so means "the seafarer."

Looking for any infusion of pre-Christian Celtic heirlooms in this regional variety of the faith, one is tempted to look for resurgence of Irish gods and heroes—whose adventures are stirringly recalled in Middle Irish literature—in the lives of the saints. The classic example is Saint Brigid, whose saint's day is February first. This is the very day of Imbolc, the spring festival sacred to the goddess Brigit,† and the Virgin Mary's day comes right along behind, on February second.

The church attempted to use this proximity to purge Saint Brigid of her pagan past: "It is said that when Mary was giving birth to Jesus, Brigid averted the eyes of the onlookers, so a grateful Mary let Brigid have her festival first."[11]

---

* The twelve also include Saint Columba, who founded the Abbey of Iona off the Scottish Isle of Mull in 563. All of them studied at Clonard Abbey, founded around 520 by Saint Finnian.

† Brigit, originally Brigantia, corresponds perfectly in Irish to an Indo-European name *bṛgantiə, which also represents a Sanskrit adjective *bṛhatī* "the great lady." This again is reminiscent of Braganza in northwest Iberia, and Bregenz in Austria. There is also Burgunt, an Old High German female name, and Bornholm, for which the Old Norse origin was *Burgundaholmr*, the supposed source of the Burgundians. The same root is seen in the Irish royal name Brian, and the Middle Welsh word for "nobles," *breint*. Brigantia, the old form preceding all these names, thus appears to have been a prehistoric celebrity across Europe. (See Mallory and Adams 2006, p. 410, and Lambert 1997, p. 96.)

But the fact that Saint Brigid was in the stable is the key point: Brigit was a goddess of animal life, and her *Vita*, penned by an admiring neighbor from Kildare, the monk Cogitosus, is full of stories of how she miraculously charmed them, getting animal produce such as butter, milk, and bacon to regenerate when needed, and birds, foxes, cattle, pigs, and one wild boar to behave according to her wishes. She also had something of a knack with building work, inspiring cooperation among rivals to build a road through bog land, rolling a millstone from the top of a mountain to where it was needed, and miraculously causing a door to fit a doorway in her church, this last well after her death. Everything in fact but preaching the Christian message, whether among pagan or faithful. These all read like popular fables, but the text is in Latin, not Irish.[12]

Irish Missions

As it turned out, the most important long-term effect of the retention of Latin—not the vernacular—in evangelizing Ireland was the potential this gave for Irish monks to return the good news of Christ to England and the rest of Europe. With the Frankish invasions (beginning in 408), Gaul had been forcibly transformed into France; and although their king, Clovis, had accepted Catholic Christianity in about 496, there was still much work to do to rebuild the Gaulish church among Franks. Meanwhile, Britain had lost its Roman culture (including the word of Christ) under an influx and spread of Saxon settlement, which persisted during the fifth and sixth centuries. Likewise in northern Italy, the church had been set back by invasions of Goths (in the fifth century) and Lombards (in the sixth and seventh centuries). Farther east, still pagan Slavs (with others such as Huns and Avars) were taking possession of central Europe, the Balkans, and even the western half of Greece.

It was all a vast invitation to white martyrdom. Another saint named Colum, this time *Colum Bán* "white dove" (latinized as Columbanus), led the first of the great Irish missions to Europe, coming (like *Colum Cille* to Iona, twenty-two years before) with twelve fellow Irish monks, and landing in Brittany in 585. Columbanus was already forty-two, and without prior experience on the continent. But Christianity, preached in Latin, was a universal message. And he stayed there, winning converts, until his death in 615.

During that period, making good use of royal connections, though naturally causing some resentment among French bishops, Columbanus was able to found four new monasteries. Three of them were close together in Burgundy, in eastern France—at Annegray, Luxeuil, and Fontaine-lès-Luxeuil (before 600). Later, after considerable travels (because he was no longer welcome in France), he founded the abbey at Bobbio in northern Italy, in 614. Discipline was founded on his own system (which became known as the Rule of Saint Columbanus), but was later replaced by the more generally accepted Rule of Saint Benedict. After his death, his colleagues and successors went on to found several more monasteries in France, Germany, Belgium, and Switzerland.*

---

* In this last country, there was founded the monastery of Saint Gall: this was precisely the place where Columbanus's younger colleague Gall (or Gallus) had resided, and it is named for him (though he had long refused the offer to become its abbot). In its library is the edition of the Latin grammar of Priscian, famous for the many Irish annotations that appear in its margins, revealing the everyday language of Irish monks in the mid-ninth century. Nearby is the city of Bregenz where Columbanus and Gallus both preached, and whose name happens to celebrate the same goddess (Brigantia) once known in Ireland as Brigit.

CHAPTER 9

The Savior as Our Chieftain
The Gospel of the War Band

| *Thuo ên thero tueliƀio,*
Thuomas gimâlda | — *uuas im githungan mann,*
diurlîc **drohtines** *thegan* —: | *'ne sculun uui im thia dâd lahan,' quathie,*
'ni uuernian uui im thes uuillien, | *ac uuita im uuonian mid,*
thuoloian mid ûsson **thiodne:** | *that ist thegnes cust,*
that hie mid is **frâhon** *samad* | *fasto gistande,*
dôie mid im thar an duome. | *Duan ûs alla sô,*
folgon im te thero ferdi: | *ni lâtan ûse ferah uuið thiu*
uuihtes uuirðig, | *neƀa uui an them* **uuerode** *mid im,*
dôian mid ûson **drohtine** . . .

Then one of the twelve, named Thomas (he was a fine man, the
Prince's staunch thane), said: "We should not berate his deed or check
his will in this matter; we should firmly stay by him, and suffer with
our **Leader**. That is the choice of a thane: to stand fast together with
his **Lord**, to die with him at the moment of doom. So let us all do it,
follow his road and set our life as worthless beside his. Close to his
war band all about him, let us die with our **Prince**!"

From the *Hêliand* "The Savior": a Gospel retelling in Old
Saxon, early ninth century[1]

THE CONTINUED USE OF Latin in the British and Irish churches had
ensured that Irish Christianity, and Irish monks, remained quite able to
communicate with, and indeed to educate, people all over western and (later)
central and eastern Europe. But Latin was their lingua franca: Irish Gaelic
continued to be their vernacular; and the marginal notes in the manuscripts
that they copied well show how lively their Gaelic life remained.

The different tradition that this preserved, especially its joy in long-distance pilgrimage and exploration, served to reinvigorate and extend the Christian faith in the seventh century, when Europe was struggling to recover from the disruption of the Germanic conquests, and the conquerors—largely German-speaking kings—struggled to institutionalize and legitimize their rule. Acceptance of Christianity was an important part of this for the victorious dynasties.

The exposure of those Germans to Catholic Christianity came about at various times, and for various purposes.

It was apparently at his own instance that King Clovis of the Franks asked Remigius, bishop of Reims, for baptism in 496, but he was encouraged by the military motive of a recent victory over another Germanic tribe (the Alemanni centered on Swabia) when he had appealed to the Christian god. He had received instruction too from Vedastus, bishop of Arras and Cambrai, and he must have received insistent pressure from his wife, Clothilde, who had been brought up a Catholic. It took up to two centuries more—eight generations—for Christianity to become the religion of all the Franks, but Clovis's successors would succeed in uniting all the Frankish realm.

Less spontaneous would have been the conversion of Æthelberht, king of Kent, who received Pope Gregory's emissary Augustine, and received baptism in Canterbury in about 600. But he too had a Christian Frank for a wife, Bertha. And he could see the political weight that might come from such a spiritual alliance with Rome. His lead was followed by King Rædwald of East Anglia and King Sæbert of Essex in 604. But the situation was touch-and-go for a generation. Both Æthelberht and Sæbert were succeeded by heathen sons, and Rædwald's recently baptized Christian son was assassinated by a heathen soon after his accession. Still within fifty-five years not only Kent, East Anglia, and Essex but Mercia and Wessex too were ruled by Christians.

A complication in the Christian conversion of England was the evangelical contest between the Irish tradition of the white martyrs from the north, and Roman Christianity coming from the south. Although there were many minor differences between these two lines of Catholicism, this focused most concretely on a difference in the formula (in Latin, *computus*) for the calculation of a date to celebrate Easter. At Whitby in 664, the contest was resolved—in Rome's favor—by King Oswiu of Northumbria, who at the time held the balance of military power in England. Then the last heathen king, Arwald of the Isle of Wight, was killed in battle in 686 with the militant Christian king Cædwalla of Wessex. England had become, in name, a totally Christian realm within the seventh century, one hundred years behind the land of the Franks. And although much of its conversion had been achieved by Irishmen, it was now avowedly loyal to creeds and policies of the pope in Rome.

Over the eighth century, two charismatic preachers from England attempted the conversion of the rest of the Germans. They were Willibrord of Northumbria and Boniface of Exeter, or Wessex. (Boniface was the pope's choice of a name for him: he had grown up as the Anglo-Saxon Wynfrith.) Willibrord (658–739) preached among the Frisians of northern Germany and in Schleswig, while Boniface (680–754) was based at Mainz, farther south, with the whole of Germany as his field. Both worked with support from Christian Frankish kings, and with a mission entrusted to them by the pope. Boniface in particular was the agent of the Frankish overlord Charles Martel, who granted him four dioceses in Bavaria and saw potential in Christianity as a means to extend his domination north and east into Saxony. Boniface's dramatic style of evangelism (he famously cut down Thor's oak at Fritzlar in Hessen) was ultimately fulfilled, a generation after his death, in twenty years of campaigning (777–797) in Saxony by the Frankish king Charlemagne (*Karl der Große*), who explicitly required Christianization of his subdued enemies. The point was made by the execution of 4,500 Saxon captives at Verden in 782. Later, his *Capitulatio de partibus Saxoniae* issued in 785 set the death penalty for anyone refusing baptism, or reneging on his baptismal vows.

This uncompromising approach to evangelism was continued by his son Louis the Pious (*Ludwwig der Fromme*), who also sent the missionary Ansgar of Amiens (801–865) on missions to Saxony, Westphalia, and beyond the limits of Frankish power into Denmark, and even Sweden. Ansgar was less successful as he went farther north (and farther from the Frankish influence), and Scandinavia largely remained heathen despite his best efforts.

Scandinavia was in fact a new field for evangelism, with even more localized nature-worship than in Germany, and less scope for making an impression on the heathen through the simple destruction of idols. Most important was the political difference: it was the locus of a power structure of warriors, the Vikings, who had never made peace with the Romans, and so were completely detached from the kingdoms of western Europe. It would not succumb to Christianity for another two centuries: until on the one hand, Danes had largely conquered (and settled) Christian England, and on the other, the Franks had extended their continental power northward and eastward into what became the Holy Roman Empire. But as it had been for the Saxons, conversion, where it was offered to the unwilling, was largely delivered in Scandinavian countries at the point of a sword or on the edge of an axe.

Military Values Come to Christ

This new approach to conversion, one based on military threat, remained important for these peoples of northern Europe, who—in their pre-Christian pasts—had largely ordered their own societies through extending war bands. Evidently, its effectiveness had a lot to do with the political associations of Christianity, by now seen as the distinctive cultural trait of the Romans (their glory largely faded in history). To be Christian was to be civilized, but also to be in fealty to the lord who had made you submit to the ultimate lord, the Lord God.

What sort of a lord was God? In Hebrew he had been אֲדֹנָי (adōnáy) "my lord" (etymologically "mighty"), to distinguish him from בַּעַל, ba'al "lord, master, owner," which had been used for so many other competing gods in Palestine. In Aramaic he was mārōyā ("the man," related to many words meaning "male," such as Akkadian māru, Arabic marʔ). In Greek he was kȳrios, the holder of authority, kŷros. In Latin he was evidently dominus, the word that conjured up the master of a household domus. And in Gothic too, he had been fráuja "lord of a household."*

All these were terms derived from the relation of head of a family, which would include relations between master and slave, father and child, and indeed (especially with ba'al) husband and wife.

For the new German-speaking converts, a different metaphor was chosen to express God's lordly nature. The words corresponding to Gothic fráuja still existed in the languages of the English (Anglo-Saxon), the Saxons (Old

---

* This was its current meaning in Gothic of the fourth century. But since it derived originally from the Germanic root *fra-, Indo-European *pro-, seen in English first, fore, Latin prīmus, Greek prōtos, Sanskrit prathamas, it was well adapted to characterize leaders generally.

Saxon) and in the southern and eastern parts of the Frankish empire, namely Hessen, Swabia, and Bavaria (Old High German)*; but they had become archaic, tending to obsolescence. For the German-speaking Franks and the Saxons, they were largely terms of address, used in the fixed phrase *frô mîn* "milord, sire"; and for the English, it was a poetic word, also often used as an intensifier for adjectives: e.g., *frēamicel* "hyper-great," *frēafætt* "hyper-fat," *frēatorht* "hyper-bright." In all the languages, its feminine forms (OHG *frouwa*, OS *frūa*, AS *frēo*) also lived on as a grand word for "lady" (and has become modern German *Frau*).

The new word for Lord was taken not from the household, but from the characteristic German institution of the war band. This institution had been described to the Romans in the great documentary work on Germania of the historian Tacitus (ca. 56 to 117 A.D.; consul in 97). He called it the *comitātus*, a term that is still used to describe this kind of social institution cross-culturally to the present day.[2]

> In battle, it is a disgrace for the chief [*princeps*] to be outdone in bravery, and a disgrace for the band [*comitatus*] to fail to match the bravery of their chief. Indeed, it means life-long infamy and dishonor to withdraw from battle and so survive one's chief. Their principal oath [*sacramentum*] is to defend him, to guard him, and to offer up their own sterling deeds too for his glory. The chiefs fight for victory, and the band-brothers [*comites*] for their chief.[3]

In a war band, as Tacitus pointed out, military bearing is carried out across a whole way of life.[4] It was not just for battle, but for a lifetime of loyalty. And this ethic, with the militarism and gaining of booty removed, was not a bad fit for the relation between Christ and his disciples—indeed their devotion after the death of their chief almost outdoes the fealty due to a warlord.

---

* Most of the Frankish empire that was conquered (by Clovis and his sons) between 481 and 614 seems to have spoken Romance, i.e., the language that was going to develop into French. The Frankish conquerors were relatively few, and were of a tradition that had been exposed to Romance for many generations. Franconian, the speech of the Franks, was itself a Low German variety, like Saxon; and the northern strains have survived into modern Dutch. But it seems to have been little used, or only for a short time in Francia as a whole. In fact, our knowledge of the spoken language in the Frankish empire is slight, but its written language remained Latin throughout. (Hen 1995, pp. 23–25.)

The Old Saxon poem *Hêliand* (meaning "Healer," i.e., "Savior"), quoted in the epigraph to this chapter, is a retelling of the Gospels in the military ethos of the war band. It was written in the early ninth century, hence just after the Saxons were finally defeated and Christianized by Charlemagne. Its Lord, then, is fitly cast as a *drohtin*, the leader of a band (in OS *werod*), as well (with some exaggeration—at least at this point in Christ's history) as a *thiodan*, a king, leader of a people (*thioda*). But the term is key. It means (by its form)[5] the leader of a band (OHG *truht*, AS *dryht*, ON *drótt*), as reflected in the corresponding terms OHG *truhtin*, AS *dryhten*, ON *dróttinn*, all regular Germanic words for "warlord" (although in Scandinavia the word would achieve greater influence as a word for royalty). And so we find in Anglo-Saxon, not just pagan uses like *eorla dryhten* "lord of earls" in Beowulf, but also *Drihtenum Gode* **domino Deo**, "to the Lord God" and *Drihtnum Críste, sóðum cyninge* **domino Christo, vero regi**, "to the Lord Christ, true king."[6]* [The words in bold are Latin glosses of the Old English.]

Wifely Virtue

However, the historical record shows that the first steps toward this outcome, each Germanic people's acceptance of Christ as if their leader in war, were not—at least originally—in the idiom of direct soldierly recruitment. In almost every case, the people signed up to Christ because their own military lord did so; and that lord often did so at the urging—perhaps even at the behest—of his wife, in consultation with a Christian priest.

---

* *Truhtin/dryhten* and their cognates were to disappear too, as Germanic society settled down. Just as the Latin word *dominus* was replaced in Romance by *senior* to express "lord" (French *monsieur/seigneur*, Spanish *señor*, Italian *signore*), so *truhtin/dróttin* was replaced by *hêrro/herra* (German *Herr*, Norse *herra*), which is by origin a comparative, and like *senior* meant older, (literally, "grayer"). This seems to have been a result of the feudal system in settled states, where hierarchy became more important than loyalty forged in battle. (Cf Green 1998, pp. 112–16.)

In English, the *drightin* word (last attested in the *Oxford English Dictionary* for 1572) was replaced in common use by *lord* (from AS *hlaford* "loaf-warden," another domestic term). Both words appear in Beowulf and *hlaford* is already used of Christ in the Anglo-Saxon Gospels of the tenth century. The *drightin* word, associated with old texts, became specialized to mean God: e.g., Dutch *Trecht*. (But in extremely archaic or dialectal German (*Kriegs*)*Trechtein* can still mean a military officer.)

Clovis, king of the Franks, had followed his wife, Clothilde, to become not an Arian (like the majority of German Christians of the day) but a Catholic, as she herself must have insisted. (His motive was, supposedly, at least partly a military one, since he believed his wife's god had saved him from defeat in battle.) A century later, Æthelberht, king of Kent, was baptized by Saint Augustine, after living for some time with his Catholic wife, Bertha. Augustine had been sent explicitly to convert him by Pope Gregory I the Great, but again the presence of a Christian wife is telling. And Bertha's daughter Æthelburh went on to marry another heathen English king, Edwin of Northumbria, on condition he convert to Christianity, accepting the mission of the Roman Paulinus; and he was duly baptized at York in 627, at the head of all his people. After her husband's death in battle, she returned to Kent, and there established one of the first Benedictine convents in England.

Why, one might wonder, were queens so often ahead of kings in acceptance of the foreign (Roman) faith? There is little evidence from the Germanic world, when the church began to impinge on it; but early Christianity was in general more benign to women than were other (pagan) cults. The church forbade infanticide and (consummated) child marriage, and in general was unenthusiastic about the remarriage of widows, allowing them to maintain their deceased husbands' estates. These practices, over time, led to a greater proportion of women among Christians than in the population at large. Admittedly, women were always excluded from the Christian priesthood (as they were not in all religions). But they could aspire to some level of authority in the church, if they were appointed deaconesses.[7] Sentimentally and maternally, women may have been more attracted to the charitable mercy enjoined in the Gospels than their male kindred, who—as Romans, Celts, or Germans alike—were brought up with harsher, military ideals. Furthermore, access to personal chaplains was one of the few ways that females could receive a literate education. And these clerics might accompany these ladies when they were given in marriage, and so might later aspire to convert their husbands. For all these reasons noble ladies, if given a degree of freedom of choice, were more likely to accept Christ than gentlemen were; and this differential was as true in Germanic, as in Roman or Celtic society.

These points all relate to an early Mediterranean Christianity, without the militaristic trappings that it would gain in the Germanic world. But Clovis, believing Clothilde's God had given him victory over the Alemanni, was explicitly so assured by Bishop Avitus of Vienne:

This vulnerability of raiment [i.e., wearing of a baptismal gown] will cause, as you have faith, O happiest of kings, it will cause, I say, that for you henceforth the force of arms will be stronger. And whatever hitherto has come to you through good fortune, it will now be conferred by holiness.[8]

Somehow the apostles to the Germans convinced the royal families, and thereby their followers, that the Christian God had power to give victory, superior to any support that Donar/Þunor, Ziu/Tiw, Wodân/Woden, or Frey might offer. It was easy enough—given a stout heart—to destroy the apparatus of these gods, their temples, sacred trees, or images, and to point out the complete failure of the gods to punish or even resist this sacrilege. (Most spectacularly in this line, Boniface cut down the great oak tree sacred to Thor/Donar in Hessen, and built an oratory to Saint Peter with the wood on the very same spot.[9]) To add insult to injury, they could even point out that the Mediterranean heartland of Christianity was (at the time) much richer than the lands in the care of the heathen gods. As Bishop Daniel of Winchester wrote to Boniface in 723, with advice on preaching technique,

this point is also to be made: if the gods are all-powerful, beneficent, and just, they not only reward their worshippers but punish those who reject them. If then, they do this in temporal matters, how is it that they spare us Christians who are turning almost the whole earth away from their worship and overthrowing their idols? And while these, the Christians, possess lands rich in oil and wine and abounding in other resources, they have left to those, the pagans, with their gods, lands stiff with cold where these exiles from the world are falsely believed to reign.[10]

Somehow the question of what the Christian god could do to show his greater power and benevolence was successfully answered, for Germanic Europe did turn Christian. But it required the timing sense of a showman, coupled naturally with the unshakeable faith of a saint, to turn the outcomes of day-to-day life and war into demonstrations of Christ's overwhelming power and mercy. Boniface was well aware that the actual influence of political lords was crucial in pulling this off:

Without the support of the Frankish prince [Charles Martel] I can neither govern the members of the church nor defend the priests, clerks, monks, and maids of God; nor can I, without orders from him and the fear inspired by him, prevent the pagan rites and sacrilegious worship of idols in Germany.[11]

The outcome was allegiance to Christ, and indeed a fierce allegiance, but perhaps not as it had previously been experienced. Some have called it the "barbarization of Christianity,"[12] in which Christ was recast as a God interested in guaranteeing the wealth, renown, conquests, and general material success of his worshippers. The apostles to the Germans, however, did not have the luxury of appealing directly to a common moral sense, which might find an echo in the paradoxes of the Gospel's Beatitudes:

> Blessed are the meek, for they will inherit the earth . . . Blessed are the merciful, for they shall be shown mercy . . . Blessed are the peacemakers, for they will be called the sons of God . . . Blessed are you when people insult you, persecute you and falsely say all kinds of evil against you because of me. (Matthew 5:5, 7, 9, 11)

These were not virtues that sustained respect for a warrior in a Germanic war band: quite the reverse. Yet such warriors (and their womenfolk) were the target audience for Willibrord, Boniface, and their successors.

They had to reach the Germans where they found them, to gain their trust—most effectively through a display of miraculous might—then baptize them (even if, like Clovis, apparently, they saw the gown for the ceremony as girly), and then hope to bring them to a true Christian sense through catechism, a long process of stylized, yet interactive, discussion that answered the questions and provided the intellectual style in which a regular Christian understanding could grow. But in practice, this catechism—perhaps because it had not been designed for the "sudden-baptism" system of Germany—was never effectively brought into the northern world: the Christian instruction that the German Christians would receive would not be much more than the homilies of their priests in church.

It has been claimed[13] that Christianity never recovered from the pragmatic misunderstanding that was caused by the circumstances of Germanic conversion. On this view, the Roman papacy became allied with the Germanic kings of the north (from the Franks through into the Holy Roman Empire), and so the charisma of Germanic kingship (the essence of *Heil*) was sanctified through a special relationship with Christ, the one true God: instead of being a world-renouncing faith—awaiting the second coming of Christ at the "setting of the era" (*occasus saeculi*)—Christianity became a status-justifying ideology, the spiritual charter for a newly defined "Christendom," identified with Christian Europe, or more specifically the world of the Latin rite.

This may well have been the outcome of the conversion of the northern lands, but politically, it was not much different from the accommodation that had been achieved between church and empire in the three centuries since Constantine and Theodosius had legitimized Christianity as the faith of Rome. The fierce particular loyalties of the war band may not have been soon purged by conversion to Christianity, but they did not survive the spread of Latin education. By contrast they were not taken up in the more ancient lands of Christendom, at least not while they remained part of Christendom.* The Germans, although they would become the center of Christendom for a millennium, were late to the feast, too late to claim responsibility for the secularization—or the Germanization—of Christianity.[14]

To witness the process by which Germanic understanding—rather than Christianity—was transformed, in the light of growing knowledge of Christian values, some of the semantic changes that came about in Germanic words are revealing.

Creed and Faith

Christianity from very early has had a creed, a set of propositions about God and the way the world works, that Christians are required to hold true. An early statement by Saint Paul (1 Corinthians 15:1–2), probably written in 57 A.D., though written rather clumsily, makes clear the importance of having these opinions:

> And, brothers, I make known to you the gospel which I gospelled to you, which also you have received, and in which you stand; by which

---

* It is arguable that the code of the *palikári*, the young rogue, in a Greek popular epic like Digénis Akrítas (Anatolia, twelfth century) is an example of the war band ethic. But this tends to show not the spread of an ancient German (or central Eurasian) ideal, but rather the social structure that arises when there is no effective central government.

also you are saved, by what word I gospelled to you, if you hold fast,
except unless you have believed in vain.

Saint Paul went on to specify the main claims of the Christian faith, summa-
rizing and headlining them in his first proposition (verses 3–4):

> That Christ died for our sins according to the scriptures; and that he
> was buried, and that he rose again the third day according to the
> scriptures.

And in the rest of the chapter he gave more details of the crucial events,
pointing out that Christians lived dangerously: if any of this was false, then
their faith was void, and nobody was going to escape death or be redeemed.

These claims were taken up and expanded in further formulations, notably
the Old Roman Creed of the second century, the Nicene Creed, agreed by
the Council of Nicaea in 325, and the Apostles' Creed from the end of the
fourth century.*

Christianity emerges as a historical and a philosophical faith: its adherents are committed to asserting certain facts about what happened in the
past, as well as a particular theoretical interpretation of them. This was—as
far as we can now conjecture—something very different from an acceptance
of Germanic gods. The German tribes' relation to their gods was better
compared with their relation to a lord, one of fealty to a person rather than
intellectual assent. Tacitus recorded that they were propitiated with regular
sacrifices—human for "Mercury" (presumed to be Woden), animal for
"Hercules" and "Mars" (Thunor and Tiw).[15]

But this progress—from personal homage to a lord, through reliance on
his help, to active belief in a divine order established by certain key acts of
the divinity—had been as much a feature of Mediterranean Christianity as
of the more recent conversion of the Germanic-speaking peoples. In the
Gospels, people are often commended for their personal faith in Christ, and
told it has made all the difference to their salvation,[16] or are upbraided for

---

* Their importance to the faith was emphasized by the word used for them in Greek and
Latin, συμβολον / *symbolum*, a word derived from the practice of breaking and then sharing
tally sticks, as an earnest of good faith. By this metaphor, the creed was the identity document for Christians, as well as their guarantee of entitlement to the rewards to come. The
word is first so applied by Cyprian, Bishop of Carthage (ca. 250).

their lack of it.[17] At one point, the Jews are told to have intellectual faith in his works, and therefore his relation with God, even if they have no faith in him personally.[18]

This faith is one mark of the true disciple, and it is displayed in the Christian form of prayer, when a believer communicates directly with God. Christ explicitly contrasted it with how the heathen pray,* noting the pithiness and lack of self-interested begging in a good prayer. But the Lord's Prayer, when it is given, is also distinctive in its total endorsement by the suppliant of whatever the Lord is, and whatever the Lord is planning, as well as its focus on the moral attitudes and status of the suppliant in person. It is a statement of faith, and of readiness for the duties entailed by that faith.[19]

This development from felt loyalty to an unseen Lord to willed orthodoxy in opinions about him is paralleled by the varied syntax of the words for "faith" and "to have faith" or "to believe": in Greek πιστις (*pistis*) and πιστευειν (*pisteuein*), in Latin *fidēs* and *crēdere*. As a noun, faith can be an asset capable of saving its holder; as a verb, believing betokens a virtuous attitude in itself, but specifically to one's Lord, to his words, or to the revealed truth about him.

In fact there is no sign in the Gothic New Testament (fourth century), nor in the Gospel Harmonies written in Old High German, Old Saxon, and Old English (ninth century), that there is any less flexibility in the syntax of the Germanic equivalents for this concept as noun and verb, viz Gothic *galaubeins ~ galaubjan*, High German *giloubī ~ gilouben*, Old Saxon *gilōbo ~ gilōōian*, Old English *geleāfa ~ gelýfan*.† So already in the ninth century, the first century in which Christianity pervaded the Germanic world, Germanic ideas of what Christian faith entailed were just as comprehensive as the antecedents in the Mediterranean world.‡

---

* He was calling them *ethnikoi*—which in another context might have been translated "Gentiles."

† Etymologically the Germanic words all have the Indo-European root *leubh, which had meant "desire, pleasure." (Other derivates include *libido* in Latin, and *love* in English.) A Germanic warrior's loyalty to his Lord was akin to rejoicing. Contrast the Hebrew duty to fear God reiterated in the book of Proverbs (e.g., 1:7, "The fear of the Lord is the beginning of wisdom").

‡ These words are the predecessors of modern German *Glaube ~ glauben*, Dutch *geloof ~ geloven*. The closest modern English equivalents *belief ~ believe* arose from a lexical byway, since they replaced the directly descended words in English, *ylefe ~ yleve*, in the fourteenth century.

There are no direct Scandinavian equivalents: synonyms in those languages are all derived from Old Norse *trú ~ trúa*, which relate to archaic English *troth ~ trow*, also kin to the noun and verb *trust* and adjective *true* (which until the thirteenth century only meant "faithful").

As we have seen, there were some early literary productions that represented Christ as a warlord, notably the Old Saxon *Hêliand*. And as that word itself reminds us, some resonance of the new German vocabulary used to describe the faith may have rung strangely. As the English abbot Ælfric himself put it:

> *Iesus is Ebreisc* [Hebrew] *nama, þæt is on Leden* [Latin] *"Saluator," and on Englisc* [Old English] *"Hælend."*[20]

And this was general: in Old High German too, the Savior *salvator* was represented as *heilant*: literally, "the healer." It has been suggested that this term had magico-religious overtones, painting Jesus as a wizard as much as a transcendental agent of salvation of mankind from sin, a conveyor of *heil* (divinely inspired, especially military, good fortune)[21] and hence "holy" (German *heilag*, Saxon *hêlag*, English *hælig*). But *heil* was the word for health (and etymologically the same thing, wholeness), and if its military associations did no harm in the early years after conversion, it was soon the regular—and quite pacific—word for Christian salvation* as attested in the English of the tenth century:

> *Ic ðær mynster on gestaðolode for mine saule hælo.* (901–909 A.D.)

> I established the monastery there for the salvation of my soul.[22]

> *To-dæg þisse hiw-ræddene ys hæl geworden.* (ca. 1000 A.D.)

> Today this household has been saved.[23]

But overall, as the direct translations of the Gospels above show, Germanic-speaking Christians did not change the content of Christian worship. What they did, rather, was to accept a trivialization of their erstwhile heathen terms in the service of their new way of life.

---

* Itself originally a Christian Latin neologism from *salvus* "whole" and *salūs* "health, safety." In the Germanic languages, newly Christianized, there must have been differences between the usage of the forms, at different times and places. In the Old Saxon *Hêliand*, for example, *hêlag* means "holy," but *hêl* is not used for anything but wholeness and (physical) health.

Germanizing the Calendar

Christianity came with new measures of time: the year marked out with holy festivals, and the week marked out with seven successive day-names.

The English church was particularly active in reconditioning pagan festivals as Christian events. This fits with the actions of celebrities such as Boniface and Willibrord—Englishmen taking their faith abroad. According to the Venerable Bede (672–735), the celebration of Christ's resurrection, called Pascha or its equivalent almost universally in Christendom—from Aramaic *paskhā*, Hebrew *pesach* "Pass-over," but conveniently reminiscent of the Greek verb *paskhein* "to suffer"—was in England renamed for the goddess Eostre[24] (of the dawn); and this name (later spelled *Easter*) was taken up in south Germany as *Ōstarun*, modern *Ostern*.[*25]

The feast of Christ's birth was generally known in Catholic Christianity as *Nātālicia* or *Nātīvitās*, viz "birthing"; but since it had been set as the new midwinter festival, it took as its English name *gēol* (later spelt Yule), a word that was used in most of the Germanic languages for the months of deep winter (English *se ærra geóla* December, *se æftera geóla* January; Gothic *fruma jiuleis* November) or (as in Norse *jól*) a twelve-day feast held at this time. This conversion was also recorded by Bede, who actually thought of both *Eostur* and *Giuli* as primarily names for months.[26] Both English and Germans, however, were much later to adopt a new name for the feast: English *Cristes mæsse* ("Christ's mass"), first attested around 1123, and German *Weihnachten*, literally "Holy Nights," latter twelfth century, which used the other pre-Christian Germanic word for "holy," *wīh*, still also seen in the verb *weihen*, to consecrate or ordain.[†27] The Dutch too moved to the name *Kerstmis*, and the Frisians to *Kristtijd*, but in Scandinavia the feast remains *Jul* to this day.

The actual transition for the days of the week is somewhat obscure, but in the Roman Empire, the seven-day week seems to have begun to replace the old Roman eight-day *nundīnum* cycle, punctuated with a *nundīna* market day, in the second century A.D., and then spread to other lands along with their Christian conversions. A seven-day cycle, punctuated by a sabbath, had been observed by the Jews at least since the fifth century B.C., so an association of

---

* Both representing the same etymology as English *east*, and German *Osten*, viz the Indo-European root **ausōs*, also seen in Sanskrit *uṣās*, Greek *heōs*, Latin *aurōra*, Lithuanian *auszrà*, all meaning "dawn."

† Also in English *witch*, and Latin *victima*.

a new calendar with Christianity, presented to the Roman world as the new reformed and universalized Judaism, would have seemed quite natural.

The naming of the original days was a complex—and ultimately inconsistent—matter. The Jews had singled out the sabbath and the day preceding it (*shishi*—preparation or *'ereb*—evening) and otherwise used ordinal numbers, from first to fifth, starting after the sabbath. The Greeks followed this (with all the ordinals feminine, since *hēmera* "day" is feminine in Greek), but often added a specific name for Sunday—for Christians, the day on which the Lord had arisen:

SUNDAY	MONDAY	TUESDAY	WEDNESDAY	THURSDAY	FRIDAY	SATURDAY
Κυριακή *kyriakē* (Lord's)	Δευτέρα *deutera* (second)	Τρίτη *tritē* (third)	Τετάρτη *tetartē* (fourth)	Πέμπτη *pemptē* (fifth)	Παρασκευή *paraskeuē* (preparation)	Σάββατο/α *sabbaton/a* (Sabbath)*

This system still prevails in Greek, and has inspired weekday names in the Slavonic world as well (although numbering the days from Monday rather than Sunday). Here, for example, is the Church Slavonic series:

MONDAY	TUESDAY	WEDNESDAY	THURSDAY	FRIDAY	SATURDAY	SUNDAY
Понедѣлїникѹ *ponedĕliniku* (post-Sunday)	Вѵторїникѹ *vŭtoriniku* (second)	Срѣда *srĕda* (middle)	Четврїтѹкѹ *četvritŭku* (fourth)	Пѧтѹкѹ *pętŭku* (fifth)	Сѫбота *sąbota* (Sabbath)	Недѣл *nedĕlja* (Not-doing)

The second day is Tuesday here, rather than Monday, and Friday now receives its own number—the fifth day. However in neither system was any deity other than the Lord mentioned, and not even that in Slavonic.

However, in the empire as a whole, astrology too had an influence, particularly so as the weekday names were constructed and handed down in Rome, and the Latin tradition. In particular, it was thought auspicious to bear in mind the planet ruling each day: and the order of the days was Sun, Moon, Ares, Hermes, Zeus, Aphrodite, and Cronos. Fixing the Lord's day as the Sun (as per the identification of *Sol Invictus* with the risen Christ[†]), and transferring to the corresponding Roman planet names (traditionally equivalent to gods), we find a new set of seven day-names, beginning with Sunday:

---

* Σαββατον is a neuter noun, but may be in the singular or the plural.

† Cf chapter 5, p. 84.

SUNDAY	MONDAY	TUESDAY	WEDNESDAY	THURSDAY	FRIDAY	SATURDAY
DIES (DAY OF)						
*Solis** the Sun	*Lunae* the Moon	*Martis* Mars	*Mercurii* Mercury	*Iovis* Jupiter	*Veneris* Venus	*Saturni* Saturn

This was the system that was introduced to the Celtic and Germanic world: it came in with their conversion to Catholic Christianity (or perhaps slightly before it, with access to merchants). The reactions to it were mixed, but curiously indifferent to the presence of pagan deities.

The British accepted it literally. All the Latin names were taken over, including the sun and the moon (which if translated would have been *haul* and *lloer*), and perpetuated, though in a British accent. Given the sound changes of one and a half millennia, it has defined the modern Welsh week without Christian interpolation or Celtic interpretation:

SUNDAY	MONDAY	TUESDAY	WEDNESDAY	THURSDAY	FRIDAY	SATURDAY
DYDD (DAY OF)						
Sul the Sun	*Llun* the Moon	*Mawrth* Mars	*Mercher* Mercury	*Iau* Jupiter	*Gwener* Venus	*Saddwrn* Saturn

The Irish, on the other hand, required obeisance to the Lord, as well as recognition of the actual landmarks of the monastic week. The moon remained recognizable, but nothing else meaningful was taken over from the Latin words. The words are here given in their Old Irish forms, but the system is preserved in Gaelic (under more cumbersome spelling patterns) to the present day.

SUNDAY	MONDAY	TUESDAY	WEDNESDAY	THURSDAY	FRIDAY	SATURDAY
DIA (DAY OF)						
Domnach the Lord	*Luan* the Moon	*Māirt* Mars	*Cēt–ain* first fast	*Dardāin (etar da āin)* between two fasts	*Ōin diden* last fast[†]	*Satharn* Saturn

---

* *Solis* may be replaced by *Dominicus* or *Dominica* (Lord's)—either masculine or feminine since the gender of *Dies* is doubtful.

† The word for fast (*āin*, Modern Irish *aoine*) is a borrowing too: it is derived from Latin *ieiūnium*.

The Celts therefore had received the days of the week, either as a meaningless mumbo-jumbo, or as an opportunity to index certain days for holy activities. When the system was transmitted to the German world, it was treated more ambivalently.

In Wulfila's Gothic Bible translation only three days figure, and they are predictably Friday, Saturday, and Sunday, respectively identified as *fruma sabbatō* ("before Sabbath"), *sabbatō dags* ("Sabbath day"), and *afarsabbatō dags* ("after-Sabbath day"). Friday also turns up in Gothic as a bare loan from Greek, *paraskaiwē* (παρασκευή "preparation"), and so it is possible that Wulfila (in the third century A.D.) knew no more than that: the Jewish week—which in any case did not distinguish anything but sabbath and day-number.*

But in transmission to the Anglo-Saxons of England, the pagan gods who put in a virtual appearance—courtesy of their astrological life as heavenly bodies—are now identified with full individuality through a novel *interpretatio anglica*.

SUNDAY	MONDAY	TUESDAY	WEDNESDAY	THURSDAY	FRIDAY	SATURDAY
sunnan-dæg the Sun	*mōnan-dæg* the Moon	*tūves-dæg* Tiw = Mars	*wōdnes-dæg* Woden = Mercury	*þunres-dæg* þunor = Jupiter	*frīge-dæg* Frige = Venus	*sætern-dæg* Saturn

Here, curiously, the (perhaps already) discarded heathen gods of England were lined up and substituted for Latin names of the pagan gods of Rome. The names are first attested quite late—approximately at the turn of the first millennium—although *sunnandæg* is an exception, in the seventh-century *Laws of Ine*.[28] This suggests that there may be some causality that kept the other weekdays from showing up in the types of literature that have survived. At any rate, they do seem to postdate the spread of Christianity among the English, yet in order to create them someone had found ancient divine equivalents for Roman deities, and then a whole population of serious converted Christians—including elites made up of monks and priests—were prepared to continue them in everyday use (to this day). The different attitude evinced by the Greeks (and their followers the Slavs), who rejected the use of false gods, shows that this is not a trivial fact.

---

* It is inferred, from some alien day-names that turn up in eighth- and ninth-century Bavarian German, that Gothic may have had more day-names on the Greek pattern: *ertag* "Tuesday" suggests Ares (Greek equivalent of Mars), *phinztag* "Thursday" suggests *pemptē*, and *pherintag* "Friday" may be *paraskaiwē* all over again. (Green 1998, pp. 310–12.)

There are difficulties with the divine equivalences chosen too. Why was Saturn left unchanged? Tiw, as the accredited god of war, seems a straightforward alias for Mars, but why was Woden the chief Germanic deity equated with Mercury (a mere messenger among the Olympians), while Jupiter the chief Roman god was identified with the blusterer Þunor? Meanwhile Frige, not a well-known goddess, is absent from Old English literature.

Both Julius Caesar and Tacitus, our chief sources on pre-Christian German culture, wrote that their principal god was Mercury. And Tacitus rated Hercules and Mars next in prominence.[29] This is usually taken as an *interpretatio romana* of gods who were really worshipped as Woden, Þunor, and Tiw. So why the discrepancy here? It seems that Woden corresponds to Mercury (both for Tacitus, and the recompositor of the Germanic weekdays) because both had the function of escorting the dead to the underworld. Both also had strong responsibility for magic and divination. Hercules made sense (for Tacitus, we conjecture) as the equivalent of Þunor because he was renowned for his strength and various adventures with giants and men. But the task for the recompositor was not to find the best Roman equivalent for Þunor, but rather to find some Germanic god that would correspond to Jupiter. As such, the fact that Jupiter was also known as *Tonans* ("the thunderer") while Þunor's name actually *was* thunder must have clinched it. As for Frige, her name meant nothing less than "love" itself (related in origin to *friend*), which was a strong indicator of Venus, evidently a goddess of sexual love.*

For speakers of Old High German in central and southern Germany, the pattern was very similar to the Old English one (from which it may well have been derived), although with one or two quirks.

SUNDAY	MONDAY	TUESDAY	WEDNESDAY	THURSDAY	FRIDAY	SATURDAY
sunnūn-tag the Sun	*māne-tag* the Moon	*zios-tag* Zio = Mars	*mittwoch* mid-week	*donares-tag* Donar = Jupiter	*fria-tag* Fria = Venus	*sambaz-tag,* Sabbath day, or *sunnūn-āband* sun-eve

---

* The name *Vĕnus* itself (in Latin, unlike English, pronounced with a short e) is a word for "charm," seen also in such words as *venustus* "charming" and *veneratio* "worship," and also seen in Gothic *wênjan* "to hope" and German *Wunsch* "wish."

The problem of motivating the selection of Frige falls away if we can focus instead on her Nordic counterpart Freyja, whose name means "the lady" rather than "love," but who does have good literary form as a goddess of sexual love.

German, rather than English, forms of the gods' names are used. But the same technique used by Slavonic avoided using a god's name for Wednesday, and Saturn too has been dropped, either in favor of "Sabbath," in a nasalized form,* or a positional reference to the day following, Sunday.

The system (with Christianity and Roman contact) must have reached the Nordic world a little later.

SUNDAY	MONDAY	TUESDAY	WEDNESDAY	THURSDAY	FRIDAY	SATURDAY
sunnu-dagr the Sun or drōttins-dagr the Lord	mānu-dagr the Moon	tys-dagr Tyr = Mars	oðins-dagr Oðin = Jupiter	þōrs-dagr Þōr = Jupiter	frjā-dagr Frjā = Venus	þvāti-dagr or laugar-dagr, both = wash-day

This Old Norse system has the distinguishing features of emphasizing the translation of *dies dominica* "the Lord's day" as *drōttinsdagr*, and also (like all Scandinavian languages since) noting the special role of Saturday as wash-day: *þvātidagr* or *laugardagr*.

But if the days of the week were so "interpreted" everywhere in the Germanic world, not so the months of the year, which—although there were previous systems—were everywhere borrowed straight from Latin, a system that had long been standard throughout the empire. (It was also adopted by the Celts and the Slavs as they were absorbed into Christendom, though with some carryovers from their earlier names.)

German Heirlooms: Tree and Cross

As well as incorporating their old pantheon in the new weekly calendar, there are also signs that the Germanic peoples carried across some elements of the style of their old religion into the new worship of Christ Jesus. Just as the Irish and British had expanded with gusto a tradition of hero-tales into lives of the

---

* This nasalized form, [sambaton] rather than [sabbaton], also underlies Slavonic *sǫbota*. It is still there in modern German *Samstag*, but also French *samedi*. We also find Hungarian *szombat* and Romanian *sâmbătă*, showing it had widespread popular currency in Europe.

saints, there was a genre of nostalgic Germanic literature that looked back to heroic, heathen times from a Christian perspective. In Beowulf, the role of God in recently converted Germanic literature was to assure the right outcome from struggle, to act as a personalized guarantor of *wyrd* "fate." God, though, still endorsed traditional displays of courage: as Beowulf himself remarks,

	Wyrd oft nereð	Fate often saves
unfaégne eorl	*þonne his*	a hero not doomed, when his
	ellen déah.	courage avails.

using the same verb *nerian* that is often used to mean Christ's salvation. And in a fragmentary epic that has survived in Old High German, another eponymous hero cries out

*"welaga nu, waltant got [quad Hiltibrant], we-wurt skihit"**

"Alas, O ruling God," quoth Hildebrand, "a woeful fate is upon us."

when he realizes that destiny is forcing an outcome (namely, for father to kill son) that neither he—nor presumably a just God—would have chosen.[30] Poets face squarely the tensions between old worldview and new.

But this tension did not always tell against a simple understanding of the new faith: heathen traditions could also, on occasion, give a new poetic force to Christian imagination.

The leader of the Germanic gods in the west—Woden, or Wotan—is not much described in literature, but his Norse equivalent, Oðin, is.† In particular, in the *Hávamal*, stanza 138, he is described as hanging himself in self-sacrifice, for nine days and nine nights, on the world-tree Yggdrasill, a name that translates as "Ygg's steed' (since he rode upon it)," where Ygg is an alias for Oðin.

Veit ec at ec hecc vindga meiði
a netr allar nío,
geiri vndaþr oc gefinn Oðni,
sialfr sialfom mer,

---

* Curiously close, in both sense and sound, to the more modern, "We are in the shit."
† The name is reconstructed for Proto-Germanic as *Wōðanaz, with an Indo-European root *vāt-, also seen in Latin *vātes* "seer," Irish *fáith* "poet," Welsh *gwawd* "praise-poetry," and German *Wut* "mania."

a þeim meiþi, er mangi veit,
hvers hann af rótom renn.

I know that I hung on a windy tree
nine long nights,
wounded with a spear, dedicated to Odin,
myself to myself,
on that tree of which no man knows
from where its roots run.

It does not take much inspiration to compare this to Christ's torment on the cross, but it could be a Germanic idea to take the cross itself, conceived as a world-tree, as a central character in its own right, and describe its feelings as it is forced to play out this elemental sacrifice.

Bæron mē þær beornas on eaxlum, oððæt hīe mē on beorg āsetton,
gefæstnodon mē þær fēondas genōge. Geseah ic þā frean mancynnes
efstan elne micle, þæt hē mē wolde on gestīgan.

Bore me there men on their shoulders, until they me on a hill set up,
fastened me there enemies enough. Saw I there the Lord of mankind
hasten with zeal great, that he me would upon ascend.

This is the theme of the Old English poem known as *The Dream of the Rood*, one of the earliest Christian poems in that language, and quite plausibly the work of the first known Anglo-Saxon poet, Cædmon.*

Although the precise form of the instrument of Christ's execution was not specified in the New Testament (it was made of wood, but the more explicit terms—Greek *σταυρός stauros*, Latin *crux*—were used more generally for stakes and gallows-trees) the cross itself had been a salient Christian symbol at least since the second century A.D. Minucius Felix, defending the faith against common critiques of his day, felt the need to deny a popular association of Christianity with the sign of the cross:†

Cruces etiam nec colimus nec optamus . . . Signum sane crucis naturaliter visimus in navi, cum velis tumentibus vehitur, cum expansis palmulis

* It is written on the Vercelli manuscript (tenth century), and partly transcribed onto a stone monument, the Ruthwell Cross, which dates to the eighth. Cædmon himself is dated to the seventh century.

† This shows, at the very least, that the belief was widespread.

labitur: et cum erigitur iugum, crucis signum est, et cum homo porrectis
manibus deum pura mente veneratur. Ita signo crucis aut ratio naturalis
innititur aut vestra religio formatur.[31]

Crosses too we neither worship nor wish for . . . Of course we see the
sign of the cross in nature in a ship, proceeding with billowing sails, or
gliding with a complement of oars: and when a yoke is set up, it is the
sign of the cross, and when a man stretching out his arms worships a
god with a pure heart. So this sign of the cross is either the basis for
physical objects, or the form of your own religion.

Meanwhile around 210 Clement of Alexandria saw T as a Christian symbol,[32]
and Tertullian about the same time accepts that Christians are called *crucis*
religiosi ("the religious of the cross"). But the knock-down evidence that
Christians were explictly using the symbol themselves only comes with the
depiction of crucifixes in religious iconography that seems to begin in the
fourth century, and to be well established by the sixth.[33]

Then Venantius Fortunatus (who lived from about 535 to about 600)
famously dignified the cross itself in a hymn that is still current in the Roman
Catholic Church:

Vexilla regis prodeunt
Fulget crucis mysterium
Quo carne carnis conditor
Suspensus est patibulo . . .

The banners of the King advance, the
Cross's mystery shines forth, in which in
flesh the creator of flesh was hanged on
a gallows . . .

Quo vulneratus insuper
Mucrone diro lanceae
Ut nos lavaret crimine
Manavit unda et sanguine.

Wounded from above by that dire edge of a
spear, to wash us of sin, he flowed with
water and blood.

Impleta sunt quae concinit
David fideli carmine
Dicens In nationibus
Regnavit a ligno Deus.

Fulfilled are the words which David sang
in a song of faith, saying: Among the
nations God has reigned from a tree
(wood).

Arbor decora et fulgida
Ornata Regis purpura
Electa digno stipite
Tam sancta membra tangere . . .

Tree of honor and splendor, decorated with
the purple of a King, chosen to touch such
holy limbs with its worthy trunk . . .[34]

But this was all well before Augustine (archbishop in 597) began the conversion of the Anglo-Saxons, and a good 150 years before Boniface (who died in 754) undertook the conversion of other Germans and Saxons.

Venantius had visited parts of Germany before settling Gaul, which in that period was just changing its name to Francia. But since Germany was still heathen at the time, there was little chance of any spiritual influence on his sense of the status of the cross. He himself was, of course, firmly founded as an orthodox Catholic, and living in a Catholic court: King Sigibert, through whom Venantius gained preferment, ultimately to a bishopric in Poitiers (Pictavis), was third in line from the first Christian Frank, his grandfather Clovis, and had in fact insisted on the Catholic conversion of his Arian bride, the Visigothic princess Brunhilde, on their marriage in 567.

Despite the unlikelihood of direct influence on or from Venantius in his poetic reverie at the Frankish court, there is plenty of evidence that Saxons and Germans, before their conversion, had long seen spiritual force in trees—a cult that may yet have a distant echo in the tradition of the Christmas tree.

Though Yggdrasill, the world-tree of the Norsemen, on which Oðin sacrificed himself by nine days' hanging, has no attested equivalent in German or Saxon literature, there are some less magnificent texts that only make sense if the unregenerate Anglo-Saxons had a tree fixation.[35]

In England, a century after Augustine's arrival, a canon wrote:

> If anyone makes an offering on trees or well or railings or anywhere except in the Church of God . . . that is sacrilege, that is, sacrifice to demons.

In the eleventh century, the comment was made:

> Some men are so blinded that they take their offerings to a stone made firm in the ground and also to trees and wells, just as witches teach them, and such a man will not understand how stupidly he acts or how this dead stone or dumb tree can help him or give him health . . .

Even the devout were not far removed from these practices, provided they were given Christian sanction. Saint Willibald (ca. 700–787) says that he had been a sickly child, but was cured when his parents took their son and "offered him before the lordly and holy cross of the Savior . . . as is the custom of the

Saxon race." Standing crosses, too, could be placed in the fields, as sites for prayer, a practice of Bishop Aldebert of Gaul, about which the pope complained to Saint Boniface in 744.

If standing crosses could be seen as particularly holy "trees"—as the Rood claimed for itself in the *Dream of the Rood* poem—

Forþan ic ðrymfæst nū	Therefore, now I rise up
hlīfige under heofenum, ond ic	glorious under heavens, and
hælan mæg	I may heal
æghwylcne ānra, þāra þe him	each one of those who hold me in
bið. egesa tō mē	awe.
Iū ic wæs geworden wīta	Formerly, I was hardest of
heardost,	torments,
lēodum lāðost, ær þan ic him	most loath to people, before I of
līfes weg	life the right path opened to
rihtne gerymde, reordberendum.	them, the speech-bearers.
Hwæt, mē þā geweorðode	Lo, me the prince of glory
wuldres ealdor	honored over all the forest
ofer hol[t]wudu, heofonrīces	trees, the guardian of the
weard!	heavens!
Swylce swā hē his mōdor ēac,	Just as he, his mother also, Mary
Marīan sylfe,	herself,
ælmihtig god for ealle menn	almighty god before all men,
geweorðode ofer eall wīfa cynn.	honored over all womankind.

(lines 84–94)

then things were very much in keeping with the ancestral European practice of the pre-Christian Germans, and perhaps of the Celtic Druids too.

A slight linguistic clue suggests that Germanic veneration of the cross was, in the beginning, a continuation of previous tree worship. This originates from the famous injunction of Pope Gregory I to Bishop Mellitus. The pope had just sent Augustine to be the apostle to England, and was now reinforcing him with this new bishop:

Tell Augustine that he should by no means destroy the temples of the gods but rather the idols within those temples. Let him, after he has purified them with holy water, place altars and relics of the saints in them. For, if those temples are well built, they should be converted from the worship of demons to the service of the true God. Thus, seeing that their places of worship are not destroyed, the people will banish error from their hearts and come to places familiar and dear to them in acknowledgment and worship of the true God . . .[36]

One result of this seems to have been that the Anglo-Saxons retained many of their own words for rituals and objects that were reinterpreted and repurposed after the Christian conversion. Baptism was called *fulwiht* "fulfillment," the altar *wigbed* "holy bed" or "holy board," and vestments *godweb* "godly weavings." By contrast, since it seems there were no pre-Christian Germanic priests or holy buildings, the terms *episcopus, presbyter, compater* "godfather," *monachus, abbas, diaconus, kyriakē* "church," *scrinium* "shrine," *missa* "mass" were taken over directly into English: *biscop, preost, cumpæder, munuc, abbud, diacon, cirice, scrin, mæsse*.

Regarding the Holy Cross, however, the seventh-century church in England was all too ready to adopt native words for tree or wood: *rōd, bēam, treow, wudu* were all in use; in fact the Latin *crūc-* only seems to have been borrowed in the eleventh century, with a palatalized second c, giving Old English *crūc*, Middle English *cruche*, and Modern English *crouch*.* Another term (and the universal word for the Holy Cross in Gothic) was *galga*, more specifically "gallows," originally meaning the curve of a bough. It would seem, then, that the concept of a holy tree was something that the Anglo-Saxons found already familiar, and adaptable.[37]

This linguistic fact about Old English Christianity is striking, giving rise to such familiar antiquities as *Holyrood House*, and Hamlet's oath to his mother, "No, by the rood, not so" (act 3, scene 4). And *rood* went on to be

---

* The word *cross* itself comes later from Norse *kross*, which had been borrowed from Old Irish *cros* (plural *crosa*), itself from Latin nominative *crux*. (The Irish word would have come through Welsh *croes*: compare the changes in *Saxones* > Welsh *Saeson* > Irish *Sásana*.) Early on, it seems to have been used mostly for place names.

It came finally to supplant the other words, as a metonym for Christianity (first attested in the twelfth century), as a pure shape (as a noun and as a preposition *across*, both twelfth century), and as a verb, to denote the making of that shape (1430), even as vaguely as going to the farther side of a river or road (1583). (Per the *Oxford English Dictionary* entry *cross*.)

Curiously, the war cry of Harold, the last Saxon king, at the battle of Hastings (1066) was "Olicrosse!" (*hálig cros*), referring to the Holy Rood of Waltham. (In Wace, *Roman de Rou* 13, 119.)

the standard word for a lifesize crucifix, which was a regular feature of medieval churches, while "the Rood" became a name for "the True Cross," the wooden structure on which Christ was hanged, and which in fragmentary form provided the holiest of all relics.

But was this holy tree of the Germanic peoples actually personified, as the Cross was in the *Dream of the Rood*? In the texts of Norse mythology, Yggdrasill—though cardinal to the structure of the universe—was never a character in his or her own right.* Despite Yggdrasill's etymology as "Woden's steed," it functions not as a sentient collaborator, but as a fixture on which the god mounts himself (i.e., metaphorically, "rides") and hangs in agony.

In fact, despite the clear background for it in Germanic pre-Christian worship, there is no known personification of a tree in any of the north European traditions of worship, even in such a form as the Christian poets Venantius and the author of the *Dream of the Rood* envisaged in describing the Cross. In the long term, the Living Tree did not survive as a Germanic heirloom in Christianity. Trees evidently had been respected, and continued to be so after the advent of the Christian faith, but they are not known to have been personified or deified.

With a perverse irony, Greek Christianity did adopt the word for cross *staurós* as a devout proper name, and Stavros is still popular as a boy's name in Greece. In Iberia too, Cruz is a girl's name. Grammatical gender seems to determine the appropriate sex of recipient; and since there is no grammatical gender in English, this has left the Beckhams free too to name their son Cruz.

---

* Tellingly, J. R. R. Tolkien, in his large-scale reworking of Germanic mythology *The Lord of the Rings*, has no word for an animated tree other than *ent*, an Anglo-Saxon word meaning "giant," itself derived from the common Germanic stem *etunaz* "giant," seen also in Norse *jǫtunn*. *Enta geweorc* "giant work" is a common phrase in Anglo-Saxon poetry, expressing uncomprehending respect for Roman antiquities (e.g., the ruins at Bath).

CHAPTER 10

"Listen, All Ye Slavs"
Orthodoxy Rejects Trilingualism

Obače svojǫ pritŭčjǫ da pristavljǫ,	Let me add my own parable,
mŭnogŭ umŭ vŭ malě rěči kažę.	Condensing much sense into a few words:
*Nazi bo vĭsi bes **knigŭ** <u>języki</u>*	Naked are all <u>nations</u> without **Scripture**
brati sę ne mogǫšte bez orǫžija	Who being without arms cannot fight
sŭ protivĭnikomĭ duši našichŭ	The adversary of our souls
gotovi mǫky věčĭnyję vŭ plěnŭ.	and are ripe for the dungeon of eternal torments.
Iže bo vraga, <u>języki</u>, ne ljubite,	And so, ye <u>nations</u> who love not the Enemy,
brati že sę sŭ nimĭ myslęšte dzělo,	And who truly mean to fight him:
otŭvrĭzěte priležĭno umu dvĭri,	Open eagerly the doors of your intelligence—
orǫžije priimŭše tvrĭdo nyně,	Ye who have now taken up the stout arms
*ježe kujǫtŭ **kŭnigy Gospodĭnje**,*	that are forged through **Lord's Scripture**,
glavǫ tĭrǫšte neprijězni velĭmi.	That mightily crush the head of the Un-friend.

Saint Constantine, aka Saint Cyril, apostle to the
Slavs (863–867 A.D.)*

---

* *Prologue to the Gospel* (863–867 A.D.), lines 77–88, translated by Roman Jakobson 1963 (substituting "Scriptures" for "their own books" as translation of *knigi*). Note that wherever the translation says "nations," the original could just as well be translated "languages."

THE FIGURE OF CHRIST on the cross did become increasingly salient in Christian worship as it was practiced in northern Europe, with roods (or large crucifixes) in churches which naturally became the focus of worship, being the most vivid and concrete representation of God, and what he had done for mankind, in the church. One would pray to Christ on the cross, and for some of the simpler worshippers, distinguishing between the two may have become difficult.

This was particularly true in the Slavic-speaking parts of Europe. Here the very word for "cross" was derived from *Christ*. The Church Slavonic word крїстъ *krïstŭ* or крѹстъ *krŭstŭ*, which has led to modern Serbo-Croat *krst*, Russian крест *krest* Latvian *krists* or *krŭsts* (all of which mean "cross"), is actually derived from Church Slavonic Хрїстъ *Xrïstŭ* "Christ."

This is odd, since in a Greek Orthodox missionary environment, there would have been no word like Latin *crux* that might lay the basis for confusion. (The Greek cross has always been σταυρός *staurós*.) But it is our first inkling that the Slavs were first approached in the name of Christ not by the Greeks, but by western Europeans—in the first instance most probably by the Irish.[1]

The Slavs' identity as a people is determined by their once-single language, known as Slavonic, although they have embraced a number of different linguistic standards in the second millennium A.D., and two alphabets, Roman or Cyrillic, depending on whether they were Christianized by the Catholic or the Orthodox church. Their ancestral tribes, located in eastern Europe, were named Veneti, Antae, and Sloveni (and other variants) by ethnographers from the ancient Mediterranean world (notably by Strabo, Tacitus, and Procopius) but they had no impact on this world until they expanded into the pasture and steppe lands of the Carpathians and Balkans, lands that were largely depopulated in the early fifth century A.D. after the (Germanic) Goths, who had lived there, had decamped to invade the more attractive Roman lands to the west.

The Goths had themselves been fleeing invading hordes from Asia; and in the fifth century, the Slavs were dominated by large companies of equestrian steppe-nomads with strong military organization, first the Huns (famously led by Attila), then in the mid-sixth century (after fresh disturbances in Asia) reorganized as the Avar Khanate. Their language—since it was not written down, nor even much quoted—remains tantalizingly unknown, though unlikely to be Slavic.

This kind of force was a perennial threat to the Roman Empire in the east. But at the turn of the sixth to seventh century the threat was realized as a full-scale invasion of most of the Balkans and peninsular Greece. Thereafter, the Slavs were able to settle most of the region—on their own terms, and without Greek interference—throughout the seventh and eighth centuries. The result was an effective barrier between the eastern (Greek) and western (Frankish) halves of Mediterranean Christendom, the region that had formerly been the northern shore of the Roman Empire.

Meanwhile, the Franks under Charlemagne (ruled 768–814)—now largely Romanized—absorbed the (fully German) Duchy of Bavaria to their east, and so gained control of northern Dalmatia (modern Slovenia and Croatia) and western Pannonia (modern Hungary), dominating the Slavs who continued to live there. Another achievement of Charlemagne (this time in concert with Moravian Slavs, in campaigns in 791 and 796) was to end the power of the Avar Huns.

For three centuries the Avars had held the military hub of the Balkans, but now they yielded this dominance to the Bulgars. These were another Asian people that spoke a Turkic language, a form of which has survived in their sister community that settled on the Volga—the Chuvash of Cheboksary. They had been entering and settling parts of the Balkans from the east for more than a century. The Bulgars would now settle permanently in the land that came to be known as Bulgaria, but without their own language. At first, taking their lead from their southern neighbors, they administered their lands in Greek. But later they assimilated in language to their Slavic subjects, and this became official in 893. Bulgarian language would thenceforth mean a dialect of Slavic.

At the dawn of the ninth century, the emperor Nicephorus I (ruled 802–811) was able to reclaim Greece for the Roman Empire, but he was defeated and killed in attempting to displace the Bulgars farther north. Meanwhile, much, much farther north, a different group of foreigners, the Norse Vikings (here known as Varangians *væringjar* "pledged men," Slavic *varyági*), were establishing themselves as a ruling elite. They became kings (*kunungar*, "men of kin," i.e, "high birth," converted in Slavic to *kŭnędzi*—Russian *knyazi*) in the new state of Rus',* a league of various cities (first notably Novgorod, then, in 882, Kiev). Trading relations began with Byzantium (and indeed the Muslim Caliphate) along the Volga river system, though this took them through the

---

* The apostrophe ' that appears at the end of *Rus'*, *knyaz'*, and some other words in romanized Russian means a palatal y consonant. So pronounce [ru:sʸ], [knya:zʸ].

potentially hostile territories of Khazar and Pecheneg Turks to their south. Like the Bulgar elite, the Varangians would gradually give up their own language and customs, and assimilate to their Slavic subjects (forming the Russian, and Ukrainian, nations).

The Moravians and Bohemians (on the western marches of the Slav area, next to Bavaria) set up their own kingdom of *Velká Morava* (Great Moravia) in the mid-ninth century: this would give the opportunity to establish the first autonomous Christian church among the Slavs. About the same time, there was missionary activity not far away to the south in Serbia, and emperor Basil I sent priests (shortly after an invasion force) in 869: the first Serbian bishopric was founded at Ras, near modern Novy Pazar.

But the turbulence of the eastern frontier returned almost immediately: another invasion took place in 895. This time it was the Magyars, in concert with Onogur (i.e., "Hungarian") Bulgars. Allowed freedom of transit by the Bulgar Khanate, they raided widely in southern Europe, to the west as far as Milan and to the south into Croatia. Most importantly, by 902, they had totally crushed and superseded the Moravian state, leaving some Bohemian fragments under the control of the Holy Roman Empire (i.e., Germany) to the west.

This insertion of a completely alien Finno-Ugric–speaking entity on the central European steppe, bordering with Francia Orientalis (modern Austria) to the west, and with the confluence of Romance-speaking Wallachians, Moldavians, and Transylvanians (i.e., Romanians) to the east, effectively meant that the Southern Slavs (Serbs and Bulgarians) would thenceforth be isolated from the vast mass of others in central and northeastern Europe.

In Bulgaria the official acceptance of the Christian faith (from the Orthodox Church) was offered by Boris I, *knyaz'* of the first Bulgarian Empire in 864. (He accepted the name of the current Roman emperor, his godfather Michael, at his baptism.) In Russia, Vladimir I, *knyaz'* of Kiev, chose to bring Rus' to the Orthodox faith in 988, likewise accepting the name of his royal Greek godfather Basil and marrying the emperor's daughter Anna into the bargain, but also entering into an immediate military alliance with him against a current revolt in the Byzantine Empire. Vladimir had supposedly previously ordered a survey of all the faiths on offer, but had chosen Orthodox Christianity when informed that his emissaries to Istanbul, on entering Hagia Sophia cathedral, "knew not if they were in earth or heaven."

In both cases there were subsequent reverses that could have threatened these new independent churches that were conducting worship in the Slavic vernacular.

In Bulgaria, the Byzantine Empire actually succeeded in reconquering the kingdom in 971; but not its church, which had been declared autocephalous— "self-headed" that is, independent within the Orthodox communion—and whose high priest had been raised from metropolitan to patriarch in 919.* As it turned out, the Greeks made no attempt to reorganize the Bulgarian church into closer union with their own, and in any case soon lost the power to do so when the Fourth Crusade effectively deposed the emperor in Constantinople. Bulgaria then began a new independence with its capital moved from Preslav to Turnovo.

In Russia, promotion of the church to autocephaly came much later. The seat of the metropolitan was moved from Kiev to Vladimir in 1299, and from Vladimir to Moscow in 1325. All three cities had been repeatedly ravaged in the thirteenth century, and in 1238–1240 were completely destroyed by the Mongol invasion of Batu Khan. Moscow, however, was able to recover in a way the others could not. In 1589 the then metropolitan of Moscow, Job, became a patriarch in his own right, with parity with the patriarch in Constantinople, and so the Russian Orthodox Church too became auto-cephalous within the Orthodox communion.

This defines the basic board on which the Christianization of the Slavs was played out. Although the northern and western areas (Sorbians, Poles, Czechs, Slovaks, Slovenes, Croats—and soon including the interloper Hungarians) were largely contacted by representatives of the Roman church, with a standard Catholic regimen of scriptures and liturgy in Latin, and catechism and homilies in the vernacular, in the southern and eastern areas (Serbian, Bulgarian, Ukrainian, and Russian) a much more radical use of the common Slavic vernacular was exploited, with distinctive results for the development of the Christian faith in its "Orthodox" form.

Irish Catholics

The first missionary activity among the Slavs for which there is evidence occurred in the latter eighth century, in the western marches of the Frankish

---

* The Bulgarian patriarchate was the first autocephalous Slavic Orthodox Church, granted autocephaly three hundred years earlier than the Serbian Orthodox Church (1217) and almost six hundred years before the Russian Orthodox Church.

domains, and although we must suppose that most of the priests were Frankish, the best-known preacher there was an Irishman, Saint Vergilius (at home probably known as Fergil), who was born around 700 into a noble family, and educated at Iona. Given responsibility for the Slavic mission by the pope in 752, he became known as the "apostle to the Carinthians." He died in 784.

As coming from the west, these missionaries were in the western tradition of the Latin rite, but the Irishmen at least would have been familiar with vernacular worship from their own practice at home in Ireland, and must be presumed to have learned to communicate in Slavonic. Consistently with this, early loan vocabulary absorbed into Church Slavonic shows that the basic linguistic exchange at this time was from Frankish (i.e., German) and Latin, into Slavonic. For example,

Frankish: loan word—*post* < *fast* "fast"; *mŭnĭxŭ* < **monĭc* "monk"; biscup < *biscof* "bishop"
loan translation—*ne-priĕznĭ* < un-hold (viz "non-friend") "enemy, fiend, devil"; *sol* < boto (viz "messenger") "apostle"

Latin: loan word—*olŭtarĭ* < *altare* "altar"
loan translation—*blagosloviti* < *bene-dicere* (viz "well-speak") "bless"; *vĕra* < fides (viz "trust") "the Faith"

The loans also tend to show that the Latin being used was delivered in a Bavarian accent; *mĭša* < missa "mass" shows the characteristic High German "hushing" of the s (cf Kirsch for kirsa "cherry"); and *oplatŭ* < oblatum "offering" shows the devoicing of b (cf Bavarian *peran* for Germanic *beran* "to bear," *upil* for *ubil* "evil"). In some cases the origin is ambiguous, *vŭse-mogy* < *omni-potens* or *all-mahtīg* "almighty," but not Greek—cf *pantokratōr*, literally, "all-strong."

This gross evidence of bilingual worship leads into the main issue that arose from the conversion of the Slavs, namely the acceptability of vernacular scripture and vernacular liturgy. We know from the Freising manuscripts, two penitential prayers and a sermon, which were produced in the ninth century, that a degree of vernacular literacy would soon be in use to develop knowledge of the faith. But in the time of Vergilius, it loomed only as a shadow.

Since Latin was accepted in the western churches as the language of spiritual authority, it must have been used ritually even among people who did not fully understand it; but this led to difficulty on the spiritual importance of getting the grammar right. Vergilius had pronounced valid a baptism where an unscholarly priest had intoned "*baptizo te in nomine Patria et Filia et spiritus sancti*," putting in the wrong words for "of the Father" (*patris*) and "of the Son" (*filii*). His bishop, none other than Boniface himself, would not support him on this. Neither would Rome.*

Initiative from Constantinople

A century of experiences of this kind of dispute between (western) religious authorities may have made the prince of Great Moravia, Rastislav, send a petition eastward, to Emperor Michael III in Constantinople. His letter, sent in 862, asked for

> a teacher capable of explaining the faith to us in our own tongue, so that other countries, seeing this, might imitate us . . .
> "By the mercy of God we are well, and many Christian teachers have come to us from the Latins, the Greeks[†] and the Germans, who teach us various things. We Slavs are simple people and have no one to guide us to the truth and teach us knowledge . . ."[2]

Evidently this is a compilation of tendentious summaries from what must have been an extended diplomatic letter. But the key requests of the prince are two: to gain a vernacular command of the faith that would belong to the

---

* Boniface died in 754, and Vergilius went on to be bishop of Salzburg in his own right. So in this case, the issue of linguistic validity was deferred.

　　Evidently, the two missionary saints never saw eye to eye. Boniface even pursued Vergilius (nicknamed "The Geometer") for heresy, on the ground that he held controversial views on the sphericity of the earth, holding that there could well be people at the antipodes who, cut off by oceans on every side, could never have heard of the saving Word of God. (Isatchenko 1963, pp. 50–53; Cooper 2003, pp. 38, 175.)

† The mention of Greeks is perplexing, since this letter, and the mission it caused, are believed to be the first collaboration between Moravia and Byzantium. Isatchenko 1963, p. 62, argues that it is an allusion to the learning of the Irish in classical languages. He mentions Vergilius's companion, another Irishman, named *episcopus Dobdagrecus*: Bishop Dobda, the Greek.

Moravians (possibly as an example to others); and to cut through the variety of doctrine that came with multiple sources of authority.

The emperor had two such men, the brothers Constantine and Michael. (They would ultimately be known to history by the sacred names they chose toward the end of their lives, Cyril and Methodius). Though Greeks themselves, they had grown up in Thessalonica with Slavic neighbors and—we infer—acquired a basic knowledge of the language, presumably in its Macedonian form. Constantine-Cyril was a philosopher, linguist, and diplomat, with experience of embassies to Samarra in the Arab Caliphate and to the khan of the Khazars. Michael-Methodius had experience in administration of a province with a Slav population, and had also accompanied the embassy to Khazaria. Although Constantine was the younger brother, by about a decade, he was generally seen as the more able of the two—not least by his self-effacing brother—and hence the leader of the expedition to Moravia. At the time he was in his mid-thirties, and Methodius in his late forties.

From a modern perspective, we would say that Constantine, a phonetician with practical experience (probably) of Arabic and Khazar Turkic, had also been working on a script for the Slavonic language. At the time, before the "grammatization" advances of the fifteenth century (in Italy and Spain), this kind of intellectual feat was seen as more a matter of divine inspiration than as practical linguistics. When Constantine had asked if the Moravians had a script (as a precondition for accepting their invitation) Emperor Michael III had told him that in the time of his father and grandfather a Slavic alphabet had been sought but not found. When first asked by the emperor to take up the challenge of "finding" such a script, Constantine had replied:

то кто можеть на водоу бесѣдоу писати или Єретичьско имѧ себѣ обрѣсти?

to kto mojetĭ na vodou besědou pisati ili Eretičĭsko imǎ sebě obrěsti

So who can write speech upon water, or find for himself the name of a heretic?*

---

* *Life of Constantine (Cyril)*, 14:11. The quip is reported in Slavonic, but the conversation of Cyril and the patriarch must have taken place in Greek.

Nonetheless, he does seem to have received inspiration.

There is no direct evidence linking Constantine-Cyril to the Glagolitic script (still in ecclesiastical use in Croatia until the early twentieth century), but it seems that this is what he came up with. Glagolitic script was built up from a selection of Byzantine cryptographic alphabets and alchemical symbols.[3] The point is made that it needed to look un-Greek, in order not to be associated with recent or contemporary Greek theology, particularly icon-oclasm.[4] Glagolitic is quite unlike the much better-known Cyrillic script. Yet Cyrillic is based on the same phonetic analysis of Slavonic made by Cyril, and for that reason alone (as well as sentiment), this name is fitting. Since it was based on the forms of the Greek alphabet, this new Cyrillic had the advantage of being much easier than Glagolitic to learn, for someone already literate in Greek or Latin.

In the spring of 863, the party of missionaries set off, bearing with them a letter from the emperor which is eloquent of the way the initiation of a new script was then seen—not as a solution to an engineering problem, but rather as a kind of miracle, or revelation from God.

> [God] . . . has now, in our time, revealed letters in your tongue, a thing
> which has not happened for a long time, but only in ancient days, so
> that you may be included among the great nations which praise God
> in their own tongue. Moreover, we are sending to you the one to
> whom God has revealed them, a virtuous and a most devout man and
> a most learned philosopher. Therefore accept a gift greater and more
> valuable than gold and silver and precious stones and all transient
> riches.[5]

When they arrived in Moravia, they immediately set to work, selecting and transposing into Slavonic the material for a lectionary (also called an *aprakos*): namely, a digest of Gospel readings, prayers, and ritual formulae for use in Orthodox worship. It is not clear that any actual translation was required[6]—there had been already a century of preaching by the Irish and Frankish clergy based in Regensburg and Salzburg—but since this involved use of a new alphabet, it called for widespread training in the new letters, as well as a vast range of decisions about applying the system piecemeal to the words, and the quite extensive inflexional system of Slavonic grammar.

The spelling system pioneered on the Macedonian dialect spoken in the extreme south, near Thessalonica, turned out to be applicable, and useful, here on the extreme west of the Slavonic-speaking area, to write the dialects that would become Czech, Slovenian, and Serbo-Croat. Linguistically, this is a significant fact.

But Constantine and Michael were laboring in a vineyard that had already received a century of cultivation. Unsurprisingly, this led to friction with the previous laborers, who naturally regarded it as their patch. Moreover, Constantine and Michael were bringing a new doctrine, which emphasized the independent use of the native language and by its very nature tended to undermine the Franks' traditional reliance on scripture in Latin. After all, if Christianity in Latin had been good enough for the Irish, the Saxons, and the Germans, why not for the Slavs too?

"Trilingualism"

The Franks' theological response to the Greek innovators was to appeal to "trilingualism." According to this doctrine, there was nothing coincidental about the choice of languages in which Christianity had first been preached to the world—Hebrew, Greek, and Latin. Rather, by an unconscious, but cosmic, irony, Pontius Pilate had even prefigured them, as he announced Jesus's status to the world in an inscription on the cross where he was crucified.

This trilingualism was in fact a well-known claim in Isidore of Seville's sixth-century encyclopaedia, the *Etymologiae*, a staple of ninth-century education;

> Now there are three sacred languages, Hebrew, Greek, and Latin, which are far the best in all the world. For in these three languages on the cross of the Lord his charge was written by Pilate.[7]

having been pointed out by the poet Prudentius in the latter fourth century;

> Declared by Hebrew pen, by Attic style,
> Declared too by a third, Italia's tongue.
> Pilate commands in ignorance: "Go, scribe,
> in three lines tell what power is crucified.
> The cross's three-fold title, in three tongues,
> let Jewry read and learn, let Greece take note,
> let golden Rome, God-worshipping, behold.[8]

while the theologian Augustine (354–430), slightly later, had detected a deeper reason for the choice of the three:

> In fact, these three languages were superior there to any others: Hebrew, for the Jews who gloried in the law of God; Greek, for the wise of the world; Latin, for the Romans who ruled many, almost all, the nations at that time.[9]

Although this belief in the special status of the three was a common doctrine at the time, it was no part of the Christian creed, much less its implication that no other language was fit for the worship of God. This last claim, in fact, had been repeatedly condemned in the West by councils at the turn of the eighth-to-ninth century.[10]

The correspondence inviting and accepting the Byzantine mission to Moravia makes it clear that what was desired, and promised, was a special script for the Slavs that would enhance their global standing as fully fledged Christians. Furthermore, as a linguist with international experience and theoretical insight from his phonetic research on the Slavonic alphabet, Constantine was not inclined to give trilingualism an ounce of credibility. Instead he produced a long poem of his own (in Slavonic) known as the *Proglas kŭm Evangelieto* "Prologue to the Gospel." In this, he pleaded quite emotionally for the supreme value of what we should now call indigenous literacy. Here is a passage from it:

slyšite nyně otŭ svojego uma,	Hear now with your own mind
slyšite slověnĭskŭ narodŭ vĭsĭ,	Hear, Slavic people all,
slyšite slovo, otŭ Boga prijde,	Hear the Word, for it came from God,
slovo že krŭmę člověčĭskyję dušę,	The Word nourishing human souls,
slovo že krěpę i srĭdĭce i umŭ,	The Word strengthening heart and mind,
slovo se gotovaję Boga poznati.	The Word preparing all to know God.
Jako besvěta radostĭ ne bǫdetŭ	As without light there can be no joy,
oku vidęštju božijǫ tvarĭ vĭsjǫ	For while the eye sees all of God's creation,
nŭ vĭse ni lěpo ni vidimo jestŭ,	Still what is seen without light lacks beauty—

tako i duša vǐsjaka bez bukǔvǔ	So it is with every soul lacking letters,
ne sǔvědǫšti zakona že božija,	Ignorant of God's law
zakona kǔnižǐna i duchovǐna,	The sacred law of the Scriptures
zakona rai božii javljajǫšta.	The law that reveals God's paradise.
Kyi bo sluchǔ gromǐnajego tǫtǐna	For what ear, not hearing
ne slyšę, Boga možetǔ bojati sę?	The sound of thunder, can fear God?
Nozdri že paky, cvěta ne ǫchajǫšti,	Or how can nostrils which smell no flower
kako božǐje čjudo razumějete?	Sense the divine miracle?
Usta bo, jaže sladǔka ne čjujǫtǔ,	And the mouth which tastes no sweetness
jako kaměna tvorętǔ že člověka.	Makes man like stone.
Pače že sego duša bezbukǔvǐna	Even more, the soul lacking letters
javljajetǔ sę vǔ člověčěchǔ mrǐtva.	Grows dead in human beings.[11]

This issue of ideals—on how best to find Christian enlightenment—was of course not susceptible to a purely rational, or even a practical, solution. But there was a political aspect to the dispute too, about the right of Slavs to convert from their previous practice (heavily dependent on Latin sources) to the new materials being created and distributed by the Byzantine mission. And this cried out for a legally binding resolution.

The human problems of introducing the new indigenous-language services were underscored by Richbald, whom the archbishop of Salzburg had appointed the proto-presbyter of Pannonia, a neighboring principality to the south of Moravia. Kocel the prince of Pannonia was an enthusiast for Constantine-Cyril's new letters and invited the two Greek brothers, setting fifty more students to learn the system. This created an impossible situation for Richbald:

A certain Greek, Methodius by name, fundamentally undermined the language and education of the Romans and the writings of the authentic Latin authors with Slavic letters, which had recently been invented; he cheapened Latin in the eyes of the whole people and to some extent also the mass, the Gospels and the church office of those who exercised it in Latin.[12]

The issue echoed on for years, for and against what the Greeks and Slavs called "the trilingual heresy," or rather (as the Greeks defended their position—with copious quotation from scripture) for and against the right of any people to worship God—in spoken and in written form—in whatever tongue they knew. It is impressive that Cyril and Methodius never allowed the level of debate to switch to the issue of a choice between Latin and Greek, which would not have been distinguished in status under "trilingualism"—though the contentious issue of jurisdiction between Rome and Constantinople over Moravia (and the rest of the Slavic world) might then have stood out with tactless clarity. Rather, they maintained the equality of all languages and peoples and the sacred right of any vernacular tongue to be used for all spiritual tasks up to the Holy Communion.[13]

There were debates in Venice, and an invitation of the brothers to Rome (867–869) that (when accepted) seemed to lead to the support of Pope Hadrian II and to Rome's endorsement of the Slavic liturgy. It echoed on past the deaths both of Cyril in Rome in 869 and (sixteen years later) of Methodius, by then archbishop of the Slavs; and it was still being actively defended (a losing battle) by their successors in Moravia against both the new prince of Moravia (Svjatopulk, who had deposed—and blinded—the original inviter, Rastislav) and the Frankish clergy, when the Magyars overran the principality in 907, effectively closing down indigenous use of the script there, and the Slavic liturgy.* The Roman Church's missionary effort would continue through the agency of the Holy Roman Empire (a German monarchy based in Aachen); and Slavic bishoprics would be established at Prague (983), at Griezno in Poland (1000), and at Esztergom in Hungary (1001). But in all these the key role of German clergy, officiating in Latin, was no longer threatened.

---

* Use of the Glagolitic script did however continue in Pannonia, Dalmatia, and Croatia, Slavic lands to the south, though conducting the Roman Catholic rite, rather than the Orthodox. Its use was officially authorized in 1248 by Pope Innocent IV and was perpetuated actively in the liturgy until the mid-twentieth century. For example, the 1935 concordat with the Kingdom of Yugoslavia anticipated the introduction of the Slavic liturgy for all Croatian regions and throughout the entire state.

In this region, then, Serbo-Croat written in Glagolitic played the role associated with Latin in the rest of the Catholic world, until liturgies using modern vernaculars spread after Vatican II (1962–1965).

Value in the Vernacular

However, the Cyrillo-Methodian ideal of indigenous literacy was picked up, now with a strong Orthodox connection, in the more southerly and easterly parts of the Slavic world, first in Bulgaria and Serbia, and then in Rus'.

According to the *Life of Saint Clement*, a Greek source, the Moravian Slavic-language staff had been dispersed with appalling lack of respect in 885, the elders turned out in the cold and the younger staff actually sold into slavery. Many were lost, but among the former, Clement, Naum, and Angelarius managed to reach Belgrade, and thence the safety and welcome of the Bulgarian court in Pliska, now defining itself as Slav and Christian. The tsar of Bulgaria, Prince Boris (to be baptized as Michael), took them in; the prince himself "read selections from the scriptures on their lips." Meanwhile, according to the Slavonic *Life of Saint Naum*, some of the slaves had the good fortune to be put up for sale in Venice just as a representative of the Byzantine emperor was there; he bought them and took them back to Constantinople, where they were treated with honor. By these and other routes, a minimal complement of students of Cyril and Methodius managed to reach Bulgaria. It is not known if any of the texts produced by the brothers were with them, but this is immaterial to the sequel. The skills of Slavic literacy, applied to Bible and liturgy translation, were saved and provided the nucleus of a new, and much less exposed, school.

The Bulgarian court set up not one but two centers of Slavic religious studies, from 886 in Ohrid, and from 893 in their new capital of Preslav. Clement, in Ohrid, became the first bishop of the Bulgarian language and spent his career translating, writing hymns, and instructing children and laity. He remained in touch with Prince Michael, and when the prince died Clement maintained ties with his successor and son Symeon. Naum too may have joined him here.

We only have supposition on which to base a picture of how things were different in Preslav: still, in the capital, greater exposure to Greek, as to other international influences, was likely. If so, this might have led to the origin of the Cyrillic script as we know it, itself really nothing more than a stylistic variant of the Greek alphabet, supplemented with extra letters from Glagolitic where these were needed to adequately represent the sounds of Slavic.

Non-Greek Cyrillic	Б	Ж	Ц	Ч	Ш	Ъ	Ь	Ѣ	Я
Glagolitic	Ⱀ	Ⰶ	Ⰱ	Ⱍ	Ⱎ	Ⰰ	Ⰱ	Ⱑ	Ⰶ
phonetic	b	ž	ts	č	š	ŭ	ĭ	æ	ē

It would have been an aid to those already literate in Greek, probably the majority of those who used it in Preslav, and through its wider accessibility—with no corresponding drawbacks—it gradually supplanted the original script as conceived by Saint Cyril. At least it still bore his name.

Bulgaria's political independence went through an extended period of eclipse under the renewed power of Constantinople (971–1185), but without damage to its church's autonomy. In 996, Vladimir I, *knyaz'* of Kiev, chose to bring Rus' too into the Orthodox fold. The Cyrillo-Methodian principles stayed good, and Rus' was under no pressure to adopt anything but the Slavic rite. More widely, the Orthodox Church, with its patriarch in Constantinople, allowed the principle of indigenous language worship to be applied much more widely: Orthodox churches have provided vernacular versions of the liturgy as the church has spread, most notably (among national churches) in Romania.

This linguistic autonomy, which has been traditional since the time of Cyril and Methodius in the Orthodox churches, had various consequences. These all result from the lesser control that the Orthodox patriarchy has been able to exert: it never required the kind of uniformity in liturgy that has characterized the Roman Catholic Church over the seventeen centuries (until the 1960s) that it remained wedded to its long-term standard language, Latin.

A Claimed Flaw

Freedom to read Holy Scripture in one's own language, the Cyrillo-Methodian ideal, seems nowadays admirable, even incontestable, as a principle. But it did hold dangers that were not wholly imaginary, dangers that were already feared by the Roman Catholic, if not yet the Greek Orthodox, establishment. Essentially, these fears were for the purity of the faith, and its protection from the infection of error. Once scripture was being received through a language uncomprehended by the established guardians of the Christian creed, mistakes could easily creep in and take root in the minds of the unwary.

To an extent, this danger was minimized by nature of Church Slavonic itself. It had been chosen as the vernacular of the Slavs, and so had been pressed into service to be the vehicle for the Slavic liturgy and scriptures, but in at least two ways it was more distant from their daily speech—and closer to the Orthodox tradition—than this would imply.

First of all, it had been "given its letters" by a ninth-century scholar and linguist who was not himself a native speaker: although Constantine-Cyril had been brought up in Thessalonica, close to the Macedonian Slavic zone, and presumably had had some occasion to hear it spoken around him, there is little doubt that he was a Greek, from an elite—hence most likely mono-lingual—family.* Slavonic was, then, characterized by a Greek academic, who may therefore (in this age before general descriptive linguistics had even been dreamed) have added to it, even unconsciously, some features of Greek grammar.

Second, Constantine had had direct experience only of Macedonian Slavic when he invented an alphabet for Slavic generally, and so must have abstracted from any special features of Slavic dialects spoken all over the Balkans and eastern Europe.

There was variety, or at least the beginnings of it, and the table below shows some aspects of that variety, at least as they developed in the following millennium. Distinct from Macedonian, the Slovenes and Czechs represent best what Slavic may have been in Moravia, while Bulgarian and Russian are self-explanatory markers of the communities to which Church Slavonic was exported.

CH. SLAVONIC (GLAGOLITIC, CYRILLIC)	MACEDONIAN (CYR. SCRIPT)	SERBIAN (CYR. SCRIPT)	BULGARIAN (CYR. SCRIPT)	RUSSIAN (CYR. SCRIPT)
otŭče našĭ *Our Father*	otče naš	oče naš,	otče naš,	otče naš,
iže esi na nebesi *Who art in heaven*	**koj** si na nebes**ata**,	**koji** si na nebes**ima**,	**kojto si** na nebes**ata!**	**suščij** na njebjes**ax!**

---

* "The city of Thessalonica . . . had a much more immediate experience of the Slav presence than any other Byzantine city . . . Each morning, when the great gates in the city walls opened . . . groups of Slavs would enter the city and pursue their affairs there . . . the [Greeks] were obliged to learn their language." (Tachiaos 2001, p. 16; and cf pp. 17 and 162, n. 37, on Constantine's ethnic origins.) It sounds like the MIT linguist Ken Hale's child-hood, listening to Spanish and Papago (Tohono O'odham) from friends in school breaks in (officially monolingual) Arizona in the 1940s. (Personal contact)

da svatitŭsē imē tvoe *Hallowed be thy name*	da se sveti imeto tvoe,	da se svti ime tvoje.	da se sveti tvojeto imje;	da svjatitsja imja tvoje;
da pridetŭ ćarstvo tvoe *Thy kingdom come*	da dojde ćarstvoto tvoe,	da dodi ćarstvo tvoje,	da dojdje tvojeto ćarstvo;	da prijdjót ćarstvije tvojó;
da budetŭ volě tvoe *Thy will be done*	da bide voljata tvoja,	da bude volja tvoja,	da bŭdje tvojata volja,	da budjet voljä tvoja;
ěko na nebesi, i na zjemli *As in heaven, so on earth*	kako na neboto, taka na zemjata.	kako na nebu, tako i na zemlji.	kakto na njebjeto, tŭj i na zjemjata	i na zemlje, kak na njebje.

Ch. Slavonic (Glagolitic, Cyrillic)	**Croatian (Glagolitic, Latin)**	**Czech (Latin script)**	**Slovene (Latin script)**	**Polish (Latin script)**
otŭče našĭ *Our Father*	oče naš,	otče náš,	oče naš,	ojcze nasz,
iže esi na nebesi *Who art in heaven*	**koji jesi** na nebesima,	**jenž jsi** na nebesích	**ki si** v nebesih,	**któryś jest w** niebie
da svatitŭsē imē tvoe *Hallowed be thy name*	sveti se ime tvoje.	posvěť se jméno tvé	posvečeno bodi tvoje ime.	święć się imię twoje;
da pridetŭ ćarstvo tvoe *Thy kingdom come*	**dodi kralje**vstvo tvoje,	přijď **králo**vství tvé	pridi **k nam** tvoje **kralje**stvo,	przyjdź **król**estwo twoje;
da budetŭ volě tvoe *Thy will be done*	budi volja tvoja,	buď vůle tvá	**zgodi se** tvoja volja,	bądź wola twoja
ěko na nebesi, i na zjemli *As in heaven, also on earth*	**kako** na nebu, **tako** i na zemlji.	jak v nebi, tak i na zemi	**kakor** v nebesih, **tako** na zemlji.	jako w niebie, **tak** i na ziemi;

1000 Years of Slavic: The Lord's Prayer (first six lines) in Church Slavonic and some modern Slav languages (changed words and morphs in bold; changed sounds underlined).

Looking at these differences, one sees that the relative particles *iže* "who" and *ěko* "as" have survived only in Czech (though in changed form), elsewhere largely replaced by the interrogative pronouns with *k-*. (Russian is distinctive here in using a present participle *suščij* "being"). Another major difference lies in the presence or absence of the definite article *(-to* or *-ta* attached to the end of a noun or pronoun): Macedonian and Bulgarian have it: the rest do not. In choice of vocabulary, in the south (from Croatian to Bulgarian), "come" *pri–ideti* ("go near") has been replaced by *do–ideti* ("go as-far-as"), while from Croatian in the south to Polish in the northwest the archetypal king is no longer Caesar (> *car-*) but Karl (> *kral-/krol-*) i.e., Charlemagne himself.

These are the differences, and they are sufficient to make comprehension difficult nowadays across the Slavic expanse, a vast, and bisected, area: it is more than a thousand miles from Moscow to Serbia, and they are divided by the intervening Hungarians and Romanians. Yet both their churches were (and have remained) heavy users of Church Slavonic, a lingua franca for Orthodoxy that has lasted more than a thousand years.

In fact, it is a mistake to see even Church Slavonic, as it was used over the course of a millenium and across half a continent, as a unitary language, with a single grammar. It was used in a variety of "dialects" (usually called "recensions" ~ редакции *redakcii*), each eclectically incorporating features of a local Slavic language. The language is often also known as Old Bulgarian, recognizing the effect of the founding developmental process that went on in the Bulgarian empire in the tenth to thirteenth centuries; and Bulgarian features (such as the definite article) are sometimes transposed into it. In this form, long before the rise of Muscovy and its empire in the mid-sixteenth century, it was also used as a common language for Slavs more widely.[14]

The existence of Church Slavonic, and its usability in both spoken and written forms, did have a pronounced effect on Slavic self-awareness, something that had been absent from the Slavic peoples in their preliterate days. But if there was anything political about this sense, it was restricted to foreign policy: the cardinal choice whether a tribe should accept Christianity from the church based in Rome or the church based in Constantinople, this in turn determining the choice of alphabet they would use to write their language, and thereafter the spiritual (and other) literature that would become available to them. By and large, Slavic princes who were free to make their own choice (Bulgaria in 865, Serbia in 880, Rus' in 988) opted for Constantinople, but others—all too far from Byzantium, but all too close to the Holy Roman

Empire—turned with dutiful gladness to Rome (Croatia in 925, Bohemia in 955, Poland in 966).

In the ninth and tenth centuries, there would have been a widespread sense—especially in the western realms, loyal to Roman Catholic Christianity—of the dangerous potential of indigenous literacy: had not the scriptures translated into Gothic given rise, and indeed three or four centuries of vigor, to the heresy of Arianism? It had died away, in fact, only when the language itself had largely ceased to be spoken in the seventh century. There was soon an apparent confirmation of this fear in the case of Old Bulgarian.

In the tenth century the heresy of the Bogomils (*bogo-milŭ* "God-dear") arose in Bulgaria, probably in the southern area that corresponds to modern Macedonia; it continued to thrive, despite Orthodox and Catholic resistance, until the fourteenth, sending out offshoots westward especially into Serbia and Bosnia, and later even into Kievan Rus' and to the Cathars in the south of France (twelfth to fourteenth centuries), collapsing only together with the Bulgarian Empire itself under Ottoman assault in 1463. It was a dualist religion, reminiscent of Manichaeism, with a good God creator of the spiritual, and an evil God responsible for the whole physical universe.

There is a famous reference to dualism in Slavic pre-Christian belief in the northern Slav land of Polabia. It was written by the twelfth-century German priest Hermold:

> The Slavs, too, have a strange delusion. At their feasts and carousals they pass about a bowl over which they utter words, I should not say of consecration but of execration, in the name of the gods—of the good one, as well as of the bad one—professing that all propitious fortune is arranged by the good god, adverse by the bad god. Hence also in their language they call the bad god *Diabol*, or *Zcerneboch*, viz the black god.[15]

Hermold's Slavic is faultless, and *černobogŭ* would indeed mean "black god." So it is just possible that the availability of Slavonic as a scriptural and liturgical language made it possible to reconstitute such ancient theological beliefs of the southern Slavs in a more modern and sophisticated theological framework, such as they were learning from Orthodox priests.

If true, this would be an example of vernacular literacy serving to unhinge a people's religious faith, with heirlooms from pagan Slavdom easily absorbed into their Christian creed. But a converse danger of this same ideal has been decried.

Could the fact that Slavs could worship in their own language, without needing to learn a metropolitan lingua franca such as Greek (or Latin), have acted as a brake on cultural development? In being content with their vernacular, were the Slavs missing a necessary stimulus?

This has been suggested by John Meyendorff, recalling the thesis of G. P. Fedotov:

> There is a vital contrast between the evangelization of Western, Germanic barbarians and the adoption of Byzantine Christianity by the Slavs: the Eastern "barbarians" received the Christian faith in their own Slavic language, whereas their Western cousins were called to study Latin . . . Rapidly and successfully "indigenized" in Slavic lands, Christianity never became a vehicle of secular learning . . . In principle, Christian Byzantium avoided hellenizing its converts. It did not impose upon them the study of a foreign language . . . culturally, [Russia]'s initiation to the foreign Byzantine civilization was limited by the language barrier . . .[16]

Likewise, Francis Thomson has analyzed the use that Orthodox Russians made of the literacy that was conferred on them. He emphasizes the limited nature of what was imparted in Slavonic, rather than the withholding of a rich secular linguistic context available in Greek. Scripture and liturgy were provided in vernacular translation—and moreover in a lectionary (апракос *aprakos*) that restricted their actual experience to short and disconnected texts that gave just the minimum required for worship. Thomson maintains that this had the effect of infantilizing Russian religion.

Since they absorbed their Orthodoxy without learning to read the Greek original texts, believers never became competent to master the higher Greek theology that was based on them, and were thereby made vulnerable targets for counterintellectual cults and approaches as they came along.

If this is true, vernacular literacy, rather than unhingeing faith, will have had the effect of impoverishing the content of an otherwise highly sophisticated tradition. Slavs in general, then, would have been the losers, from the missed opportunity to educate their elite in Greek. He writes:

> It was not the Mongols who were responsible for the intellectual isolation of Russia . . . but the fact that the form under which the Christian faith was received in Old Russia was shorn to a great extent . . . of its

intellectual content. This caused an over-valuing of ritual observance, which led inevitably to obscurantism.[17]

This is a highly tendentious conclusion. If true, it would provide some sort of explanation for the readiness of the Russian Orthodox tradition simply to accept what they received from the Greek Orthodox Church, without seeking to adapt it. Such passivity (or perhaps rather, humility) would include features of the *typicon* (τυπικόν "order of service") that seem better adapted to monastic practice than to the typical congregational worship; and the general late Orthodox (fourteenth-century) enthusiasm for *hesychasm* (ἡσυχασμός—"quietness" in Greek), which aims at a direct perception of God through meditation and personal revelation, in an ascetic and a mystical experience, rather than the more outward paths of scriptural study and communal worship typical of western Christianity.[18]

All this from the apparently reasonable proposal that potential converts to the faith should be offered scripture and liturgy in a language that they would understand directly.

These claimed effects of Slavic vernacular literacy—whether realized or not—give us some illustration of its potential, and so why it might be feared as well as desired: they give reasons why pessimistic Christians (notably the Catholics) might have resisted use of popular languages for reasons that were sincere, and not necessarily based on tradition and the protection of privilege.

But since all the evidence is purely evaluative—valuing the gross achievement of Catholic Europe as higher than that of Slavonic Orthodoxy—no firm conclusion can be drawn. Russian Orthodox practice may indeed have tended to be more conservative in thought and practice, and more contemplative in style, than that of western Catholicism. But it is a mere plausible supposition to attribute this to the difference between two styles in which Christianity was imported, one received in the (Slavic) vernacular, and another through a classical foreign language (Latin).

CHAPTER II

Conversion by the Book
The Faith Enforced in Latin America

NACIÓ Conmigo en la Religión el zelo de la conuersión de Gentiles, el qual dio
principio a esta obra, amonedado del Apóstol: <u>Volo vos loqui linguis</u>. Cor. 14.
Instrumento único, que el Espiritu Santo dio para sanar las encanceradas llagas
de la Gentilidad . . . quien podra persuadir a hazer lo que no sabe dezir?

The zeal for conversion of the Gentile, which gave rise to this work, was
born in me from the admonition of the Apostle: [*Latin*: **I wish you to
speak in tongues. 1 Corinthians 15**]. The one and only instrument given
by the Holy Spirit to heal the cancered wounds of being Gentile . . . Who
can persuade anyone to do what he cannot say?

Antonio Ruiz de Montoya, *Tesoro de la lengua Guaraní*
(1639 [1876])

ABOUT A THOUSAND YEARS after their conversion to Catholic
Christianity, the nations of western Europe were given an unprecedented opportunity.

They might enter a previously unknown and unsuspected continent, and
as they gradually discovered its dimensions, they might do to its unprepared
and unsuspecting inhabitants the two great things that the Romans had
done to their own ancestors. These were: to exploit these peoples' military
weakness to subdue them and assume ownership of their world, with all
its treasure; and—as a quid pro quo—to bring them to knowledge of the
spiritual truth of the universe as they understood it, telling them above all
about the ubiquity of sin among the human race, and the redeeming love and
sacrifice of their god, Jesus Christ.

In the taking of America, though, these two steps would occur almost together, rather than with the lapse of centuries that had punctuated Rome's double conquest of Europe.

The first to be offered this implicit deal were the coastal peoples of Europe ruled by the monarchies of Spain and Portugal. And to this deal the Spanish and Portuguese monarchies reacted quite precipitately, in the last decade of the fifteenth century. Somehow, even before any substantial discoveries of land had been made, they had come to believe that a colossal fortune was for the taking across the Atlantic.

Between 1492 and 1500, they had entered claims for all of any lands, sight unseen, from the Caribbean to Brazil, and had them adjudicated, at least officially, by the pope in Rome. At the time, they called the conjectured continent *Terra Firme*. Everyone at the time believed that the serious content of what was being assigned was the right to the domination of India, whether approached by sailing west or sailing east. But the Spanish monarchy's instructions to Colombus, as well as the papal bull of 1493 that justified Spanish ambition, had stressed that the aim in building an empire was to spread the Gospel to the heathen.[1] The stage was set—although no one yet knew it—for the (Catholic) conversion of the Americas.

The challenge was immense, dwarfing at first even their own overweening ambition. As Columbus groped his way around the Caribbean in 1502–1504, he soon realized that each bay at which he landed seemed to be home to speakers of another language: "They no more understand one another than we do the Arabs." Having experienced Taino in the islands of Hispaniola and Cuba, he would have encountered four distinct Chibchan languages—Paya, Miskitu, Guaimí, and Kuna—even in his short run along the coast of what is now Honduras, Nicaragua, and Panama. Later voyagers (Córdoba in 1517, Grijalva in 1518) would have been among the first Europeans to hear some of the many Mayan languages (now called Yucatec, Yok'otan, Huastec), as well as Zapotec and Totonac in southern Mexico, while Cortés in 1519 opened up the interior and revealed that the most widely spoken language was none of these, but Nahuatl. Yet even this was just the masters' language: there were a variety of other mother tongues spoken by peoples under the Aztec dominion across central Mexico: Zoque, Tarasco, Huave, Lenca, Otomí, Chichimeca, Chinantec, Mixtec, and Popoluca being only the biggest.

This was not even an exceptionally multilingual part of Terra Firme on which the Spanish had chanced to make landfall. Ultimately in 1892, the count of la Viñaza would list 493 languages identified by Spanish linguists over three and a half centuries of research in the Americas. (Nowadays, missionary organizations, such as SIL International estimate the original number of indigenous languages spoken in the Americas at the time of contact as more than three times this total, about two thirds of them still spoken.) To spread the Gospel, then, there was an immense task of communication: all the more, given that a new language to learn means a new community to contact and conciliate, with a group identity all its own.

But there was one mitigating circumstance. The Americas had their local tradition of imperialism, particularly in the places that the Spanish conquered first, Mexico and Peru. In both these areas, lingua francas—what the Spanish would call *lenguas generales*, the Portuguese *linguas gerais*—had spread so that there was a degree of bilingualism with a common language. South of Peru too, other lingua francas had their spread, though less evidently from military conquest: Aymará across into Charcas (what is now Bolivia),[2] then Guaraní down across Paraguay toward the drainage of the Rio de la Plata;[3] and to the east and north, widely across Brazil in both the Paraná and the Amazon river systems, there was Tupi, a very close relative, almost a dialect, of Guaraní.[4]

Fundamentally, as the peoples of the American continents rapidly succumbed to the Hispanic conquistadores and their invasion forces, the problem became how to bring an uncharted diversity of tribes and cultures, all radically new to the European world, to a common faith in the Christian (specifically, the Roman Catholic) God.

The profusion of languages was just the beginning. Diversity continued with the territories and political affiliations of the people living there, the ways of life and economy, and the belief systems. These sometimes posed radical challenges to any European sense of human decency. The American natives included peoples like the Aztecs, the Maya, and the Chibcha, whose dominant tribes routinely cut open the chests and plucked out the hearts of captives in sacrifice; like the Taino, Caribs, Arawak, and Tupi peoples of the South American coasts on the Atlantic who practiced cannibalism on members of enemy tribes; and (less horrendous—but still shocking or sensational to civilized Europeans) the stark nudity practiced by many tribes in Brazil in their everyday life. Everywhere too there seemed to be practices more familiar from heathendom in the old world: formal polygamy as well as sex apparently regardless of discipline, divination based on animal life and the weather, and worship of pagan idols in temples and shrines.

The solution, as it presented itself to the invaders, was first of all to take military control, and endeavor to stamp out unacceptable practices as and when they came to the notice of the European authorities. If, indeed, they survived: after Columbus's discovery of the Caribbean Islands, and the uncontrolled colonization that followed, the whole indigenous population went extinct within a century. Cortés in Mexico, Pizarro in Peru, Jiménez de Quesada in the northen Andes, had each deposed the thitherto legitimate authority and set up his own regime in the name of his king. The distancing that was intrinsic to confrontation with an uncontacted people gave a power and compulsion to their promotion of the faith. This was not how the Catholic missionaries had proceeded across the Roman Empire, and beyond into the farthest extremities of Europe.

Since the Spanish and Portuguese began their entry into the Americas with military invasions, there was no early conciliation of native pagan custom, as had happened a millennium before in most parts of northern Europe: the Goths and other Germanic peoples, after all, had commanded respect for their traditional, and still all too dangerous, military prowess, as well as their social dignity as kings and war bands, even as they gradually yielded piecemeal to the greater spiritual prestige of the Roman clerics.

The second step after military imposition was to begin direct contact with the thinking—and speech—of the people. This involved two tasks: to identify their languages, and to analyze them so as to make them tools of communication.

As it happened, Europe in this period was for the first time giving recognition—and then effective grammatical analysis—to all its vernacular languages.* Appropriately, too, this intellectual movement—like the conquest of the New World—was centered on Spain. Its charismatic leader was the linguist Antonio de Nebrija, who had presented his brand-new analysis of Castilian Spanish, *Gramática de la lengua castellana*, the first ever, to Queen Isabella before the departure of Christopher Columbus to seek new realms for the Spanish crown to conquer. This work had followed his similarly elegant teaching grammar of the Latin language, *Introductiones latinae*, whose use had been taken up at schools to become the favored path to classical literacy in Spain. Intellectually, language analysis was all the rage; and (for the first time in history) literate scholars set themselves to work on new, unknown languages, to find their rules, and so make them learnable.

---

* A movement known as *grammatisation*, and described at length in Auroux 1994.

So the skill of grammar-writing—and experience of how the use of grammars can accelerate the learning of new languages—was present. Translation was becoming a technology, rather than a miracle to be prayed for. And as it became clear that large-scale lingua francas were current in significant parts of the Americas, the task of encoding and then diffusing the novel message of the Lord began to look feasible. Reaching most of the population of Iberian-controlled America, innumerable as were its tongues, was not so unreasonable after all.*

In fact the bilingualism that was achieved—and the Spanish-dominated Mexican society that arose—was not based on study, but was the predictable result of the taking of indigenous brides and concubines by the Spanish conquerors and immigrants: mixed-language households became widespread, as did bilingual children who grew up in them. But for the active propagation of the Christian faith, which depended on exact knowledge of written language, the early attempts by the missionaries at linguistic fieldwork cannot be overlooked.

Learning and Teaching the Languages

From what had been close to a zero base in 1520[†]—the year the Spanish conquest of Mexico was achieved—conscious language learning was begun. A notable opening event was the landing in May 1524 of a group of Franciscans, who became known as "the twelve apostles of Mexico." A month later, they had reached the region of the capital, Tenochtitlán, and the neighboring land of Tlaxcala, and founded four separate monasteries. Here they set about their mission, preaching and teaching, all the while attempting

---

* Furthermore, especially in Mexico, there were other languages besides Nahuatl, which had large populations, and relatively large communities: Tarasco (now called Purépecha), Mixtec, and Zoque in the southwest, and a closely related group of Mayan languages, led by Huastec, Quiche, Yucatec, and Kaqchikel, in the southeast. These also were early analyzed and utilized by missionaries.

† Already in 1500 a Franciscan mission had reached Columbus's first landfall, Santo Domingo in the Caribbean, but the native (Taino) population first contacted there died out, through illness and abuse, almost before their language could be observed, let alone learned and used for preaching. So Taino and its related dialects in the Antilles (so-called "Black Carib") were never the subject of the Spanish missionaries' grammatical analysis.

to learn the ambient language, which in all these places was Nahuatl, the principal language of the previous Aztec empire.

The chronicler Gerónimo de Mendieta, writing three generations later, offers some nice testimony of the methods employed:

> Letting go for a time their personal dignity, at break times they would play with [the children] with straws and pebbles, to get beyond any awkwardness in communication. And they always had paper and ink in hand, and when they heard a word from an Indian, they would write it down, and the intent with which he said it. And in the afternoon the priests got together and talked over their scripts, and did their best to agree on the apparently most suitable Spanish equivalent for these words. And it could happen that what they thought they had heard one day appeared wrong the next.[5]
>
> ... Some of the children who were a bit bigger came to understand what they were saying; and as the children saw the friars' desire to get hold of their language, they not only corrected their mistakes, but also asked them many questions, which gave them great satisfaction.[6]

It was ever thus; and not only for Nahuatl, but concurrently for a number of other languages beyond, through Yucatán and Guatemala, and much farther south into New Granada (modern Colombia), Peru, the Chaco, and Brazil. Twelve Dominicans arrived in 1525, a year after the Franciscans, and then in 1533 twelve Augustinians. The Jesuits, only founded in 1534, first arrived in the Americas in 1549, at Bahía in Brazil, and soon created a reputation for pressing back the borders of the Christian mission.

Soon effective study of the local native language would go from being an impressive achievement to a minimum requirement. The Second Church Council of Mexico, in 1565, contained the determination:

> We order that all the priests [curas] set themselves with great diligence to learn [deprender] the tongues of their districts, under penalty that, if they are negligent in this, they will be removed from the village [pueblo] in which they are, and will not be provided with another.[7]

And by 1578 the Council of the Indies, the King's executive arm in the colonies, could issue a requirement that all parish priests, as a condition of tenure, learn the language of their parishioners.[8] The stakes were thereby raised: priests must not just exhibit due diligence, but must actually be competent.

After a generation of familiarity, Spanish clerics at last felt that they had sufficient mastery of some of the languages to write them up as grammars and dictionaries. There is a report of an early grammar of Nahuatl by the first bishop of Mexico, Juan de Zumárraga, from 1532, but it has not survived. The first work still extant was written in 1547: Andres Olmos's magisterial analysis of Nahuatl,* smartly followed by other grammars, on Huastec (1548), Mixtec (1550), Kaqchikel (1553), Tarasco (aka Michoacán and now Purépecha; 1555), Quiche (aka Utlateco; 1556), Quechua (1560), a joint work on Chiapanec, Zoque, Tzeltal, and Chinantec (1560), and Zapotec (1564).

These books were just the beginning. The first manuscript work on a language was usually a *Doctrina christiana*, providing a translated version of basic prayers, a creed, and a catechism. Later there would be an *Arte*, or grammar, and a lexicon or *Diccionario*. The *Doctrina* could be put straight into the hands of native speakers, once they were taught to read; perhaps more often, it might simply have been read to them by Europeans who were themselves as yet uncomprehending of the American languages on the page. By contrast, grammars and dictionaries were only of use to fellow missionaries. Some works were entitled *cartilla*, primer or introductory reader, but these were themselves constructed as a compilation of basic religious texts, listing the beliefs and the duties required of a good Christian. This clearly shows the clerics' view of the first, and probably the only, purpose of literacy for Indians.

Soon the printing presses were brought into service of these newly analyzed languages. The first grammar to appear in print was Santo Tomás's work on Quechua, *Grammatica o arte del la lengua general de los Indios de los Reynos del Perú*, published from Valladolid, Spain, in 1560. The first Nahuatl grammar to come out in a printed edition was Alonso de Molina's *Arte* in 1571, published on the spot in Mexico City. Other significant first-edition printed grammar-dictionaries, of interest for the promotion of Christianity to large numbers in the Americas, were those of the Portuguese José de Anchieta on Tupi (termed on its title page as *lingoa mais usada na costa do Brasil*), in Coimbra, Portugal, in 1595; of the Italian Ludovico Bertonio on Aymará, in Rome, in 1603; of Bernardo de Lugo on Muysca (aka Chibcha)

---

* Friar Olmos reputedly became fluent in Nahuatl, Totonac, Huastec, and Tepehuá. In 1560 he produced a trilingual grammar and dictionary of the former three.

in Madrid, in 1619; of Juan Coronel on Maya, in Mexico City, in 1620; and of Antonio Ruiz de Montoya on Guaraní, also in Madrid, in 1639. Only the linguists of New Spain (modern Mexico) had access to a printing press in their own country.

The fact that learned and reliable analyses of languages were becoming available did not mean that all, or even most, of the friars and priests active in the American colonies would profit from them. Throughout the three centuries that the empire existed, the typical Spaniard was notorious even among Europeans for his lack of interest or competence in foreign languages,* and the religious were no exceptions to this rule. Although the State required competence in the vernacular as a condition of appointment for priests, one of the recommendations of the Third Lima Council in 1582–3, providing for the actual state of pastoral care of the Indians, was that they should take care to spread the good linguists around the parishes: incompetent priests were still a problem.

In general, the clergy in the church hierarchy were less diligent in acquiring language skills than were the friars; but even the Jesuits, whose reputation was unmatched for bilingualism in the Americas, had a provincial head in Lima who in a 1601 letter to headquarters in Rome argued that Quechua competence was an unnecessary luxury for the order's elite. (His case was rejected, following the 1594 ruling that all Jesuits were obliged to study their local language.)

The issue came to a head in Bogotá in 1606, when the president of New Granada, Juan de Borja, required all clergy there thenceforth to preach in Chibcha. For nigh on three decades, it had been a scandal that few priests spoke the language, and this despite the compulsion on all of them to attend at least one year of language classes. Continuing failure to make progress with conversions was attributed largely to this language barrier. Borja actually named just fifteen Spaniards as having competence in Chibcha in 1606. Still, the new decree was ineffective, despite the grammars produced in this period by Jesuit José Dadey (probably over 1605–1620[9]) and the Dominican Bernardo de Lugo (1619). A major additional problem that particularly

---

* This "silence of Pizarro" is illustrated in painful detail, across Europe and the Spanish colonies, in Kamen 2002, pp. 494–506. One anecdote from Mexico in the 1570s: a Spanish judge Alonso de Zorita asked a Nahuatl speaker why the Indians were so prone to evil ways: "Because you don't understand us," he replied, "and we don't understand you and don't know what you want."

afflicted New Granada seems to have been rapid decline in the population of the language's native speakers, precisely documentable for the city of Tunja to the north. A generation later, in 1641, a new royal decree recognized a new situation, ordering the replacement of Chibcha by Spanish in official use.[10]

In practice, the competent linguists (known as *lenguas*, or *lenguaraces*) were channeled into field missions, while the plum positions in theology or administration went to others: in Brazil, Jesuits were said to face a career choice between Tupi and theology.[11]

But language requirements would continue to rankle, even if they were largely circumvented in practice. It is notable that when, in a later age, the decree went out on April 16, 1770, for all languages but Spanish actually "to be abolished," its only concrete requirement was for bishops thenceforth to appoint curates regardless of their competence in other languages.

But whatever the practical constraints from human failings on becoming multilingual, those grammar books demonstrate that the language barrier was no longer impassable. The real work of conversion could begin—a process that was known without embarrassment as *adoctrinamiento* "indoctrination." And it would continue for at least two centuries, from the middle of the sixteenth century until that famous royal decree of 1770, to abolish the use of native languages.

American Values

In the sixteenth and seventeenth centuries a sustained attempt was made to convert a whole continent's sense of right and wrong in favor of Catholic Christianity, an attempt that was backed up with a self-righteous determination, where persuasion failed, to use extreme force, not excluding torture and the death penalty. From a modern perspective, this seems a morally dubious enterprise, at the very least.

And some scruples did get expressed. The unquestioned spiritual benefit of conversion was used as a justification, granted specifically by the pope (such as Pope Alexander VI's *Inter caetera* of 1493), for Portuguese and Spanish arrogation of power, through armed invasion, into otherwise peaceable and nonthreatening kingdoms. But the activist humanitarian Bartolomé de las Casas (1484–1566), who had begun his career as a colonist in the Caribbean, went beyond protesting at the gratuitous cruelty he knew to be practiced on the Indians to reject the kind of mass conversion to which they were being subjected, especially by the Franciscans. His belief that baptism was invalid without full understanding, and his respect for the convert's reason, was actually asserted in the papal bull *Sublimis Deus* of 1537.

José de Acosta (1539–1600), himself a Jesuit active in conversion before becoming an apologist for overall policy, insisted that the Spanish were the pope's agents in converting this part of the world, directly comparable with Saint Mark, sent by Saint Peter to convert Egypt, or Augustine sent by Pope Gregory I to convert England. The fact that they did it through use of an empire, rather than a peaceful mission, was an "historic instrument of Providence."[12] He did not overlook the injustices committed by Spaniards, but triumphantly used them as an argument in favor of the valid conversion of the Indians, since "men who have suffered serious wrongs from Christians still have not cast Christ aside." (The Stockholm syndrome, whereby victims find themselves in thrall to their abusers, was evidently inconceivable to him, and probably to his audience.)

The Spanish remained concerned about the ethics of their treatment of the Indians, resulting in the passing of many Laws of the Indies, including the Laws of Burgos (1512) and the New Laws (1542, explicitly inspired by the protests and appeals of Bartolomé de las Casas): however, both these codes proved unenforceable when they met with armed resistance on the ground from the Spanish *encomenderos*, the very private interests that they had been drafted to control. Overall, it is arguable that the Spanish and Portuguese discoveries in the Americas, by opening them up to adventurers from Europe, created some of the modern world's first revolutionary political orders, dynamic situations of shifting power that they could not fully understand, and that even their (formally unchallenged) royal authority was unable to dominate.

This failure to enforce their highest standards did not at any point lead to doubt in the moral monopoly of the Catholic faith. By the nature of things, the clear failures were seen as due to the fallen human nature of the settlers, perhaps even of the missions, not to any inadequacy of the religion being preached, nor indeed any unsuitability to the situation of the subject population, taken unawares though they had been after unknown eras of separate existence from the rest of humanity.*

---

* Amazingly, José de Acosta was already conjecturing in 1590 that the Americas had been populated from Asia in the distant past. (Prieto 2010.)

Spain and Portugal, the two major powers—which were undisputedly Catholic—were pathbreakers in their access to the Americas, their zones of exploration demarcated to the west and east by the Treaty of Tordesillas in 1494; and from 1580 to 1640 they were even under a common crown. Although the powers of northwestern Europe (France, England, and the Netherlands)— where Catholicism was, to say the least, disputed—would increasingly challenge them after 1600, they largely had central and south America as their exclusive field of operations during the sixteenth century. There was some irritation from "Antarctic France," a Protestant foundation by the French in the area of Rio de Janeiro from 1555 to 1567, but this was riven by its own confessional dispute (over the Eucharist—between Huguenots and Calvinists) and later eliminated by the Portuguese.

In Europe, these contending powers all had reason to blacken Spain's name and reputation for its colonial policy. In the north, they were establishing Protestant reformed churches to be free of the abuses they associated with Catholic powers like Spain. France, the great central power of western Europe, resented the great and growing powers to its south, especially at the turn of the fifteenth to sixteenth century, when they seemed to have closer links to the papacy. Spain and England were tied by a marriage alliance over the period 1554–58, partly to balance France; but in England, Spain became increasingly unpopular, and from 1585 to 1604 they too were at war. Meanwhile, the Netherlands had begun eighty years of a bitter independence struggle from Spain in 1568. Bartolomé de las Casas's original denunciation of the Spanish early treatment of the Caribbean Indians (*Brevísima relación de la destrucción de las Indias*) had been written in 1542 and first published in 1552 for domestic consumption. The Netherlands ensured that the Dutch translation did not go out of print between 1578 and 1648.[13]

This horrendous record of abuse of innocent natives was a handy, if not very fair, stick with which to beat the Spanish.* Its impact was combined with tales of heartless autos-da-fé of the Inquisition, show trials and public executions to stamp out any deviance from Catholic orthodoxy (though in

---

* None of these powers—except perhaps Spain's fellow Catholics, the French in Canada— when they gained American colonies of their own, were distinguished for better treatment of the indigenous people than the Spanish. It was almost as if fear, intolerance, and unbridled exploitation were inseparable from European first contact with American First Nations. But perhaps more to the point ethically, none of the other powers aspired to match Spain's legal efforts, albeit ineffective, to safeguard the natives' interests and well-being in the Americas.

all honesty, the indigenous populations of America were largely left immune from this organ of the Spanish church). The Spanish, to this day, resent *La Leyenda Negra*, the black legend, which was put about to discredit them and their colonial empire. But although Catholic evangelism could have been represented as an essential part of a Spanish-Catholic conspiracy to carve up the world, the Europeans' propaganda war against the Spanish failed to engage with the ethical question of forcible conversion in the Americas.

Decent Obscurity

Various reasons explain why the European outsiders were never able to focus unfavorable attention on Spain and Portugal's propagation of faith to their Indian subjects. The Spanish missonaries found various ways to isolate the new converts in a sort of Christianity to which the rest of the world, and specifically Spain's enemies and neighbors in Europe, had no access.

First, the process was managed in a local language, usually the *lengua general* or command language of the region, certainly a language of wider communication of a kind, but only within some zone of the Americas. Especially in the early days, there would also have been much rote learning of prayers and creeds in Latin; but this would not have expanded into any general capability in that language, which might have allowed common access to outsiders. Notable, too, by its absence from the process was the vernacular of the colonists themselves, whether Castilian Spanish or Portuguese. This was laughingly noted as a means to keep the worst elements of contemporary life out of the Indians' way: but of course, it also kept them well away from the uncontrolled discourse of Europeans.

Second, conversion was largely in the hands of the mendicant orders, under particular "rules." These were charitable foundations made up of "regular clergy" who had taken vows of poverty, chastity, and obedience, and not integrated into the secular church hierarchy. These were, principally, the Orders of Saint Francis, Saint Dominic, Saint Augustine, and Our Lady of Mercy, and the Society of Jesus—better known as the Franciscans, Dominicans, Augustinians, Mercedarians, and Jesuits. Having an autonomous status that linked them directly to the papacy, and no geographical infrastructure of dioceses and parishes, they were able to spread their efforts over the Americas as a whole and target communities, often on the frontiers of Spanish settlement and control, where they saw particular need for evangelical work and pastoral care. So, for example, the whole Mayan region of Yucatán in the southeast of Mexico was designated in the 1560s as the province of the Franciscan order; and in 1609 the Jesuits received, from the government in Asunción, a commission to set up a chain of settlements along the Paraná River (on the borders of modern Paraguay, Argentina, and Brazil), armed for self-defense, principally against raiding slavers from São Paulo, known as *bandeirantes* ("banner-men"). By 1641 these Jesuit outposts had established themselves as the famous *reducciones*, which functioned like an autonomous Jesuit republic until the expulsion of the order from the Americas in 1767. All over the Spanish Americas, from California to Tierra del Fuego, missionary work continued in remote communities while the cities and towns were westernized through the day-to-day commercial and economic activities of mestizos, increasingly in Spanish rather than indigenous languages.

Third, the kind of Christian written materials which the missionaries used for their work were not the common scriptures of the Holy Bible. In the first generation after conquest there had been much encouragement of natives to commit to memory the prayers from the *Doctrina* (chiefly the Apostles' Creed, the Lord's Prayer [*Pater Noster*], the *Ave Maria*, and two sets of commandments—those of the Lord, and those of the Catholic church—which listed the required observances of a Christian) in Latin or Spanish. But after the 1560s much greater emphasis was placed on presenting the faith in language comprehensible to the converts—the process known straightforwardly as *adoctrinamiento*, "indoctrination."

Doctrinas Instead of Scripture

The essential was to ensure that, whatever the language, they should be presented only with doctrine that was correct. A major step in this direction was the Third Council held in Lima, Peru, in 1582–83. This agreed a form of words for the principal documents used in the Americas to propagate the faith, derived from those propounded by the recent Council of Trento in Italy in 1545–63. The Roman Catholic Church would thenceforth have a common form of written document on which to base its propagation of the faith in the Americas—soon to be translated into Quechua, Aymará, and a host of other indigenous languages. But this was a derived and composite set of texts, resulting from traditional prayers and theological debates down the ages, and designed to be useful for pastoral care of Christian souls.

It comprised:

1. the Catechism (in short and long forms, and including the prayers of the *cartilla* and a number of lists—of commandments, sacraments, and acts of mercy, but usually many more;
2. the Confessional (organized according to the Ten Commandments, but customized with characteristic Andean sins); and
3. a set of short, model Sermons.

The first two elements, Catechism and Confessional, were in question-and-answer format, with a notional priest asking the questions, and the believer supplying the right answers. But in practice and in theory, the believer was expected to memorize it all.

These texts—or close analogs to them—as translated into the other general languages of the Americas, became the basis for Catholic instruction throughout the Americas for the next two centuries. Their use was combined with sacraments, homilies, and pastoral care supplied by priests in indigenous languages and in Latin.

It is interesting—from a more general Christian perspective—that the church did not make any direct use of the accepted original scripture, namely the Holy Bible itself.

The reason for this rather surprising policy of the Roman Catholic Church was a doctrine on the proper use of authority. Since Roman Catholics hold that the church itself is the proper source of authority on the Christian faith, they hold that the church must be actively involved when Holy Writ is interpreted, for fear of error. Hence it discouraged independent reading of the Bible by lay Christians—and was long content to leave its text in the decent obscurity of a language that had become impenetrable to the public: Latin. This conveniently unified the texts consulted by all priests, but equally conveniently made it accessible only to them, who were trained in its proper interpretation.*

---

* A Spanish New Testament (from Erasmus's Greek) was printed, dedicated, and delivered to Carlos V in Brussels in 1543, but was swiftly condemned and destroyed.

The first complete Spanish-language Bible to be published in Spain came out only in 1793, although a papal decree of 1757 had permitted the reading and printing of vernacular Bibles under some conditions (Ellingworth 2007, pp. 120).

This was actually anticipated by the first printed Bible in Portuguese. This was produced in parts from 1719 to 1751, not in Portugal, nor Brazil, but in Batavia in the Dutch East Indies—at much the same time as the Bible in Malay, 1668–1758 (Ibid., pp. 130, 129).

It was always an embarrassment to have Holy Scripture on the *Index Librorum Prohibitorum*, so clear bans on printing or reading the Bible are hard to find. The clearest are some of the rules of the Index, authorized by Pius IV (1564):

> **Translations of the New Testament** made by authors of the first class of this Index, **are allowed to no one, since little advantage, but much danger, generally arises from reading them** . . . Inasmuch as **it is manifest from experience that if the Holy Bible, translated into the vulgar tongue, be indiscriminately allowed to every one, the rashness of men will cause more evil than good to arise from it,** it is, on this point, referred to the judgment of the bishops or inquisitors.[14]

This belief, that the church holds the valid interpretation of the Bible, explains another doctrine of the Council of Trento, namely that authority rests with Jerome's Latin translation, the Vulgate, rather than the Hebrew, Aramaic, and Greek originals of its various constituent books. The essential thing was to insist on a single supreme source of authority, and not to recognize different sources that, through fallible, human understanding, could give rise to conflict.

The net effect of this was to deny any need for versions of original Scripture in vernacular languages, especially not if intended for those who had been judged unworthy to aspire to ordination. The only texts we can consider as effective "scriptures" in the time of the Roman Catholic conversion of the Americas were the Catechism, the *cartilla*, and the Confessional. All these could be translated into general languages of wider communication—and at need into other vernacular languages—without too great concern that authoritative, and hence potentially disruptive, texts were being created.

In creating this basic, new "scripture for learners," the church had made a signal, and creditable, effort to accommodate the indigenous languages of the Americas, and so too the indigenous and mestizo people who grew up speaking them. But this effort to reach out and embrace them in their true diversity never succeeded in reaching the further goal of fully integrating and accommodating the Indians, or even the mestizos, into a single Christian community on a par with the Spaniards and Portuguese and their fully European progeny.

One effect of translating the faith into the newly learned languages of America was the rise in importance of the *Doctrina*, as defined at Trento and promulgated in Lima. It provided a common semantic interpretation (legible in Spanish or Portuguese) for a set of parallel texts that introduced, and largely defined, the Christian faith for Catholic congregations. The unity of these texts was a product of the common need to project this extended, abstract subject matter to many different indigenous peoples, diverse communities who yet had two things in common: the fact that they had suddenly become subjects of the Spanish or Portuguese king, unknown across a vast uncrossable ocean; and a set of compulsory propositions that they were required to believe and obey, on pain of punishments that threatened to be literally endless.

Doctrinal Effects

Besides causing a common form in which the faith would be put into them, was there any other way in which the indigenous languages affected the content of the Catholic faith? The faith itself, what we have called *Ecclesia Ritus Latini*—the Church of the Latin Rite—had been defined over centuries in various parts of Europe and the lands to its east, and was not available for modification either for the Iberian part of Europe, or—much less —for the inhabitants of the American continents who found themselves, for reasons beyond their own control, new members of the Catholic church. The church would not formally compromise, or even temporize, with its newest converts. The process of *extirpación de idolatrías*—"uprooting of idol-worship"—which was a constant background to the church's mission throughout the Americas between 1570 and 1660 and was prosecuted (if irregularly) with grim vigor, reminds us how severe the missionaries could be in defending orthodoxy as they saw it.

On the other hand, the church did aspire to win the devotion of its new communities, not simply to enforce their conformity and sullen obedience. And for this to happen, new miracles were needed, new creative acts of the Holy Spirit that would bring the souls of American natives and mestizos to see that their salvation lay with Christ, and so to accept it humbly. And yet surprisingly few additions of this kind were inspired by the American languages and the shared imaginations—of rituals, ethics, and even spirit reality—on which their understanding was built.

Some (notably Bernardino de Sahagún) viewed the Virgin of Guadalupe, already popular as a saint, as the Aztec goddess Tonantzin in poor disguise.

Whatever the truth of this, the cult was there, and the church used it to the
greater glory of Christ. In other cases an analogy seems to have won its way
into Christian practice in Mexico, without being offically sanctioned. The
Aztecs had used pictographic scrolls, in place of hieroglyphic or alphabetic
writing, in their communications—most famously to record tribute lists.
That use had been much more general, and continued for some generations
after the conquest, even though Nahuatl itself was soon being used in alphabetic script. But these pictograms also appeared on the new church buildings
that were going up, apparently giving a new resonance to old icons. Serge
Gruzinski, influential recent analyst of the Aztec conversion, has pointed
out:

> The eagle [*quauh-tli*], or greenstone ... ["jade"—*chalchiuh-tli*] and
> the Fifth Sun *Nahui Ollin* ["sun of the earthquake"] decorate
> numerous Christian sanctuaries ... was it not necessary, to delay the
> death of the fifth and last Sun, to feed it with the precious water
> (*chalchiuh-atl*), water that was none other than the blood of the pris-
> oners of the sacred war (*atl-tlachinolli*), whose glyph (which inter-
> twines water and fire) also crept onto church façades?
>
> Could it be ... an indigenous interpretation or transcription of
> Christian themes? This was undoubtedly the case when the glyph for
> precious water was associated on Franciscan coats of arms with the
> blood of Christ rather than with the blood of sacrificial victims.[15]

However, this proceeding was not taken up as a tactic for spiritual contact
with the pagans' souls, wherever they might be found. The identification,
even the mere association, of a Christian personage with spirits worshipped
in a previous era was not accepted by Catholic missionaries as a useful intermediate step on the way to full orthodoxy. This was despite the fact that the
missionaries noticed a large number of surprising parallels between cult
objects and symbols of the pagan past and the practice of Christianity.

The Mayans had had an initiation ceremony reminiscent of baptism,
known as *zihil* "birth," or *caa put zihil* "two times birth,"* which was recognized as such by their great persecutor, bishop Diego de Landa.[16] They also
set up monumental crosses, of various sizes, which are representations of

---

* The Aztecs too had an analogue to baptism, *nequatequiliztli*, involving a combination of
  washing and name-giving.

a world-tree, known as *yax-che'* "first tree" or *yax cheel kab* "first tree in the world."*[17] The slightly different word *ya'x* means green, and this is the color of the center, reminding that there is a further world-tree (each of a different color) in each of the four cardinal directions.[18] These trees—ritually identified with ceiba trees, also called *ya'xché*—are symbols of the universe, but not instruments of redemption; yet in the Mayan creation myth recorded in the *Popol Vuh*, it is on a calabash tree (*tzima*) that a slain god's skull is hanging when it miraculously spits fluid to impregnate a virgin (*Xkik'* "Blood Woman"): she conceives Hero Twins, Jun Junahpu and Xbalanke, who will save the world from the power of Death and the Underworld (*Xibalbá*).

The major turning points of the Hero Twins' subsequent struggle with and triumph over the Lords of Death match not only in quality, but actually in Mayan diction, the passions of Christ, as reported in the creed within the K'iche' *Doctrina*.

So we have in the K'iche' *Doctrina* (spelling modernized, and with a literal gloss)

uchí Poncío Pílato	suffered under Pontius Pilate
*x-q'axq'obik x-**rip**ik*	was-nailed <u>was-spread</u>
chu-wach Cruz	on-face Cross
xq'amik	died
xmuq'kiq'	was buried
<u>*xq'ah chi xibalba*</u>	<u>descended to Hell</u> (lit. place-of-fear)
*rox q'kih x-u**q'aztah** ríb*	third day was-<u>revived</u> for-himself
chik'ixol e q'amínaq'	from-among the dead
<u>*x-aq'am chi q'ah*</u> . . .	<u>ascended to sky</u>

while correspondingly in the *Popol Vuh*, we find

Ta xkik'ulawachij kiwach	Then they faced each other
*Xki**rip** kiq'ab' kikabichal*	both of them <u>spread their arms</u>
E pu jupujuj ta xebek pa choj . . .	and head first they went into the pit oven . . .
<u>*Xeqaj chi xibalba* . . .</u>	They <u>descended to Hell</u> (lit. place-of-fear) . . .

---

* The Aztecs too had a symbol of the cross, *nepaniuhtoc* (cf *nepantla* "in the middle"), representing the confluence of the four directions.

Nabe chikikamisaj kib	First they would kill themselves
Xa wi xere lib'aj chik'astaj	then immediately they would
wi chi u–wach . . .	<u>revive</u> in their face . . .
Ju suk'u xe'aq'an chi kaj.	Then at once they <u>ascended into the sky</u>.
Jun k'u q'ij	One of them is sun
Jun nay pu ik' chike.	and the other one is moon.[19]

Just as Jesus was crucified (in a spread-eagled position), then descended into Hell, then rose again, and finally ascended into Heaven, so the Twins fell to their deaths in a spread-eagled position, descended into Xibalba, were then revived (as fish faces), and rose up to the sky (where they became the sun and the moon).

The first known text of the *Popol Vuh* "Book of Council" dates from 1701–1703, a copy made by a Spanish friar named Francisco Ximénez, but it is presumed to reflect a much older original that could well predate the conquest of the Maya (which was not completed until 1697, after two centuries of campaigns). If so, this shows that Christ's passion was told in very similar terms to the native scripture of heroic victory over death; if not, it suggests that the oldest and most complete Maya scripture that we have is itself a composite that has already been profoundly influenced by Christian themes.

Farther south toward the center of South America, the Tupi and Guaraní had believed in an *yby marā-e'ӱ* (Guaraní *yvy mara-eӱ*), a "land without evil," where there was no more death and one could meet one's dead ancestors; indeed they had devoted great efforts to pilgrimages in order to find it.[20] They also had a cultural hero Sumé, a white man with a long beard, who had brought the good law (*tekokatu*), possibly the wide-ranging apostle Saint Thomas (São Tomé to the Portuguese). This same saint (an apostle known to have wandered far) was also claimed for Inca prehistory, both by Pachacuti Yamqui in the early 1600s and identified with the deity Tunupa, the storm-god of Titicaca, by Francisco de Avila around 1647.[21]

The Aztecs even had a myth in which a god, Nanāwātzin "the one covered in sores," laid down his life willingly in order to save the world. As a result he was burned on a bonfire, and ascended into the sky as the fifth sun, illuminating the world until the present day. Although the myth itself, taking place in a polytheistic heaven, may not be given an *interpretatio Christiana*, the association of Christ with the sun *tonati-uh* ("shining/warming goes") was used in early evangelism at least metaphorically, for the source of our sustenance.[22]

Yet while many of the leading themes of Christianity had at least a spiritual resonance, for Americans who found themselves subjects of his Catholic Majesty, the King of Spain, the missionaries in the Americas were not willing to accommodate any of this as a *praeparatio evangelica*,* even if it were suitably redescribed and cast into a Christian view of world history. Indeed, the Inquisition had burned at the stake Francisco de la Cruz, one of the most prominent Dominican friars in Peru from 1561 to 1578, merely for willingness to incorporate Inca religious songs, known as *taki*, into Christian worship, as per early missionary practice:

> The most unusual of these dances was that of the nobles called Incas, and the highest noble among them sang the words, very soulful, with four syllables to each verse. And it suddenly struck the Spaniards and priests present that the words contained epithets very suitable for Our Lord. And when [the Spaniards] asked where they came from, [the Incas] said that the same ones they had formerly given to the sun and their king they had converted to the praise of Jesus Christ, taking material from what they had heard preached. (From the *carta annua* for 1571).[23]

It appears that Counter-Reformation Spain was more anxious to stress boundaries between the sacred and the secular than to fuse them, and was suspicious of any attempt to smuggle traditional rituals into Christian service. The Third Lima Council included an explicit ban on *taki*.[24]

Christian Forms in Idolatry

If there was any compromise between Christianity and indigenous beliefs in the Americas, it ran in the opposite direction, through a moderate acceptance of Christian symbols into native practice, in those places where the latter survived the periodic campaigns of *extirpación de idolatrías*.

---

* I.e., a prefiguring, in early thinking, of the full truth revealed in the Christian Gospels. This idea was as old at least as the philosopher Clement of Alexandria (ca. 150–215), a convert to Christianity who had seen Plato's work as a preparation for Holy Writ.

This began very early. A collection of songs current in the sixteenth century, known as the *Cantares Mexicanos*, includes inexpert efforts to offer up praise to the new Spanish gods, but in terms that show, at the very least, the memory of their American predecessors. Here the Holy Spirit replaces Huitzilopochtli (the war god, "Humming-bird of the Right"):

yztac huexotl aya yztac tolin	Here to Mexico, the place where
y ye imanica mexico nica	the white willows and white
huiya	reed grasses are
timatlalaztatototl tipatlantihuitz	You, the blue heron bird, come flying
tehuan titeotl	You Who are the God
***spiritu santo** ohuaya eta*	Who are the Holy Spirit
i anca ye tehoatl aya ypan ticçohua ya	So You unfold
ypan ticyectia in ye mocuitlapil ye ye matlapal aya	so You arrange Your tail and Your wings,
ye momacehual.[25]	Your vassals.

And the insertion of Christian identities into ancient American cults has continued to this day.

Pachamama is the earth-mother, or time-mother, of the Andes, an Inca goddess of fertility who presides over planting and harvesting, and causes earthquakes. Her children include the sun Inti and the moon Killa. Since before the spread of Inca power, she had had a major cult center at Copacabana, a peninsula jutting into Lake Titicaca, with attendant temples to the sun and the moon on neighboring islands. But with the arrival of the Spaniards, Copacabana was converted to a shrine to the Virgin Mary. An image of Maria Candelaria was ritually instated on February 2, 1589, the Feast of Candlemas. Augustinian friars then substituted holy processions, and harvest blessings, for the old rain rituals. Celebrations of Saint Maria ad Nives also take place on August 5, a feast that was at the time only a generation old, having been inserted into the General Roman Calendar in 1568. But August 5 had also been the great feast of Pachamama, and the rites observed for this include to this day a libation on a rocky outcrop in honor of the surrounding holy mountains, with the attendance of a shaman. Offerings are therefore made not just in prayer to the Christian pantheon, but in kind to the ancient *wak'a* of the land (spirits, holy things), the fundamental focus of Inca reverence.

The identities of Mary and Pachamama are fused more widely. A "mass" for Pachamama is celebrated at Lampa in the Peruvian region of Puno, to "enable" the feast of Mary's Immaculate Conception on December 8. And Pachamama herself is addressed in Quechua as *Maria llumpaqa* ("Mary the pure") and *santa tira wirjina* (i.e., Spanish "Santa Tierra Virgen"), "Holy Earth Virgin." Meanwhile, Mary is known as *Mamacha* or *Mamanchis* "Mommy, our Mom." The Bolivians of the Callawaya group address the two together *Uywiri, Pachamama, tierra María*: "You who nourish us, Earth Mother, Earth Maria."[26]

In Guatemala, traditionalists at Santiago Atitlán have preserved the system of *cofradías* "fraternities," an institution originally brought to them from Spain by Franciscan missionaries; these are the clubs of laymen who stage the religious processions and festivals, at least once a year. They have developed their religion in different directions, and arguably in conformity with pre-Hispanic tradition, since the departure of the friars. The characters *Ma-Nawal JesuKrista'* (Jesus Christ Emmanuel—though the first name may also be translated "Mr. Ancient," also "man my-son"),* his father the Sun (*Ti-Tixel*, also *Qil-Ta* "Our Father"), and his mother Madre An-Dolores (aka *Ya-Lor* "Ms. -Lor-") are recombined into a Mayan-flavored tale of his sufferings, sacrifice, and resurrection as a man of maize. Other characters include his disciple John (*San Juan Karajo*—recognizable as the Spanish for prick), John the Baptist (*San Juan Bauktista*, or *Ajuan* for short, now with baby jaguar and ancient book), and Jesus's brother the apostle Saint James, *Santiago Mayor*. Santiago rides a wind horse (*xlaj jyu kiej*) and carries a sharpened sword, but beneath it all has become a trickster.[27]

None of this would have been acceptable to the friars who first brought the word of God to the Tzutujil people of *Chi Ya* "beside the water," now known as Santiago Atitlán. But the *cofrades* who keep this adjusted tradition alive are the same body of *saqristanes* who also organize the conventional events of Catholic Holy Week in the village. And the tradition does have the advantage of relating directly, if not rigidly, to the mishmash of Mayan

---

* This word *nawal* is an ancient word indeed. Within Nahuatl, it was once used to refer to a sorcerer, or spirit familiar: also the beast into which a shaman can transform himself. It is clear that many Nahuatl words were borrowed into Mayan; but the latter concept in Mayan languages such as Tz'utujiil was expressed by the word *way*. (Coe 1992, pp. 256–57.)

community life as experienced over the past millennium—perhaps, as the *Popol Vuh* itself did three hundred years before.

The Catholic church in the sixteenth century was not going to accept any supplements or adjustments in its faith that stemmed from association with the pre-Christian imaginings of new converts. Nor was it going to put the ancient scriptures of the faith into the hands—let alone minds—of these new converts. The Holy Creed was not up for restatement, nor the Holy Scriptures for reinterpretation.

The Inquisition

If there were any lingering doubts about this, they could be put to rest by Spain's evident reliance on *La Santa Inquisición*. This judicial instrument for ensuring conformity of faith within Catholic Christendom was not given its permanent seat within Spain's American empire until fifty years after the conquest. Philip II placed one tribunal in Lima in 1570 and another in Mexico City the following year; a third was established in Cartagena, on the Caribbean coast of New Granada, a generation later in 1610. Each was possessed of two inquisitors, one attorney (*procurador*), a secretary, a bailiff (*alguácil*), and an accountant with a network of auxiliary contacts for each throughout their regions. They were charged by the king not only to protect orthodoxy among the faithful, but also to block the entry of foreign heresies. An apparent indulgence was extended to the Indians: they were not to be subjected to the Inquisition, whether for reasons of immaturity as Christians, or incomprehension of the full purport of dogma. But everyone else, including mestizos and black slaves, would feel its weight; and its condemnations fell particularly hard on any Jews that might be uncovered, or shipwrecked sailors of enemy powers, who had the misfortune, often, to have been unacceptably brought up as Protestants.

The immunity of Indians may have been partly pragmatic, to stop the courts being swamped with the cases of unripe Christians, still in thrall to many aspects of their own unacceptable upbringing. But they can have been in little doubt that other means would be found to punish them, if idolatry was exposed. Before the Inquisition came to the Americas, in 1539 one Aztec lord of Texcoco, don Carlos Mendoza Ometochzin, had famously been arraigned for having kept up his ancient traditions, proclaiming his faith in the old gods, and denouncing the right of Spaniards to be in "New Spain" at all. Arrested on these charges, he had been condemned by Juan de Zumárraga, Mexico's first bishop, and in consequence burned at the stake. In this, intolerance of religious faults provided welcome cover for suppression of political resistance. No one would defend rejection of Christ, even if they had ethical doubts about Spain's right to rule over a foreign people that had presented no threat.

This stench of oppression and aggression was compounded with a racism toward the native inhabitants of the Americas, which only became more entrenched over time. It even came to be a part of the accepted rules of the church in the Americas. Within both the Spanish and the Portuguese empires, the natives of America were never adjudged worthy themselves to be consecrated as priests. In 1583 this prohibition was added as a formal text of the Third Council of Lima, overruling the claim (that had been urged by the friars at the Council) that among the native population, the mestizos were the only people who could transmit the faith to those who spoke remoter languages, since these were languages not taught in the Catholic seminaries.[28]

The Franciscans themselves, first missionaries in Mexico, had long nurtured the ambition to bring up an indigenous priesthood, and indeed founded a special college for Indian youth in the 1530s at Tlatelolco near Mexico City; and throughout South America, Jesuits stoutly maintained that native or mestizo converts were no different from Spaniards before the Lord.* There was some attempt to realize these ideals in legislation, and the mestizo right had even been asserted in a brief from Pope Gregory XIII to the Lima Council. But nonetheless, these ideals were set aside at the crucial moment when the council reported, and then faded with time, in competition with the mundane and self-interested norms being established by European criollos.[29]

The ban on admission of nonwhites to Holy Orders remained in effect. For the Almighty, the salvation of American souls may have been on a par with that of their European brothers (and sisters); but the hierarchy of the

---

* They did entertain some doubts about their intellectual equality, however. Father José Cardiel, a Jesuit of the last generation in Paraguay (expelled in 1767), opined: "Things which consist in memory, like learning to read, write and routine duties, and getting by heart any role in a foreign language, they do with greater facility and readiness than we. Understanding and debate, very weak and lacking. [*Entendimiento y discurso, muy débil y defectuoso.*]" (Ballesteros 1979, p. 23.)

new Catholic church in the Americas remained, generation after generation, as firmly under the control of the invading Spaniards and Portuguese as was any other aspect of the colonial government.*

Expressing the Faith in a New Language

What then of the American languages in the service of the church? How did the Gospels fare, as expressed in them?

There was some initial skepticism, at the highest level, about their expressive power. In 1596, even as the Jesuits were setting up *reducciones* for Guaraní speakers, the Spanish king was decreeing for Río de la Plata that only Spanish should be used, on the ground that indigenous languages "would not allow the expression of the mysteries of the faith with propriety and without imperfections."[30] And part of the reason that Chibcha had been unable to gather momentum as a *lingua general* in the latter sixteenth century had been opposition by superiors of the Franciscans, Dominicans, and Augustinians to use of the language, who asserted,

> these dialects [are] extremely poor in vocabulary, lacking such terms as *Christ, charity, grace, contrition, penitence* etc. [and] they possess indecent expressions for terms such as *incarnation* and *virginity*.[31]

Although they are fairly typical of the uninstructed views that tend to prevail before much research has been done on little-known languages, these dismissive or patronizing attitudes were not shared by Europeans who had any direct linguistic knowledge. Rodrigo de la Cruz, in a letter to the Spanish emperor Charles V in 1550, wrote of Nahuatl, the Mexican language, "that in

---

* It is tempting to see an analogy here with the persistent theological inferiority of the Slavic Orthodox (both priests and laity) within the Orthodox Church as a whole, unlike the parity achieved by Germanic congregations, who had been largely schooled by Catholic missionaries through Latin—the phenomenon discussed at the end of chapter 10.

  Is there inevitably something of a dignity deficit, something patronizing, in delivering a faith exclusively in translation, especially if the texts are not original, but a special set of adapted media? (This method was applied for evangelism both in Orthodox eastern Europe, and Catholic America.)

  Or are these just examples of apartheid, the kind of demeaning treatment inevitable when one language community refuses fully to usher another into its spiritual space?

every village today there are many Indians who know it and learn it easily, and a very great number who confess in that language. It is an extremely elegant language, as elegant as any in the world."

Another priest, Francisco Ximénez (1666–1730), described the Mayan language K'iche': "What I say is that, having penetrated these languages, of all those I have knowledge, among Latin, our Castilian, German, Italian etc., there is no language more proper, nor more genuine, nor more ordered, nor regular . . ."[32]

In Paraguay, when the Jesuits were attempting to take on board the new requirements from the Third Lima Council in 1584, the provincial wrote to the father general of the order: ". . . the Indian tongue is in great part brilliant for the propriety of its vocabulary. Which in truth was of great value, since thus the Indian could be adequately acquainted with the truths of our faith, when before there had arisen errors and difficulties . . ."[33]

Later, in 1639, Antonio Ruiz de Montoya, the principal grammarian and lexicographer of Guaraní, reflected on his thirty years' study of the language:

> studies which effectively revealed a tongue so copious, and elegant, that gives it cause to compete with the tongues of repute. So proper in its meanings, that we can apply the words of Gen. ii: [*Latin*: Whatsoever Adam called every living creature, that is the name thereof.] So proper is it that things, being naked in themselves receive from it clothes of their own nature.[34]

In the New Kingdom of Granada, Bernardo de Lugo, grammarian of Chibcha, headed his work with uncompromising praise for his subject:

> Who are you who fly so light?
> I am the Chibcha tongue. Where are you bound?
> From the new Kingdom, to exotic lands,
> Which will take my truths for new ones.
> You well say that you enlighten us all
> With your depth; say, what do you imagine?
> That by studying you will know what you intuit,
> That the learned Lugo is foremost in my schools.
> He put me in a Grammar, since I am intricate.
> And from a rude thing he made me so urbane
> That I cause admiration throughout the world . . .[35]

The grammarians may perhaps be forgiven for their exuberance in praise of the languages that they devoted their lives to explaining, but they also endeavoured to substantiate their claims by pointing out particular features for admiration.

Francisco Ximénez wrote of the rationality of K'iche' thus: "[the words] are like natural signs with such order and correspondence that I do not find any other language more ordered or even as much so, so that I have come to believe that this language is the first in the world."[36]

An example of such signs would be the tense markers for nouns that the Portuguese and Spanish linguists discovered in Tupi and Guaraní.[37]

Tupi and Guaraní are interesting in that no routine distinction is made between present and past in verbs; nouns, however, may be marked for past and future. In Tupi the past ending was *-pwera*, and the future *-rama*. Guaraní, as usual presents somewhat eroded equivalent forms: respectively *-kwer* or *-kwe*, and *-ram* or *-rã*. They make a noun refer to a former state, now ended, and to a state intended or foreseen, which is not yet achieved at the time of the utterance. Interestingly they can co-occur on the same noun, usually in the order future+past, hence Tupi *-rambwera* and Guaraní *-rangwe*. This is what Guasch calls the "frustrated future," indicating an unfulfilled state that might or should have been.[38]

To summarize in a clear set of examples taken from Tupi:[39]

Ayapó xe-rembi'u-rama	I am preparing my food (which is not yet ready).
Ayapó xe-rembi'u-pwera	I prepared my food (which I have already eaten).
Kunumĩ o'u xe-rembi'u-rambwera	The child ate my food (which I never got).

According to Ruiz de Montoya (1640, p. 30), it is also possible to combine them in the opposite order, to yield Guaraní *-kwerã*, characterizing something that "turned out," i.e., might not or should not have happened, but nevertheless did.

These markers can, it turns out, also be used as independent words, much as English can talk of *has-been*s, *might-have-been*s, *yet-to-be*s, and *never-was*es. As such they were used to give a more philosophical exact, and less figurative, translation in Tupi of Christ's famous words in the Garden of Gethsemane. "O my Father, if it be possible, let this cup pass from me:

nevertheless not as I will, but as thou wilt ... O my Father, if this cup may not pass away from me, except I drink it, thy will be done."[40] In Tupi there are no cups to be drained. Jesus instead says:[41]

T'i	ram-bwer	iã	xe-remimborará-rama,	xe rub-y gûé!
May-be	FUT-PAST	this	my-suffering-FUT,	my Father O
May these my sufferings to come be an unfulfilled future, O My Father.				

Aipó	xe re'õnama	rambwera	abai-me,	t'o-nhe-monhang	umẽ	xe-remimotara.
This	I my-death	FUT-PAST	difficult-as	may it-PAS-SIVE-do	not	my-will
As my death is difficult to make unfulfilled, may my will not be done.						

It would be interesting to know whether Montoya's favorite examples in his grammar and dictionary of Guaraní, aba-kwe-rã [man+PAST+FUT] "he who was not to have been a man and then was," and omano-bae-ran-gue [dead+thing+FUT+PAST] "he who was to die, but did not,"[42] are intended as contributions to Christology; and if so, whether they would have been orthodox for the Council of Nicaea.

Tupi and Guaraní might have been elegant vehicles for theology, had their speakers ever been admitted into the ordained, and hence influential, body of the church as a whole. But as it was, use of American languages within the church remained a means of pedagogy only, without implications for understanding of the faith as a whole. These languages were used primarily for instruction in the Doctrina (hence requiring accurate translations of all the Christian terminology). They would also be used for ancillary purposes, which might develop people's personal faith and understanding of Christian history, such as the writing of hymns and prayers, or for the performance of religious drama.

However, even if we stick to the Doctrina, there was some difficulty with vocabulary. This occurred even though these low-level scriptures were all rewritten in the languages with a new audience of fresh converts in mind.

In Peru, Quechua has no word for evil, and the language makes do with what is literally "not good" mana allin; and so, for example, the Lord's Prayer

(*Pater Noster*) ends rather weakly *mana alli-manta quispichihuaycu* "Deliver us from the not good." Chibcha, the language to the north, had a similar gap, so that in most expressions "bad" is rendered as *achuen-za* "it is good—not."[43] But there is another word for harm or hatred, *guahaica*, so the Pater Noster in Chibcha ends <u>guahaica</u>-z *chihas aguynzacuc chie choc maquyia* "<u>harm</u> by-us for-there-not-being us well please-make" (i.e., "deliver us from evil").[44] This word had other pertinent relatives: *guahaiansuca* "be corrupted, damaged" and *guahaia* "corpse, dead person."[45] There was some risk of confusion in identifying Satan, sworn enemy of the Christian god, with a pre-Christian Chibcha spirit, *Guahaioque*, which might be etymologized as *guahai a-uque* "image of the corpse" or *guahai ioque* "skin of the corpse." He may (like the Devil) have been associated with a serpent, but serpents in Chibcha myth were symbols not of deceit, but of origins from a watery world. Another authority has conjectured that the name is in fact derived from *guaha ioque* "deer skin," with theological implications completely unknown to us.[46] Yet the word is summarily equated with *Diablo* and *Demónio* in the *Diccionario y Gramática Chibcha* attributed to the Jesuit José Dadey (ca. 1605–1620); and in the same book we find *Guahaioque sis muysca agotac abta* "Guahaioque deceived these people" as part of the story of the serpent's temptation of Adam and Eve in the Garden of Eden.[47]

In this same relation with the Chibcha people, the church was apparently happy to let its clergy be known by the very term that had previously dignified pagan priests, namely the word *chyquy* (pronounced šikɨ). As the chronicler Friar Pedro Simón (1574–ca. 1630) put it (using Spanish spelling):

> *Jeque* is the priest (*sacerdote*) of the Idols, he who fasts, and makes sacrifice; it is a word corrupted by the Spanish, because it is properly called *cheque*, and is the same as *mohán* in other provinces.[48]

In the contemporary *Diccionario y Gramática Chibcha*, the word for "priest" (*Sacerdote* or *Padre*) is given as *Chyquy* in Chibcha, and on page 152v of Fray Bernardo de Lugo's confessional (dated to 1619) we read:

> *missa quisqua **chyquy** atabe a-bohoza um-mi-gua? missa a-bquysqua-za* **chyquy** *atabê . . .*

> Have you had [carnal] knowledge of a priest who says Mass . . . some priest who does not say Mass?

with the immediate note "One has to ask in this way, because the primitive Indian woman [*la India chontal*] cannot tell which is ordained and which not, and so it is enough to ask what is set down here, which will allow her to understand."[49]

When the priests of the old cults, even if formally suppressed, were still a conscious memory, it was useful to think of them as some inferior substitute for, or predecessor to, real clergy, rather than something else altogether, mere wizards or witches. On the same lines, we also find the term *quymuy* "steward" used, for example in the parallel questions of the Confessional:

> *Ipquabe Chibchazhum, Bochica suetyba aquymuy miguecha miguaia hocagaia mue ocasac umgueoa? Chyquy Dios aquymuy mihoc aguesca ocasac mgueoa?*[50]

> Something that the <u>stewards</u> of Chibchachum, Bochica, or *Suetyba* ("Yellow-Bird") taught to your forefathers and foremothers, have you affirmed? What the priests <u>stewards</u> of God (Dios) have taught, have you affirmed?

In the Andean lands of South America, there was agreement to use the loan word *Dios*, for the Deity Himself. (As Dadey's dictionary remarks tersely, under this entry,[51] "There is no general name for their false gods.") This was the practice in Chibcha, Quechua, and Aymará. But in other lands and languages, especially Mexico, the missionaries often agreed to use a native word, reconditioned naturally to remove the connotations of its pagan past. So in Nahuatl, he is referred to as *Dios teotl* ("the god Dios"), later as *Teotl* ("God"). In Yucatec Mayan he is *Dios Citbil* ("Dios almighty"), but also *hunab ku* ("the one god") or simply *Ku* ("God"), while his pagan predecessors are written off as *u kuul ah ma ocolalob* (*dioses de gentiles*—literally, "the gods of those who do not believe").[52]

In Brazil and the Chaco, the friars adopted a much more radical strategy, to identify the One True God with a preexisting deity, *Tupã*. This identification goes back to the first missions of Christians, led by Manuel de Nóbrega (1517–70), among the Tupi people on the coast of Brazil. He wrote:

> No definite God, but they call the thunder "Tupana," which is as one who calls a thing divine (observe the root Tup is also in the very name of these Indians); and so the Fathers found that this should be the word most adequate to express the name of God in the Christian

concept "Paí Tupana" [father Tupana], even if the Indians find difficulty in apprehending the concept of God as Spirit, and ask if he has a head, or a body, whether he is a woman and what he looks like. They do not have idols; nonetheless there are those among them who make themselves holy and promise them health and victory against their enemies.[53]

In some situations, a new language was called on to translate a central theological term when there is no equivalent word. In Tupi and Guaraní, there was no single word to translate Latin *filius*, Spanish *hijo*, English *son*, the most important attribute of Jesus Christ. In most languages, and certainly those of the Middle East and Europe, there is a single word that means male offspring, in relation both to father and to mother, and contrasts with *daughter*, the exact female equivalent. But in these two languages of South America, there is one word for a father's son (*ta'yra*), another for a father's daughter (*tajýra*), and a third word, which means the offspring of a mother, regardless of whether male or female (*membyra*).*

Jesus, then, is the *ta'yra* of God, but the *membyra* of the Virgin Mary. This seems clear enough, although it might complicate the theology of Sonship in the Trinity. But there was some squeamishness in using the terms, because their biological basis could be foregrounded. Both have a suffix -*ra*, which in Guaraní is lost in the vocatives: *che-ra'y*, *che-memby* "my son!". But without its suffix, *ta'y*- also literally meant testicles or semen. With the addition of -*pug*-, the word for burst, it connoted wet dreams and masturbation too, both of which in Catholic Spanish are usually termed *polución*. For example, in Montoya's *Guaraní Confessional*, we read:

Ere-poko pa kuña angaipa habari rae? Nde-ra'y-opug eí akóiramo rae?

Did you touch a woman sinfully? Did you willfully ejaculate from that?[54]

Meanwhile *memby* was conjectured by Montoya, the first grammarian and lexicographer of Guaraní, to be derived from *mē*, meaning male, with the

---

* The word for "daughter" is pronounced [tayɨra] in Tupi, but [tažira] in Guaraní. Linguistic note (in order to explain some phrases below in Tupi and Guaraní): many words (including *ta'yra* and *tajýra*) have a first consonant that "oscillates" among t, r, and s, depending on the word that precedes.

passive suffix -*py*, so *memby* might be etymologized as "what a man did to me." A bishop, Bernardino de Cárdenas, reading the works of Montoya, thought both of them inappropriate, since Christ's conception had been pure, without human seed and without the intervention of any man.[55]

There was little to be done about this, of course, short of refusing to talk of God the Father (*Tupã Tuvâ*), God the Son (*Tupã Ta'yra*), and Mary Holy Mother of God (*Maria Tupã-sy Marangatu*) in these languages at all. Conceivably there might have been an agreement to use only loan vocabulary (Portuguese *pai, filho, mãe* in Brazil ~ Spanish *padre, hijo, madre* in Paraguay—Father, Son, Mother): there was, after all, a wide agreement to call the third Person of the Trinity *Espiritu Santo*, without any attempt at vernacular translation.

Montoya himself dismissed this concern as beside the point: who thinks of etymologies in everyday conversation? In any case does not Saint Paul himself speak of Christ as *semen Abrahae* "the seed of Abraham" (Hebrews 2:16), and *ex semine David* "of the seed of David" (Romans 1:3)?

Yet the argument among churchmen has gone on, and the case for keeping carnal etymologies, even if they are present, in their (restricted) place is still being buttressed to this day by the foremost scholar of Guaraní, Bartomeu Melià. It is arguable that the theology of Christianity gets its power from adopting these fleshly terms and giving them a new purified meaning.[56]

CHAPTER 12

Gloria Tlatoani
Christian Literature among the Indios

The devil Anhangusu speaks:

Oporombo'ea'u	He teaches people lies
Tupã nhe'enga ra'anga.	uttering the word of God.
I xy mombe'uporanga	The lovely declaration of His Mother
xe moingotebẽngatu,	cuts me to the heart
omombuk-y bé xe akanga.	and pierces my head.
Sãi xe îukame'ymi	It almost killed me,
Tupã sy rera abaîté.	terror of the name of the Mother of God.
Serenduba rupibé,	When I hear her name,
amõngoty xe nhemimi,	I go to hide somewhere else
xe putunusu pupé.	within my great darkness.

Father José de Anchieta, *Na Aldeia de Guaraparim* lines 6–15
(Brazil, sixteenth century)

T HE INDIGENOUS LANGUAGES OF America—even those that were designated for use as "general languages"—were not accepted as fit vehicles for Holy Scripture. Any search for complete translations of the Bible, or its constituent books, is vain, although key passages were extracted for use in liturgy, or to illustrate the documents that spelled out Catholic *doctrina*.

But this left open the option that newly converted speakers of these languages might write their own literature to express their faith, by composing prayers, meditations, sermons, and indeed poems and dramas. Such works gradually appeared in the sixteenth and seventeenth centuries, as the conquered elite of Mexico and Peru received instruction in literacy using the Roman alphabet.

More immediately, the missionaries themselves, though relative beginners in the languages, could start writing an "indigenous" literature for the edification of the new congregations.

Sahagún in Nahuatl

Fray Bernardino de Sahagún (1499–1590), one of the first great missionaries to Mexico (who also effectively organized an encyclopaedia of pre-conquest Aztec culture in his *Historia General de las Cosas de Nueva España*) attempted to combine the fondness of Mexicans for song and dance with his own knowledge of their language and culture to produce, in 1583, a volume called the *Psalmodia Christiana*. He explained his motivation:

> [The Indians of New Spain] ... in most places, persist in going back to singing their old [songs] in their houses or their palaces (which arouses a good deal of suspicion as to the sincerity of their Christian Faith); for in the old [songs] mostly idolatrous things are sung in a style so obscure that none can understand them well except they themselves ... In order easily to counteract this mischief, ... these [songs] have been printed in the [Mexican] language so that they will immediately abandon the old [songs], a penalty being imposed applicable to any who go back to singing the old [songs].[1]

In doing this, Sahagún had forerunners. One of the very first missionaries in Mexico, Pedro de Gante (Peter of Ghent), who arrived in 1523, had had the idea of reaching the commoners—who were not being educated by the friars, unlike the children of nobles—through song and dance, since that seemed to be basic to their worship of their own gods:

> For when they were to sacrifice for any purpose ... before they killed them, they had to sing before the idol. When I realized this and that all their songs were dedicated to the gods, I composed some very stately verses concerning God's law and the Faith, and how God became man in order to save the human race, and how he was born of the Virgin Mary though she remained pure and immaculate.

He had found this most effective in building enthusiasm, and continued it throughout a whole celebration of Christmas. The children proved gifted in picking up the new songs, and there was some spontaneous creation of others.

Despite its name, Sahagún's work, written more than fifty years later, was arranged not around the Biblical book of Psalms, but around the feast days of the Catholic calendar. This means its content could range freely over significant moments in Christian history, provided only they were linked with some saint. It was a purely Christian work, with no allusions to the original Psalms of King David. But although, as a kind of Christian almanac, it could hardly recall the characteristic spirit of Aztec poetry—elegant despair before an unyielding universe—it is a highly competent stylistic pastiche of it.[2]

Sahagún's flair for Nahuatl style entailed its own theological risks. To give a flavor, we might say: "That lifeboat-man, that lion, did sail close to the wind; by the skin of his teeth he skirted around phrases and allusions that would directly honor some of the Aztec deities. Sometimes, perhaps, he fell right in."

The traditional telling of the myth of the five suns, in which Nanāwātzin immolates himself to become our present sun, begins:

In quenin **tzintique** *in teteuh . . .*	How the gods had their **beginning . . .**
in **oc iovaian** *. . .*[3]	when there was **still darkness . . .**

But almost the same phrase is used at the Feast of Saint Thomas Aquinas, describing the darkness before God was pleased to create Saint Thomas Aquinas and Saint Bonaventure, especial sponsors of Dominicans and Franciscans respectively.

In **oc iouaia**, *in aiamo* **tzintzi** *cemanaoac, iuh tlatlalilli, iuhca dios itlatoltzi*[4]	When all was **darkness**, before the world **began**, such was the commandment, such was the word of God

This seems bathetic, even if the Aztec and Hebrew concepts of a time before the world's creation are, necessarily, rather similar: "in the beginning . . . darkness."

He also writes, of Christ's epiphany:

Ca in gloria tlatoani, omopā acico	The glory of the King has come
	to reach you
Ca oamopan tlathuic,	above you it has dawned,
oamopan tlanez	above you it is bright.
ma xicmottililiti in amotlauil,	Go to see to glorify your light,
in amocouh,	your torch,
in amoapocio	your **smoke**
in coioac **tezcatl** *in necoc xapo,*	the broad **mirror** pierced through
iehoatzi in Iesus.	which is Jesus.

where the emphasized elements show a direct allusion to Tezcatlipoca, the god of obsidian mirrors and smoke. But unlike *Tonatiuh*, the sun, a deified heavenly body that is clearly real, and hence available to be (metaphorically) equated with Christ, Tezcatlipoca is uniquely something from the Mexican pantheon, and any equation with Jesus would seem a betrayal of the Christian faith: at any rate, on another occasion, Sahagún equated him with Lucifer, the devil himself.[5]

By contrast, the sun analogy seemed revealing, since Christ is the source of enlightenment, and was often iterated,

Ma ticmauiçocain	Let us pay honor
itlamauiçollachiualtzi, in	to the wondrous works, the love,
itetlaçotlalizi, in	of our divine **sun**, Jesus.
*toteu***tonatiuh** *in Jesus.*	

Psalmodia Christiana, fourth psalm for the
Feast of Saint Thomas the Apostle

and

In iquac oualmomā **tonatiuh** *in*	When the **sun**, Jesus, came
Iesus, etetl **tonatiuh** *in momanaco:*	forth, three **suns** came out.
iece ca tlamauiçoloc, auh onoceppa	But it was a miracle, and
cecenteti	they all were one.

Psalmodia Christiana, third psalm for the second day of the
Nativity of Christ

Although there were problems of this kind in Sahagún's attempt to Christianize Nahuatl traditional songs, it seems that the text was a popular one. It began to circulate in 1564; later, after surviving review by the Inquisition's Holy Office (as his major life's work, the *Historia General*, did not), and lavishly illustrated with images of saints, it was published in 1583. Unlike most of the *Doctrina* texts (and indeed Sahagún's *Historia General*), it was published without a facing translation, so the orthodoxy of its content had to be taken on trust by clerics without functional Nahuatl.

After that, it continued in use for five or six generations until the eighteenth century, when it was denounced; almost all copies were then destroyed. Apparently, it was censored not for pagan influences, but for containing passages that read too much like a translation of Scripture. That is rather hard now to substantiate; indeed it is denied by its twentieth-century translator, who had read it all with Bible in hand.[6] By the time of its condemnation, however, its well-intentioned and harmless directions on the Christian faith would have long outlived the memory of the Nahuatl songs, from which it had originally been intended as a diversion.

Anchieta in Tupi

While Sahagún was laboring in the Colegio de Santa Cruz de Tlatelolco to Christianize the Mexicans and document their ancient traditions, another European, José de Anchieta (1534–1597), was preparing to lay the foundations of religious literature in a very different American language. He was working in much less peaceful conditions, among cannibals and amid a minor colonial war, in the new Portuguese colony in Brazil; and his mission was to bring the Gospels to the speakers of Tupi.

A native of Tenerife in the Canary Islands, Anchieta had studied at Coimbra, Portugal, and was received into the Company of Jesus—the Jesuits—in 1551, at the age of seventeen. Two years later he had come out to Brazil, to join the foundation that Manuel de Nóbrega had established in 1549. He was shipwrecked on the way there, but—unlike Pedro Fernandes Sardinha, the unfortunate first bishop of Brazil in 1556—he was not captured, clubbed, and eaten by the coastal people. Arriving delayed but safe, he was posted at the village of Piratininga and was present at its refoundation as São Paulo in 1554.

Anchieta was noted for his pioneering skill in learning the local language, and he became much in demand as an interpreter in the long series of hostilities and negotiations between the competing Portuguese (Catholic) and French (Calvinist) colonies of the region in the period 1553–1567. The tribe known specifically as Tupi was allied with the Portuguese, but most of the local people had sided with the French: these, unlike the Portuguese, had not attempted to ransack their villages nor enslave them. Nonetheless the French settlers ultimately lost the war. Nóbrega, Anchieta, and the Jesuits were notorious (among the Portuguese settlers) for their sympathy with the Tupi peoples, but still in the war they sided actively with the settlers. (They were, after all, fellow Catholics, as well as compatriots.)

Anchieta was multitalented, noted among much else for his skill as a surgeon and physician. But he was probably most distinguished at the time for his humanity and courage as a missionary: in 1563 he offered himself up as a hostage in order to maintain a truce with the Tamoyos (Tupi: "elders"), an alliance of tribes against the Portuguese. These practiced cannibalism on their enemies, and were no friends of the Portuguese at the time. Threatened by a group of natives on the beach—where he was composing, in the wet sand, an ode in Latin elegiacs to the Virgin Mary—he is said to have saved the situation by replying in sorrowful tones, but with a supernatural warning in his ready Tupi,

Ko 'ara-pupé pe-puka-puka;	In this world you are laughing;
pe re'õ riré pe-yase'o-se'o-ne	after your deaths you will be crying.

Navarro 2004, p. 327

Anchieta remained with the Tamoyos for seven months, and he completed the ode.

After the war, a Jesuit college was founded farther north in Rio de Janeiro, under the direction of Nóbrega. Anchieta was appointed to teach there. He succeeded Nóbrega as principal upon his death in 1570, and seven years later became provincial superior to the Jesuits throughout Brazil as well.

Anchieta's arrival in Brazil had come a generation after the Franciscan start with Nahuatl in Mexico, so he was not one of the first grammarians in the Americas, even if he was in Brazil. But he lost no time in studying the Tupi language, producing a grammar (*Arte*), a Catholic doctrine (*Doutrina*), and a dictionary in the 1550s. He was the first to write on the Tupi language, although his work (the *Arte* and the *Doutrina*, at least) were only published just before his death—back in Coimbra, Portugal, in 1595. These works he wrote in Portuguese, not in his native Spanish.

He was not just an academic and missionary, however. He had been exposed to the lively dramas of Gil Vicente in his college years at Coimbra. Vicente, dubbed "the Portuguese Plautus," had died around 1536 and had been at the height of his posthumous fame and popularity in Anchieta's student years. Many of his plays have a strong religious or allegorical content, and this is characteristic of Anchieta's work.

Anchieta's dramatic sense may also have been stimulated by the *Spiritual Exercises*, which were the formation for Jesuits recommended by their founder, Ignacio de Loyola, and involved imaginative self-involvement by the subject in the key events of Christianity. In a very different context, the twentieth-century "Method" school of acting is related. Imagined impersonation was central to Anchieta's dramatization of spiritual and infernal forces.

Arriving in Brazil, he (like all the Jesuits) was struck by how susceptible the natives were to song and dance—as Bernardino de Sahagún was finding at much the same time among the Mexicans. Consequently, dramatic refrains and choruses, as well as dance numbers, came to have an important place in Anchieta's creations.

These various influences and insights bore fruit in the plays Anchieta wrote—largely in Tupi—in the latter years of his life, plays that focused on the life-and-death struggle between demons and angels that lay behind the missionary endeavor.

These plays paint a different world from that of the *Doutrinas*: they are not legalistic statements of Christian claims about the world, together with systematic checks on what sins an individual has committed in a recent tract of time. Rather they are explorations of the interaction of good and evil—where the outcome seems to hang in the balance even to the point of creating suspense. Furthermore, the main characters are not human beings, although their fate often hangs in the balance, but powers and principalities, usually of evil in the form of devils, but also the souls of saints and guardian angels. The settings are local in the extreme, with most of the devils taking names of native chiefs that Anchieta had known in his long and unsettled career among the Tupi, and the names of places he knew well on the coasts of Brazil. They brought Christianity out of legalistic theory, and into a world of danger and adventure.

This world, and the thoughts of players in it, were largely articulated in Tupi, the favored language of devils (*diabos*) and individual souls, as well as guardian angels. These are the characters with whom indigenous people will feel in direct contact. Many of the grander characters, however, speak Spanish, including figures from Ancient Rome—whether martyr saints or harsh emperors, but also noble principles that are given a voice, such as the Fear of God and the Love of God. There is little Portuguese spoken, but an angel, pontificating in the style of the Holy Creed, sometimes gets away with it.

The grandeur imputed to (Castilian) Spanish—logically, it should have been to Latin—is quite conscious. One demon deliberately assumes the language,

porque el español ufano	because haughty Spanish
siempre guarda cortesía	always keeps up courtliness

Auto de São Lourenço lines 868–69

When the emperors—who are being arraigned for the martyrdom of Saint Laurence—first realize that they are in serious trouble, their Castilian slips, and they find themselves breaking into Guaraní (known at the time as Carijó) briefly (*Xe akaî*—"Ah me!") and then into Tupi for special pleading against a fellow accused.

Aûié, xe îuka îepé!	Enough of this! You are killing me!
Na s-etá-î xe angaipaba.	My sins are not many.
E-îá-te xe r-ubixapa!	Why not take my boss?

Auto de São Lourenço lines 892–94

Their avenging demon is not fazed: he remarks (in Castilian) that he knows all languages, and the emperors speedily fall back into Spanish, with the resigning phrase:

¡Oh miserable de mi	Oh woe is me,
que ni basta ser tirano	that it is not enough to be a tyrant
ni hablar en castellano!	nor to speak in Castilian!

Auto de São Lourenço lines 897–99

This use of languages specific to the Brazilian situation, especially Tupi, allows Anchieta to focus on features of the culture, and weave them into a Christian approach. Evidently considerable importance was attached to the name (*r-era*) used. In *Auto de São Lourenço*, the devils are tasked to take lethal vengeance (by smashing heads and devouring) on the Roman emperors for the cruel martyrdom by roasting of Saint Laurence. They remark that they will need to change their names:

Abá-pe ia-'u raē-ne?	Whom shall we devour first?
São Lourenço r-upiar-ûera.	The old enemies of Saint Laurence.
Akó t-ubixá-nē-mbûera?	Those old putrid kings?
A-ierok kori s-esé-ne.	I'll change my name today, for them.
Ta s-etá-katu xe r-era!	May my names be many!

Auto de São Lourenço lines 734–38

This was the custom in Tupi society whenever someone killed another person. It meant that the victim's angry soul could not find the killer to take vengeance; but it also marked the transition to a new stage of life. In *Na Aldeia de Guaraparim* ("In the Village of Guaraparim"), by contrast, a soul is accused by devils of refusing to be baptized:

Nd'o-ie-erok-i, erimba'e	He was not named [baptized], in the past,
o-gû er-umana r-aûsupa	loving his former name
s-ere'yma r-esebé.	together with the nameless [pagans]

Na Aldeia de Guaraparim lines 498–500

S-ere'yma "nameless" is the Tupi word for pagan, intended to indicate someone lacking Christian baptism. So preexisting Tupi ethics, elaborated for murder and cannibalism, gave an unexpected special force to a universal Christian rite of passage.

The plays give a devil's-eye view of Christianity: and they did not like what they saw in this "new law."

Xe moaîu-marangatu,	It bothers me greatly
xe moŷrō-eté-katû-abo	annoying me very much indeed
aîpó t-eko-pysasu . . .	this new law . . .
Xe r-eko i porang-eté	My law is very fine,
n'a-î-potar-i abá s-eîtyka,	I don't want men to cast it out,
n'a-î-potar-i abá i mombyka.	I don't want men to give it up.

Auto de São Lourenço lines 21–23, 37–39

Guaixará, the devil speaking here, defines his observances, in a good-hearted way reminiscent of the European devil's maxim: "Do what thou wilt" shall be the whole of the Law. It starts in good fun, but ends up decidedly antisocial:

Moraseia é i katu,	Dancing is what is good,
îe-gûaka, îe-mpyranga,	dressing up, applying rouge,
s-a'-mongy, îe-tymaã-gûanga,	plumage, dyeing one's legs,
îe-moúna, petymb-u,	blacking up,* smoking,
karaí'-monhã-monhanga . . .	preaching heaven on earth . . .†
îe-moŷro, mor-apiti,	getting wild, mass-murder,
îo-'u, tapuîa r-ara,	eating people, catching foreigners,
agûasá, moro-potara,	taking girlfriends, having sex,
manhana, sygûaraiŷ—	pimping, whoring—
n'a-î-potar-i abá s-eîara.	I don't want anyone to give them up.

Auto de São Lourenço lines 52–61

Sex and the Sixth Commandment

These were evidently the besetting sins of the Brazilian, as seen from the sixteenth-century Jesuit standpoint. The list gives us an idea of what the missionaries of Christ were asking people to give up from their traditional way of life, and compares with another—much more widespread—means of inventorying sins, namely the confessional.

The Lima Confessional, copied throughout Latin America, began with the words:

> Are you cohabiting? For how long? Did not the priest tell you when you confessed that you should leave her? Why did you not do it? This person with whom you are cohabiting, is she married or single?

So it was general practice to foreground cohabitation in assessing the state of a confessor's soul, before coming on to more specific sinful choices that he or she had made.

---

* One of the preparations for a cannibalistic feast.

† This is literally "keep on with prophetism," with *karaíba*, traveling prophets who inspired crowd frenzies and trances. They were the evangelists of the "land without evil."

And perhaps it is not a coincidence that in Anchieta's play *Na Aldeia de Guaraparim* the closest the devils come to a successful arrest of the soul they are pursuing is when they accuse him of incomplete confession of his amours:

Na nde ruã–te–p'akó kunhã ri ere–îe–momotá?

But weren't you certainly attracted by women?

Kûese nde r–emirekó manhan–amo ere–î–mondó endébo s–erur–uká.

Just a few days ago, you sent your wife as a procuress, to get her to bring them to you.

To, anhẽ kó a–îkó emonã! Kunhã–yba xe r–aûsu.

Ah. This is what I was really doing with them. The sweet girls were in love with me.

A'e–pe ere–î–mombe'u a'e r–esé nde mondá?

And did you confess you had deceived them?

Xe r–esaraî–te–katu. A–nh– angerekó îepé, aípó supé n'a– basem–i. Anhẽ, na xe r–emo'em–i.

In fact, I clean forgot. Although I was interested in them, I never turned up to meet them. Honestly, I am not lying.

A'ã, s–enotĩ–amo é, i mima, nd'ere–nosem–i!

No. The truth is you were ashamed of them, and kept them hidden; you would not let them come out with you!

Xe r–esá pupé–katu a–s–epîak nde i mim–ag–ûera.

I see plainly that you kept them hidden!

E–î–pysyk, Moroupîarûera!

Seize him, Morupiaruera [Past Enemy of Man]!

E–î–pytybõ, Mboî–usu!

Lend a hand, Mboiusu [Great Cobra]!

E–s–apy, Tatapytera!

Burn him, Tatapitera! [Heart of the Fire]!

Tupã sy, nde ma'enduá xe ri! . . .

Mother of God, remember me! . . .

Na Aldeia de Guaraparim lines 635–56

This might seem to reinforce an emerging picture of clerical obsession with sex. But within the drama, the soul's slip here, when he fails fully to rebut the devils' cross-examination, gives the playwright an opportunity to display the mercy of the Virgin Mary: the soul can appeal successfully to her, and receive forgiveness and hence salvation. Christianity needed to be shown as an instrument not just of righteousness, but also of forgiveness.

The ubiquity of this kind of sexual offense, and its lack of malice, may have made it a suitable case to bring up. The examination of such a theme in an entertaining play—and through use of a language that the converts would have known well—gave a human face to religious demands, and so could win hearts better than the quasi-judicial process so well documented in the universal confessional. Sex may only be prominent because it gets to the nub of human relations, both for the dramatist, and for the priest.

Still, the focus of the confessional, once it fixed on intimate relations, was remarkably unremitting—especially since this was a questionnaire that, if it was more than a sham, must have elicited evasive answers, which would have needed subtle follow-up.

The idée fixe continued (under the sixth commandment):

> Are you married or single? Since you last confessed, have you known another person than her with whom you are married? How many of them? Married or single? How many married women? How many times have you gone with each of the married women? How many single women? How many times have you gone with each of the single women? Have you known a maiden? Did you corrupt her? How many times did you go with her? Have you been with any relative?

Questions followed about bestiality and homosexuality, and then the focus changed to impure thoughts:

> Have you had a pollution when asleep? Did this happen because you talked or thought of some woman? Have you had a voluntary pollution? Have you looked with longing [afición] on any persons, or impurely [deshonestamente]?

After ten more detailed questions, we read:

> Has some person, or your wife, been a procuress at your request?

This is precisely the type of behavior that almost damned the soul in Anchieta's play. It is worth mentioning that traditionally, recruiting other wives was an expected and respected duty of the first wife, should it become necessary—for example, if the household became too large for a single mistress.[7] Such arrangements, evidently, did not win the church's blessing.

And finally:

> Have you known [carnally] any priest? Have you known any father who does not say mass?

This was the longest and most detailed single theme in the Lima Confessional, with instructions how the questions must be adjusted to the sex of the respondent. The questioning in the indigenous language allowed the priests—if they knew the language well enough to understand and query—to probe, and in so doing to show more about the true nature of Catholic Christianity (as it emerged) than could ever be stated in the approved theoretical statements of the *Doutrina*, even if buttressed by the (fixed) question-and-answer format of Catechism.

In these works of Sahagún in Nahuatl, and Anchieta in Tupi, the vernacular language could be used in relatively open, if not really informal, literature to give a more heartfelt and humane understanding of the hopes and fears touched by the Christian law, beyond what was stated clearly in black and white in the *Doutrina*. Some of the themes touched would be present in the *Doutrina* but could be treated in a more lively, even lighthearted manner. It also enabled the priests to use music, song, and dance to enlist enthusiasm, and so engage the hearts of converts.

Pérez Bocanegra in Quechua

For popular worship, the indigenous languages were used as long as they stayed strong in their communities, and Quechua is a fine example. This part of the service remained an adjunct to the central rites of the mass, which—as in the rest of the Catholic church—remained unchangeably in Latin.

Here is part of a hymn to the Virgin Mary, written in about 1622 by the parish priest Juan Pérez Bocanegra of Belén in Cuzco (who also wrote six volumes in Quechua on church history). He was—in opposition to Jesuits—very keen, where possible, to use native Quechua terms rather than loans from Spanish or Latin (though *santo*, *angel*, and *anima* all appear, even in this short extract). His work in this hymn was intended for Quechua-speaking peasants, and so it was accepted.[8]

Some cultural, rather than religious, background in legend and myth could be included in the mix of ideas, so that *Supay*, a generic name for the ruler of the Inner World,* is identified with the Devil; *uthurunku* (properly a jaguar) is recast as the Serpent in the Garden of Eden; and the author made free to play with different metaphors to bring home the central truth of Christ carnally present in Mary's womb—a royal inn, a walled garden of delights, and many other images.

Qan quyaman, pillan, paqtan	To you, O Queen, the equal
tukuy santokunamanta	of all the saints
llapa angelkunamanta	of all the angels
supaypa umanta waqtan	Supay's head is broken
jallp'aman tupuqta t'aqtan.	and spread over the earth:
Sutillayki.	With just your name.
Ñujñu ruruq chunta mallki	Sweet fruiting palm plant
runakunaq munay kallcha	revered by all people
pukay pukay sumaq phallcha	red red fine gentian
sut'arpu tukuchiq kallki	turning ash to bricks [or killing evil?]
t'ituyachiq ñawillayki	your eyes shining
qhispiwanpu.	life-boat [or translucent nave?]
Qanmi kanki qhapaq tanpu	You are the royal inn
may may kamapas uyaylla,	accepting come who may,
qhatiqiykipaq munaylla,	beloved by your followers,
jatun sunqupas ayranpu,	for mighty-hearted a cactus,
k'umuykuqkunapaq llanp'u	for the humble soft,
waqcha quya.	caring for the poor.

---

* Garcilaso de la Vega (1539–1616), in his *Royal Commentaries of the Yncas* (Part 1), wrote that *Ucu Pacha* was the "lowest earth, where they said that the wicked were sent; and to describe it more clearly they gave it another name—*supay-pa-huasin*. This word means *devil's house*." But the grammarians Domingo de Santo Tomás and Antonio Ricardo were aware that this latter phrase was a Christian coinage. (MacCormick 1993, p. 255.)

wisq'aykusqa kusi muya,	Enclosed joy garden
qhapaq yayq yaykuna,	entered by the royal father's command,
yapay t'ika aqllakuna,	beautiful flower of choice,
Jesús purichiq uruya,	the sling-bridge to Jesus,
pilku ch'antaq k'anchaq quya,	weaving colorful amulets,
suyakuyniy.	my hope.

. . .

Animayta uthurunku	My soul, the Jaguar
qallu llulliniwan llullaspa	with deceiving tongue, deceitful,
pallqu kawsayman pusaspa,	drew to a lying life
muyupuwan chunku chunku	(Demons), they compass it about,
chayña maywaq intuykunku	encircling it with shows of love
wantunanpaq . . .[9]	to carry it off . . .

Yapuguay in Guaraní

After three examples of European missionaries who wrote original literature in American languages, and their effects on the Catholic faith in the Americas, we turn at last to a native speaker, one born and raised there, who continued his own language's literature by writing on Christian themes.

Nicolás Yapuguay was, as the tradition proudly records, a distinguished musician, and a *cacique** (i.e., from an indigenous noble family). Born around 1680 in the Jesuit mission town of Santa María la Mayor, on the border between modern Paraguay and Uruguay, he naturally grew up speaking Guaraní as his first language, although he learned Latin and Spanish too in the course of his education, at which he excelled.

His claim to fame is his work with the Italian Jesuit, Father Paolo Restivo. A keen exponent of the Guaraní language, Restivo had produced in 1724 a new edition of the classic grammar and dictionary published by Antonio Ruiz de Montoya in 1639–40. Yapuguay certainly worked with him on this edition, but he also produced two works of his own, *Explicación del Catecismo* and *Sermones y Ejemplos*—despite their titles written in Guaraní

---

* *Cacique* [kasíke] is a word borrowed from Taino—the first American language encountered by Christopher Columbus in the Caribbean—and became a general term for chieftain in Spanish and Portuguese. The Guaraní equivalent would be *mburuvichá* "superior." (Cf Tupi *morobixaba*.)

throughout. They have both survived, in a strangely uneven printed version, which shows that they were printed on the Jesuits' own press, established by self-help in the mission when they could get no delivery of a commercial printing press.

Eloquence was a fitting attribute of a *cacique*, and had been so noted by the linguist Montoya in his description of the "Spiritual Conquest of Paraguay":

> Many are ennobled by eloquence of speech (so highly they value their language, and rightly, because it is worthy of praise, and to be renowned among languages of repute) and with it they gather people and vassals, with whom they and their descendants remain ennobled.[10]

This link was aptly stated in Guaraní:

amongue aete oñe'ẽ porã etéramo, ñõte jepe omono'õ ava reta

If he truly speaks well, only so can he gather a multitude.[11]

From the titles, and from their laudatory but unexcited reception, it is clear that Yapuguay's works were not pathbreaking in their content. They were pastoral texts derived from study of the catechism, and elaborations, from memory, of the Gospel sermons that he had heard each Sunday. Still, his Jesuitical comrades were deeply impressed by the style, *purissima Guaraniorum lingua*. And Father Paolo Restivo "kept him at his side as an interpreter whenever he wanted to explain something in Guaraní more elegantly."[12] He also arranged the printing of Yapuguay's collections as books, and while Father Paolo's name did not appear on the title page, Yapuguay insisted on adding *con dirección de un religioso de la Compañía de Jesús.*

These works, elegantly written as they were, aspire to nothing more than a fluent exposition of practical Christianity for the Guaraní-speaking congregation. They were never translated into Spanish or Latin to find a wider and less parochial audience, even though, as one commentator put it, *nil elegantius a Jesuita ullo scriptum fuerat*—"nothing more elegant had been written by any Jesuit." Elegance, it seems, was not enough to justify translation.

Since Yapuguay is praised as the best writer on Christianity that the Guaraní speakers produced, this in effect condemns the whole Jesuit enterprise along the Paraná River, utopian as its missions there are often said to be. The summit of their education was to produce prize students, not original scholars. The comparisons intended to honor Yapuguay only succeed in patronizing him. Guillermo Furlong, writing a preface to his work in 1953, wrote: "so much more notable in that the Indians, though supremely skillful in copying, were not so in creating. Their short attention span, or their embryonic mental development, did not allow them to soar mentally, although when in contact with the earth they were (like the mythical Antaeus) dauntless and matchless. There was not an European object that they did not imitate to perfection . . ."[13] Even his friend and greatest supporter, Father Paolo Restivo noted, "well known and superior to what can be conceived in an Indian is the ability of this Nicolás Yapuguay, *cacique* and musician of Santa María, much praised in all his compositions—and rightly—for the exactness [*propiedad*], clarity and elegance with which he happily makes his points, even in matters touching on God, which is not something easy to find in other Indians."[14] Again, the backhanded reference to Indian standards stands out.

The case of Yapuguay, then, can be seen as a more subtle example of the kind of racism that kept indigenous Americans out of the priesthood— a policy that was not questioned again after the Third Council of Lima. Catholic Christianity, led on the ground by Spaniards and Portuguese (though other Europeans might be smuggled into their ranks), assigned them a place, but one that ranked below the top table. And the Iberian elite claimed—no doubt quite sincerely—to have evidence derived from experience that there is where the Indians belonged. The judgment applied, even in the extreme case where an Indian appeared to have the qualities that justified elite status, both social and intellectual.

Meanwhile, Christianity—however sincerely believed and elegantly expressed by the odd exceptional individual—could not wash away the racial difference of lineage, a dividing line that was helpfully reiterated by language. Souls might be equal before God—indeed there was no ground, in Christianity, for them to be anything else; but facts of origin, family, or favored tongue carried implications that Man would not forget.

These few, scattered examples suggest that it would have been possible to develop theology, and to control the higher functions of the church, in the indigenous *lenguas generales*. They could have played a role analogous to that of Spanish and Portuguese. But it was not to be. They were instead used by Christian missionaries as contact languages to make conversions—at whatever level of understanding—and for routine pastoral care, in which an annual confession of sins, conducted individually, was deemed essential. Even in the Jesuit missions, where Tupi or Guaraní was the universal language for everyday use, it did not give rise to parity of esteem for its users, and hence for their concerns, in the community. While there were still speech communities defined by indigenous languages, they never became full parts of the Catholic Christian church.

❦

CHAPTER 13

Extirpación de Idiomas?
Asserting Monolingualism

*Si alguno hubiese de hablar con Dios debería ser en español por la majestad
de la lengua.*

If anyone had to speak to God it should be in Spanish, for the majesty of
the language.

Carlos V, King of Spain and Holy Roman Emperor (died
1558), cited with approval by Manuel José de Ayala (1728–1805)
in his *Recopilación de las leyes de Indias*
("Digest of Laws of the Indies")[1]

E VER SINCE THE FIRST generation of settled Hispanic rule in the
Americas, in the second third of the sixteenth century, the Christian
empires had followed a policy of separate development, seeing the status and
regime of *la república de españoles*, or more truthfully *la república de blancos*, as
something quite different from *la república de indios*.

Subjects of the former polity—*súbditos*—were more or less on a par with
those of the European homeland although, given Spanish conservatism,
a very real difference in status developed between those born in Iberia,
peninsulares (known locally as *gachupines* "dry stumps" or *chapetones* "cork-
cloggies"), and the later generations (*criollos* "home-reared").[2]

Subjects of the latter, however (more likely to be classed as *vasallos* than
súbditos), had a rather special status, reflecting the lack of Christianity in their
past. This meant that the Hispanic kingdoms were duty-bound to offer them
the opportunity of salvation—understood, without contest, as conversion to
the Catholic faith (and that, free of the attentions of the Inquisition)—but
in return they must lose their freedom of self-determination, being liable

to directed labor (*encomienda* or *mitá*) where so commanded by Spanish governors, or to *reducción*, i.e., resettlement into villages where they would be organized and enlightened by religious clergy. They must also pay a special tribute to the crown.

The traditional rulers of indigenous societies, everywhere known as *caciques*, were a partial exception, absorbed into the system as holders of Iberian offices, like *gobernador*, *alcalde* (mayor), or *regidor de cabildo* (president of the council), and had many other privileges, such as the right to bear swords and firearms, and to ride horses.

This was the theory. In practice people's status was much less determinate, especially given the high degree of pairing during the early years of incoming peninsular men with native women, and the general ferment of irregular unions as the unruly "New World" settled down to foreign management. The resulting *mestizos*, despite their numbers, never fitted clearly into the system, but were left vying for position, largely as would-be criollos at the tail end of the queue. And black slaves from Africa were another important part of the mix in many parts of the American continent and islands, but as slaves: at least in the first generation, they had only obligations, and no rights at all.

The separate identity of the *indios* (or *naturales*) was marked for two centuries (at least seven generations of Ibero-America) by the survival, and vigorous use, of the indigenous languages, either their own mother tongues, or—in *reducciones*, *encomiendas*, and Indian *barrios* of cities—the so-called "general language" of the country, whatever it was, but which was nowhere Spanish or Portuguese. It was these indigenous languages that had in practice been used—after the first generation of conquest—to convert the Indians, and the twists and turns of this conversion process have been the story of the last two chapters.

By the early eighteenth century, a certain equilibrium had been achieved, with a horizontal social structure largely independent of the different regional *audiencias*, as the provincial governments were called. The *república de blancos*, with its mestizo and slave appendages, everywhere spoke Spanish or Portuguese; and the *república de indios* spoke a local language. Written language—evidently a necessity for religious and civil administration, and to a lesser extent for trade—was largely confined to Spanish or Portuguese; but in the large centers of settlement, the missionaries' hard-won command of indigenous languages had been translated—by educating the children of

noble families—into indigenous literacy, notably in Nahuatl and Quechua.*
The Jesuits' *reducciones* along the Paraná River and into Brazil, also meant
that speakers of Guaraní and Tupi could often read and write. The *lenguas
generales* had never become official for Catholicism anywhere: but they were
the principal languages for indigenous people in all the settlements, where
worship was uncontestedly Catholic.

In the middle of the eighteenth century, this balance was overturned,
ending the traditions of indigenous literacy, and replacing it with Spanish
and Portuguese.

The motive was external, inspired by new ideas of the European
Enlightenment, which suggested that rulers might increase both general
well-being, and their own wealth, by intervening to rationalize the way their
realms were governed. Linguistic diversity, an apparently needless complication, was an immediate target. So was the temporal power of the Catholic
church, identified as it was with the traditions that needed reform.

Three archbishops of Mexico oversaw the change.

Under Manuel José Rubio y Salinas (in office 1748–1765), there was a surge
in the provision of schools teaching Spanish: in the two years 1754–1756, they
went from 84 to 262, the archbishop commenting:

> I believe that . . . they will manage to forget their languages and with
> the creation of the schools they will acquire a taste for reading and
> writing . . . to ennoble their spirits and escape from the neediness,
> nakedness and wretchedness in which they live.[3]

The next incumbent, Francisco Antonio de Lorenzana y Buitrón (in office
1766–1772) likewise felt he was acting in the Indians' own best interests. In
1769 he opined that those who did not support the extension of Spanish,

> leaving them shut up in their own language, are to my thinking the
> declared enemies of the natives, of their policy and their nationality.

---

* There was a chair of Quechua at the University of Lima from 1579 to 1784.
  In Mexico, the Franciscans' Colegio de Santa Cruz de Tlatelolco, intended to prepare
  native Mexicans for the priesthood, functioned only between the 1530s and 1550s. After
  three unfulfilled royal *cédulas* ("decrees") in 1580, 1582, and 1614, a chair in Nahuatl (and
  Otomí) was only established at the University of Mexico in 1640.

Warming to his theme, he pithily identified its disadvantages:

> This is a constant truth: the maintenance of the language of the
> Indians is a folly (*un capricho*) of men, whose fortune and learning
> is restricted to speaking that tongue learnt even as a child: it is a
> contagion, which separates the Indians from the conversation of
> the Spaniards; it is a plague, which infects the Dogmas of our
> Holy Faith; it is a prejudicial marker to separate the natives of some
> villages from others by diversity of their tongues; it is an increased cost
> for the parishes, which require ministers of different languages in
> their same domain; and it is an impossibility for the governance of the
> bishops.[4]

He then received, in 1770, a royal decree from King Carlos III "in order that
at once may be achieved the extinction of the different languages . . . and the
sole use of Castilian" (i.e., Spanish, and throughout the empire). Although
there was little concrete force to this beside abolition of the requirement for
bishops to appoint parish priests with regard to language knowledge, the tide
was turning against the status quo.

During the period of office of the next archbishop, Alonso Núñez de
Haro, from 1772 to 1800, anything that tended to disadvantage the monolingual Spanish speaker was exposed, disputed, and finally abolished. All
official support of American language schools ceased. The chair of Quechua
in Lima was discontinued in 1784.

Revolution meanwhile was also coming to the other end of the American
empire. Most influential in South America, in the *reducciones* where Tupi
and Guaraní were spoken, were the Jesuits. Their loyalty to the pope was
the root of their undoing, since the papacy was waging a losing battle
for influence with the Catholic monarchs of Europe. And so, for reasons
largely unconnected with their actual activities in America, they were
formally expelled by the Portuguese crown from Brazil in 1759 (with con-
comitant banning of the Tupi *língua geral*), and from the whole Spanish
empire in 1767. The *reducciones*, left under Indian management, very soon
collapsed.

In the next generation, the early nineteenth century, the ideas of the
Enlightenment went even deeper, so far as to make not just conservativism,
but kings and empires themselves seem an irrelevance. Liberation strug-
gles convulsed the whole of Ibero-America, and the result everywhere was

the victory not of the indigenous, but of the criollos, the Americans who felt they were being demeaned by the presumptions of their European cousins across the Atlantic. Although some lip service was paid to the human roots of the American countries (for example, in Mexico's cult of *indigenismo*), the role of the indigenous languages (and the communities that spoke them) was everywhere even further reduced. In the new Mexico, independent in 1821, for the first time the courts became closed to pleas in Nahuatl. In 1810, 45 percent of Mexicans were of the *república de españoles*, with Spanish as their first language: in 1995 the proportion had doubled to 88 percent.

The global effect of these changes was to withdraw the support that the church had been giving, by default, to the indigenous languages of the Americas. New generations of Latin Americans would be expected to cope exclusively in Spanish, in their religious life as in everything else. It was no longer acceptable to pray, and to confess, in other languages—at least, one could not expect to find a priest who would understand. Services would retain their Latin, but all the vernacular parts, where the priests try to communicate actively with the congregation, would take place in Spanish or Portuguese. Thenceforth Americans monolingual in anything but one of these two languages would become fewer and fewer, and the religious community of Latin America would become disjoint from the oldest, indigenous, speech communities.

The *república de indios* had kept its indigenous-speaking members in the status of permanent minors, with neither the full rights nor the full responsibilities of their criollo and mestizo fellow subjects of the crown. Now—whether it suited them or not—they would have to grow up: but at the cost of their languages. In another sense, they would have to wake up: to lose their easy familiarity with their people's traditional worlds.

The church was more united, in a sense that had been desired by those three archbishops of Mexico; but it had become so by denying direct access to those who thought in Nahuatl, Quechua, Guaraní, and many, many other languages. As a result, it was also, in a human sense, impoverished.

It was able to wash its hands of many issues: the fitness of other languages' terms to express Christian thinking, the significance of analogies between their spiritual traditions and the Christian centers of sin and resurrection, the basis—whether anthropological or ethical—for denying Holy Orders to whole communities of people because of the language that they spoke, or that their ancestors had once spoken.

The indigenous languages of the Americas had become an irrelevance. But by the same token, the church itself became smaller, no longer needing to reconcile the different approaches to sin and salvation that Spanish and Portuguese imperialism had once made it confront.*

---

* It is interesting that the current pope, Francis, discussed this very issue with Bishop Díaz from Chiapas, Mexico, in December, accepting translations of scripture and liturgy into the Mayan languages Tzotzil and Tzeltal. Mexican religious analyst Elio Masferrer notes that since the 1960s, the church has believed that "the Revelation of the Word be delivered in keeping with the culture of each people." ("Mexico's Indigenous Languages Get Nod from the Church": http://www.bbc.co.uk/news/world-latin-america-25445819)

CHAPTER 14

"Back to the Sources"

God's Word and Translation

Quemadmodum desiderat cervus ad fontes aquarum:
ita desiderat anima mea ad te Deus.

As the hart panteth after the water brooks, so panteth my soul
after thee, O God.

Psalm 42:1

Sed in primis ad fontes ipsos properandum, id est graecos et antiquos.

Above all, one must hasten to the sources themselves, that is, to the
Greeks and ancients.

Erasmus, "On the Plan for Study, Reading, and
Interpreting of Authors"[1]

PREVIOUS CHAPTERS HAVE RECOUNTED important changes of
language in the history of the spread of Buddhism and Christianity, all
of which had impact on the content of the faith, or on the self-image of the
faithful. In the modern age, when instruction—and usually scripture and
liturgy too—in world faiths is available in all the major languages of wider
communication, these effects seem oddly parochial.

The Internet provides some useful information on numbers: as of
November 2014, the full Bible has been translated into 531 languages, as
well as being partly available in 2,352 more.[2] The Qur'ān has been translated
into at least 63.[3] Mahayana Buddhist sutras are available in at least twelve
languages, but these are dominated by the half-dozen of its traditional Asian
heartlands (Sanskrit, Chinese, Korean, Japanese, Tibetan, Mongolian); for

European languages (except for English) they can be read in small and very various quantities.[4]

Despite carryovers of racial discrimination in many parts of the world, this linguistic *smørgåsbord* is revealing of today's openness of world faiths to new converts, and the parity of respect that they are likely to receive nowadays if they decide to join the Christian church, the Muslim *ummah*, or the Buddhist *sangha*, in whatever primary language they use. Although theological discussion, if it does take place, may be preferred—for practical reasons—in a few better-known languages, there is no longer any sense that choice of linguistic medium, and hence language community, can affect the fundamentals of the religion, or the status of converts.

This chapter will look at how this new, apparently language-neutral, approach to religion came about. We might call it "language transparency." Essentially, it dates back to the European Reformation of the sixteenth century, and the general fixation on translations, of scripture and liturgy, that came in its wake.

This transition was original to Europe, and quite autonomous. No newly converted population was involved. All the significant actors were Christian clergymen (interacting with princes and their governments); and all belonged to nations of northwestern Europe that had been accepted, and had considered themselves, as parts of Roman Catholic Christendom for the past several centuries.

Furthermore, although the change co-occurred with the period of western European explorers' discovery of the New World and of the sea route around Africa to Asia—the first half of the sixteenth century—there was no obvious way in which these discoveries had prompted a new attitude to Christian faith, let alone textual support for faith in personal study of the scriptures. The discoveries were after all largely made by mariners from Spain and Portugal, countries where the Reformation had failed to take root.

It is perhaps arguable that "grammatization" did play a role—the process whereby modern languages, such as Italian, Spanish, German, French, and English (as well as many others), were for the first time seen as distinct entities deserving description with their own grammars (respectively 1441, 1492, 1534, 1550, and 1586),[5] and each with a significant written literature of its own. At the very least, this literature would, in the Protestant north of Europe, soon include a full printed translation of the Holy Bible into each vernacular (German 1522, Dutch 1526, French 1530, Czech 1549, Danish 1550, Polish 1563, and English 1611*). But the right to make these Bible translations was at first highly contested by the Catholic church and its traditionalist supporters, to the extent of burning some early translators and publishers at the stake (notably William Tyndale, for a partial edition of the English Bible, in 1536). So the new linguistic attitudes to expression of the scriptures must be seen as separate from the new, more simply patriotic, attitudes to extending the coverage of grammar books from Latin to the various nation-states' vernaculars.

Yet the change in intellectual climate in western Europe that occurred in the sixteenth century was expressed doubly in new attitudes to translation. Not only did the process begin of attempting to translate the Christian scriptures into the vernacular of every Christian community; but the clergy who would encompass these translations had previously begun to take an interest in the authenticity of the text of the scriptures as they knew them.

This was a development wholly unprecedented in the West for more than a millennium, since Jerome had sealed his "Vulgate" translation in 405. The Church of the Latin Rite had accepted this Latin text as the closest they needed to come to an authentic text of the set of the cardinal books, even though they had all been written in Hebrew, Aramaic, or Greek. This official view was firmly reasserted after many vernacular translations had already been completed, in the canons and decrees of the Council of Trento of 1546:

> the sacred and holy Synod . . . ordains and declares, that the said old
> and vulgate edition, which, by the lengthened usage of so many ages,
> has been approved of in the Church, be, in public lectures, disputa-
> tions, sermons and expositions, held as authentic; and that no one is
> to dare, or presume to reject it under any pretext whatever.[6]

---

* This was King James's Authorized Version for England and Scotland, based on the original languages, and clarifying a rather murky situation for Bibles in English.

Myles Coverdale had actually published a full text based on a variety of other translations,
none of them Hebrew or Greek, in 1535. Coverdale's place of publication was outside England,
probably Marburg or Cologne. It was adopted as the core of the "Great Bible," "one book of
the whole Bible of the largest volume in English," ordered by Henry VIII to be set up in
every parish church in England in 1538. But Coverdale's Bible was then prohibited by the
king in 1546. It was reissued, with less controversial notes, as "the Bishops' Bible" in 1568.

In Scotland, the Geneva Bible, published in 1560 and of Calvinist inspiration, had been
most popular. (Ellingworth 2007, p. 116–17.)

But a new attitude to classical texts had developed, in what is now called the Renaissance. Fifteenth-century scholars in Italy had founded and developed the discipline of textual criticism, a means to distinguish and select the best quality amid hosts of copies. The new science could have political as well as literary implications. Some, among them the great humanist Lorenzo Valla (1407–1457) —whose *Elegantiae* had used empirical methods to get Latin back to the classical style of Cicero—had even used stylistic arguments to debunk the authenticity of the *Donation of Constantine*, a text that had been used for seven centuries to legitimize the church's temporal power. When the professor Angelo Poliziano (1454–1494) sat down to formulate the principles of textual criticism and classical philology (in his *Miscellanea* 1489), he was laying down rules for a new standard of skeptical and evidence-based research.

The copyist's tradition had preserved all the ancient literature that still survived, whether holy or secular, from the classical era, but now—with the invention of printing, and consequent proofreading and long, identical, print runs—there was the possibility of establishing the best text once and for all. Monks copying sacred texts could be as fallible as when they were reproducing history or poetry. Why should the products of Jerome's labors on Holy Writ be exempt from this? Indeed, why not use the best methods to establish the best of all texts, Holy Scripture?

Some influential figures in the church seemed to take account of this implication of the new technology. Most notably, the Spanish cardinal Jiménez de Cisneros (1436–1517) commissioned the *Complutensian Polyglot Bible*, the first edition of the Hebrew, Latin, and Greek texts to be printed in parallel.* It was edited over a period of fifteen years by a team of scholars expert in the different languages, and led by Diego López de Zúñiga, who knew them all. Jiménez's reputed motive for the work was "to revive the decayed study of the Sacred Scriptures," though it is clear that no actual emendation of the Latin text was envisaged as a result of comparing it with the two older versions that surrounded it. Rather—being associated with the languages of deviant religious sects, Judaism and Greek Orthodoxy—they were seen as "robbers" nailed up on either side of the (true Catholic) Vulgate, as the editors apparently joke in their preface.[7]

Of course, the Vulgate in the sixteenth century was not just a text. As presented by the Catholic church, it was compassed about with interpre-

---

* It was named for its city of origin, Complutum, the Roman name of Alcalá de Henares.

tive commentary. It was above all to preserve the validity of the vast web of authoritative notes, built up over centuries, that the church resisted all emendation of the text.[8] The Complutensian Polyglot starts with some rough, but ancient, hexameter verses on varieties of interpretation:

> *Littera gesta docet: quid credas allēgorīa.*
> *Moralis quid agas: quo tendas ānagōgīa*

> The letter teaches what happened; allegory what to believe;
> moral [interpretation] what to do; anagogy where to make for.[*]

Compare this with the principles proposed by Hrabanus Maurus seven centuries before: he had distinguished *historia*, "literal interpretation," from *allegoria* "figurative meaning," *anagogia* "mystical meaning," and *tropologia* "moral guidance."[9]

This same verse was picked up by Nicholas of Lyra, who showed how it might apply, for example, to the place-name Jerusalem: literally a city in Judaea, but morally the faithful soul; anagogically, it is the Church Triumphant; allegorically, though, it is life itself, or whatever is necessary for salvation.[10]

By the latter fifteenth century, the Catholic church had had a thousand years to build up a store of insights that it delivered in a package with the Bible's text. Besides the coherence of this inherited conglomerate, the church could also claim (as in the learned sneering of the Complutensian Bible's preface) that the source texts of the Bible themselves had been transmitted by unreliable witnesses. Particularly in the case of Hebrew, these were the treacherous Jews who had refused to recognize the Messiah when He came, and would not be above perverting their text to justify their error.[†] How

---

[*] I have marked the vowels with the popular (but wrong) quantities (¯ long, ˘ short) to make the verse scan (e.g., túm-titty-túm-tum at the end of each line). Allegory—properly ἀλληγορία *allēgoria*—may be etymologized as "otherwise-speech," and usually connoted a reference to prophecy. Anagogy—ἀναγωγία *anagōgia*—Greek for "leading up," meant interpretation with an eye on heaven and the afterlife.

[†] This was the explicit view of Nicholas of Lyra, who had been born a Jew himself, and perhaps spoke with "the zeal of the convert":

> *In hoc tamen valde cavendum est, quantum ad locos Scripturae Veteris Testamenti, qui de deitate Christi ac de consequentibus ad hoc loquuntur: quorum aliquos Iudaei corruperunt ad defensionem sui erroris, ut partim declaravi in quadam quaestione de divinitate Christi . . .*

> In this much care is needed, as far passages in the Old Testament that speak in passing of the godhead of Christ and its consequences: some of these the Jews have corrupted to

much better, therefore, to trust the Vulgate, with its revelation elaborated by the devout over a millennium of meditation!

Criticizing the Vulgate

It was a formidable edifice, which must have seemed proof against piecemeal attack by individual skeptics, or even (as most of the critics actually were) devout seekers after fresh aspects of God's truth. But it proved vulnerable to intellectual examination.

First of all, the critics armed themselves with new language skills, in Hebrew and Greek, which had not been available to earlier generations of West Europeans, at least not outside Italy.

Johann Reuchlin (1455–1522), for example, the first fully competent scholar of Hebrew in northern Europe, was a German monastery official's son from the Black Forest, who was sent as a young man with an aristocratic party to Paris, where he could learn Greek, and somewhat later (at thirty-seven) was sent on another mission to Linz, where he met a Jewish physician from whom he could learn Hebrew. Supporting himself as a legal copyist, he began to research the sources of the Bible, though limited by the scarcity of Greek and Hebrew texts that were yet available. He was not a trained theologian, and his main motivation seems to have been the sheer joy of linguistic exporation. As he wrote in the preface to his final work, "I have pursued the study of many foreign languages with such an exertion as well as eagerness that I have no doubts about having followed the beacon of the Genius consuming me."[11]

A decade younger, Desiderius Erasmus of Rotterdam (ca. 1466–1536) was likewise educated at a monastic school, Deventer in the Netherlands, and was lucky enough to be in the first generation taught Greek at school. He took holy orders, but like Reuchlin supported himself in the early stages of his career as a secretary and copyist. Erasmus was much more a self-conscious "Renaissance man," or to use the contemporary term, *humanista*— as his double-barreled Christian name suggests, containing words for "love" in both Latin and Greek (the first part being his own invention).

---

defend their own error, as I have partly declared in a certain question of the divinity of Christ . . .

Prolegomena to Walafrid Strabo, in *Patrologia Latina* cxiii, 29–30

He never held a permanent academic post, but spent periods of his life at universities in Paris, Leuven, England, Italy, and Basel and became so intent on revising the Latin text of the New Testament that he resolved to learn Greek properly, something he achieved largely through self-study in about 1500–1503. He spent 1506 to 1509 in Italy, improving his Greek and elaborating an edition of the New Testament (with parallel Latin translation) which came out as *Novum Testamentum Omne* and went through five editions between 1516 and 1535. The third edition (1522) was probably used by Tyndale as the basis for his English translation, even though textual criticism of the Greek—especially, in the selection of the best manuscripts—was never a major virtue of Erasmus's text.

These two self-made scholar-linguists proceeded to call in the old-world original Old and New Testaments—the Hebrew *Tanakh* and the Greek *Καινη Διαθηκη* (*kainē diathēkē*)—to redress the balance of the (slightly newer) world of the *Editio Vulgata*. Their own motives were not combative, although some queried their modesty: Zúñiga, for example, believed it was only because Erasmus was *laudis potius cupiditate ductus* ("led more by greed for praise") that he needed to bring out a new text, and so openly damn the church's translation, rather than content himself with annotations.[12]

Still, the novice linguists immediately turned up suspicious translations when they compared originals with passages of the Vulgate.

One of the clearest was in Psalm 130. Here the text of verse 5 read:

כי־עמך הסליחה למען תורא, i.e.,

ki-omk he-şliọheh l-m'on	but-with-you (is) forgiveness, so-that
thiware	you-are-feared

But the last word here (on the right in the Hebrew characters) looks very much like תרוה i.e., *torah*, Hebrew for "law." Sure enough the Vulgate of this verse read:

Quia apud te propitiatio est;	Because with you is propitiation; and
et propter legem tuam,	because of your law,

suggesting that some translator had misread this word as *legem* "law" and possibly also deformed the syntax of the conjunction *l-m'on* "so that" before it.

Reuchlin used this example as evidence that (as is now well known) the translators of the Septuagint (which has a similar error here, reading ενεκεν του νομου "because of the law") must have lacked vowel-pointing in their Hebrew text: once that is inserted וְתֵרָא *thiware* looks very different from תּוֹרה *torah*.

Reuchlin in fact found more than two hundred such cruces as this, where comparison with the Hebrew Old Testament suggested errors in the Vulgate. Against the persistent Christian barracking that the Jews had deliberately falsified their text, he argued that this would have been almost impossible given that the number of verses, and even letters, in every book of the Old Testament is counted. Furthermore, the several exemplars of the text that are available to consult are identical.[13] He was also impressed by the sheer antiquity of the material, as far as anyone knew at the time, the ultimate *Urtext*:

> The mediator between God and man was, as we read in the Pentateuch, language, yet not any language but only Hebrew; God wished his secrets to be known to mortal man through Hebrew.[14]

Reuchlin clearly wanted to attribute merit to the Hebrew tradition—hardly surprising, since he had, uniquely among European Christians of his day, taken the trouble to acquire the ability to read it—but one can also see that he was a textual critic to his fingertips. He wished like his humanist peers to return *ad fontes*—back to the sources—and quoted the following simile, neatly enough from Jerome himself:

> Wine that is often drawn off the cask loses in splendor. The same applies to translations: the original language of every work is sweetest.[15]

This implied a preference for the testimony of the Hebrew and Greek texts of the Bible, but on the best possible textual-critical grounds. He did not elaborate on whether this special sweetness of the original is of accuracy and authenticity, or rather of literary sparkle and inspiration. He was even able to cite Augustine himself on his side:

> Augustine says in his *De Vera Religione* that the language of Holy Scripture should be understood according to the peculiarity of every particular language, for each language has its own particular

manner of speech ... when one language is translated into another, then everyone believes that it makes no sense and does not sound right.

The kind of argument Reuchlin was promoting through his career tended to look for truth in a sense of the day-to-day world, in the way written language works, and in such principles as human sciences can discern at work there. These were practical sciences, among which textual criticism could justly claim a status as a new addition to the scholar's equipment. The Roman Catholic Church rightly discerned that this was a threat to the kind of authority the church itself had built up over the past millennium, whereby it had acted as the unique, infallible judge of truth and virtue.*

But the Old Testament was merely a background to Christianity: only through allegorical or anagogic interpretation could it be consulted for the truths of the faith itself. Far more penetrating, and ultimately more damaging, testimony was going to be given when the New Testament was subject to the same comparative critique. This is what Erasmus would do with his new Greek edition, accompanied helpfully with a new Latin translation based on it. Surprisingly, perhaps, the Greek text (which became known as the *textus receptus*) was not up to the highest critical standards: the oldest available manuscripts had not been used, and for the last few verses of Revelation, it had even been reconstructed by translating the Vulgate back into Greek! But it served. The most significant revisions came in passages that were not in textual dispute.

Most famously, Erasmus proposed a new translation for the command of John the Baptist, the "voice crying in the wilderness" in Matthew 3:2.

In Greek, he cries out μετανοειτε, which is derivable from *meta-* "after" and *noeō* "think, use *nous*," and the verb is in the present imperative plural form. Erasmus suggests it should be rendered as *resipiscite* or *ad mentem*

---

* In the church's defense, it should be noted that it was not alone, in this era, in seeking to establish truth within a closed world, a world for which it alone set the rules. I have pointed out in my book *Ad Infinitum* (see especially pp. 226–30) that the essence of learning as developed in Latin was not to leave the truth open-ended and available for development through research, as might be our modern ideal, but to close it in a set of *summae*, statements of principles for each field that would characterize them once and for all. For if knowledge (*sapientia*) is revisable at some point in the future, how can it really count now as knowledge?

redite, either of which would mean "come to your senses." In his commentary, he notes how neat Greek is in placing repentance in afterthought, not in the confession; but this is to forget the real meaning of μετανοειτε, which—like the other verb beginning with μετα, μεταμελει—may have begun by meaning "change your mind" but very clearly meant to repent of, or be sorry for past actions (and not just in Christian Greek).

The usual verb for this in Latin is *paenitet*, but being impersonal (as if in English one had to say "it repents me of my sin"), it has no imperative, and so one can see why Jerome was reduced to using the auxiliary *agite* "do" with the verbal noun *paenitentia* as object, so translating as *paenitentiam agite*. The problem came when this phrase began—in the light of church practices—to change its meaning: no longer "to be sorry," but "to show your regret by doing penance" and mortifying the flesh. This is what *paenitentiam agite* meant in the Middle Ages, often reinforced by changing the spelling to *poenitentiam agite*—suggesting a link (otherwise hard to defend) with *poena* "punishment."

Erasmus's new translation undercut the church's traditional approach to make amends for sin, and the whole sacrament of penance, but on the grounds of half-understood Greek, and ignorance of how the Latin expression itself had moved in meaning since Jerome bestowed it.

At Luke 1:28, when the Angel Gabriel greets the Virgin Mary, Erasmus would not accept *gratia plena* "full of grace" as an adequate translation of κεχαριτωμενη, which is literally "graced." Erasmus suggested *gratificata*, also pointing out that this is not a standard greeting, and that Mary herself was left pondering what kind of greeting it might be.

The net implication was that Mary herself was not a repository of grace, but one whom the Lord had graced: not, therefore, an appropriate recipient of worship in her own right. Nor, as Erasmus would have it, was she an advocate who could (now as ever) prevail on her son. He noted that when Jesus returned home from the temple with his parents (Luke 2:51), he was said to be υποτασσομενος αυτοις *subditus illis*, i.e., "obedient to them." This Vulgate translation just betokens a well-run family, where members knew their place—and did not preclude occasions when Joseph or Mary might have obeyed their son. It was not, as commentary on the Vulgate would have it, a license for the faithful to plead with Mary, so that she could instruct her son.

The kind of linguistic points that Erasmus picked up on did not expose rank mistranslations of the New Testament into Latin, but rather pointed out that the details of the Vulgate's phrasing, when they went beyond the implications of the New Testament Greek original, were not robust enough to bear the weight of interpretation that the church traditionally hung on them. In Erasmus's own mind, he was attempting to separate truth from authority, to enhance the church by recognizing and eliminating accretions and abuses.

Erasmus was not, however, in thrall to the Greek text, in preferring it to the Latin: in occasional cases he thought that the Vulgate might be closer to the original content—as when he disregarded the Doxology ("For thine is the kingdom, the power and the glory, for ever and ever" οτι σου εστιν η βασιλεια και η δυναμις και η δοξα εις τους αιωνας), which appears at the end of the *Pater Noster* "Lord's Prayer" (Matthew 6:13) in all the Greek manuscripts—but in none other, including Jerome's own translation. This was a result of his extra policy, announced in his dedicatory letter to the pope, "to run through all the writings of the old theologians and to trace from their quotations and expositions what each one of them had read and changed."[16]

In short, Erasmus and Reuchlin's policy was to base the reconstruction of the Holy Scripture on historical evidence, wherever they could find it, and not solely on the authority of the church, whether traditional or current. This suggests that, in the Reformation created by this "philological" view, scholarly rigor would be preferred as a guide to truth, over faith in the inspiration of the heroic translators of the past.

Luther's Approach

However, the new accessibility of the Hebrew and Greek testaments was taken up most influentially not by a philologist, but by an inspirational preacher who declared that his whole life's career, and his whole understanding of Holy Scripture—which took him, along with much of northern Europe, out of communion with the Catholic Faith—was based on an inspired understanding of one verse of the Bible: Romans 1:17:

> *Justitia enim Dei in eo revelatur ex fide in fidem: sicut scriptum est: Justus autem ex fide vivit.*

or as he later phrased it in his own language:

Denn darin wird offenbart die	For therein is revealed the
Gerechtigkeit, die vor Gott gilt, welche	righteousness <u>that avails</u>
kommt aus Glauben in Glauben; wie	<u>before</u> God, <u>which comes</u> out
geschrieben steht [(Habakuk 2,4):	of faith into faith; as is written
aber] der Gerechte wird aus	[(Habakkuk 2:4): but] the
Glauben leben.	righteous man <u>shall</u> live out
	of faith.

This was the German friar Martin Luther (1483–1546). His concept was that the key to the Scriptures lay in the thesis of salvation by faith; and he went on to translate the whole Bible with this in mind. He was an inspirational, rather than a strictly accurate, translator (as comparison of this little bit of German with the Vulgate reveals, with underlining that shows what Luther added, and square brackets what he deleted). But he was so by design, repeating words of Saint Paul:

> I have not received the Gospel from man but from heaven.[17]

In general, he believed that advanced understanding—such as could only come from an enlightened theologian—was required to give a good translation, and that could only be a free one:

> A real translation is the application of sayings in a foreign language to one's own language.[18]
>
> Languages themselves do not make a theologian, but they are of assistance, as it is necessary to know the subject matter before it can be expressed through languages.[19]
>
> It is not enough to know grammar, but one must pay attention to the sense: for the knowledge of the subject matter brings out the meaning of the words.[20]

Luther, therefore, was happy to use the aids that Reuchlin and Erasmus had made available, to give a deeper linguistic basis to his new insight into the real essence of Christian salvation, not leaving him trapped in the Vulgate and the Septuagint.

Since he was convinced of the rightness of his overall interpretation, and he believed in offering a translation that was simple and clear, he supplemented the text slightly where he judged it necessary. This was most famously true in his version of Romans 3:28:

<table>
<tr><td>Arbitramur etiam justificari
hominem per fidem sine
operibus legis.</td><td>So halten wir nun dafür, daß der
Mensch gerecht wird ohne des Gesetzes
Werke, <u>allein durch den Glauben</u>.</td></tr>
</table>

Here the Vulgate, like the Greek New Testament, says, essentially word for word: "So we believe that man is justified [Greek δικαιουσθαι] by faith without the works of law." But Luther's German has inserted an extra word *allein* "only" before "by faith" (*per fidem*) and put *durch den Glauben* "by faith" at the end of the sentence, giving it stronger emphasis as the crucial point, quite validly for those that believed as he did.

Luther's translation into German included the Old Testament as well as the New, although the evidence of how much Hebrew he learned from Reuchlin's works is obscure. In both Hebrew and Greek he was actively learning in his thirties (1513–1519), essentially ingesting commentaries on texts rather than actively learning the languages' grammars as such. He wrote:

I am no Hebraist according to the grammar and rules, for I never allow myself to be bound, but go freely through it.

The phrases and manner of speaking, and construction, how one should connect and express the words, that one cannot give nor teach, for the construction often changes the meaning of the words ... I have learned more Hebrew whenever I, while reading, held one passage and saying against another, than whenever I have judged it only according to the grammar.

He was, however, closely in touch with his younger friend, the German humanist Philipp Melanchthon (1497–1560), who was extremely well founded in all the relevant languages,* and followed him in believing that without the help of the Holy Ghost no understanding was possible.[21] Collaboration with him undoubtedly was a major help to Luther as translator—an advantage

---

* Melanchthon had been given his Greek surname (a translation of his given name, Schwarzerdt, meaning "black-earth") by none other than Johann Reuchlin, who as his great-uncle had also supervised his education. Melanchthon went on to a starry career as the foremost educationalist in his country, and was awarded the title *Praeceptor Germaniae*.

that he even defended theologically, since the main fault of Jerome's translation, for Luther, was that he undertook it alone. Such work necessarily lacked the support of the Holy Ghost, he held,[22] following Matthew 18:20:

> For where two or three are gathered together in my name, there am I in the midst of them.

And so he could write Jerome off in these terms: "But I am amazed that at that time, scarcely three hundred years after Christ, so great a blindness was found in the Church together with so great a knowledge of languages."[23]

Besides believing that the combination of inspiration from the Holy Ghost and attention to original texts was the key to valid translation of the Scriptures, Luther also dismissed another principle of interpretation that had been a major prop to the Catholic church's teaching. This was the elaborate fourfold exegesis of the Holy Text, literal, allegorical, moral, and anagogic.

"Nothing is clearer than God's word if read in the original languages and without reference to the exegesis of the Fathers," he opined.[24]

Luther jettisoned the traditional, church-defined approach to interpretation in his *Lecture on the Galatians* of 1516–1517. But in doing so, he cut the ground from under a central claim of the church for the Virgin Mary. The doctrine of Mary's perpetual virginity was not in the Gospels or letters of Paul. Furthermore, it could be pointed out that two passages of the Gospels clearly showed that, at home, Jesus was well known to have both brothers and sisters. The simple interpretation of this is clear.[25] The doctrine was buttressed in Scripture only by a misreading of Isaiah 7:14, and an allegorical reading of Ezekiel 44:1–3, which, on the face of it, was a description of the interior of the temple in Jerusalem:

Et convertit me ad viam portæ sanctuarii exterioris, quæ respiciebat ad orientem : et erat clausa.	Then he brought me back the way of the gate of the outward sanctuary which looketh toward the east; and it was shut.
Et dixit Dominus ad me : Porta hæc clausa erit : non aperietur, et vir non transibit per eam, quoniam Dominus Deus Israël ingressus est per eam : eritque clausa	Then said the LORD unto me; This gate shall be shut, it shall not be opened, and no man shall enter in by it; because the LORD, the God of Israel, hath entered in by it, therefore it shall be shut.

Principi. Princeps ipse sedebit in ea, ut comedat panem coram Domino : per viam portæ vestibuli ingredietur, et per viam ejus egredietur.	It is for the prince; the prince, he shall sit in it to eat bread before the LORD; he shall enter by the way of the porch of that gate, and shall go out by the way of the same.

A certain kind of faith had been needed to follow Augustine,[26] and so inter-pret this as a description of the Virgin's womb yet to come. But it was not the faith held by the new German translators.

And yet, despite considerable unease in Protestant quarters about excesses in the cult of Mary, all the translators and notable theologians held back from denying Mary's virginity. Erasmus was the most explicit about the situation: "We believe in the perpetual virginity of Mary, although it is not expounded in the sacred books." But the actual Protestant reformers, among them Luther, Calvin, Zwingli, and Bullinger, preferred to draw a veil over the whole matter, accepting the relevance of the Ezekiel passage to Mary, without noting that its message could only be allegorical—and thus, in their terms, non-Scriptural.[27]

Translations for All

The result of the humanist- and Protestant-inspired revolution in Bible translation was, paradoxically, to lessen the value of the translated Bibles that it produced, at least as authoritative evidence for the creed.

The Vulgate had been a translation that, in the traditional view of the Roman Catholic Church, had inherited all the authority of the original sources—indeed exceeded their authority through having been evaluated and interpreted by the church itself. But for the humanists and Protestants, the authority rested with the evidential texts, the sources themselves— though they could be clarified and illuminated through the translators' inspired understanding. The new versions produced, whether into Latin (like Erasmus) or the variety of modern European languages that came after Luther's German Bible, were simply aids to comprehension by the faithful: they could not replace God's word itself.

Hence although many of these translations achieved a special relationship with the nations who could read them—one thinks especially of Luther's

Bible in Germany, and the King James Authorized Version in England—there was no sense in which they redefined the faith in those congregations. That theological duty—as and when it was required—was the concern of the source languages only; and the profusion of tongues in which the translations allowed God to be worshipped and understood were purely of sentimental and educational value for the different Christian populations.

So, in his *On Translation: An Open Letter*, written when he had finished his version of New Testament and was still engaged in the Old, Martin Luther wrote:

> We do not have to inquire of the literal Latin, how we are to speak German, as these asses do. Rather we must inquire about this of the mother in the home, the children on the street, the common man in the marketplace. We must be guided by their language, the way they speak, and do our translating accordingly. That way they will understand it and recognize that we are speaking German to them.[28]

Luther's populist focus was rewarded by results. His great adversary Johannes Cochlaeus lamented on the "amazing multiplication by printers of Luther's New Testament, so that even tailors, women, and random idiots who had somehow learned to read a little German, were reading it with great enthusiasm as the source of all truth."[29]

In a sense, for the Protestants, the vernacular Bibles gained something of the same status as the *Doctrina* had in early modern Latin America. Knowledge of them was the mark of a pious Christian, ideally the heritage of every Christian: but for serious study by scholars or priests, there was something else.

For the Catholics, this "something else" remained the Vulgate in Latin; for the Protestant world—the rest of western Christianity—it was the Old and New Testaments in their original languages. The Scriptures might be read for convenience and enlightenment in the vernacular, but when authority was required, these originals had to be consulted. Theology, not the requirement for a foreign translation, now determines how a religion is reinvented, or received by a new population.

Language Transparency in a Worldwide Mission

Thus the main question of this book—how the major faiths changed in the course of reinventing themselves for understanding in new languages—is

disarmed for the half-millennium in which the vast majority of Bible translation has been done. For in the Protestant churches, which would indeed
dominate worldwide Christian missonary evangelism from the eighteenth
century onward, there was never a question of reinterpreting any aspect
of the faith on the strength of a new translation. Certainly, Scripture needs
to be understood, and mass literacy is everywhere encouraged, not least
to this end. But as a religion that makes claims about what happened
specifically in history, Protestant Christianity is held by the authority of
the original sources. Somehow, after Luther, western Christianity changed
to being a faith that understood itself in historic terms that must stand for
eternity, no longer a contemporary system under the day-to-day control of
the church.

This is not to say that the western church has remained united in the
aftermath of the linguistic scruples of the Reformation. But the grounds for
the ultimate splitting of the church itself were not based on language. The
main doctrinal differences are sometimes called the five *sola*s:

1. *sola scriptura*—only Scripture may be trusted as a source of doctrine;
2. *sola fide*—salvation is by faith alone, not by good works;
3. *sola gratia*—salvation is by God's grace, freely given, not earned by
   merit;
4. *solus Christus*—the believer's relation is directly with Christ alone,
   not mediated through priests;
5. *soli Deo gloria*—there should be no cult of the saints, angels, or the
   Virgin Mary.

Of these, only the first, *sola scriptura*, is about language, or specifically a
set of texts, the Holy Bible. Yet there is no dispute on what texts the Bible
contains (most recently specified, ironically enough, by the Catholic church
at its Council of Trento); only on who is to interpret them, and whether the
Vulgate translation has independent authority.

The fourth difference, *solus Christus*, tends to undermine the status and
function of the priesthood, although there are many references in the New
Testament to the sacred leader of worship (Greek ἱερευς or ἱερατης, Latin
sacerdos) but much fewer to the "elder" (Greek πρεσβύτερος, Latin *senior*),
from which as it has happened most of the western European words for *priest*
(cf German *Priester*, French *prêtre*) are derived. Nevertheless, in the early
church, it was the "elder" who led the small groups that actually gathered for

worship, and aided the bishops (ἐπίσκοποι—overseers) in church organization; hieratic "sacred leaders" were not in evidence except as an aspect of
Christ himself, or of the church as a collective. Other officers of the church
were known as servants (Greek διάκονοι, Latin *ministri*). Apparently the
first of these roles, the hierophant mediating between church and godhead,
was what the Protestant reformers wished to eliminate; and this would be
compatible with the general movement toward a direct relation with Christ,
of which vernacular access to the Scriptures was another manifestation. The
higher rank of "bishop" was also abolished in the more egalitarian Protestant
churches. But even they mostly retained some form of ministry or priesthood, with enabling roles befitting "elders."

One other doctrine, known as transubstantiation, has also divided the
Catholic church from the Protestants since the days of the Reformation.
This is a philosophical matter, concerning any change in being—according
to the Aristotelian doctrine of substance and accidents—that the bread and
wine may undergo in the course of Holy Communion. Arguably, this could
be a matter of linguistic interpretation (What did Jesus mean by "This is my
body," "This is my blood," "Do this in remembrance of me"?) But if so, the
difference in truth-conditions of the various interpretations do not depend
on the language (e.g., Greek versus Latin versus German) in which they are
expressed.

And the new sects that multiplied out of the schism of the Reformation—
among them Lutherans, Calvinists, Reformed churches, Methodists, Baptists,
Pentecostals, Adventists, and Moravians—did not polarize around specific
languages, and though they evidently used their local vernacular or lingua
franca, they certainly did not make it official for their worship and scriptures.
These sects could not be described as language communities organized for
worship, even if Martin Luther preached and wrote in his native German,
John Knox and Thomas Cranmer in English, and Jean Calvin in French.

The only exception to this would be the Church of England, which always
played a bit fast and loose as a Protestant church—most saliently because it
never abolished the office of bishop. Language-wise, it was explicitly a faith
for a nation (not much different from a speech community), and was initiated
with two major new scriptures written in the English language—the Book
of Common Prayer (1549) and the Thirty-Nine Articles of Religion (1563).
The particular link that this seemed to forge between Anglicanism and the
English language may have contributed to the special esteem—for a mere
translation—that has been given to the King James ("Authorized") Version

of the Bible, which dates from 1611, but which replaced the Great Bible (ca. 1537), and then the Bishops' Bible (1568), which had been appointed for use in all churches at the actual time of the English Reformation (initiated by the excommunication of King Henry VIII and Archbishop Cranmer in 1533).*

Any global effects of the Reformation in northwestern Europe turned out to be delayed for about two centuries, because European imperialism was a two-stage process, undertaken first by (Counter-Reformation) Catholic powers, and only pursued effectively by some of the Protestant lands of the northwest, the Netherlands and Britain, from the eighteenth century. Even then, the East India companies, British and Dutch, did not themselves favor missionary activity; and Protestant missions had to await the rise of missionary societies, which became a major force for foreign-language evangelism in the 1790s.

By the early seventeenth century, the two Catholic imperial powers, Spain and Portugal, had reached the maxima of their expansion across the Americas and Asia. For Portugal, this turned out to include bases all the way across the Indian Ocean, from Mozambique (1512) to Ceylon (1517), Goa (1534) and Malacca (1558), Macao (1575), and even Vietnam (1659); for Spain, it would include not just the Americas from Florida to Chile but other possessions gained by crossing the Pacific westward from Mexico, notably the Philippines (1565). In general the Catholic missionaries were even more wide-ranging than the pioneering merchants and imperialists, entering the major Asian empires where Spanish and Portuguese interests as such would not be welcome. Both shared too in a century-long, but ultimately blocked, attempt to convert Japan in 1549–1650.

All these places were evangelized with the kind of methods used in Central and South America, without use of vernacular scriptures. Clerics wrote grammars and dictionaries for the (wide variety of) vernacular languages involved,† and produced *doctrinas* and *confesionarios* to introduce the basics of the faith. As always among Catholics, no provision was made to translate the Bible into these languages.

---

* Much later in its career, in the eighteenth century, after the beginnings of British involvement in India, English would even be known marginally in the East as "the Christian tongue." See Ostler 2010, pp. 141, 294.

† See Zwartjes 2011, for accounts of grammars and dictionaries of Tamil, Konkani, Bengali, Marathi, and Hindi in India; Japanese; Tupi and Kiriri in South America; Kongo, Kimbundu, and Sena in Africa; as well as dictionaries in Chinese, Vietnamese, and Malay, all written between 1550 and 1800 by Portuguese scholars.

In some cases, especially Goa and the Philippines—which were under the temporal power of Portugal and Spain—this evangelism was extremely effective. But it proved rather ineffective where Asian political control remained strong. This was likely because Catholic missionaries, concerted by authorities in the Vatican, were compelled to be rather uncompromising on any social or cultural differences with local circumstances and sensibilities. As Latin was preserved for the liturgy, so no accommodation was tolerated in alien creed or ritual.

In China, a promising start had been made by Jesuits, notably Matteo Ricci (in the period 1601–1610), in establishing benign relations with the Ming government, though this involved accepting "practices favorable to Chinese custom," including use of a liturgy in Chinese. But the Catholic church later decided, first in 1704 and again in 1742, to exclude its converts from taking part in any Confucian rites: and the result was a ban by the Chinese government on any Catholic presence, which lasted from the early eighteenth century until 1939.

In Mughal India, despite a presence by the British East India Company from 1600, there were only a few missionaries, almost all Catholic, until the nineteenth century. Abbé Jean-Antoine Dubois, a French Catholic, spent 1792–1823 in south India, attempting—at the behest of the company—to rebuild the Mysore Catholic community after the crushing of Tipu Sultan's disastrous liberation struggle (which had emphasized Islam). Dubois was famed for his cultural embrace of Hindu society, adopting their style of dress and certainly their languages, and trying to make himself sensitive to their finer concerns. It was these social sensibilities—notably total abstinence, vegetarianism, and caste-consciousness—he felt, that limited any future for Christianity in India, and so he dismissed any Protestant view that what he called "the naked text of the Bible" would yet be persuasive, since it would just expose Indians directly to Christian enthusiasm for communion wine, fatted calves, and carpenters and fishermen. When informed that William Carey at Serampore had achieved the translation of the Scriptures into twenty-four Asiatic languages, he said he doubted "that these twenty spurious versions . . . will, after the lapse of the same number of years, have operated the conversion of twenty-four pagans." Ultimately, speaking in 1823, he believed Christianity in India to be facing defeat. It had indeed lost half its strength in India during the eighteenth century, declining from about one million to 475,000.[30]

But then the energy of the Protestant missionary societies hit the vast tracts of the world that were under European imperial control. The beginning of the nineteenth century witnessed a sudden, and sustained, surge in vernacular translations of the Bible. And in its train came a great advance of success in Protestant Christian conversions, if not the total conquest that the optimists might have hoped for. Half a century after Dubois had given up on the Catholic mission in despondency, India in 1881 contained 417,000 Protestants, 129,000 of them full communicants.[31]

Worldwide, three dozen languages had received translations in the three preceding centuries, beginning with the Reformation-inspired translations into German, Dutch, and English. All but half a dozen of the translations made in that period had been into European languages.* But now, between 1800 and 1900, another sixty-one were added, most of them in the Indian subcontinent (forty-three—including Pashto in Afghanistan), but many too in the principal languages of Africa (eight), the Pacific (eleven), and Southeast Asia (four—including Burmese). Given that the propagation of God's Word was distinctively a Protestant priority in missionary practice, and that Britain was by far the biggest empire with a Protestant religious culture, the areas under British rule were naturally the most prominent. But other major additions in that century included modern Russian, Mandarin Chinese, Thai, and Japanese.[32]

Since then, other Protestant organizations (notably Wycliffe Bible Translators) have added 430 more, so that the current score (as of November 2014) is 531 languages with a full edition of the Bible.[33] This is still rather small, as an attempt at complete coverage of the almost seven thousand languages spoken in the world today. But if the Bibles are targeted broadly at the languages with the largest populations, it means that all those with a million or more speakers have at least been covered.

ᗺᑕᔕᗡᗺ

---

* The honorable exceptions were Wampanoag in 1631 (by the Englishman John Eliot in Massachusetts); Tamil in 1728 (by the Dutchmen B. Ziegenbalg and B. Schultze, in Tranquebar, South India); Malay in 1758 (by the Dutchmen M. Leijdecker and P. van der Vorm, in Batavia, Java).

  Arabic, Syriac, Persian, Armenian, and Georgian all received new Christian translations in this relatively early period, though there were older texts from their long Christian pasts, not necessarily organized as per the Council of Trento's specification for Holy Scripture.

After the Reformation, western Christianity—outside the Catholic church—
was no longer inclined to identify the faith with a particular language.

Within these reformed churches, the importance of an inherited, organized community—a traditional Church—was devalued while the importance of Scripture, and individual acquaintance through Scripture with
Christ, was enhanced. The whole could be seen as a kind of democratization
of Christian faith, with a far greater stress on individual conscience as moral
arbiter. And crucial to the whole was the availability of God's Word in a
form accessible to the believer, namely a reliable translation into the local
vernacular language.

So, in a way, Christianity's reinvention of itself as an assertively multilingual faith had its own effect: not to make the faith quite as diverse as it was
multilingual, with a new creed in each new language that expressed it; but to
liberate it from a creed necessarily expressed in any particular language. And
so Christianity—at least, in any of its Protestant sects—was made open to a
congregation anywhere in the world.

❦

CHAPTER 15

God and Language Beyond Imitation
One Enough

كِتَابٌ فُصِّلَتْ آيَاتُهُ قُرْآنًا عَرَبِيًّا لِقَوْمٍ يَعْلَمُونَ

kitābun fuṣṣilat āyātu-hu, qurʔānan ʕarabiyyan li-qawmin yaʕlamūna (3)

A book whose verses are explained in detail,
the Qur'ān in Arabic for people who understand.

(*Qur'ān* 41:3)

وَلَوْ جَعَلْنَاهُ قُرْآنًا أَعْجَمِيًّا لَقَالُوا لَوْلَا فُصِّلَتْ
آيَاتُهُ أَأَعْجَمِيٌّ وَعَرَبِيٌّ قُلْ هُوَ لِلَّذِينَ آمَنُوا
هُدًى وَشِفَاءٌ وَالَّذِينَ لَا يُؤْمِنُونَ فِي آذَانِهِمْ
وَقْرٌ وَهُوَ عَلَيْهِمْ عَمًى أُوْلَئِكَ يُنَادَوْنَ مِنْ مَكَانٍ
بَعِيدٍ

Walaw jaʕalnāhu qurʔānan aʕjamiyyan, laqālūʔ
"lawlā fuṣṣilat āyātu-hu, aaʕjamiyyun wa-ʕarabiyyun?"
Qul "huwa lilladīna amanūʔ hudan wašifaʔun;
wa-alladīna lā yuminūna fī adanihim waqrun;
wa-huwa ʕalayhim ʕaman ʔulaika;
yunādawna min makānin baʕīdin." (44)

Had We made it a Qur'ān in a foreign language, they would have said,
"If only its verses were made clear." Non-Arabic and an Arab?
Say, "For those who believe, it is guidance and healing.

But as for those who do not believe: there is heaviness in their ears,
and it is blindness for them.
These are being called from a distant place." (44)

Qur'ān 41:44

ISLAM INCARNATES A PARADOX. As a religion, it is notorious for not
tolerating translation of its holiest scripture, the Qur'ān. This scripture, a
work delivered in Arabic only, is central to its message, and arguably more
important within Islam than the Bible within Christianity, or the Tipiṭaka
within Buddhism. Yet as a faith it has been able to win converts throughout
Asia and Africa, and far beyond the zone where Arabic is a native language,
or even where it has been used as a lingua franca of trade and later of
conquest. Remarkably, Islam as a world faith has managed to overcome—or
transcend—the language barrier that its Arab founders erected, without ever
losing its loyalty to the local language of Arabia.

Superficially, the question this book asks can get no purchase on Islam.
If Islam has held steadfastly onto Arabic, what sense can it make to ask:
"What is the effect on a religion of spreading into communities where they
speak a new language?" But somehow the sense of what was preached and
prayed in Arabic was transmitted to those who—at least previously—had
had no knowledge of this language, and who would go on to make a place for
Arabic worship in language communities where God—or gods—had been
addressed in quite different tongues. Just possibly, this process of transmission to a wider multilingual world might have marked the varieties of Islam
that we find in the modern world.

The Arabs—that is to say, the Arabic-speaking tribes, which surged
out of southern Arabia in the seventh century A.D. and deposed the last
Sassanid from the empire of Persia, as well as detaching from the Byzantine
Empire every one of its southern and western Mediterranean provinces—
had a simple answer to the question. We hear vanishingly little of how their
faith got established, or indeed of what was actually believed by the early
conquerors at least until the ninth century. But they retained a simple faith
in the superiority of revealed monotheism (summarized in the one word
Islām, meaning "submission" to the will of *Allah* "God"). And although the
Arabs, their impoverished desert life, and their language had been almost
unknown, even to their close neighbors, in preceding centuries, they had
no lack of national, religious, and linguistic pride once they had established

themselves as the masters of the Levant, even to Khorasan in the east and al-Andalus in the west.

Apocryphally, Muḥammad himself is said to have remarked: "Love the Arabs for three reasons: because I am an Arab, because the Qur'ān is in Arabic and because the inhabitants of Paradise speak Arabic."[1] But even in the Qur'ān itself, we find flattery—or at least reassurance—for the Arabs:

> You are the best nation [*ummah*] ever brought forth to men, bidding
> to honor, and forbidding dishonor, and believing in God ... (3:110)

(followed by a remark that People of the Book—implicitly other such people—have been a disappointment). As for their language, although the Qur'ān remarks more than once that it has been sent down from heaven deliberately in Arabic,* it does not actually say that the language is better than others.

The Qur'ān itself is said to bear the proof of its genuineness in its inimitability (*iʿjāz*), in that no one could write anything like it, even if humans and spirits (*djinn*) were to collaborate on the task (27:88). But it does not say exactly what aspect of the Qur'ān is beyond reproduction: presumably not the simple fact of being in Arabic—unusual as that may have been for an extended text when the Qur'ān was first written down.

It was left to Arab scholars to theorize that Arabic is particularly excellent as a language, and hence too good to be translated effectively. The jurist known as the "Sheikh of Islam," Imam Al-Shafi'i (767–820—hence some 150 years after Muḥammad), declared that "No human being, unless he is a prophet, can be the compete master of Arabic ... He who learns this language, made by God the language of the Seal of the Prophets and the medium through which was revealed His last book, would gain an advantage ..." The linguist Ibn Qutaibah (828–885) held that it was specifically Arabic's richness in metaphor that made it impossible for any translator to put its text fully into any other (though such translation could perfectly well be done for the gospel from Syriac into Ethiopic or Greek, or indeed the Hebrew Torah and Psalms into Arabic).[2] For the Brethren of Purity

---

* E.g., "so that you may understand [*taʿqilūna* 12:2, 43:3] ... upon your heart, for you to convey warning in plain Arabic language [*ʿalā qalbika, li-takūna mina almundireena bi-lisānin ʿarabiyyin mubīnin* 26:194–95].

(*ixwān al-safā*), a secret society of Muslim philosophers in Basra, Iraq, of the eighth century, Arabic represented "perfection of human language" (*tamāmu l-luyati l-insāniyyati*). The preeminent theologian Al-Ghazālī (1058–1111) was also impressed by the singular metaphorical expressiveness of words in Arabic, and the danger this posed (in misdescribing the divine attributes) for any attempt to reproduce this in apparently equivalent words in Persian or Turkish.[3]

It hardly mattered whether God's choice of Arabic for the scripture had been made because of Arabic's intrinsic excellence, or conversely, Arabic had come to be blessed with these advantages as a result of carrying God's revelation: the net effect was that the Qur'ān's truth, and its expression in Arabic, were totally bound up with each other. Hence, those who relied on other languages would get no closer to the revelation than partial aspects that might emerge from a commentary. A translation would never be "the real Qur'ān," even if its words were the closest that could be found to the Arabic originals. Certainly a Muslim could not conceive of dropping the original text, and working exclusively with a translation, as—for a good millennium—western Christianity had done with the Latin Vulgate edition of its own scriptures. In Islam, the language of scripture cannot be changed without, illegitimately and perhaps unconsciously, changing details of the faith itself.

This is the core doctrine of the Qur'ān's untranslatability, which was and is sustained in Islam, but it went through different interpretations in different eras.

Early on, the concern was how much could be expected of converts who had no previous exposure to Arabic. For the first century after the Arab conquests, the chief exposure of Islam to a non-Arab population was to the Persians. Some Arabs, among them notably the eminent jurist Abū Ḥanīfah (who lived from 699 to 767, three generations after the Prophet), maintained that it was permissible to recite the Qur'ān in Persian, even in prayer, though most who accepted this believed that this was justified by a lack of knowledge of Arabic.[4] This license seems to have been conceived in order to get over a transitional stage in the spread of the faith.

Much later, a comparable situation would be experienced, when a Muslim congregation under pressure could find that too little knowledge of Arabic and the Qur'ān was on hand to support proper worship: this was the predicament of the Moriscos, Muslims who remained in Spain in the fourteenth to sixteenth centuries but were being overrun, and increasingly suppressed, by the Christian *reconquista*. They endeavored to hold on to worship in Arabic, but were often defeated by individuals' personal ignorance of its meaning. As a result, they annotated their copies of the Qur'ān heavily, with glosses and partial translations in their Romance vernacular Mozarabic: this was essentially Spanish, but written in the Arabic alphabet in what is called *aljamiado* style.*

After 1567, when all further use of Arabic was formally banned by royal decree, Moriscos translated all prayers and the sayings and wrote them too as *aljamiado*, providing an effective hiding place for their records of Qur'ānic verses, noted in the same script, but (invisibly to their persecutors) in the original Arabic. This discretionary policy—characterizable as "Needs must, while the Devil drives"—was an example of what Muslims call *taqiyya* "precaution," finding measures to hide one's true faith from unbelievers.⁵

In between these stages at which translations were of use to Islam, characteristic of growing and declining Muslim communities respectively, there seems to have been little need for translations of the Qur'ān to support propagation of the faith. Rather, the *ummah* of the faithful grew through the close presence of controlling and/or influential Muslims. This is the process that the late historian Jerry Bentley called "voluntary assimilation," and it worked because Muslims turned out to excel in the arts both of war and of trade.⁶

Non-vernacular Arabic

The Arab conquests of the seventh and eighth centuries in west Asia and north Africa, followed in the tenth to thirteenth centuries by the Turkish conquests from Central Asia across to Anatolia and southward into India, placed Muslim elites in power in large parts of the Old World. But the power of their sword was only one aspect of the advance of the *ummah*. Arabs had long been great traders, across Arabia and around its coastal seas. Soon, and at the latest from the eleventh century, a significant body of enterprising Muslim merchants was entering Africa from Zanzibar. (The term *Swahili* is from Arabic *sawāḥiliyya* "coasters.")

---

* *Aljamiado* is none other than a borrowing into Romance of ʿajamiyya, the word much used in the Qur'ān to mean "non-Arab."

One feature of the Arab advances in two generations after the Prophet was their domination of the Berber peoples of North Africa, including those like the Tuareg (then known as the Sanhaja) who were at ease in crossing the deserts. On these long journeys, their merchandise was notably kola nuts, salt, gold, ivory, leather, dates, and slaves. They followed various routes around and across the Sahara, and so penetrated the *Saḥel* (conceptually another "coast," but of the desert), a forested zone that extended westward as far as Senegal and the Atlantic Ocean. The zone was the setting for a rich political history under Muslim influence, including the empires of Ghana (750–900), Gao (tenth to thirteenth centuries), Mali (1230–1600), and Songhai (1464–1591). The Almoravids or Marabouts (*al-Murābiṭīn* "those posted as a garrison") were a dynasty (1043–1157) of the Sanhaja, centered at Marrakech, whose empire extended south to Senegal and northward into southern Spain (al-Andalūs).[7]

Major centers of this trade were the legendary Timbuktu and its competitor Djenné (in what is now Mali), which had been founded as cities early in the twelfth century. Timbuktu also became a considerable Muslim academic center.

A new field for Muslim trade would also open up at the other end of the Indian Ocean. Turks from Central Asia had long been raiding and ultimately conquering northern India: what began in the first decade of the tenth century as Ghaznavid incursions into Punjab, Sindh, and Gujarat ultimately led to the establishment of a sultanate at Delhi in 1206 and a territorial empire covering the whole Indo-Gangetic plain. One effect of this was that the principal ports—both Gujarat's Broach (Bharuch) in the west and Bengal's Tamluk in the east—came under Muslim control. Muslims—mostly Persians, probably—began to take advantage of these ports, trading first with Sumatra and Malaya, and later farther east. It must have helped that Arabs and Persians had participated in Indian Ocean trade since at least the Umayyad era, in the century leading up to 750 A.D.[8]

The trade had comparable social and religious effects on the new populations brought into contact with Muslims, though these customers were quite different from their African clientele, being largely Hindu and Buddhist. But once again, the Muslims were able to attract elite support, and then full popular conversions, by their wealth and savoir faire; by the early seventeenth century, a network of Muslim-dominated trade, and hence sympathy for Islam, had spread across the whole of southeastern Asia.[9] Linguistically, there was little effect on the commercial lingua franca, which remained

Malay, as it had been since the seventh century, when Śri Vijaya had spread its trading empire across the archipelago from Sumatra. But now the taipans of trade, from the Straits of Malacca to the South China Seas, were making their prayers in Arabic.

All over north and central Africa, west and south Asia, and southeastern Asia, the ruling and trading elites became Muslim. As a result, Islam defined the social code for elites in this vast area of the inhabited world—itself something of a surprise, since Muslim ethics and accessibility tend toward the egalitarian. The Muslims created an open elite, and the vast populations close to them wanted to be like them: Muslims were seen as discriminating, and as a people who knew how to achieve worldly power and wealth.

Amid this polyphony of ambient languages, from Turkic to Bengali across Asia, and from Hausa and Mande in west Africa, through Swahili to Sudanese and Malay in the east Indies, it mattered little that their scriptures were written in Arabic, another impenetrable foreign language, and that they allowed no translation of it in the practice of their religion. If they made a favorable impression—as they seem to have done everywhere—they would attract recruits and disciples from an early age, and in only a generation or two the locals would be providing their own experts on Arabic and the Muslim faith.

Some Muslim missionary activity did occur, often associated with the mystic wing of the Muslims known as Ṣūfī, in many parts of the Islamic world. This they called daʕwah, "summons, invitation." But given the social attractions of the Muslim community as it spread itself across the world, one can easily see how the language barrier created by Koranic Arabic was crossed.

Translating the Qur'ān

The mature doctrine, which seems to have emerged once Islam was widely established in the non-Arabic speaking world, was that translation of the meaning of the Qur'ān was acceptable as an aid to explaining or understanding the faith, but not for any function that could be seen as substituting for the holy text itself. Interlinear translations were fine, since they simply presented guidance on a possible interpretation of the original text; and vernacular commentary (tafsīr) likewise. By contrast, any use of the translation in prayer would not be acceptable, since this would usurp the Qur'ān as the word of God.

Outside the *ummah*, the first full translation of the Qur'ān into a Western language fulfilled none of these conditions, since it was made not by an aspiring Muslim, but by Christians concerned to "know the enemy." Peter the Venerable, abbot of Cluny, commissioned Robert of Ketton, an Englishman otherwise well known for scientific translations, to produce the *Lex Mahumet Pseudoprophete*, a Latin translation in 1143. Its title (viz "The Law of Mahomet the False Prophet") proudly advertises bias; and its inaccuracy was reputed among Western scholars over most of the last eight centuries: e.g., Hadrian Reland in 1717 termed it *"pessima Alcorani versio Latina,"* the worst of transla-tions. But a title may be assigned by others than the author; and criteria of translation quality can change. A recent analysis judges it an honest attempt to convey the meaning of the text, often informed by contemporary *tafsīr* (commentaries) although it did permit itself some license, e.g., moving verses around within a *sūrah* (chapter). A more literal, and arguably more accurate, translation into Latin by Mark of Toledo, written fifty years later, dispensed with such Muslim expertise, but by the same token made itself much harder to interpret.[10]

To give one simple example, at surah 22, verse 1, the text reads: *yā ʔayyuhā al-nāsu ittaqū rabbakum inna zalzalata al-saʕati shayʔun ʕaẓīmun.* This is literally in English: "O sons of-man, fear your-lord; indeed earthquake of-the-hour thing terrible." Mark renders: *O vos homines, timete creatorem vestrum quia terre motus hore est magnum* "O ye men, fear your creator because the earthquake of the hour is a great thing." This is literally correct (though adding a gratuitous detail about the Lord, as humanity's creator). More specifically, Robert translates: *Genus humanum, Deum time, quoniam hore maxime terremotus est timendus die resurrectionis* "Human race, fear God, for the earthquake of the greatest hour is to be feared on the day of resur-rection." The words underlined are not in the Arabic, but they signal the uncontested Muslim interpretation of this verse, fixing it as a sign of the end of the world.[11]

Points like this recall the Muslim tradition's view that the Qur'ān is commentable but untranslatable.

Besides knowledge of the Qur'ān, widespread literacy among Muslims, at least the elite, meant that many knew supporting literature known as the *aḥadīθ* (usually in English hadith), literally "happenings, reports." This included the *sīrah*, "travels" (i.e., biography of the Prophet), *sunnah* "prac-tice" (of a Muslim), and many elements of *šarī'ah* "road," i.e., law. These documents are voluminous, and are available in different sets that are given different degrees of authority—not least because different sects of Muslims accept different collections of them. In particular, this is true of the *ši'ah*—Shia—who recognize Ali as the true successor to Muḥammad, and a subsequent succession of imams as spiritual leaders of the *ummah*, the community of the faithful. Since the source and transmission of the hadith—for all their potentially deep spiritual import—is agreed to be human, they are not subject to any prohibition on translation, even if they are usually consulted in Arabic: naturally so, since with the Qur'ān always there in the background that is the common language of Islam.

Sources of Scriptural Authority

Reviewing the status of scripture in the various faiths we have considered in this book, we can distinguish at least three major approaches to the source of its authority.

One approach is to view scripture as owing its authority to sanctification by the spiritual leaders of the community, that is to say, by the church itself. A good example of this is the Roman Catholic Church of the Latin Rite, and its singling out of the Latin translation of scripture, the Vulgate, as the one authoritative source, as against all the original texts (and other translations) that were available in various languages. But the relationship of the Hebrew Old Testament or *Tanakh*—an acronym—TaNaKh—of *Torāh* ("Teaching" or "Law"), *Nəbī'īm* ("Prophets"), and *Kətûbîm* ("Writings")—to the Rabbinic tradition in Judaism is another comparable case: although language was not an issue (nor were Hebrew translations of the Aramaic sections, in Daniel and Ezra, ever supplied), a decision had to be made on which of many books would constitute the canon. The precise time and agency of this decision is not recorded; but in historical times, the Hebrew *Tanakh*—like the Catholic Vulgate—came surrounded with a wealth of authorized commentary. For historical and practical reasons, due to language change in the Middle East, this was delivered in Aramaic, not Hebrew, the whole being known as *Targumim* "the translations." Hence the *Tanakh* was not seen as a lonely monument of a text, much less as a source of authority independent of the Rabbinical tradition that interpreted it.

In practice, both the Vulgate and the *Tanakh* came to be impenetrable to their own congregations, and were understood only as they were interpreted by priests or rabbis. This kind of scripture is not directly accessible to the faithful, nor self-standing, even if all accept in principle that the importance of this text is as a direct link to the truth of the faith. In the case of the Catholic church, as we have seen, this de facto impenetrability, due to the fact that vernaculars changed while a fixed text (in Latin) did not, was made a virtue in itself, and defended by papal decree.

The European Reformers of the mid-sixteenth century—Reuchlin, Erasmus, Luther, Tyndale, and many others—needed to conceive a new source of authority for Christian Scripture. Having identified and accepted evident mistakes in the transmission, whether of text or translation, they could no longer believe that authority resided in the traditional interpretation of the text itself, and even less in Jerome's Latin translation of that text. Once all this—translation and interpretation—was seen as fallible and even on occasion misleading, a new criterion of valid testimony was needed. It was discovered in the standards of classical philology and textual criticism. This could be directed to find the simple truth of the correct reading in the original language, and the correct interpretation—in whatever language, ancient or modern—of that reading.

This was, and remains, Scripture for the Protestant churches of Christianity. It represents the Word of God itself, and hence the paramount—for some even the sole—source of authority about the faith. The text has become an ideal in itself, yet not one known by simple observation of a copy that happens to be before you: it must be sought out from fallible human testimony. The true Word of God must be established through study. But since this process of establishment is independent of the church tradition, it is at least possible that errors of transmission and translation once detected may lead to revision of the text, and even of the doctrine. The Scripture, once identified as the Word of God itself, begins to assume an authority greater than that of church tradition, and traditions without reference in Scripture become open to criticism: hence Luther's scepticism about the value of pilgrimage, the purchase of indulgences to save time in Purgatory (what Purgatory?), the need for a sanctified priesthood, and indeed the very possibility of earning salvation through good works.

Yet on this view the Word of God—even if hard to establish through good scholarship—is still fit to be put directly into the hands, and the hearts, of believing Christians. This is the role for vernacular translations, not as authoritative repositories of the Word, but as an accessible means to propagate it, and the more accessible the better. There is a certain democratic, *vox populi vox Dei* tone to this theology: the Word of God is best discovered

through an open process of research and translation, and the main requirements of the vernacular translation are faithfulness and clarity. As opposed
to the first model, there is no reason for the church to control, filter, or interpret the resulting message.

This is related to the third model of authoritative scripture, which is the
Islamic view. Here the origin of the text is believed to be miraculous, and so
not subject to inquiry or scholarship. The Qur'ān (*qurʔān* "recitation") is a
transcript of the proverbial *lauḥ maḥfūẓ* ("safely-preserved tablet") in heaven,
which was revealed to Muḥammad over many years, memorized piece by
piece by many who knew him, and eventually collated and edited as a written
text under the authority of ʿUthmān ibn ʿAffān, the third of the caliphs (or
successors, vicars of the Prophet), who reigned from 644 to 656. Every detail
of the text is supposed to be correctly fixed—both in writing and in pronunciation, although the writing system has been made more exact since this
era (distinguishing both consonants and vowels more precisely). Unlike the
hadith, there is no dispute among Muslims about which parts of the Qur'ān
are correct.

Among the faithful, textual criticism or philological deconstruction of this
one text are not permitted, so that the kind of disputes that have convulsed
western Christianity during the Reformation have not occurred. However,
the modern Islamic community, based on the Qur'ān, cannot be seen as a
successful implementation of the kind of authority that the Catholics of the
Latin rite were then attempting to establish.

This is for at least three reasons. First, the Qur'ān—unlike the Vulgate—
is an original, which unlike the Bible cannot be referred back to primary
sources. Second, it is unitary, and as such more authoritative than any of the
variety of Muslim sects that endorse it.* And third, it is independent and

---

* These three different views of scripture's authority seem fairly independent of the actual
descent of the documents recognized as scripture.

    The current standard text of the Qur'ān was fixed only on July 10, 1924, at Cairo, Egypt,
but is almost universally accepted throughout Islam. (This also superseded a previous scholarly standard set by Gustav Flügel in 1834.) It is a recension of the *qirāʾah* ("reading") of
Ḥafṣ from ʿĀṣim, which was one of seven (or perhaps ten, or fourteen) *qirāʾāt* ("readings")
all declared of equal validity by the scholar Abū Bakr Ibn Mujāhid in the tenth century.

    There has never been a reconstruction of the Qur'ān on text-critical principles; and an
attempt to do this in the 1930s–40s (by a succession of German scholars) failed, owing to a
series of adverse events. (See Reynolds 2008, pp. 2–7.) A very early manuscript of the Qur'ān,
from the seventh or eighth centuries (but independent of ʿUthman's standardization), was
recently discovered in Sana'a, Yemen, and is published in Sadeghi and Goudarzi 2012.

open to all (subject to the minor constraint of knowing Arabic!), both for study and for intonation in worship. As a result its thick garb of preexisting interpretation does not constrain access to it, as the Vulgate's commentaries did when it was accepted as the Bible for western Europe. Translation and interpretation remain possible, but they remain distinct from the Qur'ān itself, the real thing, steadfastly set out in Arabic.

The advantage of this third model of scriptural authority over the first (e.g., the Vulgate) lies in its independence of any sect; and its advantage over the second (e.g., the Protestant Bible) lies in its determinacy. What the Qur'ān says does not depend on the results of the best philological research, an activity that can never ultimately be closed.

The core of the faith (and the creed), then, remains secure. But this firm center creates a corresponding disadvantage. The supporting hadith documents, which in many cases are all that is available to clarify the historical background or legal interpretation, are open to selective acceptance and rejection, and indeed may be configured as the basis of different sects. The Qur'ān cannot be used to distinguish between the validity, say, of Sunni, Shia, or Ibāḍi; and historically it has been compatible with considerable variation when new peoples were gathered into the Muslim *ummah*.[12]

Muslim Communities

The Arabic language was, as we have seen, self-consciously intrinsic to the Qur'ān, and so—as its basic scripture—to orthodox faith in the religion that became known as Islam.

> We have indeed sent it as a Qur'ān in the Arabic language, so that you may understand. (43:3)

This means that the Arabic speech community, which may be called *ummat al-ʿarabiyyah*, has an intrinsic link with the world-body of the Muslim faithful, what is termed *ummat al-islamiyyah*. Islam, according to the Qur'ān, is the result of God's decision to give the Arabs their own prophet.

> We have therefore made this Qur'ān easy upon your tongue, for you to announce glad tidings with it to those who fear, and warn those who are quarrelsome. (19:97)

> And whereas before this exists the Book of Moses, a guide and a
> mercy; and this is a Book giving testimony, in the Arabic language, to
> warn the unjust; and to give glad tidings to the virtuous. (46:12)

This was a wonderful thing for those who spoke Arabic natively, and
made it possible for the vast majority of these Arabs very quickly to identify
themselves with this revelation which directed itself to their community,
and none other. The prohibition on translation, such as it was, can also be
seen as a means of guaranteeing this association, and allowing it to be
granted to others who spoke other languages only if they were prepared
to learn enough Arabic to take part. These people, in the early centuries
of the caliphate (seventh and eighth A.D.), were known as *mawālī*
"clients" in the entourage of powerful Arabs, and made up the majority
of the forces in the Arabian army; they spoke principally Persian, but
also Kurdish, Berber, and (latterly) Turkic languages. These last may
also—starting in the reign of al-Muʿtasim (833–842)—have joined the
caliphate as *ghilmān* "lads," slave-soldiers attached directly to the household
of the caliph.

For all these, Arabic was a holy language (as well no doubt as a medium
for sheikhs and senior officers), and they took Islam pretty much as they
found it. Their obligations were the five *arkān al-dīn*, pillars of the faith,
viz *šahādah* "witness to the faith," *ṣalāt* "ritual prayers five times a day,"
zakāt "almsgiving," usually reckoned at 2.5 percent, *ṣawm* "abstinence
during Ramadan," and *ḥajj* "the pilgrimage to Mecca," once in a lifetime, if
possible.

Recruitment was always attractive, especially for the young, unattached,
and above all ambitious, as the *Dar al-islām* (Islamic Court) spread its military control over first western Asia, and then north Africa and Spain—all
within two generations of the Muslims' breakout from Arabia. However, a
unique brake on conversions operated from the Arab side. Non-Muslims
(*ðimmī* "under protection") were subject to a poll tax (*jizyā*), the rate of which
varied over place and time but which was higher than the *zakāt* charged to
Muslims. For this there was specific Qurʾānic authorization:

> *Qatilū allaðīna la yuminūna bi-Allahi, walā bi-al-yawmi al-āxiri, walā
> yuḥarrimūna mā ḥarrama Allahu wa-rasūluhu, walā yadīnūna dīna
> al-ḥaqqi, mina allaðīna ūtū al-kitāba ḥattā yuʿaṭū al-jizyata ʿan yadin
> wa-hum ṣāyirūna*

Fight those who believe not in Allah nor the Last Day, nor hold that forbidden which hath been forbidden by Allah and His Messenger, nor acknowledge the religion of Truth [even if they are] of the People of the Book, <u>until they pay the Jizya</u> with willing submission, and feel themselves subdued. (9:29)

Consequently, mass conversions were not welcomed by local governors, who saw an immediate reduction in their tax take. For some time, an informal conformity of interests between the Muslim authorities and other religious leaders (Zoroastrian, Christian, or Jewish) combined to moderate—and in some cases, even to reverse—mass conversions.

Increasingly, though, the peoples under Muslim control were converted, and needed to be instructed in the faith. One outcome of this was the appearance of translations and commentaries (*tafsir*) on the Qur'ān, but only into the languages of subject (*dhimmi*) peoples that already had a literary tradition, Persian and Greek.

The Persian tradition was initiated* by three full translations, all undertaken in Khorasan or Central Asia. But interestingly, they were produced only after the Islamic Caliphate had been established for a good two centuries, and indeed—through the Abbasid revolution—had largely been taken under Persian management.

The first of the three was done at the Bukhara court of the Samanid king Manṣūr (ruled 961–976), as part of a complete translation of the Arabic commentary *Tafsir al Ṭabari*; the second appeared in the eleventh century in the context of a new Persian commentary, by Abū Manṣūr Abdullah al-Anṣāri of Herat (on the border of Afghanistan); and finally in the twelfth century a third was written by a theologian from Transoxania (modern Uzbekistan), Abū Ḥafṣ ʿUmar an-Nasafī. These books are all available today.

The Greek translation of the Qur'ān is less well known, and is from an earlier era. It cannot have been any later than the mid-ninth century, but may have been much earlier, since the author seems conversant with

---

* There are two hadiths that report that the very first translation into Persian—but only of a very short passage—was by Salman the Persian, a disciple of the Prophet himself. He rendered the opening surah (literally the *sūrah al-fātiḥa*), and allowed it "to be used by Persians for recital in prayer, until their tongues softened." This work of Salman reportedly "was not disapproved by the Prophet." (Tibawi 1962.)

Greek administrative language; and the Umayyad Caliphate's administration of Syria (which lasted from 661 to 750) was conducted in Greek.
Unfortunately for the conjecture, our main witness of that administration, John of Damascus, does not give any evidence of knowing of this
translation.[13]

This Greek Qur'ān (referred to as τὸν Κουρᾶν—closer to the Arabic than
the usual name in Modern Greek, το Κοράνιο) seems to have been a skillful
work,[14] by someone literate in both Arabic and Greek, and capable of exer-
cising judgment to leave terms in transliteration when a technical meaning
would not have been clear in Greek.

The work was used for reference by the Byzantine scholar Nicetas in
his *Refutatio* written between 855 and 870, and in another, unknown, scholar's *Abjuratio*, both anti-Islamic works written in Greek. But—unlike, for
example, Robert of Ketton's Latin version—it was probably not itself deliberately created for polemical reasons.

The intriguing question, however, arises of why it was written at all. The
main scholar to examine it[15] has suggested three possible motives:

1. within a scholarly circle (with a polemical aim),
2. as the product of a religious community whether for liturgy, for
   missionary activities, or as a help for the non-Arab believer, or
3. as an administrative tool in a Muslim, but (at least partly) Greek-
   speaking, state

although he discounts the first. If he is right this suggests that there
were Greek-speaking converts in this early period, who needed guidance
on the meaning of the Holy Qur'ān, whether for its spiritual or its legal
content.

Those who benefited from this Greek translation of the Qur'ān were,
however, in a radically different position socially than those who would
read and study the Persian versions. Although only native speakers of
Arabic could look at the Muslim scripture, and see it as intrinsically
belonging to them, by the tenth century people familiar with Persian
could also see their language community as incorporated body and soul
into the *ummat al-islamiyya*. There were small outlying populations of
Zoroastrians and Christians, Manichaeans too, but overwhelmingly the
kalemrau-e-zabān-e-fārsī ("where the writ of Persian language ran") was
everywhere a part of Islamdom. Persian speakers could see their language

as firmly attached to Islam, even if the scriptures could never (validly) be consulted in it.

By contrast, Greek was everywhere associated with the Greek Orthodox Church of Christianity, the established faith of *Rūm* (the Roman Empire) as seen from Arabia and its caliphate, and hence the tongue of the *Kāfir* "unbeliever" and *Mushrik* "associator"—one denying recognition of absolute supremacy to Allah.

Like the other prime *ahlu-l-kitābi* "people of the book," the Jews (who were allowed some license as aspirant worshippers of the same God), these people would never be accommodated in the *ummah*, for two good reasons—stated in verses of the Greek Qur'ān that have been preserved. (The Greek is quoted to demonstrate its fluent and literate style.)

First, they believed that Christ was put to death before he ascended into heaven:

> And because the Jews said: "We killed Messiah, Jesus son of Mary, Gods messenger." They did not kill and they did not crucify him, but it seemed to them (as if). Those who are doubtful due to uncertainty concerning him have no knowledge about him, only acceptance of a belief. And in reality they did not kill him, rather God exalted him to Himself. (4:157–58)*

In addition, they attributed progeny to the Almighty, an impossible thing when the truth that had been presented to them is so very simple: God is One.

> The Jews say that Israel is the son of God. And the Christians say that Messiah is the son of God. This is their speech through their mouths. They liken their speech to the deniers of old. God will kill them, because of the things they deny. They have taken their messengers and priests to be lords beside God, as well as the Messiah,

---

* Καὶ τοῦ λέγειν Ἰουδαίους, Ἡμεῖς ἐφονεύσαμεν τὸν Χριστὸν τὸν Ἰησοῦν υἱὸν Μαρίας ἀπόστολον Θεοῦ· οὐκ ἐφόνευσαν αὐτὸν οὐδὲ ἐσταύρωσαν αὐτόν, ἀλλ' ὡμοιώθη αὐτοῖς. οἵτινες δὲ ἀμφιβάλλουσι δισταγμῷ ἐξ αὐτοῦ, οὐκ ἔχουσιν εἰς αὐτὸν εἴδησιν, εἰ μὴ ἀκολουθίαν τοῦ νομίζειν· καὶ οὐκ ἐφόνευσαν αὐτὸν ἐν ἀληθείᾳ, μᾶλλον ὕψωσεν αὐτὸν ὁ Θεὸς πρὸς ἑαυτόν.

son of Mary. And they were commanded to serve only one God."
(9:30–31)*

This latter is tantamount to *širk*, the unforgiveable sin of regarding some
other entity as a "partner," i.e., a conceptual equal of Allah. And in the Arabic
this last verse does conclude by stating explicitly:

> *Ittaxaðū aḥbara-hum wa-ruhbana-hum arbaban min dūni Allahi wa-al-
> Masīha ibna Maryama. wa-ma umirū illa liyaʕbudū ilahan wahidan. <u>lā
> ilaha illa ḥuwa. subḥāna-hu. ʕammā yušrikūna</u>* (9:31)

They have taken their messengers and priests to be lords beside God,
as well as the Messiah, son of Mary. And they were commanded to
serve only one God. <u>There is no God but he. Praise be unto him.</u>
<u>But they demean him</u> [where the verb used is the verbal form of the
noun *širk*].

The essential failing of the Jews and Christians, as criticized here, is that
they allow substitutes—representative figures—to play important roles in
the relation of believer with God. True worship of Allah, by contrast, requires
accepting the true path to communication with him, namely the words he
has made manifest in the Qur'ān.

The Demand for Direct Authenticity

Abhorrence of all indirect, hence misdirected, worship is why Islam rejects
any translation of the Qur'ān that is significant. On the one hand, this
excludes any translation of the Qur'ān that causes the worshipper to lose
touch with the original text; but on the other, it excludes idolatry, known
explicitly as *waθanīyah* from *waθan* "graven image." In both cases, a substitute is being offered, either for the word of God, or for godhead itself. Allah

---

* Λέγουσιν Ἰουδαῖοι ὅτι Ἰσραήλ ἐστιν υἱὸς Θεοῦ· καὶ λέγουσιν οἱ Χριστιανοὶ ὅτι ὁ Χριστός
ἐστιν ὁ υἱὸς τοῦ Θεοῦ· τοῦτό ἐστιν ὁ λόγος αὐτῶν διὰ τῶν στομάτων αὐτῶν· ἰσοφωνοῦσι
τοῖς λόγοις τῶν ἀρνησαμένων ἐκ πρίν· φονεύσει αὐτοὺς ὁ Θεός, ἕνεκεν τῶν ἀρνοῦνται·
ἐπελάβοντο τοὺς ἀποστόλους αὐτῶν καὶ τοὺς ἱερεῖς κυρίους πάρεξ Θεοῦ· καὶ τὸν Χριστὸν
υἱὸν τῆς Μαρίας· καὶ οὐκ ἐκελεύσθησαν δουλεύειν εἰ μὴ Θεοῦ ἑνός.

has expressed himself in the Qur'ān and in his creation: it is *širk* to attempt to redo either of these expressions, either with supposedly equivalent words, or with images that in some way claim to represent what Allah has caused to be, because the only way to do this is to attempt to remake them.

This prohibition on images is called aniconism. An analogous word for the prohibition on use of equivalent words in place of Allah's Arabic, i.e., on indirect signing, would be "asemism." Aniconism is distinct from iconoclasm, which is the practice of destroying images already made. This is explicitly approved by the Qur'ān (21:51–68), which tells the story of how Abraham destroyed his tribe's idols. When questioned, he denied what he had done, and then ironically asked the idol-worshippers to ask the one remaining idol about who had destroyed the others. When they protested that it was unreasonable to expect an idol to talk, he countered with a question: "How they could possibly worship a being that did not even do that?" Their reaction was to attempt to protect their remaining idol but to burn Abraham, which Allah says he frustrated.

Images of gods, then, are fair game for the Muslim to destroy, at least if Abraham is a good role model: but when the Qur'ān talks specifically of *širk*, it is concerned not with graphic representations, but about a misplaced reverence that in effect demeans Allah. In fact, the Qur'ān does not explicitly propose aniconism or asemism in general. The doctrine—which is certainly lively in some parts of the *ummah*—is based rather on a number of hadith, such as:

> Narrated Aisha (wife of the Prophet):
> I bought a cushion having on it pictures (of animals). When Allah's Apostle saw it, he stood at the door and did not enter. I noticed the sign of disapproval on his face and said, "O Allah's Apostle! I repent to Allah and His Apostle. What sin have I committed?" Allah's Apostle said, "What is this cushion?" I said, "I have bought it for you so that you may sit on it and recline on it." Allah's Apostle said, "The makers of these pictures will be punished on the Day of Resurrection, and it will be said to them, 'Give life to what you have created [i.e., these pictures].' The Prophet added, "The Angels of (Mercy) do not enter a house in which there are pictures (of animals)."[16]

In some parts of the Islamic *ummah*, then, there is, or has been, a prohibition both on figurative representation, and on translation. Islam has been, in some periods and places, both aniconist and asemist. This equivalence has analogues in a number of other religions.

During the first five hundred years of Buddhism, iconography (until the late first century A.D.) did not include depictions of the Buddha himself, as is clear at the shrine of Sanchi. This had been founded by emperor Aśoka in the third century B.C., but was not completed until the first A.D. In the rich profusion of symbolism carved here, the *buddharūpa* (Buddha-form) is nowhere to be seen, but the presence of Buddha is conveyed by many associated images: the Bodhi-tree where he received enlightenment, the great wheel of dharma (itself a metaphor for his teaching), a stupa (containing precious relics), the vision of a white elephant (which inspired his miraculous conception), a riderless horse (for his escape from domestic life) and—most widespread of all—a pair of vast footprints. Other ways of portraying the Buddha without showing him include an empty throne, and the symbol of the *triratna*, "the three jewels"—of Buddha (the sage), dharma (the law), and *sangha* (the church). As the sage Nagasensa famously pointed out to king Menander:

> The Blessed one, O king, has passed away by that kind of passing away in which nothing remains which could tend to the formation of another individual. It is not possible to point out the Blessed one as being here or there.[17]

This is not exactly aniconic—there is a profusion of images and associations, but not direct depiction. It has been claimed that this is not aniconic at all, but rather a series of presentations of the sacred sites, where lay devotion was practiced.[18] But the absence of direct representation of the Great Man (*mahāpurisa*) still stands out painfully.

The Buddha himself, while alive, had decried any fixation on personality or physical presence. He is said to have reproached his old disciple Vakkali who, on his deathbed, wanted to see him one last time: compassionately he turned up, but with the words: "O Vakkali, why do you crave to look on this body of impure matter? Vakkali, one who perceives dharma perceives me. One who perceives me perceives dharma."[19]

The Buddhist literature, however, contains very little to document this apparent ban on graphic representation. Yet in one passage in the Tipitaka, it is taken for granted: "World-honored one," the Buddha is asked, "if images of yours are not allowed to be made, may we not at least make images of

Bodhisattvas in attendance upon you?" Which the Buddha then graciously permits.[20] He explicitly forbids, however, "figures of men and women coupling."[21] And in another passage,[22] the Buddha is concerned about possible erotic effects of art: it is forbidden for "the monastery walls to be adorned with figures of men and women." These forbidden images are called *paṭibhāna-citta*, which means something between "lively" and "racy": sexual suggestiveness seems to be a characteristic flaw in decorative pictures. But nothing forbids pictures of gods or life forms, as such, or even forbids the worship of idols—which in Pali is called *paṭimā-pūjā* "counterpart devotion." It is a central practice of Hinduism.

In a different chapter of the same text, known as the *Cullavagga*, Buddha was asked if it was permitted to tell the teaching *chandasi*, meaning "in Sanskrit verse." He replied that it was not, adding:

> *anujānāmi bhikkhave sakāya niruttiyā buddhavacanaṃ pariyāpunituṃ.*
>
> I give you, O Monks, permission to learn the word of the Buddha in own dialect.[23]

The Buddhists in central and south India and Śri Lanka, who developed into the *Theravāda* school ("Doctrine of the Elders") took this to mean "in the Buddha's own language," and they have continued the use of Pali as their religious language until the present. Their doctrines, then, have been preserved in the language of original transmission, just as Islam has in Arabic. And the Theravada school too is famous for restricting its iconography, essentially permitting only the Buddha himself to be represented, and only in familiar poses, whether seated in order to bless or teach, or lying on his side, preparing to enter into *parinirvāṇa*. They maintain the doctrine that Buddha was not a deity but a brilliant human being, hence that they too are not worshippers of idols, but simply use these effigies to focus their attention.

After the second century A.D. the figurative representation of the Buddha became more accepted and widespread. One center of production for these statues was Gandhara (modern southern Afghanistan) where they were transformed by Greek sculptural style; and another was Mathura, south of Delhi, which seems to have risen independently.[24] The famous two great Buddhas of Bamiyan, formed in 507 and 554 A.D., were naturally in the Gandhara tradition.

Despite all the previous aniconism, when the Muslims and Buddhists came into contact, in Sogd to the northeast of Iran in the latter seventh century, and the word Buddha was first borrowed into Arabic, it meant nothing more or less than "idol."* This was how the "Gandhara-style" effigies of the Buddha must have been seen, with Muslim horror at evident idolatry overwhelming any perception of a deeper similarity in how divinity was to be respected. A Tibetan tantra records: "In keeping with the teachings of those whose women wear veils . . . the hordes of Tayi [i.e., Arab] horsemen destroy in battle any statues of gods there be, without exception."[25]

But as shown by Persian, which outside Iran was also the lingua franca of Muslims in Central Asia and northern India, there was more ambivalence about graphic images, in their potential for beauty as against distraction: the range of Persian miniatures, for example, somehow had to be reconciled with Islam. This ambivalence never left the name of Buddha: his statues were things of beauty, and this was not lost on Persians. The name came first into Persian through connections in the northeast, notably Sogd, where it is spelled *pūt*. (Sogdian, although a related language, lacked the sounds [b] and [d]). Farther west, in Iran, it was borrowed as *but* (or with a Persian accent *bot*).†

In the conventions of Persian poetry, largely established at the Samanid courts in Samarkand and Bukhara, *bot-i zībā* "idol of loveliness" and *bot-i māh-rūy* "moon-faced idol" became stock images for the beloved's beauty, with *češm-i bādāmi* "almond eyes" and *lab-i qūnče* "rosebud lips," all of them reminiscent of a Buddha statue. And *navbahār ḥasan* "beautiful as Nava Vihāra" (referring to the monastery in Balkh, but standing for them all) was another Persian commonplace, so it was understandable that poets found their Buddhist neighbors' past bittersweet. The mixed feelings about Buddha images may be summed up by two of them:

---

* For example, Al-Jāḥiz was using *budd* to refer to the idol of Kuvera in the early ninth century, and Ibn Durayd, writing a dictionary in the late ninth, defined the word as *ṣanam*, i.e., "idol." Al-Dimaški's *Cosmographie* (early fourteenth century) termed *budd* the principal stones at Somanath, which Mahmud had famously desecrated as idols in 1026 (quoting Qur'ān 53:20). They were actually fertility symbols, male and female (Vaux 2012).

† In modern Turkish, "idol-worship" is still *put-perest*, once borrowed from Persian; but in modern Persian, this word has long been dropped in favor of *paykār-parast*, literally, "face-worship."

bot–i peresti girifteh im hamehin jahān čun bot-ast u–mā šaman–im

We are all idol-worshippers: the world is the idol and we śramans (i.e., Buddhist monks).

Rūdakī (who died 940), in Bukhara

zi Islām–i majāzī gašt bīzār:	If one from feignèd Islam
keh rā kufr–i haqīqī šod padīdār?	turned in scorn:
darūn har bot–i jānī ast panhān;	What true belief in infidelity
beh zēr–i kufr īmānī ast panhān	might be shown?
	Inside each idol there is hidden
	a living soul.
	Under the infidelity, there is a
	hidden faith.

Mahmūd Shabistarī, Sufi poet from Tabriz (1288–1340),
from *Secret Rose-Garden* (*Gulšān-i Rāz*)[26]

❊❦❊

Closer to home for Islam, early Judaism also maintained strong prohibitions against images, and linked this with a ban on polytheism.

Famously, these are the first and second of the Ten Commandments:

• You shall have no other gods above me.
• You shall not make for yourself an idol, or any likeness of what is in heaven above or on earth beneath or in the water under the earth. You shall not worship them or serve them ... (*Tanakh—Exodus* 20:3–5)

More explicitly than in the Qur'ān, and far more strictly than early Buddhism ever suggested, the representation of any living creature is also forbidden. God's motive in requiring this appears to be simply a matter of loyalty, rather than the saving of the Israelites from the embarrassment of pledging their service to something that is not there anyway. God goes on:

• for I, the Lord your god, am a jealous god, visiting the iniquity of the fathers on the children, on the third and fourth generations of those who hate me; but showing loving kindness to thousands, to those who love me and keep my commandments.

God is requiring loyalty, not a denial of the existence of any competitors. This may be why he requires the people to have no gods **above** him. In Hebrew, this is *'al pānā-ya* "above face-mine" rather than "in my place." But it is hard to see why this should extend to banning all representation of any living thing, unless this is meant as a piece of preventive legislation, to deny any potential backsliders the excuse that an image in question was not for actual worship, but only to look at or admire. There are two kinds of created object that are forbidden, as specified in Hebrew: *pesel*, the "graven image," i.e., something wrought of metal, wood, or stone; and *temūnah*, the likeness or image, which would be defined more conceptually as a representative form. It is also rather clear, and basic, what the people are forbidden to do with the idols: *lō tištaḥweh lā-hem*, "ye shall not bow down to them" (from *šāḥāh* "to prostrate onself"). This is an act of worship rather rare in modern Christianity, but still basic to Islam. The following point ("nor serve them either"—*wa-lō tā'ăḇǝdêm*) is not so clear: how can one be a slave (*'eḇed*) to a graven image? Perhaps this last clause is a mere rhetorical reinforcement.

In the end, the requirement of the Ten Commandments is clear. And the immediate upshot—of what happened when the people lost faith in God and asked for new gods, and how their worship of a golden calf, which Aaron cast for them, severely offended God—is also clear. Strict monotheism remained a duty of the Israelites, and with them the Jews, ever after: but the ban on any figurative art that might re-create living creatures seems to have dropped out of the Jewish consciousness. A vivid exception to compliance is the synagogue abandoned around 250 A.D. of Dura Europos in eastern Syria. Discovered essentially intact in 1932, it was vividly decorated with fifty-eight scenes of narrative art, although originally there were probably close to a hundred. They include the Sacrifice of Isaac, Moses leading the children of Israel out of Egypt, Moses receiving the Two Tablets on Mount Sinai, the visions of the prophet Ezekiel, and the story of Esther. Particularly interesting is the fact that it includes partial representations of God himself: his hand shows divine intervention or approval in many of the paintings.

On the language side, Hebrew not only remains the authoritative language of the *Tanakh* (Law, Prophets, and Writings) but is still the language of common prayers in synagogue: the central prayer *Shema Yisrael* "Hear, [O] Israel"), *Tefilat ha-Amidah* the "Standing Prayer," and most others. Jews are advised to say their personal prayers in Hebrew too, if they are able. This is recommended for various reasons. The language of the original is said to be safer—since no translation can be perfect—and Hebrew is in any case the "Holy Tongue," chosen by God himself to reveal himself to the prophets.*

A third reason is more idiosyncratic. After the Babylonian captivity and exile, the main language of Jews in Syria and Palestine was Aramaic, no longer Hebrew: in this period, even the *Tanakh* was largely discussed on the basis of a *targumah* (translation) into Aramaic. Aramaic, then, was the vernacular. Neverthless, the part of the Talmud called the Gemara, at Sotah 35a, defends the saying of prayers in Hebrew rather than Aramaic by the claim that "the angels do not understand Aramaic." Angels, it transpires, are needed to carry our prayers on high.

There is more special pleading too. The *Shema* is required to be in Hebrew because it incorporates large portions quoted from the Torah. The *Amidah* may be in any language, since it is a communal, not a solitary, prayer, and this has a potency allowing the angels to be dispensed with. This is the doctrine, current to this day.[27]

The gross fact, then, is that in the centuries after the return from Babylon, until the dispersion under Roman rule and perhaps later, the Jews' belief in both compulsory use of the language of revelation in prayer and the prohibition on depiction of living creatures was analogous to Muslim strictures. Furthermore, early Buddhism had many of the same tendencies, perhaps the more striking because they arose in a religious tradition unrelated to the Semitic cousins, Judaism and Islam.

By contrast, Christianity through the ages has been largely tolerant both of icons and of translation.

In the first few centuries A.D., the church did take a hard line against idolatrous use of images by pagans: and subsequently, there have been periods of iconoclasm directed even at orthodox Christian imagery: notably, in the Greek Orthodox Church in the mid-eighth and early ninth centuries, and in Protestant churches after the Reformation.

But these periods of violent reaction have remained as exceptions within a tradition that has seen iconography as a useful aid to Christian knowledge and piety, especially among the illiterate. Pictures of Jesus are known (from literature) since the second century; and the Catacombs, Christian cemeteries outside Rome built from the late second century, can be seen to this day decorated with colorful scenes from life and carved reliefs on tombs.

---

* These reasons are clearly very reminiscent of Muslim disquisitions on the place of Arabic, e.g. by Imam Al-Shafi'i and Ibn Qutaybah (cf p. 266).

As for translation, the preaching of the Christian faith was always predicated on the possibility that new converts can approach Christianity through a new language. This is the characteristic Christian stance, as familiar to the Greek Orthodox Church as it is to the full range of Protestant sects.

A partial—but very significant—exception was created by the Roman Catholic Church's strong attachment to Latin, which for sixteen centuries it kept supreme as a liturgical language, even if never imposed universally. Meanwhile the Scriptures were defended from vulgar acquaintance by restriction to the decent obscurity of (the same) learned language. But this policy—although rigorously enforced in Catholic Christendom, even on occasion to the burning of those who defied it—could only be defended on practical, rather than theological, grounds.

These two features of the use of Church Latin are reminiscent of Arabic in Islam, and perhaps make Latin and Arabic socio-culturally similar as confessional languages. But on the acknowledged facts of history, Latin could never be defended as the ancestral language for Christianity, as Arabic was—and is—for Islam.

There is a reason why Christianity has broadly endorsed images and multilingual worship while Islam, early Buddhism, and Judaism have abhorred them.

The common feature shared by images of spiritual truth and translations of the word of God is that they are mediated attempts to represent the focus of religious faith: they are indirect ways of getting at a relationship that—arguably—is only valid if it is sincere because it is direct and unmediated.

Islam requires attention to the word of God as originally dictated to the Prophet, and submission to God's revealed will. The Buddhist needs to concentrate (*samādhi*) on dharma, and so ultimately achieve *mokṣa* (release) through his own focused meditation, guided by the texts offered by the *Tathāgata* "the Thus-Gone" *sakāya niruttiyā* "in his own language." The children of Israel were given austere commandments in their own language, the first two of which were not to accept any lesser gods, nor to represent the form of living beings, or anything else in the creation of the Living God. This was given in their own language, which must be recalled, even after it had ceased to be the medium of daily conversation for believers.

In each of these religions, direct relation with God or ultimate reality is required. Nothing less is sincere worship or right concentration.

But Christianity is by comparison a tissue of mediations, between the worshipping soul and God on high. In most churches before the Reformation an ordained priesthood undertook the rituals of the faith. And then a hierarchy of spiritual beings made up the hosts of heaven. Most distant from God, yet in many sects essential for communication with him, are the saints, the holy departed. Closer in is the Virgin Mary, mother of God, who is also a willing channel for prayers to the Almighty. The spirit of God abroad in the world is the Holy Spirit, one of God's three persons, yet which proceeds from the other two, the Father and the Son. And then there is the Son, who descended specially to restore the full relation between Man and God: not only by what he could impart through his presence on earth, but above all by allowing himself to be sacrificed to pay the price of the sinful breakdown between the two parties.

Everywhere, there are relations between the Christian and his or her God that are communicated through the appearance of a third party. In such a moral universe, what could be the harm in an image that might use our visual sense to help the fallible mind focus on spiritual truth? How could conversion into a still different language, to bridge the transit of the universal truth to distant souls, lead to a loss of directness or sincerity, when different aspects of God's revelation have already come down to Man in various languages, Hebrew, Aramaic, and Greek?

There is, in some ways, a similar character in the highly illustrated—and translated—form of Buddhism that descended from Gautama's original in the Gandhara area and through into China, Mahayana. This is a kind of Buddhism where the human being is not left to struggle toward salvation through his or her own resources, but can turn for refuge to an array of bodhisattvas, as well as lesser gods, who, through a multitude of rebirths and concurrent worlds, will aid a devout believer's passage to paradise, while awaiting the ultimate fate for all beings, the attainment of nirvana. In every Mahayana temple (with the exception of Zen) there is a profusion of images, and indeed unashamed idols; and the cults have been developed over two millennia, in parallel, in the principal literate languages of eastern Asia. This is close to being the polar opposite of the austere faiths that direct attention to the primal Buddha, to the Lord Yahweh, and to Allah.

The value of directness, then, and the absence of any opportunity for distraction, seem to be the underlying reasons for aniconism and asemism. They presuppose that God, or the ultimate, is humanly accessible: prayers and worship do not need to be cloaked in dissembling descriptions, in illusory images, or in a language that is familiar to the worshipper. God— or nirvana—in these religions is something quite stark and absolute, but ultimately on the human wavelength, capable of direct contact. This god is not as the Greek Semelē found Zeus: a being of such shocking effulgence that sight of him in his true glory destroyed her.

In the Islamic tradition, Allah (literally, "the god") has ninety-nine names. Knowing these names is—besides attention to the Qur'ān—one of the few ways of knowing him directly. Notably, only two or three of them are frightening—*al-mumīt* "The Bringer of Death" (though immediately balanced by *al-muḥyī* "The Bringer of Life"), *al-muntaqim* "the Vengeful," *aḍ-ḍarr* "the Distresser"—while at least twenty refer to God's mercy, approachability, and beneficence, beginning with the two best known, *ar-raḥmān* "the Compassionate," and *ar-raḥīm* "the Merciful," but including *al-ɣaffar* "the Forgiving often," *al-ɣafūr* "the Forgiving much," *al-barr* "the Beneficent," *al-laṭīf* "the Gentle," *al-ḥalīm* "the Indulgent," *aš-šakūr* "the Grateful," *al-wālī* "the Patron," and *al-hādī* "the Guide." God, so viewed, is nothing if not approachable.

❦

The Enduring Marks of Language Conversions

道可道 非恆道；名可名 非恆名。

dào kě dào, fēi héng dào; míng kě míng, fēi héng míng.

The way that can be spoken is not the enduring Way;
The name that can be named is not the enduring Name.

Lǎozǐ: Dào Dé Jīng 1 (**老子道德經**) *

T HIS BOOK HAS BEEN not about states, but about transitions. For three faiths that see themselves as universal, we have examined the first steps they took toward finding expression in new languages, as they sought (or sometimes demanded) admission to new language communities.

Every language is a large system of concepts with words to express them, in effect like a woven tissue or fine cloth; but a tissue not of colored threads, rather of meaningful associations, of words to things in the world, and one to another. The language was there first: it preexisted the faith that sought expression in it, seeking to have its own ideas woven into this ancient network. Did this process of fitting faith into language leave its marks on the ideas of the religion itself?

Each religion too was a great tradition, and it had existed already expressed in the languages of previous worshipers. After long experience in other parts of the world, it had means to repair itself, if it was torn or deformed by this process of translation. Early translations may have involved misunderstandings, or overextensions of half-digested ideas (as when early Christians

---

* Literally, this reads more like: "Way can say, not true way; name can name, not true name." The first clause depends on a pun, in that 道 *dào* means both "way" and "say."

were believed to be cannibals, from misguided interpretations of Holy Communion). So not all of the first steps will have left a long-term trace. Have we been able to find some that did? Did languages, then, really, at least in part, reinvent the world's missionary religions?

In the case studies that make up the chapters of this book, we have focused on five aspects of the languages that received the religious incomers. Everywhere we were looking for changed—and changing—elements, in its vocabulary, its grammar, its scripture, its heritage of preexisting heirlooms, and its speaker communities. Did these innovations, as they came into contact with the religion, affect its content?

In each case, we found influence of surprising depth and scope.

Buddhism was projected into Gandhara, in a north Indian dialect not vastly different from the Buddha's own Magadhi (the probable basis for liturgical Pali). This change of expression—almost of accent and nothing more—was sufficient to broaden its community, and so lay the faith open to cultural influences from the northwest, Greek and Iranian, which revolutionized its iconography.

When—against the Buddha's express command—teaching of the faith was developed scripturally in Sanskrit, a whole new philosophy entered the faith: compassion became a higher goal than personal enlightenment, and the concept developed of the bodhisattva (buddha-to-be), who was a timeless spirit rather than a mortal, patiently awaiting salvation for all.

As merchants took the faith into China, the substantial program of scholarly Chinese translation not only gave Buddhism a history with dates, and linked it with the preexisting philosophy of the Dao. It also legitimized the Chinese to be Buddhist sages with unrivaled access to scripture, recentering the faith outside the monasteries of India, and ultimately licensing its spread around China's satellite civilizations in east Asia.

The history of linguistic changes affecting Christianity was no less radical. Christianity had been founded by a speaker of Aramaic, but it traveled around the Roman Empire radically translated into Greek, and after a couple of centuries, into Latin too. This brought in first the Jewish diaspora and then Gentiles in overwhelming numbers: but the fact that it was transmitted by these two principal languages of the empire meant that it could not long keep its distance from secular power: European Christianity, embraced by Constantine and his successors, became an arm of the Roman state.

That was the political side; but theologically, its creed became entangled with Greek philosophy, and a series of eastern synods aimed at unifying the faith succeeded only in creating permanent schisms with all the different churches eastward from Egypt, each identified by its own provincial or national language.

A little later, the effort was made to propagate the faith into western Europe. Where the effort came from the Latin-speaking west of the empire, the unspoken politics of Rome meant that Latin assumed a sacred—but theologically baseless—importance as the language of the church centered on Rome.

Where the effort came from the eastern church in Constantinople (projected to the Goths and the Slavs) it set up something new, a respect for linguistic autonomy in the Orthodox church; but the resulting lack of a common language meant that the Greek-speaking metropolis never created cultural communion with its daughter churches among the Slavs and Romanians.

These were the transitions that, broadly, determined the religious conversions of Europe. The need to induct, or reconcile, new languages to the new dispensation had left its mark on all of them. There followed almost a millennium of religious and linguistic stability, until the next great time of religious—and linguistic—ferment, the sixteenth century.

The conquerors of the New World were, as it happened, well primed with new linguistic theories to match the challenge of propagating the True Faith to a benighted continent. In a magnificent achievement, they used the new tools of grammars, dictionaries, and indigenous lingua francas to contact the peoples of the Americas in their own tongues. But the ethical vision of the conquerors proved to be less robust than their military and administrative savoir faire. The converts were contacted in the vernacular, and many became devout worshippers in it over two centuries: but governance of the church remained immovably—and fatally—in the hands of those who grew up with Spanish or Portuguese.

Back in Europe, linguistic transitions—and indeed revolutions—seemed to be occurring for their own sake, perhaps caused by another linguistic technology: the printing press. A breed of turbulent monks and priests arose who questioned the purity of the tradition—for doubts about translations made more than a millennium before. On the one hand, they demanded a return to the source languages of Scripture, to restore the purity of the tradition; and on the other, they demanded that the new interpretation be divulged to the general public, through vernacular translations and (what became) mass literacy. The unity of church was shattered by the simultaneous blows of this scholarly double whammy.

Finally, we looked at Arabic within Islam. This was another approach to ensuring purity of tradition, but this one through outlawing translation of the scripture. Since Islam was a religion that would expand beyond the Arabic speech community it should have been impossible in principle: yet it worked. It led to a new doctrine, which actually admitted translations as potentially helpful for foreigners, but ensured that original and translation remained different in status, the latter merely at the level of commentary. Islam required linguistic immediacy, a fundamentalist kind of directness that also required absence of figurative images. This guaranteed linguistic purity, but at some cost to worshippers' comprehension of the language in use.

⊱⋅⊰

This last uncompromising stance is a kind of logical extreme point for the inquiry of this book. It is fittingly attached to Islam too, since this also happens to be the youngest of the missionary faiths examined here. It has the feeling of a last resort. Changing language, while trying to retain a religion, is just too dangerous (as all the other Buddhist and Christian experiences demonstrate). How much better simply to stick unswervingly to the original so that there can be no argument!

This book has striven to be neutral among faiths. We have demonstrated that even in the simplest language transfer there is the potential for a divisive or a diverting influence on a religion in a new community, even if the religion is well defined by a worldwide cult. But this influence is never enough to subvert the human need to worship, and to do this in company with the clergy—and under the instructions—of the accepted ruling power or economic elite. Conversion by voluntary association is an amazingly strong pull, especially for those who have not previously belonged to a missionary faith. Once attachment to a missionary faith has been established, though, religious conservatism may keep it in place for many generations, without any other motive. Buddhism, Christianity, and Islam are all long-term beneficiaries of this human tendency.

As to the languages, which have been the main characters in this story, their hold on their communities' loyalties have, historically, been less secure than the religions' hold on congregations. The languages of the ancient world have died or changed beyond recognition, but many of the revealed faiths of the Axial Age are still with us. Some languages indeed—Pali, Sanskrit, Coptic, Syriac, Latin—owe most of their continued existence to the religions they serve.

But through their varied cultural pasts, and the active modern life that most of the languages retain, they are a source of unending variety, which the formal loyalties of religious cults find it hard to match. This is one reason for the unreliability of languages, which would be one reading of the gross facts revealed in this book. "Traduttore traditore" runs the Italian proverb (translator = traitor), and it is an engaging fact that the word *tradurre* itself (standard Italian nowadays for "translate") owes this meaning to a mistranslation by the Italian humanist Leonardo Bruni, in a classical Latin passage about the deceptive nature of word origins. Latin *traducere* meant to derive or borrow a word from one language to another, not to translate it: to bring in more than just its meaning.[1]

Words from the original language can be borrowed as religious technical terms into a vernacular, and we have seen many examples, for one religion or another; but the vernacular, with its different hinterland of associations, is capable of illuminating them in various lights. It took Syriac to make Christ a *hmayra*—hostage human body, offered to God; Saxon to make him *werodes drohtin*—leader of a war band; Nahuatl *toteu-tonatiuh*—our lord the Sun.

Not all those with a religious faith value metaphor: some demand a straight statement of the supernatural from their scripture; some damn all images verbal or figurative. Some such fundamentalists can be found attached to every one of these missionary faiths. Yet ultimately, every religious tradition is far wider, and deeper, and more encompassing of human life. And the human instinct for worship finds people of every persuasion to take up different stances within a broad faith. All human life may be here, somewhere.

But these broad faiths—Buddhism, Christianity, Islam—whose creeds have been the main subject of these pages, are not the only channels for worship. Before the Axial Age, and long before the global missions inspired then that are still active today, there were others who also loved the world, and the variety of its creatures. They did not aspire to preach, or make universal claims, but simply to honor their local spirits. Called animists, pantheists, or traditionalists, less sympathetically called pagans or heathens, many of them are still there. They welcome the world's adornment and beauty, and treasure a striking image as honey in the heart, without seeking to work it into a theology.[2]

Kiil utziil; nimlaj taq kaslimaal; majun loulo; oxlajuj matioxiil

Long life; honey in the heart; no evil; thirteen thank-yous.

They too have their faiths. And since they are not seeking to persuade others far away, these faiths are unlikely to be transformed by the need to be presented in a foreign language. They simply subsist, in their own terms.

Down the ages, the missionary religions have endeavored to exclude such innocent gladness and simple piety, and replace them, each with their own new, revealed truth, however simple or however arbitrary. But if they still do this now, then despite all their boasted revelations and world populations, they lack the most fundamental virtue: human charity.

Notes

Epigraph

1. Verses cited by Diego de Torres Rubio, 1700, *Arte y vocabulario de la lengua general de los Indios del Perú*, Lima. English translation based on Jesus Lara's Spanish, given by Cáceres et al. 1990, p. 84.

Introduction

1. English translation (and parentheticals) mine.
2. The religious use of the Greek term comes from the Septuagint, *parádeisos*, translating "Garden" [of Eden] (Genesis 2:8ff). Originally a Median word, *pairidaēza* (literally, "walled around"), it was also borrowed into Akkadian as *pardizu*. In Persia it broadly applied to storage space, orchards, stables, vineyards, and tree farms. Later, it meant a hunting park for the aristocracy, hence a park attached to a palace. Bremmer 2008.
3. Luke 23:43.
4. *Qur'ān* 13:23, 18:107. *Jannah* alone is the usual word for "paradise" in Arabic, corresponding to Hebrew *gan* in "Garden of Eden" (*gan ʕēden*) (Genesis 2:8ff).
5. They are described, e.g., in Edgerton 2004, Kruger 1975, Thackston 1999, Ostler 2007 chapter 7, Cooper 2003, Durston 2007, Hanks 2010, and Melià 1997.
6. Cf e.g., Green 1998, pp. 283–85.
7. See e.g., Everett 2009.
8. From "Saving the Indigenous Soul: An Interview with Martín Prechtel," Derrick Jensen, *The Sun*, April 2001 (www.floweringmountain.com/indexSUN.html).
9. Sentences cited in Armstrong 2009.
10. Sentence cited in Armstrong 2009.
11. Hanks 1990, p. 259.
12. Monod-Becquelin 1997, pp. 102–03, 114–15.
13. Reid Baer: Interview with Martín Prechtel (www.menstuff.org/columns/overboard /prechtel.html).

Chapter 1

1. Sahagún 1993, p. 31 [from "The Ten Commandments of God, Fourth Psalm"].

2. Sahagún 1988, vol. 2, p. 808.
3. Sahagún 1988, vol. 1, p. 39.
4. Karttunen 1990, p. 294.
5. Citation and translation (largely) of Dibble 1974, p. 232, who adverts to the prayers to Tezcatlipoca in Sahagún, vol. 1, p. 307, ff (Book 6, "Of the Prayers which they Prayed to their Gods . . ."). 1576 [1988].
6. The original is Ausías Izquierdo Zebrero's *Lucero de Nuestra Salvación* ("Beacon of Our Salvation"). This comparison is due to Louise Burkhart, who noted the exact parallelism of the Spanish and Nahuatl scripts. Burkhart 1996, 2000.
7. Sahagún 1576 [1988], vol. 1, p. 459.
8. *Breve y más compendiosa doctrina christian en lengua mexican y castellana, que contiene las cosas más necesarias de nuestra sancta fé cathólica, para aprovechamientodestos indios naturales y salvación de sus ánimas.* 1539; *Sermones en mexicano* 1540.
9. Apparently from his commentary on Saint John's gospel, chapter 19. This would fit with verses 19–20, which give the inscription on the placard, and state that the placard was in Hebrew, Greek, and Latin.
10. Lockhart 1992, p. 248.
11. Taylor 1987, p. 11.
12. E.g., in Alva 1634.
13. Poole 1981.
14. Lockhart 1992, pp. 210–29.

Chapter 2

1. Geiger 1916 [1943], pp. 6–7, referring to the *Cullavagga* vol. 33, pt.1. This reads, in full: *na bhikkhave buddhavacanaṃ chandaso āropetabhaṃ yo āropeyya, āpatti dukkaṭassa. anujānāmi bhikkhave sakāya niruttiyā buddhavacanaṃ pariyāpunitun ti:* "O Monks, do not render the word of the Buddha into *chandas*. Whoever does so, is guilty of an offense. I give you, O Monks, permission to learn the word of the Buddha in own dialect." (*Vinaya Piṭakaṃ 2:139*) The phrase is actually singular (so literally "dialect" not "dialects"); and there is no explicit pronoun, so whose "own" dialect is not stated.
2. Derived from entries in Stefan Baums's and Andrew Glass's online *Dictionary of Gāndhārī* (gandhari.org).
3. *Khara-* "ass," *oṣṭha-* "lip," and an adjectival ending *-ī*. The script is mentioned as the second of sixty-four (after Brāhmī) in the Lalita Vistara, a third-century-A.D. biography of the Buddha in Sanskrit. In the nineteenth century, the script was rediscovered independently of its name, but the two were married up on the strength of a Chinese Buddhist encyclopedia, the 法苑珠林 (Fǎyuàn Zhūlín, i.e. the "Dharma Garden Gem Forest") of 668 A.D. This identified the script written right-left as invented by one 驢唇 (lǘ chún), but the characters mean "ass lip." (Banerji 1920, p. 193; Bühler 1895, p. 22; Terrien de La Couperie, 1886–7, p. 59). The word Kharoṣṭhī is now seen as an attempt to represent some forgotten Old Iranian name in Sanskrit (Glass 2000, p. 11) so the etymology is probably gratuitous. Terrien de la Couperie, not unreasonably, thought he could discern a relation to *Kuruš* (i.e., Persia's founding king, Cyrus).
4. Sims-Williams 2012, p. 77; Harmatta 1994, pp. 417–40.
5. Salomon 2007, p. 180.

6. It occurs in chapter 3 of the sutra. The Lotus Sutra, developed in the period 100 B.C. to 200 A.D., is more authentically the *Sad-dharma-puṇḍarīka-sūtra*, the "True-Law-Lotus-Sutra."

7. The idea is due to Seishi Karashima, speaking at the University of Hamburg on May 8, 2012: "Vehicle (yāna) and Wisdom (jñāna) in the Lotus Sutra—the Origin of the Notion of Yāna in Mahāyāna Buddhism" (http://tinyurl.com/q8efgcl). We do have another example of precisely this mistake being made by Lokakṣema, a Kuṣāṇa translator of the second century A.D. Lokakṣema's mistake was also detected by Karashima 1992, and signalized in Boucher 1998, p. 491.

8. Strabo xi.8.2; Ptolemy vi.16.5 and 8, with extensive discussion in Tarn 1951, esp. pp. 285–87 and 516.

9. Johnston 1936, part II, p. xviii.

10. Harmatta 1994, p. 436; Thakur 1996, pp. 216–17, Edgerton 2004.

11. Bronkhorst 2011, p. 129.

12. Salomon 2001, p. 248–51.

13. Harmatta 1994, p. 434.

14. Jan Nattier concludes from a survey of the literature so far discovered: "Buddhist literature in Central Asia appears to have been transmitted exclusively in Indian languages prior to the beginning of the 6th century." Nattier 1990, p. 212.

15. The Greek equivalent selected for *dharma* is *eusebeia* "reverence, piety" (having to do with worship); in Aramaic, it is *qšīṭā māqšiṭ* "rectitude practicing-rightly," where the metaphor comes from *qšṭ* "shoot, hit the mark." But the original word *dhamma* is itself literally about "holding firm." If this is typical, early translations of Buddhism were fairly free.

16. *Milindapañha*, iv.1.47 (Rhys Davids translation).

17. Majjhima-Nikāya ii.149: Assalāyana Sūtta vi. *Sutante: yonakambojesu aññesu ca paccantimesu janapadesu dveva vaṇṇā, ayyoceva dāso ca: ayyo hutvā dāso hoti, dāso hutvā ayyo hotiiti.* "Have you heard this? In the Yona, Kamboja and other border countries, there are only two varṇas, ārya and dāsa; and that an ārya becomes a dāsa, and a dāsa becomes an ārya."

18. Lalita Vistara x. *Lipi-śālā-sandarśana-parivarttā* "Chapter on Attending the Writing Class." Each of the sixty-four scripts is named, in one long recitation; the first is Brāhmī and the second Kharoṣṭhī. Few of the others are recognizable.

19. *Milindapañha*, iii.7.1 (Rhys Davids translation).

20. *Saddharmapuṇḍarīkasūtra*, chapter 10 (Buddhist Text Translation Society).

21. Schopen 1985, p. 126.

22. Veidlinger 2006, p. 411; Beal 1884, Si-Yu-Ki II, pp. 146–47.

23. "The earliest known archeological evidence of this practice [viz the use of this formula in reliquary inscriptions] is a Kharoṣṭhi inscription from the Hurram Valley in Peshawar. It was discovered on a copper relic casket 'shaped like a miniature stūpa with harmikā and umbrellas, all complete.'" Boucher 1991, quoting Konow 1929. A *harmikā*, literally a summer-house, is the superstructure on a stupa.

24. Mahāvaṃśa xii.3–5: *Theraṁ Kasmīra Gandhāraṁ Majjhantikam-apesayi: "Patiṭṭhāpehi tattheva raṭṭhasmiṁ Sāsanaṁ." iti . . . tathāparantakaṁ Yonaṁ Dhammarakkhita-nāmakaṁ . . . Mahārakkhitatheran-tu Yonalokaṁapesayi* He sent the Elder Majjhantika to Kasmīra-Gandhāra, saying: "Have the Dispensation established there in the country" . . . and the Greek named Dhammarakkhita to the West . . . And he sent the elder Mahārakkhita to Yona territory.

25. There is still dispute on whether the earliest Buddha statues are found in Gandhara or Mathura in central India, but both were in the Kuṣāṇa empire. Krishan 1996, pp. 28–50.
26. Sims-Williams 2000.
27. Reported as a prophecy from the past in Kṣemendra's *Stupavadana* lvii, 15. Sarat Chandra Das, n.d.
28. Von Hinüber 1996, p. 83.
29. Cribb 1980.
30. Maitreya, in Pali guise as Metteya, appears in the Pali Tipitaka, *Dīgha Nikāya* 26, which recounts the history of mankind, thus future as well as past.
31. Warder 2000, p. 335–36.
32. Williams 1989, pp. 29–31.
33. They are what Pāṇini's grammatical system calls *nāmāni* "names" or *suB-anta* (in virtue of their nominal morphology, coded as *suP*). Crucially, they are not verbals (*ākhyāta*, or *tiŋ-anta*).
34. *Khiḍḍāpadosika deva* (Sanskrit *krīḍāpradoṣikā devāḥ*), in Dīgha Nikāya i. 19, 20 = Commentary i.113.
35. Sadakata 1997, pp. 56–57, 125–26.
36. Developed expansively in Liu 1988, pp. 88–102; Elverskog 2010, pp. 14–19, 25–27.
37. Herodotus vii. 65. The tips have been discovered on the field of Marathon in Greece, presumably discharged by Indian troops in Darius's army in 490 B.C. Forbes 1964, p. 239.
38. Thapar 2004 (p. 144) expresses some skepticism about this, at least beyond the Gangetic Plain. But archaeological evidence for iron is inevitably diminished by rust. And there is a Buddhist text from the early Theravada canon showing that metal plows certainly were in use in this period: (*Sutta Nipāta* i.4.7: "for as a plowshare that has got hot during the day when thrown into the water splashes, hisses and smokes in volumes . . .").
39. Rangarajan, 1992, pp. 235–36: specifically, *Arthaśāstra* 2.1.19; 2.1.38; 2.21.25; 2.16.8–9.
40. Salomon 1998, p. 138.
41. Neelis 2011, pp. 24–25.
42. E.g., Stark 1996, pp. 20–21.
43. Nattier 1990, p. 218, quoting a personal communication of Richard Salomon.
44. Mahāvastu i 49 (p. 41 in Jones 1949–56 translation, vol. 1).
45. Liu 1988, pp. 93–94.
46. Liu 1988, p. 95.
47. Mahāvastu ii 365–66 (p. 332 in Jones 1949–1956 translation, vol. 2).
48. But unlike Chinese with some of the *sapta-ratna*, Indian languages have not absorbed Chinese loans for silk. *Paṭṭa-* is a borrowing from a Dravidian language such as Telugu, where it means "tree bark." Balkrishna 1925 points out a general absence of Chinese, or European (**sēr-*), loans in the Sanskrit vocabulary for silk.

Chapter 3

1. Quoted in Zürcher 1972, p. 48. (I have adjusted the last sentence.)
2. Zürcher 1972, pp. 24–29.
3. Bentley 1993, pp. 9–11: this process is proposed as a general phenomenon in populations who come into contact with merchants from other cultures, essentially as a means of

cementing their human relations with a respected source of wealth, and perhaps of other good things, from abroad. This seems the only option for the Chinese conversions to Buddhism within Bentley's worldview, since his alternative models (conquest and assimilation) do not apply.

4. This is similar to what Rodney Stark (1996 pp. 19–21) has proposed in order to explain the growth of Christianity in the early Roman Empire.

   Stark is following other claims made by Robin Lane Fox (1987) and Peter Brown (1988) on the Christian conversion of the Roman Empire, but also his own and others' empirical research on the spread of Mormonism, and of the Reverend Sun Myung Moon's Unification Church (the "Moonies").

   Stark calls this process "growth through social networks," more specifically "through a structure of direct and intimate interpersonal attachments." Faiths grow, he claims, through networks of friends and relations, within open networks. For this explanation to work in the Chinese context, there must have been a context for Indian (and other Buddhist) merchants to make friends—presumably beyond the limited mutual familiarity and trust of business contacts—on the trade routes into China.

5. 天竺國一名身毒，⋯ 修浮圖道，不殺伐，遂以成俗 It is no clearer in the original. 浮圖 is modern [fóu tu] with an Early Middle Chinese pronunciation [buwdɔ].

6. Hulsewé and Loewe 1979, pp. 109, 128.

7. Sims-Williams 2001, p. 49: this is a detail from Ancient Letter no. 2, which for sixteen centuries actually got no closer to its addressee in Samarkand than a Chinese watchtower just west of Dunhuang's Jade Gate to the Silk Road. It was rediscovered—and published to the world—by Sir Aurel Stein in 1907.

8. More biographies can be found in Rong 2000, and Vaissière 2006.

9. Rong 2000, pp. 121–23.

10. Boucher 1998, pp. 497–98.

11. Zhuangzi http://www.acmuller.net/con-dao/zhuangzi.html#note—5#ixzz2a2yNeC66.

12. This has been shown by the scholar Seishi Karashima, who has produced (e.g., 1992) glossaries of the terminology used, especially for the Lotus Sutra, known in Sanskrit as *Saddharmapuṇḍarīkasūtra* and in Chinese as 正法華經 *Zhēng Fǎ Huá Jīng*, both of which are more exactly "Lotus Sutra of the True Law." Daniel Boucher (1998) has gathered examples, specially from the work of Dharmarakṣa.

13. Zürcher 1972, p. 65: He lived ca. 266–308, and Zürcher rates him as "the greatest Buddhist translator before Kumārajīva" (who was active a century later).

14. Cited in Boucher 1998, pp. 485–86, with full references to the early sixth-century bibliography, Sengyou's *Compilation of Notices on the Translation of the Tripiṭaka*, from which this is drawn. The interpolations in brackets are my summaries and interpretation of proper names, and Boucher's of the date.

15. Identified by Karashima (1992) and Boucher (1998).

16. Norman 1983.

17. But this naturalization of Buddhism into a Chinese form did not exclude intellectual influence in the opposite direction, coming from India to affect Chinese culture more generally.

   Technically, there was little scope for Indians to predominate, since the Chinese were then in the scientific vanguard of humanity: by the second century A.D., they already had mechanical systems of gearing for chariot axles, loom building, and even a seismograph (Zhāng Héng 78–139), and would go on to develop kite flying, woodblock printing, the compass, and gunpowder, all without Indian assistance.

But the Indians did have one strength unmatched at the time: linguistic analysis. They brought the Chinese to see the advantages of an alphabetic script (the Siddha, a descendant of Aśoka's Brāhmī), which was used for writing all the Sanskrit sutras in China. The experience appears to have stimulated a new—nongraphic—view of Chinese characters, organizing them into tables on phonetic principles. This is the pioneering work of Lù Fǎyán (601 A.D.). (Xing 2013.)

It is also maintained by Victor Mair and Erik Zürcher that Indian (Buddhist) influence in the long term promoted an increasing tolerance in the Chinese for vernacular style in literature. This ultimately undermined "literary expression" (文言 wényán), i.e., Classical Chinese, which viewed language as an unchanging system of graphic symbols, whose semantic interpretation was unanalyzed and transparent. (Boucher et al. 2006, Zürcher et al. 1996.)

18. In Chinese the *Jingang Bore-boluomiduo Jing* 金剛般若波羅蜜多經 in which the second word, then pronounced [pa-ñia-pa-la-mi-ta], is just an attempt to represent *Prajñā-pāramitā*: so 金剛經 *Jīngāng jīng* or "Diamond Sutra" for short.

19. Paul Harrison (2010) has compared the translations at selected points, with an ancient Sanskrit original (independently preserved in Japan, since it was apparently sent home to Japan by the sage Ennin in the mid-ninth century). He notes that all the texts but those by Kumārajīva, Dharmagupta, and Xuanzang seem to have been compiled derivatively from predecessors, though often with some extensions or attempts at clarification.

20. Sen 2002, p. 74.

21. Li and Beal 1914, pp. 22–23.

22. Nattier 1992.

Chapter 4

1. The original language here is somewhat confused. Only the Greek text of the Septuagint, not the Tanakh's Hebrew nor the Vulgate's Latin, employs this elegant variation and does not repeat the metaphor of deep lips and heavy tongue (literally translated from Hebrew).

2. 1 Corinthians 15:8–10.

3. Bickerman 1949.

4. Russell 1991–2012 says only that this difference in reference "has been suggested," but the Zoroastrian high priest Kartir (fl. ca. 240–93) distinguished the two named groups (KLSTYD'N and N'ĆL'Y) in a list of misbelievers, on a par with Jews, (Buddhist) Śramans, Brahman (Hindus), (probable) Mandeans and Manichaeans, in the inscription of Naqsh-e-Rostam. For him, they were all following "teachings of Ahriman"— the demonic Adversary. Baumer 2006, p. 65.

5. Acts 24:5; de Blois 2002, p. 11; Matthew 2:23. The word probably underlies the usual Arabic word for Christians too, *naṣrānī*, although as de Blois pp. 11–12 points out, there are unresolved problems in just taking it as a demonym from *an-Nāṣirah*, the Arabic for Nazareth. Nazareth was in Galilee, so semantically, it may also underlie the term *Galilaeus* "Galilean," used by pagans in the era of Julian (late fourth century A.D.) as another contemptuous term for *Christianus*. Supposedly the last words of the emperor

Julian (who had attempted to undo the establishment of Christianity) were: *vicisti, o Galilaee* "You have won, Galilean."

6. 1 Corinthians 14:2–4, 14.

7. He seems to imply that he knows various languages at 1 Corinthians 14:18: "I thank God, I speak more in tongues than you all." However, this uses the expression *glōssais lalō* ("in tongues I speak") which may refer more to inspired speech (or glossolalia) than actual knowledge of foreign languages.

8. Acts 26:14.

9. Acts 21:18–28; 39–40; 22:1–3.

10. 1 Corinthians 1:22–23.

11. Acts 23:11.

12. Acts 19:21; he also assures the Romans themselves of his determination to come (Romans 1:15) in an epistle dated to this same period, 58–59 A.D. (Ornsby 1865, p. 330).

13. Acts 18:2; this act of Claudius (who reigned 41–54 A.D.) is independently attested by the Roman historian Suetonius: *Life of Claudius* xxv.4: *Iudaeos impulsore Chresto assidue tumultuantis Roma expulit.* (As the Jews were making constant disturbances at the instigation of Chrestus, he expelled them from Rome.)

14. Stark 1996, pp. 132–35.

15. Acts 28:31.

16. Tacitus, *Annales*, xv, 44; Suetonius, *Nero*, xvi, 2 (both writing ca. 115 A.D.); Cassius Dio (*Roman History*, lxix, 15,3; writing ca. 230 A.D.) by contrast omits this, and dates the first imperial interest in the Christians to the time of the emperor Antoninus Pius (138–161)—almost a century later.

17. Lugdunum suffered a major persecution of Christians in 177, Karthago had a bishop Agrippinus ca. 197, Massilia had a martyr Saint Victor under Maximian (250–310), Seville had a bishop Sabinus in 287.

18. Turcan 1992, pp. 6–7. Bizarrely, those grade-names are ΚΟΡΑΞ "raven," ΝΥΜΦΟΣ "male bride," ΣΤΡΑΤΙΩΤΗΣ "soldier," ΛΕΩΝ "lion," ΠΕΡΣΗΣ "Persian," ΗΛΙΟΔΡΟΜΟΣ "sun-runner," and ΠΑΤΗΡ "father," each under the protection of a different heavenly body (respectively, Mercury, Venus, Mars, Jupiter, Moon, Sun, and Saturn). Jerome (*Epistula ad Laetam*) quotes the grades in Latin, and Celsus (cited in Origen, *Contra Celsum* vi, 22) the planets, sun, and moon. The different grades occur sporadically in inscriptions, especially epitaphs. Cf Metzger 1945 for some more details, especially regarding the possible confusion or alternation of ΝΥΜΦΟΣ with ΚΡΥΦΙΟΣ "hidden" for the second grade, and the Greek name for the third grade.

19. Origen, *Contra Celsum* vi, 23.

20. Origen may have been the first to coin the title *theotokos*. (Vermes 2012, p. 220).

21. Exodus 4:22; Hosea 11:1; Deuteronomy 32:18–19.

22. Matthew 3:17, Mark 1:11, Luke 3:22; Matthew 17:5, Mark 9:7, Luke 9:35.

23. John 1:14, 18; 3:16, 18.

24. Homer tells of how the *parthénos* Astyoche bore a child to the god Ares (Iliad ii. 513–15), and it is also used naturally of an unmarried mother who has no option but to expose her child (Aristophanes, *Clouds* 530).

25. John 1:1.

26. As distinguished by the Liddell-Scott-Jones Greek-English lexicon.

27. Vermes 2012, pp. 149–50.

Chapter 5

1. Edict of Milan (Lactantius de Mortibus Persecutorum xlviii.8): *Et quoniam idem Christiani non [in] ea loca tantum ad quae convenire consuerunt, sed alia etiam habuisse noscuntur ad ius corporis eorum id est ecclesiarum, non hominum singulorum, pertinentia, ea omnia lege quam superius comprehendimus, citra ullam prorsus ambiguitatem vel controversiam isdem Christianis id est corpori et conventiculis eorum reddi iubebis. . .*

2. Edict of Thessalonica, February 27, 380: . . . **cunctos populos, quos clementiae nostrae regit temperamentum,** *in tali volumus religione versari, quam divinum Petrum apostolum tradidisse Romanis religio usque ad nunc ab ipso insinuata declarat quamque pontificem Damasum sequi claret et Petrum Alexandriae episcopum virum apostolicae sanctitatis, hoc est, ut secundum apostolicam disciplinam evangelicamque doctrinam Patris et Filii et Spiritus Sancti unam deitatem sub parili maiestate et sub pia trinitate credamus. Hanc legem sequentes Christianorum Catholicorum nomen iubemus amplecti, reliquos* **vero dementes vesanosque iudicantes haeretici dogmatis infamiam sustinere nec conciliabula eorum ecclesiarum nomen accipere, divina primum vindicta, post etiam motus nostri, quem ex caelesti arbitrio sumpserimus, ultione plectendos.** . .

3. Tertullian, *Adversus Praxean*, v, 2–3: *[Deus] habebat enim secum quam habebat in semet ipso rationem, suam scilicet. rationalis enim deus, et ratio in ipso prius, et ita ab ipso omnia: quae ratio sensus ipsius est. hanc Graeci dicunt, quo vocabulo etiam sermonem appellamus: ideoque iam in usu est nostrorum per simplicitatem interpretationis sermonem dicere in primordio apud deum fuisse, cum magis ratio competat antiquiorem haberi, quia [non] sermonalis a principio sed rationalis deus etiam ante principium, et quia ipse quoque sermo ratione consistens priorem eam ut substantiam suam ostendat.*

4. Cyprian, *Adversus Iudaeos*, ii, 3; ii, 6.

5. Boyle 1977, p. 166.

6. Tertullian, *Adversus Praxean*, xi–xii: *[xi, 9–10] his itaque paucis tamen manifeste distinctio trinitatis exponitur: est enim ipse qui pronuntiat spiritus, et pater ad quem pronuntiat, et filius de quo pronuntiat. sic et cetera, quae nunc a patre de filio vel ad filium, nunc a filio de patre vel ad patrem, nunc a spiritu pronuntiantur, unamquamque personam in sua proprietate constituunt . . . [xii, 6] qui si ipse deus est secundum Ioannem—Deus erat sermo—habes duos, alium dicentem ut fiat, alium facientem. alium autem quomodo accipere debeas iam professus sum, personae non substantiae nomine, ad distinctionem non ad divisionem.*

7. Ambrosiaster on Paul, 1 Corinthians 14:14.

8. Ambrosiaster on Paul, 1 Corinthians 14:24–25.

9. Paul, 1 Corinthians 1:26.

10. Stark 1996, pp. 29–47: Chapter 2, *The Class Basis of Early Christianity*. This is despite a lack of actual evidence, even anecdotal. After a parade of ancient historians who have reached the same conclusion (pp. 30–32), Stark's actual argument is based on the sociology of modern conversion to cults (new faiths), rather than sects (ultra-ist breakaway groups within a religion). Evidence is drawn from study of converts to cults such as the Mormons and various New Age groups, whose average level of education is higher than that of sectarians (Jehovah's Witnesses, Worldwide Church of God, etc.). The presumption is that Christianity after the Resurrection was a cult rather than a Jewish sect.

11. Juvenal iii.76–78.

12. Arnobius Afer, *Adversus gentes* i.59.5.

13. Augustine, *De doctrina christiana* ii.13.19.

14. Watson 1969, p. 133.
15. Constantius of Lyon, *De vita Sancti Germani*, is the hagiographical source for this.
16. Augustine, Confessions 1.13.20: *quid autem erat causae cur graecas litteras oderam, quibvs puerulus imbuebar? ne nvnc quidem mihi satis exploratum est. adamaveram enim latinas . . .*
17. Jerome, *Letter to Augustine* 172 (CSEL 44, p. 639, lines 6–7) *grandem latini sermonis in ista provincia . . . patimur penuriam. Commentarii in iv epistulas Paulinas* ii.3 (ed. Migne, Patres Latini 26, 382c) *sermone graeco quo omnis oriens loquitur . . .*
18. Libanius, *Speeches* 43.4.
19. Ammianus Marcellinus, xv.13.1, xviii.5.1.
20. Johannes Lydus, *On the Magistracies* iii.42. The prophecy was transmitted by Fonteius, otherwise unknown. Rochette 1997, p.138.
21. *Novella Constitutio* xv.preface (in Greek) (I. p.80 von Lingenthal): "and we have written the law not in the paternal voice (Latin), but this common Helladic one (Greek), so that it be known to all for ease of interpretation."
22. Sulpicius Severus, *Chronica* ii.3: *urbibus atque provinciis permixtas barbaras nationes* "barbarous nations mixed up in their cities and provinces"; Jerome *Commentary on Daniel* i., vision 2. The Bible's Book of Daniel, chapter 2, was popular reading at the time, detailing Nebuchadnezzar's vision of the idol with feet of iron and clay mixed, and about to come crashing down. It was interpreted, by both Sulpicius Severus and Jerome, as the result of insufficient integration of the new Germanic immigrants, whether socially, or in the army.
23. This is a theme I have defended at some length in Ostler 2007.

Chapter 6

1. The Aramaic text used is the Peshitta, published by the British and Foreign Bible Society in 1905/1920, as published at dukhrana.com.
2. More exactly, the Greek has "the holy wind" whereas the Aramaic "the wind of holiness." This latter, a more archaic style in Aramaic but unknown in native Greek, is sometimes seen in Christian Greek too, suggesting a direct borrowing: e.g., Paul at Romans 1:4 κατα πνευμα αγιωσυνης.
3. Stark 1996, 133.
4. Acts 21:39–40; 22:1–3; 26:14.
5. Zakka I Iwas 1983.
6. Text accessible at http://www.ccel.org/l/lake/fathers/ignatius-smyrnaeans.htm.
7. Zakka I Iwas 1983.
8. Some caution is needed in distinguishing these two, "Aramaic " and "Syriac." In modern works, "Syriac" means the Aramaic dialect orignally of Edessa, which became a literary language for some Christian communions, especially those based at Antioch and Seleucia-Ctesiphon. But until the late nineteenth century, "Syriac" (because of its explict link with Syria) was often used for Aramaic more generally, and indeed translates *'aramit* in Daniel 4:2, where the text explicitly says (in Hebrew) that it will continue in Aramaic. (Jack B. Tannous, personal contact.)
9. Curran 2000, chapters 3 and 4.
10. Properly *Frithusgairns*.
11. Nersessian 2007, pp. 27–28.

12. Rapp 2007, pp. 138–39.

13. Anderson Scott 1885, pp. 151–52.

14. Lietzmann 1979, pp. 469–70; Driver and Hodgson 1925, p. 3. The latter notes, in footnote iv to Introduction iii: "At the end of the thirteenth century it is clear from the catalogue of the Bishop of Nisibis that most of Nestorius' works in Greek and Latin had disappeared; only a Syriac version of his *Tragoedia*, his *Letter to Cosmos*, his *Liturgy*, a volume of letters, and another of sermons, besides *The Bazaar of Heracleides*, survived at that time (op. cit., pp. vii–viii)."

15. He was born at Germanicia, in Syria Euphratensis (modern Kahramanmaraş), about 150 miles northeast of Antioch. His career pre-Constantinople was as a priest and a monk in the monastery of Euprepius, outside Antioch.

16. Brock 1996 [2006-III], p. 169.

17. Brock 1996 [2006-III], p. 174, n. 53. I have replaced his translation "tabernacle," which has no clear sense in modern English, with "come to rest." It corresponds to Greek ἐσκήνωσεν, a word that implies taking up a temporary dwelling. The Syriac equivalent *(a)ggen* is a root that fundamentally refers to lying down (cf *gnona* "bridal chamber"), but as a verb often connotes God's miraculous intervention, e.g., also when Christ was conceived (Luke 1:35), or when hearers reflect on Peter's sermon (Acts 5:15); and latterly, in the liturgical tradition, of the Holy Spirit at Christ's baptism and the miracle of tongues at the Pentecost. (The word is discussed in Brock 1993 [2006-XIII]).

18. Brock 1996 [2006-III], p. 175, n. 52.

19. Baumer 2006, p. 47, citing the French translation of Nestorius 451: *Le Livre d'Héraclide de Damas*, 1910, pp. 77–81.

20. Letter to Cosmas §2 in *Patrologia Orientalis*, xiii, 276.

21. The original Greek word seems to have been πραγματεία, i.e., "business" or "treatise," which the Syriac translator rendered *ta'gūrtā* "business" or "merchandise." Nestorius 451 [1925], introduction.

22. The full text is recorded at Evagrius Scholasticus, *Ecclesiastical History*, iii. 14.

23. This clear correlation of language group with Christian confession in the seventh to eighth centuries is too pervasive to be dismissed, as some have tried, e.g., by pointing out that there were always some Syriac speakers who adhered to Dyophysitism (the Melkites, already mentioned), and Miaphysites who still knew Greek well into the ninth century (e.g., Dionysius I Telmaharoyo, Patriarch of Antioch, d. 845). The boundaries of human groups are not clear-cut, especially at the elite level.

Likewise, the link of creed with language remains immune to Jones 1959's famous denial (based on lack of positive evidence) that ancient heresies such as these were national or social movements, rather than—as they were presented—purely doctrinal loyalties. Shared languages, especially in popular use, set centers of easy communication, around which solidarities will coalesce. Languages do not require a self-conscious spirit of nationalism to have this effect, a spirit that admittedly only arose in the modern period.

24. Gregory of Nyssa, *On the Deity of the Son* [Patrologia Graeca, xlvi, 557b].

25. Zacharias of Mityle, *Syriac Chronicle*, iii. 3–5; Evagrius Scholasticus, *Ecclesiastical History*, ii, 5.

26. Evagrius Scholasticus, *Ecclesiastical History*, ii, 5; Zacharias of Mityle, *Syriac Chronicle*, iii. 2.

27. φόνους τε τολμηθῆναι μυρίους καὶ αἱμάτων πλήθει μολυνθῆναι μὴ μόνον τὴν γῆν ἀλλ' ἤδη καὶ αὐτὸν τὸν ἀέρα. Evagrius Scholasticus, *Ecclesiastical History*, iii. 14.

28. Sarkissian 1975, p. 167.
29. Sarkissian 1975, pp. 206–07.
30. Adalian 2010, s.v. *Dvin*, p. 286.
31. Suny 1988, p. 26.
32. It has been claimed, for example, that Armenian lacked the vocabulary to express the subtle distinction implicit in the dispute about the Natures of Christ.

Sarkissian 1975 attributes this view to J. M. Neale, who says that the Armenians were disadvantaged by not having been able to attend Chalcedon: "Their nearest neighbors, the Syrian Bishops, misrepresented the Council; and unhappily, the Armenian language facilitated the misapprehension; one word only being employed to express the two senses of Nature and Person." The word for "nature" is consistently, in Armenian, *bn-ut'iwn*, whose etymological meaning is "trunk-support," as of the wood that holds up a tree. Inevitably, there must have been a progression in the metaphorical use of the word before it could be used of the nature of a deity. Whether this word ever meant "person" or not, no competent bishop who was aware of Nestorianism—whatever his language—could have assumed that to equate natures with persons was safe when talking of the essence of Christ.

Édouard Dulaurier, however, pointed out that the Armenian translation of Pope Leo's Tomus was misleading, using the expression *vomn iev vomn*, literally "someone and someone," to refer to Christ's two natures, divine and human. This happened also to be the usual Armenian phrase for "the one and the other," specifically referring to people, not things or abstractions; and this would naturally be taken as referring to two individuals (i.e., different persons or hypostases). This alone might have been enough to suggest to Armenian bishops that the pope was slipping into Nestorianism. [Dulaurier 1859, pp. 28–31.]

But a work such as Dorfmann-Lazarev 2004 shows, by its fine analysis of doctrinal discussion in Greek and Armenian at the Council of Širakawan in 862, between the patriarch of Constantinople Photius and Armenian *catholicos* Zak'aria, that the Armenian language would gather vocabulary in the four centuries after Chalcedon that made it just as subtle and precise as Greek. It is not plausible that a mistranslation—if any occurred, early on—would persist in obscuring subsequent debate and reasoning. As it happened, both Armenian and Georgian derived their words for "nature" from a root borrowed from the Persian language Pahlavi (their common neighbor), viz *bun*, meaning "bottom, foundation, root, origin or principle." In both languages we have derivates of this word for nature that mean "consubstantial": Armenian *bn-ut'iwn* > *hama-bun*; Georgian *bun-eba* > *ert-bun-eba*. So a single word covers Greek οὐσία "being, substance" as well as φύσις "nature." [Dorfmann-Lazarev 2004, pp. 108–09.]

This Pahlavi word (MacKenzie 1971, s.v.) is from the common Indo-European root of Latin *fundus*, English *bottom*, Greek πυθμήν, and Sanskrit *budhna-*, Avestan *būna*. (Buck 1949, s.v. BOTTOM.) This is all very well, and does not seem to have caused confusion: but it must be noted that use of this term did not determine, or even influence, the theological outcome. Armenian ended up being a vehicle of Miaphysitism, while Georgian (perhaps partly to reinforce its independence of the Armenian church) ended up Diophysite, indeed staunchly Chalcedonian.

33. Brock 1993 [2006-IV].
34. Ammianus Marcellinus, xxvii.12.16.
35. Lee 1991, p. 369.
36. Brock 1993 [2006-IV], pp. 483–4.

37. 13.... *we(ʾ)t̠ə̄t̠emtūn bərūḥā dəqūd̠šā damlīk̠ā (h)wāt̠. 14. hāy di(ʾ)yt̠ēh rahḇūnā dəyārtūt̠an* ...

13.... ἐσφραγισθητε τῳ πνευματι της ἐπαγγελιας τῳ ἁγιῳ. 14. ὁς ἐστιν ἀρραβων της κληρονομιας ἡμων ...

13.... and were sealed with the Spirit of Holiness who was promised; 14. who is the earnest of our inheritance...

38. Translated by Sebastian Brock (Brock 1982 [1992-XI]), p. 13. The stanza is taken from Ephrem, *Hymni de Nativitate* xxiii.13.

39. Brock 1982 [1992-XI]), p. 16.

Romans 13:14 "But put ye on the Lord Jesus Christ..." "ἀλλὰ ἐνδύσασθε τὸν κύριον Ἰησοῦν Χριστόν" (from ἐνδύομαι "put on clothing")
/ ʾellā **lūḇšu̱(hy)** ləmāran yešūᶜ məšīḥā (from *lbs* "clothe"); likewise Galatians 3:27 "For as many of you as have been baptized into Christ have put on Christ."
ὅσοι γὰρ εἰς Χριστὸν ἐβαπτίσθητε, Χριστὸν **ἐνεδύσασθε**.
/ ʾaylēn gēr dəḇa-mšīḥā ᶜəmadtūn lamšīḥā **ləbeštūn**

40. Maximus Confessor, *Letter to Marinus*, in Migne's *Patrologia Graeca*, xci.136: Μεθερμηνεύειν δὲ τὰ οἰκεῖα, τοῦ τὰς ὑποκλοπὰς χάριν διαφυγεῖν τῶν ὑποπιπτόντων ... παρεκάλεσα τοὺς Ῥωμαίους ... οὐκ οἶδα τυχὸν εἰ πειστεῖεν. Ἄλλως τε καὶ τὸ μὴ δύνασθαι διακριβοῦν ἐν ἄλλῃ λέξει σὲ καὶ φωνῇ τὸν ἑαυτῶν νοῦν ὥσπερ ἐν τῇ ἰδίᾳ καὶ θρεψαμένη, καθάπερ οὖν καὶ ἡμεῖς ἐν τῇ καθ᾽ ἡμᾶς τὸν ἡμέτερον. Γενήσεται δὲ πάντως αὐτοῖς, πείρᾳ τὴν ἐπήρειαν μαθοῦσι, καὶ ἡ περὶ τούτου φροντὶς.

41. Some of the milestones in this process are listed in Ostler 2007, pp. 89–90.

42. Eusebius, *Oration in Praise of Constantine*. ed. Heikel. vii.13. Extended analysis in Runciman 1977, chapter 2.

43. These were the familiar contents of "The New Testament": the Letters of Paul (and certain other Apostles), the Gospels of Matthew, Mark, Luke, and John, the Acts of the Apostles, and the Revelation of John, all written before 150 A.D. The list of twenty-seven books has been largely uncontested since the middle of the fourth century, although until 616 the Syriac Peshitta still omitted Revelation and the letters 2 Peter, Jude, and 2, 3 John.

Chapter 7

1. Matthew 28:18–20, Mark 16:15 and Luke 24:47. In other places (John 22:23, Acts 1:8), Jesus emphasizes the sacred power that comes with this commission. Mark does not speak of "the nations," but of going "into the whole world-order" (εἰς τόν κόσμον ἅπαντα) and preaching "to all creation" (πάσῃ τῇ κτίσει). Acts, perhaps showing the limits of contemporary Jewish imagination, speaks of witnessing "in Jerusalem, and all Judaea and Samaria, and to the extreme of the earth" (ἕως ἐσχάτου τῆς γῆς).

2. Matthew 27:19, Mark 16:15–16.

3. E.g., Stark 1996, pp. 20–22.

4. The story is given at length in Eusebius's *History* v.1, quoting a letter of the noted theologian Irenaeus: in it, he claimed to have become the second bishop of Lyon, after his predecessor Pothinus, then aged ninety, had been martyred along with five others.

5. Heather 1986. Valens had, in fact, been the last Roman emperor to embrace Arianism, a heresy officially condemned at the Council of Nicaea in 325, half a century before this mass conversion to it of the Goths.

6. Photius's summary of Philostorgius, *Historia ecclesiastica* ii.5 (Migne, Patrologia Graeca, xlv, columns 467–70).
7. Green 1998, pp. 364–65.
8. The same passage quoted above, in chapter 4, p. NN.
9. This was conjectured by Sophus Bugge (1895), on pp. 178–80, with ideas most easily accessible at Oxford English Dictionary, s.v. *heathen*.

Chapter 8

1. Prosper Aquitanus, in his *Chronicon*, dated to the consulship of Bassus and Antiochus (viz A.D. 431), reports: *Ad Scotos in Christum credentes ordinatus a Papa Celestino Palladius primus Episcopus mittitur.* "To the Irish believing in Christ, on the orders of Pope Celestine, Palladius is sent as first bishop."
2. McManus 1991, p. 41; Chadwick 1970, p. 200.
3. Jackson 1953, pp. 70–71; 122–137. More recent modulations of this seminal work, illuminating and correcting details of the actual process of borrowing, can be found at McManus 1983 and 1984, but the basic evidence is only in the original.
4. Quatrain from the margin of Codex Boernerianus, a ninth-century text of the epistles of Saint Paul. (MS Dresd. A. 145b) Stokes and Strachan 1903, p. 296.
5. See DIL, at the various entries for these words.
6. *Story of Mac Datho's Pig,* §16. The original is believed to go back to ca. 800, and may be an extreme parody of earlier tales of heroic violence.
7. Cahill 1995, p.151: "Ireland is unique in religious history for being the only land into which Christianity was introduced without bloodshed." Implausible as this seems, it is indeed difficult to find the name of a single ancient Irish martyr.
8. Tardif 1852.
9. Stancliffe 1982.
10. Bradley 1999, pp. 68–69.
11. Robert Jerome Smith, *Festivals and Calendar Customs*, as quoted in Dolan 2005, p. 21.
12. Latin text available at Corpus Corporum, Universität Zürich, as Cogitosus, *Vita Brigidae.* (http://tinyurl.com/kwefxqn, http://tinyurl.com/kr8eps8)

Chapter 9

1. Verses 3993–4002, with emphasis added to military titles in the English translation. The source of the *Hêliand* is not the New Testament, but Tatian's *Diatessaron*, a harmony of the four gospels. This passage, however, seems to be a tendentious interpretation of John 11:16: Then said Thomas, which is called Didymus, unto his fellow disciples, "Let us also go, that we may die with him."
2. Tacitus *Germania* xii–xv; and for the institution across Eurasia see Beckwith 2009, pp. 1–28, "The Hero and his Friends." Beckwith sees this all over Central Asia and Europe, among Scythians, Mongols, Vedic Indians, Hittites, Persian Achaemenids, Khwarizmians, Huns, Germans (pre- and post-invasion of the Roman Empire), Sassanids, Koguryo, Japanese, Turks, Khazars, Uighurs, Sogdians, Tibetans, Slavs, Khitans, and others. It was adopted briefly by Byzantines and Chinese, but permanently by the Abbasid Muslims, in their culture of slave soldiers or *ghilmān*.

3. Tacitus *Germania* xiv, init. *Cum ventum in aciem, turpe principi virtute vinci, turpe comitatui virtutem principis non adaequare. Iam vero infame in omnem vitam ac probrosum superstitem principi suo ex acie recessisse. Illum defendere, tueri, sua quoque fortia facta gloriae eius adsignare praecipuum sacramentum est. Principes pro victoria pugnant, comites pro principe.*

4. Tacitus *Germania* xiii, init.: *Nihil autem neque publicae neque privatae rei nisi armati agunt.* "They do nothing in either public or private life unarmed."

5. The -n- ending is also significant, widely used in Indo-Europeans languages to mean "leader of." Cf Gothic *kind-ins* "provincial governor," *þiudans* "king of a people (*þiuda*)," Latin *dominus* "lord of a household (*domus*)" and *tribūnus* "head of a tribe (*tribus*)," Old Norse *herjann* "lord of armies (*herja*)," and even perhaps the god Woden/Oðin derived from **Vātinaz*, lord of Vates (prophetic spirits).

6. *Beowulf*, v. 1484; *Anglo-Saxon and Old English Vocabularies*, Thomas Wright (2nd ed., R. P. Wülcker, London, 1884), 253, 8; *Benedictine Rule* 1, 9.

7. All these points are made by Stark 1996, chapter 5: "The Role of Women in Christian Growth."

8. *Epistula* 46 Alcimi Ecdicii Aviti: *Faciet, sicut creditis, regum florentissime, faciet inquam indumentorum ista mollities, ut vobis deinceps plus valeat rigor armorum. Et quicquid felicitas usque hic praestiterat, addet hic sanctitas.* Monumenta Germaniae Historica: Auctores Antiquissimi, ed. Rudolf Peiper, vol. 6, part 2 (Berlin: Weidmannsche Buchhandlung, 1883). Also at http://www.flsh.fr/lettres-sciences-humaines/chp/pmb/opac_css/doc_num.php?explnum_id=198&PHPSESSID=1e522dfaa46b679ab45c863be8b2af91

9. Willibald, *Vitae Sancti Bonifatii archiepiscopi moguntini.* Ed. Levison, Wilhelmus (1905). Available at http://en.wikipedia.org/wiki/Donar_Oak

10. Boniface, *Epistolae* xxiii: *Hoc quoque inferendum: Si omnipotentes sunt dii et benefici et iusti, non solum suos remunerant cultores, verum etiam puniunt contemptores. Et si hec utraque temporaliter faciunt, cur ergo parcunt christianis totum pene orbem ab eorum cultura avertentibus idolaque evertentibus? Et cum ipsi, id est Christiani, fertiles terras vinique et olei feraces ceterisque opibus habundantes possident provincias, ipsis autem, id est paganis, frigore semper rigentes terras cum eorum diis reliquerunt; in quibus, jam tamen toto orbe pulsi falso regnare putatur.*

11. Boniface, *Epistolae* 63. *Sine patrocinio principis Francorum nec populum ecclesiae regere, nec presbiteros vel clericos, monachos vel ancillas Dei defendere possum, nec ipsos paganorum ritus et sacrilegia idolorum in Germania sine illius mandato et timore prohibere valeo.*

12. Sullivan 1954, pp. 28–30.

13. As by Russell 1994: *The Germanization of Early Medieval Christianity.*

14. Contrast Russell 1994, Part II, with Green 1998, p. 283. Green insists that the relations between Christian missionary and German converts needed to include a variety of approaches, from militant insistence on church doctrine to a more tolerant style, accommodating German traditions; but that ultimately the faith was transmitted. Russell stresses rather the long-term effect on the faith and the community of accepting German converts who still held different beliefs and priorities, resulting in some Germanization of Christianity.

15. Tacitus *Germania* ix: *Deorum maxime Mercurium colunt, cui certis diebus humanis quoque hostiis litare fas habent. Herculem et Martem concessis animalibus placant.*

16. Mark 5:34, Mark 10:52, Luke 17:19: "Thy faith has made thee whole."

    John 20:28–29: Thomas answered and said to Him, "My Lord and my God!" Jesus said to him, "Because you have seen me, have you believed? Blessed are they who did not see, and yet believed."

17. Matthew 8:26: And he saith unto them, "Why are ye fearful, O ye of little faith?" Then he arose, and rebuked the winds and the sea; and there was a great calm.

18. John 10:37–38: "If I do not the works of my Father, believe me not. But if I do, though ye believe not me, believe the works: that ye may know, and believe that the Father is in me, and I in him."

19. Matthew 6:5–13.

20. Ælfric *Homilies* ii. 214.

21. Green 1998, pp. 16–19.

22. *Charter of Eadweard* in Kemble, John Mitchell, *Codex Diplomaticus Aevi Saxonici* v. 163.

23. *West Saxon Gospels: Luke* (Corpus Christi Cambridge Manuscript) 19:9

24. Bede, *De temporum ratione*, cap. xv. *Eostur-monath, qui nunc paschalis mensis interpretetur, quondam a dea illorum quae Eostre vocabatur, et cui in illo festa celebrabant, nomen habuit, a cuius nomine nunc paschale tempus cognominant; consueto antiquae observationis vocabulo gaudia novae solemnitatis vocantes.*

25. Green 1998, pp. 351–53.

26. Ibid. *Menses Giuli a conversione solis in auctum diei, quia unus eorum praecedit, alius subsequitur, nomina accipiunt.*

27. Oxford English Dictionary, *sub verbis* Yule, Christmas; Mackensen 1966, *sub verbo* Weihnachten.

28. An early source for all the days of the week in English is Byrhtferth's *Enchiridion* ("Handbook"), a general spiritual guide to the universe, which dates around the turn of the millennium.

29. Caesar, *De Bello Gallico*, vi.17.1; Tacitus, *Germania* ix,1. However, Caesar was explicitly describing the Gauls, not the Germans, and puts Apollo, Mars, Jupiter, and Minerva in the second rank.

30. Beowulf 572–73; *Hildebrandslied* 49.

31. *Octavius*, xxix.

32. *Stromata* xi. "They say, then, that the character representing 300 [viz T] is, as to shape, the type of the Lord's sign, and that the Iota and the Eta indicate the Savior's name [viz the first two letters of "Jesus"]."

33. Christ and two thieves are depicted on the doors of Santa Sabina in Rome, a church constructed by Celestine I (422–433 A.D.). The doors are apparently original. But the figures are shown "standing" on the base of the panel, with crosses hardly visible, so the crucifixion itself is obscured.

   The first preserved manuscript with a clear depiction of the crucifixion is in the Rabula Gospels, created in Syria in the sixth century: the Syriac text is signed by Rabula and dated 586 A.D. at the Monastery of Saint John of Zagba. (Information from http://phdiva.blogspot.co.uk/2011/08/early-images-of-crucifixion.html)

34. And Venantius returns to the theme of the Cross as a virtuous participant in Christ's passion in his hymn *Pange lingua*, addressing it: *Crux fidelis, inter omnes arbor una nobilis* . . . "Faithful Cross, the one and only noble tree among them all . . ."

35. The following examples are marshaled, with more bibliographical detail, in North 1997, pp. 275–77. Their sources are, respectively: *Ancient Laws and Institutes*, ed. B. Thorpe (London 1840) vol. ii. 34 (§27.18); Halitgar *Penitential*, ii. 22; *Vita Willibaldi episcopi Eichstetensis*, §88; *Die Briefe des Heiligen Bonifatius und Lullus*, ed. M. Tangl, Epistolae selectae, 4.1, p. 104.

36. Bede, *Historia Ecclesiastica*, epistle lxxviii.

37. This argument is taken, with some lexical elaboration, from North 1997, p. 275.

Chapter 10

1. The word does appear with the meaning "cross" in one of the earliest Slavic texts, the ninth-century Freising manuscripts from Slovenia (written in Roman script). ["I confess my sin . . ."] *i suetemu crestu* "and to the holy cross." (Freisinger i, 2–3, cited in Isatchenko 1957, p. 64.)

2. This is a combination of clauses from two accounts of the letter, the former from the Slavonic *Life of Cyril*, and the latter from the Slavonic *Life of Methodius*, as translated in Tachiaos 2001, p. 57.

3. Tachiaos 2001, pp. 72, referring to Granstrem 1955.

4. Tachiaos 2001, p. 72.

5. Tachiaos 2001, p.75, translating from the Slavonic *Life of Cyril*.

6. Cooper 2003, pp. 56–57.

7. Isidore, *Etymologiae*, ix.1.3: *Tres autem sunt linguae sacrae: Hebraea, Graeca, Latina, quae toto orbe maxime excellunt. His namque tribus linguis super crucem Domini a Pilato fuit causa eius scripta.*

8. Prudentius, *Apotheosis* xi, 377–85: *Hebraeus pangit stilus, Attica copia pangit, | pangit et Ausoniae facundia tertia linguae. | Pilatus iubet ignorans: I, scriba, tripictis | digere versiculis quae sit subfixa potestas, | fronte crucis titulus sit triplex, triplici lingua | agnoscat Judaea legens et Graecia norit | et venerata Deum percenseat aurea Roma.*

9. Augustine, *In Iohannis evangelium tractatus* cxvii, 4: *Hae quippe tres linguae ibi prae caeteris eminebant: Hebraea, propter Judaeos in Dei Lege gloriantes; Graeca, propter Gentium sapientes; Latina, propter Romanos multis ac pene omnibus jam tunc gentibus imperantes.*

10. Tachiaos 2001, pp. 78, 177, quoting Thomson 1992 for exhaustive reference.

11. *Prologue to the Gospel* (ca. 863–67 A.D.), lines 23–42, translated by Roman Jakobson 1965. It is possible that the text was written not by Constantine-Cyril himself, but by a like-minded disciple later on, perhaps Bishop Constantine of Preslav in Bulgaria (Cooper 2003, pp. 88, 198). At any rate, this is clearly Cyril's sentiment and thinking.

12. H. Wolfram, *Conversio Bagoariorum et Carentanorum* (Latin history written in Salzburg in the 870s), p. 56: *quidam Graecus Methodius nomine noviter inventis Sclavinis literis linguam Latinam doctrinamque Romanam atque literas auctorales Latinas philosophice subducens vilescere fecit cuncto popylo ex parte missas et euangelia ecclesiasticumque officium illorum, qui hoc Latine celebraverunt.*

13. Jakobson 1965, pp. 221–23.

14. Cooper 2003, p. 101.

15. Helmoldus (1581), cap liii. In *Reiner Reineccius. Chronica Slavorum*. Frankfurt. p. 44: *Est autem Slavorum mirabilis error; nam in conviviis et compotacionibus suis pateram circum-ferunt, in quam conferunt, non dicam consecracionis, sed execracionis verba sub nomine deorum, boni scilicet atque mali, omnem prosperam fortunam a bono deo, adversam a malo dirigi profi-tentes. Unde etiam malum deum lingua sua Diabol sive Zcerneboch, id est nigrum deum, appellant.*

16. Meyendorff 1989, pp. 22–23. His authority is Fedotov 1946, 1966.

17. Thomson 1999, p. xvii.

18. Cooper 2003, pp. 108–10.

Chapter 11

1. Although most of the instructions for Columbus's four voyages from the Spanish crown concerned his authority in command and rights for distribution of treasure (firstly, the *Capitulaciones de Santa Fe* of April 17, 1492), the second year's expedition was also under the auspices of the papal bulls *Inter caetera* of May 4, 1493, and *Piis fidelium* of June 25, 1493. *Inter caetera* notes, before assigning territorial limits to Spain and (implicitly) Portugal, "this assuredly ranks highest, that in our times especially the Catholic faith and the Christian religion be exalted and be everywhere increased and spread, that the health of souls be cared for and that barbarous nations be overthrown and brought to the faith itself." And *Piis fidelium* appointed Fray Bernardo Boil as vicar apostolic of the New World, with authority to preach to the natives.

2. Aymará has been spoken in southern Peru and the area of modern Bolivia from time immemorial. Mannheim 1991.

3. "It is no marvel that this language is spoken with gusto in so many kingdoms of America; so many Indian nations, almost giving up on their own languages, prefer the speech of the Guaraní." Filippo Salvatore Gilij, *Della lingua dei Guaranesi*, in 1782 (cited by Melià 2003, p. 103).

4. Tupi, derived from the coastal language Tupinambá, spread in two forms into Brazil, at least as observed by the Portuguese: as *língua geral paulista* (LGP), up the Pará River from São Paulo, starting in the 1530s; and as *língua geral amazônica* (LGA) up the Amazon from the seventeenth century. The latter had more influence from the inland Tupi speakers known as Tapuia (from *tapy'yia*, as they called themselves). Rodrigues 2010, pp. 36–43.

5. Mendieta [1596] 1980, pp. 219–220, cited in Nagel Beilicke 1994, p. 423.

6. Mendieta [1596] 1980, p. 220, cited in Nagel Beilicke 1994, p. 423.

7. *Concilios Provinciales I & II*, México, 1555 and 1565; pub. Mexico: Antonio de Hogal, 1769, vol. i, p. 41; cited by León Portilla 1992, p. 295.

8. Francis 2006, p. 448.

9. González de Pérez 1987, p. 57.

10. Francis 2006. The grammars produced by Dadey (probably González de Pérez 1987) and Lugo (1619 [2010]) are extant, and are our main sources on Chibcha.

11. Durston 2007, pp. 134–36, citing Castel-l'Estoile 2000, pp. 141–69, on the situation in Brazil.

12. Acosta, 1588 [1984], p. 387.

13. Schmidt 2001, p. 97.

14. *Sacrosanctum Oecumenicum Concilium Tridentinum: additis declarationi-bus* ... Jean Gallemart, Agostino Barbosa, Giovanni Battista De Luca (cardinale) eds., 1762, Madrid: Joachim Ibarra, pp. 430–31:

    Reg. III: **Versiones vero novi Testamenti**, *ab auctoribus primae classis hujus Indicis factae* **nemini concedantur**, *quia utilitatis parum, periculi vero plurimum, lectoribus, ex earum lectione, manare solent* ... Reg. IV: *Cum* **experimento manifestum sit, si sacra Biblia vulgari lingua, passim sine discriminatione permittatur; plus inde ob hominum temeri-tatem detrimenti, quam utilitatis oriri,** *hac in parte iudicio Episcopi, aut Inquisitoris stetur*... (emphasis mine).

15. Gruzinski 1985 [1993], pp. 38–39. Some skepticism is in order. There are globules to represent water on the Franciscan coat of arms. But it is unnecessary to associate them with any Aztec glyph.

16. Landa 1566 [1985], pp. 83–86; cf Hanks 2010 pp. 130–31, which shows that it remained as one expression for Christian baptism, which was more standardly known as *oc ha* "enter water."

17. Knowlton and Vail 2010 illustrate how the *yax cheel kab* was identified with both the Christian cross and the Tree of Good and Evil in the Garden of Eden, as well as having multiple Mayan associations.

    For the sense of the Aztec cross, see Azoulai 1993, pp. 80, 217.

18. Miller and Taube 1993, p. 186; Freidel et al. 1995, pp. 251–52.

19. Sachse (forthcoming). This whole analogy has been revealed by Frauke Sachse. The relevant passage of the *Popol Vuh* is folios 23v–32v.

20. Clastres 1975 [1995], p. 76.

21. Durston 2007, pp. 144, 169, 300; on Tunupa aka Illapa, who was also identified, curiously, with Santiago Saint James, see Baumann 1994, pp. 68, 284, also Salles-Reese 2010, p. 57.

22. Burkhart 1988, pp. 238–39.

23. Cited in Durston 2007, p. 324, as an event at the celebrations of Corpus Christi in 1570.

24. Durston 2007, pp. 64–65.

25. Bierhorst 1985, pp. 204–06; translation by Arthur J.O. Anderson 1984, p. xxi.

26. Baumann 1994, pp. 58–60; Salles-Reese 2010 passim.

27. Stanzione 2003.

28. Durston 2007, pp. 87–88.

29. See, for example, Bakewell 2010, p. 177; Durston 2007, pp. 83, 88; Ricard 1966, p. 230.

30. Zajicová 1999, p. 151.

31. Triana y Antorveza 1987, p. 414.

32. Ximénez ca. 1710, cap. iv, folio 34 recto; ed. Chinchilla, p. 70.

33. *Monumenta Peruana* iii, 624, cited in Melià 2003, p. 47.

34. Montoya 1640 [1876], *A los Padres Religiosos* . . .

35. Lugo 1619 [2010], p. 53, as translated by the author in Ostler 1995.

36. Ximénez 1929, vol. i, chapter xxv.

37. The system is analyzed, for both Tupi and Guaraní, in Bossong 2009, pp. 7–13.

38. Guasch 1996, p. 53, discussed by Bossong 2009, p. 8.

39. Due to Navarro 2004, p. 109.

40. Matthew 26:39, 43; Mark 14:36; Luke 22:42.

41. The passage is taken from Antonio de Araújo, 1618, *Catecismo na lingoa brasilica*, foll. 52v–53, quoted and analyzed by Navarro 2004, pp. 415–18.

42. Antonio Ruiz de Montoya, 1640, *Arte y Bocabulario de la lengua Guaraní*, Madrid: Juan Sánchez, p. 30.

43. Ostler 1994, pp. 221, 227.

44. Ostler 1999, p. 43; Ostler 1994, p. 211.

45. González de Pérez 1987, pp. 221, 281.

46. These conjectures are due, respectively, to: Diego F. Gómez (http://muysca.cubun.org/guahaioque, consulted Nov. 25, 2014); Facundo Saravia (personal contact, Nov. 21, 2014); María Stella González de Pérez 1996, p. 53.

47. González de Pérez 1987, p. 363, l.1, translated in Saravia 2014, p. 88.

48. Mantilla Ruiz 1986, pp. 70–71.

49. Lugo 1619, p. 152v.

50. González de Pérez 1987, p. 351 (folios 136v–137r).

51. Ibid., p. 291 (folio 59v).

52. Hanks 2010, pp. 131–33.

53. Leite, *Monumenta brasiliae* I (1538–1553) 1956, p. 16–17, cited in Otazú Melgarejo 2006, p. 140.

54. Montoya 1640 [1876], p. 298. The official Spanish translation was: *Has tenido toca-mientos con alguna muger? Tuuiste entonces polucion?*

55. Melià 2003, pp. 215, 231: Bernardino also had problems with the word *Tupã*, it must be said, in which he detected the name of a demon proscribed by Pope Zachary at a council in the eighth century.

56. Melià 2003, pp. 242–49.

Chapter 12

1. Sahagún 1583 [1993], pp. 6–7 (adopting Anderson's translation, but with "Mexican" for *Nahuatl*, and "songs'" for *canticles*). The points that I make on this work are derived largely from Anderson's fascinating Introduction.

2. It makes copious use of the *difrasismo*: a zeugma of two items stands for a third, or a pairing of two metaphors focuses a single idea that lies behind both.

3. This is preserved only in Sahagún's encyclopedic work *Historia General de las Cosas de Nueva España*. vii. 2 pp. 4v–4r.

4. Sahagún 1583 [1993], pp. 78–79.

5. Sahagún 1579, *Apéndice de la Postilla*: "this Lucifer whom you call Titlahuacan," viz Tezcatlipoca. Cited in Sahagún 1583 [1993], pp. xx, xxxix.

6. Anderson 1984; Sahagún 1583 [1993], pp. xxxii–xxxiii.

7. Anchieta 1597 [1999] Navarro: p. 208, n. 151.

8. Mannheim 1998, pp. 390–92. The original setting of the music can be heard at http://www.sunisapis.com.ar/pagina.php?id=recursos (accessed Dec. 20, 2014).

9. The hymn as a whole is called *Janaq Pachaq Kusikuynin* "Heaven's Bliss." Besides Mannheim 1998, it is given with different spelling, and Spanish and French translations, in Cáceres Romero et al. 1990, pp. 116–23.

10. Montoya 1639 [1892], p. 49 (translation mine).

11. Melià 2003, p. 307, citing Paolo Restivo's Guaraní translation of Montoya 1639.

12. Yapuguay 1727 [1953], *Introduction* by Guillermo Furlong (my translation), p. vi, citing Father José Peramás, but following Furlong's reinterpretation of Peramás's testimony. The citations in Latin are all by Peramás, reflecting the contemporary reception of Yapuguay.

13. Yapuguay 1727 [1953], p. vi (my translation from the Spanish).

14. Yapuguay 1724, Preface (my translation from the Spanish).

Chapter 13

1. Zabala 1977, p. 65, cited by Triana y Antorveza 1987, p. 531

2. Etymologies from Corominos 1987, s. vv., (my translation).

3. Gruzinski 1985 [1993], pp. 271–72.

4. Lorenzana, *Cartas pastorales y edictos*, Mexico 1770, quoted in Triana y Antorveza 1987, p. 504

Chapter 14

1. *De ratione studii ac legendi interpretandique auctores*, Paris 1511, in: *Desiderii Erasmi Roterodami Opera omnia*, ed. J. H. Waszink et al., Amsterdam 1971, vol. i–2, pp. 79–151.
2. http://en.wikipedia.org/wiki/List_of_Bible_translations_by_language.
3. http://en.wikipedia.org/wiki/List_of_translations_of_the_Quran.
4. http://mbingenheimer.net/tools/bibls/transbibl.html.
5. Auroux 1994, pp. 183–89.
6. Canons and Decrees of the Council of Trento, Fourth Session, April 8, 1546. *Sacrosancta Synodus . . . statuit et declarat, ut haec ipsa vetus et vulgata editio, quae longo tot saeculorum usu in ipsa Ecclesia probata est, in publicis lectionibus, disputationibus, praedicationibus et expositionibus pro authentica habeatur, et ut nemo illam reiicere quovis praetextu audeat vel praesumat.*
7. Ehrman 2005, p. 76.
8. Schwarz 1955, p. 50.
9. *Enarrationes in epistulas Pauli* xv.4 cited by Piltz 1981, p. 30; Hrabanus, dated to around 780–856, was archbishop of Mainz in Germany.
10. *Patrologia Latina*, cxiii, 28–29.
11. *De Accentibus et Orthographia Linguae Hebraicae* 1518, p. ii verso. Translated by Schwarz 1955, p. 70.
12. Prologue to the Complutensian, First Decad, p. i recto: *Quod si aliquibus in locis a grecis exemplaribus, qui passim circunferuntur, veterem translationem discrepare Erasmus senserat: si que per librariorum aut incuriam aut inscitiam errat progressu temporis codices nostros subintrarunt, reformanda videbantur: extrarium id operis futurum erat: seorsum illa erant annotanda non totum sacre scripture corpus denuo transferendum: non immutanda vetera:* "But if in some places Erasmus had perceived that in some passages the old translation clashed with the Greek texts, which are available everywhere: and if such things through the inattention or ignorance of booksellers, over time, had crept into our texts, they were clearly to be reformed. This would have been something foreign to the work: they should have been annotated separately, not the whole body of Holy Scripture to be changed from scratch: the old was not to be altered . . ."
13. Reuchlin, *Augenspiegel*, p. xvi recto-verso, quoted in Schwarz 1955, p. 74.
14. Letter of October 11, 1508 (no. 102 in his collected letters), cited by Schwarz 1955, p. 83.
15. Letter no. 15 in his collected letters, cited by Schwarz 1955, p. 71; cf Jerome, preface to the Book of Proverbs, *Patrologia Latina*, xxviii, 1244 *Si cui sane Septuaginta interpretum magis editio placet, habet eam a nobis olim emendatam. Neque enim sic nova cudimus, ut vetera destruamus. Et tamen cum diligentissime legerit, sciat magis nostra intelligi, que non in tertium vas transfusa coacuerint, sed statim de praelo purissime commendata testae, suum saporem servaverint.* "If anyone really prefers the Septuagint edition, he has it as I once emended it. For we do not hammer out our new wares so as to destroy the old. And yet when he has read it with full attention, may he better understand our work which has not gone sour from being drawn off into a third vessel, but which has kept its flavor, bottled in the greatest purity straight from the press."

    This thousand-year-old metaphor of Jerome's was used again by Reuchlin in 1512 in his work *In Septem Psalmos Poenitentiales*, p. a viii recto: *Non enim tanquam vinum est in tertium vas transfusum quod facile coacescit, sed de prelo mustum de racemis pressum. de veritate inquam hebraica effigiatum in illa ipsa lingua omnium linguarum matrice ut scribit Hieronymus. quam sanctam vocant, quam Origenes divinitus esse traditam asserit, quae sola est ante confusionem linguarum orta, quae nihil impuritatis continet ut Moyses aegyptius dilucide tractavit.* "For it is not like wine drawn off into a third vessel which easily goes sour, but liquor pressed from grapes from the press. From Hebrew truth I say it has been fashioned, in that very language which is the mother of all languages, as Jerome writes. He calls it holy, and Origen states it was handed down divinely, the only language to have arisen before the confusion of tongues [at Babel], which contains no impurity as Moses of Egypt lucidly employed it."

16. Schwarz 1955, p. 145.

17. *Dasz ich das Euangelium nicht von Menschen, sondern allein vom Himmel durch unsern Herrn Jesum Christum habe (Gal. i. 10ff)* . . . Letter to Kurfürst Friedrich, March 5, 1522. (Letters, vol. ii, 455, 39–43). Cf Saint Paul at v. 12 of the quoted passage: "for neither I received it of man, neither was I taught it, but by the revelation of Jesus Christ."

18. Martin Luther, *Tischreden* ii, # 2771a (Sept. 28–Nov. 23 1532)

19. Martin Luther, *Tischreden* ii, # 2758a, b (Sept. 28–Nov. 23 1532)

20. Martin Luther, *Tischreden* iv, # 5002 (May 21–June 11 1540)

21. "I have not the mistaken view that the holy can be penetrated through the industry of human talent. There is something in the holy that nobody can ever see unless it is shown to him by God: and Christ cannot be known to us without the Holy Ghost teaching us." (Melanchthon, *Encomium Eloquentiae*: cited by Schwarz 1955, p. 195.)

22. Martin Luther, *Tischreden* i, #961 (written 1530–1535). (Schwarz 1955, p. 202.)

23. Martin Luther, *Tischreden* iv, #5009 (written 21.v–11.vi.1540). (Schwarz 1955, p. 203.)

24. *Luthers Werke*, Weimarer Ausgabe, xv. pp. 37–41. (Schwarz 1955, pp. 195–96.)

25. Matthew 13:54–57: "Having come to his own country, he was teaching them in their synagogue, so that they were astonished, and were saying, 'Whence to this one this wisdom and the mighty works? is not this the carpenter's son? is not his mother called Mary, and his brethren James, and Joses, and Simon, and Judas? and his sisters—are they not all with us? whence, then, to this one all these?' and they were stumbled at him [Greek ἐσκανδαλίζοντο ἐν αὐτῷ—Vulgate *scandalizabantur in eo*]. And Jesus said to them, "A prophet is not without honor except in his own country, and in his own house:" Mark 6:3 is almost identical.

26. Augustine, *De Annunt. Dom.* iii: "What means this closed gate in the House of the Lord, except that Mary is to be ever inviolate? What does it mean that 'no man shall pass through it,' save that Joseph shall not know her? And what is this—'The Lord alone enters in and goeth out by it'—except that the Holy Ghost shall impregnate her, and that the Lord of angels shall be born of her? And what means this—'it shall be shut for evermore'—but that Mary is a virgin before His Birth, a virgin in His Birth, and a virgin after His Birth?"

27. MacCulloch 2003, pp. 101, 613–14; Heal 2014, pp. 4–6.

28. Luther 1530: "Ein sendbrief D. M. Luthers. Von Dolmetzschen und Fürbit der heiligenn" in *Dr. Martin Luthers Werke* (Weimar: Hermann Boehlaus Nachfolger, 1909), Band 30, Teil II, pp. 632–46: *Denn man mus nicht die buchstaben inn der Lateinischen sprachen fragen wie man sol Deudsch reden wie diese Esel thun Sondern man mus die mutter ihm hause die kinder auff der gassen den gemeinen man auff dem marckt drümb fragen und den selbigen auff das maul sehen wie sie reden und darnach dolmetschen so verstehen sie es denn und mercken das man Deudsch mit ihn redet.*

29. Commentaria Ioannis Cochlaei de actis et scriptis Martini Lutheri Saxonis 1522, p. 55: *mirum in modum multiplicabatur per chalcographos Novum Testamentum Lutheri ut etiam*

sutores & mulieres, & quilibet Idiotae, qui Teuthonicas literas utcunque didicerant, Novum illud Testamentam tanquam fontem omnis veritatis avidissime legerent.

30. Moffett 2005, pp. 176–78, and citing Henry Townley, 1824, *An Answer to the Abbé Dubois: In which the Various Wrong Principles, Misrepresentations, and Contradictions, Contained in His Work, Entitled "Letters on the State of Christianity in India," are Pointed Out; and The Evangelization of India Is, Both on Sound Principle and by Solid Fact, Demonstrated to be Practicable*, London: R. Clay.

31. Moffett 2005, p. 177.

32. Ellingworth 2007; Delisle and Woodsworth 2012, pp. 169–222. The first complete and widely distributed translation into Mandarin Chinese was by the missionary Robert Morrison, issued in 1823. This was actually preceded by the work of Joshua Marshman in 1813, who had been working with William Carey's Serampore group of Bible translators in India. For classical Chinese, the first was by Archimandrite Guri (Karpov) in 1846, under the title 新遺詔聖經.

33. https://en.wikipedia.org/wiki/Bible_translations, consulted January 25, 2015.

Chapter 15

1. Hadith 5751, Mishkat vol. 3.
2. Ibn Qutaibah, *Tā'wil al-Mushkil al Qur'ān*, 16.
3. Examples derived from Tibawi 1962.
4. Tibawi 1962, pp. 7–8.
5. Chejne 1974, pp. 51–53.
6. See above, p. 45. For speculation on why Islam was such an attractive proposition, see Hodgson 1974, vol. ii, pp. 533–42.
7. Bentley 1993, pp. 128–31; *Spice Digest*, Spring 2009, http://spice.stanford.edu; Hodgson 1974, vol. ii, pp.551–55.
8. Arnold 1913, p. 363ff; Hourani 1951, p. 61ff.
9. Kamal Hassan and bin Basri 2005, pp. 12–13; Hodgson 1974, vol. ii, pp. 542–51.
10. Burman 1998; cf the comparisons in d'Alverny 1946–1948, Bobzin 1993.
11. Burman 1998, p. 719.
12. See, e.g., Crone 2012, on how various pre-Islamic faiths contributed to the development and character of Islam in greater Iran after the Muslim conquest.
13. Høgel 2010, p. 73; cf Ostler 2010, p. 189.
14. As assessed by Høgel 2013.
15. Høgel 2010, pp. 72–74.
16. Muhammad al-Bukhari, *Sahih al-Bukhari*, iii.34.318 = vii.62.110.
17. *Milindapañha* iii.5.10.
18. E.g. Huntington 1990.
19. *Samyutta Nikāya* 22.87.
20. Arthur Waley, *Mélanges chinois et bouddhiques*, vol i, 1931–1932, Juillet (July) 1932, p. 354: "A definite embargo on the representation of Buddha is referred to in the Chinese Tripiṭaka. In Chapter 48 of the Vinaya of the Sarvāstivādins (Shih Sung Lu, *Taishoo Tripiṭaka*, xxiii, 352) there is a long passage which deals with the decoration of monasteries. Anāthapiṇḍika says to Buddha . . . [as quoted]."
21. Soper 1950, p. 148. Quoted from Shih Sung Lu, xlv, Nanjio no. 1115 (the Chinese translation made in 404 by Punyatara and Kumārajīva of the monastic regulations, *Vinaya,*

of the Sarvāstivādin sect); reprinted in the Japanese Tripataka, Daizōkyō, xxiii, no. 1435, p. 323. This is the same text read by Waley, though perhaps in a different translation.

22. *Cullavagga* vi.3.2.

23. See chapter 2, note 1.

24. See, for example, the convenient summary of a century's debate on the origins of the *buddha-rūpa* at Verma 2007, p. 3.

25. The Essence of the Further Tantra of the Glorious Kalachakra Tantra (*dPal dus-kyi 'khor-lo'i rgyud phyi-ma rgyud-kyi snying-po*, aka in Sanskrit *śrī-kālachakra-tantrottaratantra-hṛdaya*), cited at http://www.berzinarchives.com/web/en/archives \/study/islam/general/historical_survey_knowledge.html?query=idol (Feb. 19, 2015).

26. Credit to Vaziri 2012, pp. 37–38, for these examples; translations mine.

27. Rabbi Menachem Posner, *Must I Pray in Hebrew?* at www.chabad.org (accessed Feb. 19, 2015).

Conclusion

1. Sabbadini 1900 on Aulus Gellius: *Noctes Atticae* i.18: *quod vocabulum Graecum vetus* traductum *in linguam Romanam, proinde atque si primitus Latine fictum esset, resolverit in voces Latinas ratione etymologica falsa.* ". . . because he had resolved into Latin stems by false etymological reasoning an old Greek word which been borrowed into Latin, just as if it had been originally created in Latin." Apparently L. Aelius had provided a folk-etymology *levi-pes* "light-foot" for *lepus* "hare," when a Sicilian cognate λεπορıν suggests it is Greek.

2. This blessing in Tzutujil, a Mayan language, is drawn from Prechtel 1998.

Bibliography

Acosta, José de, 1588, *De procuranda indorum salute*, ed. Luciano Pereña, Madrid: Consejo superior de investigaciones cientificas [Reprint 1984]

Adalian, Rouben Paul, 2010, *Historical Dictionary of Armenia*, Washington, D.C.: Scarecrow Press

Anchieta, José de, 1597, *Teatro* [1999: selected and translated by Eduardo Navarro], São Paulo: Martins Fontes

Anderson, Arthur J.O., 1984, "The 'San Bernardino' of Sahagún's Psalmodia." *Indiana. Contributions to Ethnology and Linguistics, Archaeology and Physical Anthropology of Indian America.* Berlin: Gebr. Mann Verlag, no. 9

Anderson Scott, Charles A., 1885, *Ulfilas, Apostle of the Goths: Together with an Account of the Gothic Churches and Their Decline*, Cambridge: Macmillan and Bowes

Arakawa, Masaharu, 2011, "Aspects of Sogdian Trading Activities under the Western Turkic State and the Tang Empire," *Journal of Central Eurasian Studies*, vol. 2, pp. 25–40

Armstrong, Grant, 2009, "On the Copular Sentences in Yucatec Maya," *Proceedings of CILLA IV*, www.ailla.utexas.org/site/cilla4/Armstrong_CILLA_IV.pdf

Arnold, T.W., 1913, *The Preaching of Islam*, Delhi: Low Price Publications [Reprint 2006]

Auroux, Sylvain, 1994, *La révolution technologique de la grammatisation: introduction à l'histoire des sciences du langage.* Paris: Mardaga

Azoulai, Martine, 1993, *Les péchés du Nouveau Monde: les manuels pour la confession des Indiens XVIe–XVIIe siècles.* Paris: Albin Michel

Bakewell, Peter, 2010, *A History of Latin America to 1825*, Third Edition, Hoboken NJ: Wiley-Blackwell

Balkrishna, 1925, "The Beginnings of the Silk Industry in India," *Journal of Indian History*, April 1925, pp. 42–53

Ballesteros, J.C. Pablo, 1979, *La educación jesuítica en las reducciones de Guaraníes*, Paraná: Universidad Nacional de Entre Ríos.

Banerji, R. D., 1920, The Kharosthi Alphabet, *Journal of the Royal Asiatic Society of Great Britain & Ireland (New Series)* vol. 52, no. 2, October 1920, pp. 193–219

Baumann, Max Peter, 1994, *Kosmos der Anden: Weltbild und Symbolik indianischer Tradition in Südamerika.* Munich: Diederichs

Baumer, Christoph, 2006, *The Church of the East: An Illustrated History of Assyrian Christianity*, London and New York: I.B. Tauris

Beal, Samuel, 1884, *Si-Yu-Ki: Buddhist Records of the Western World*, Delhi: Low Price Publications [Reprint 1995]

Beckwith, Christopher I., 2009, *Empires of the Silk Road*, Princeton, NJ: Princeton University Press

Bentley, Jerry H., 1993, *Old World Encounters*, Oxford: Oxford University Press

Bickerman, Elias J., 1949, "The Name of Christians," *Harvard Theological Review*, vol. 42, no. 2 (April), pp. 109–24.

Bierhorst, John, 1985, *Cantares Mexicanos: Songs of the Aztecs*, Palo Alto, CA: Stanford University Press

Bobzin, Hartmut, 1993, "Latin Translations of the Koran: A Short Overview," *Der Islam*, vol. 70, pp. 194, 200.

Bossong, Georg, 2009, "The Typology of Tupi-Guarani as Reflected in the Grammars of Jesuit Missionaries. Anchieta (1595), Aragona (ca. 1625), Montoya (1640), and Restivo (1729)," *Historiographia Linguistica*, vol. 34, 2/3, pp. 225–58

Boucher, Daniel, 1991, "The *Pratītyasamutpādagāthā* and Its Role in the Medieval Cult of the Relics," *Journal of the International Association of Buddhist Studies*, vol. 14, no. 1, pp. 1–27

Boucher, Daniel, 1998, "Gāndhārī and the Earliest Chinese Buddhist Translations Reconsidered: The Case of the *Saddharmapuṇḍarīkasūtra*," *Journal of the American Oriental Society*, vol. 118, no. 4, pp. 471–90

Boucher, Daniel, Neil Schmid, and Tansen Sen, 2006, "The Scholarly Contributions of Professor Victor H. Mair: A Retrospective Survey," *Asia Major*, vol. 19, pt. 1–2, pp. 1–10

Boyle, Marjorie O'Rourke, 1977, "Sermo: Reopening the Conversation on Translating JN 1,1," *Vigiliae Christianae*, vol. 31, no. 3 (September), pp. 161–68

Bradley, Ian, 1999, *Celtic Christianity*, Edinburgh: Edinburgh University Press

Bremmer, Jan, 2008, "The Birth of Paradise," in *Greek Religion and Culture, the Bible, and the Ancient Near East.* Leiden/Boston: Brill

Brixhe, Claude, 2004, "Phrygian," in Roger D. Woodward, ed., *The Cambridge Encyclopaedia of the World's Ancient Languages*, Cambridge: Cambridge University Press, pp. 775–88

Brock, Sebastian, 1982 [1992-XI], "Clothing Metaphors as a Means of Theological Expression in Syriac Tradition," Section XI in *Studies in Syriac Christianity: History, Literature and Theology*, Aldershot, Hants, UK: Ashgate

——, 1996 [2006-III], "The Christology of the Church of the East," Section III in *Fire from Heaven: Studies in Syriac Theology and Liturgy*, Aldershot, Hants, UK: Ashgate

——, 1993 [2006-IV], "Christ 'the Hostage': A Theme in the East Syriac Liturgical Tradition and Its Origins," Section IV in *Fire from Heaven: Studies in Syriac Theology and Liturgy*, Aldershot, Hants, UK: Ashgate

——, 1993 [2006-XIII], "From Annunciation to Pentecost: The Travels of a Technical Term," Section XIII in *Fire from Heaven: Studies in Syriac Theology and Liturgy*, Aldershot, Hants, UK: Ashgate

Bronkhorst, Johannes, 2011, *Buddhism in the Shadow of Brahmanism*, Leiden: Brill

Brown, Peter, 1988, *The Body and Society: Men, Women and Sexual Renunciation in Early Christianity*, New York: Columbia University Press

Buck, Carl Darling, 1949, *A Dictionary of Selected Synonyms in the Principal Indo-European Languages*, Chicago and London: University of Chicago Press

Bugge, Sophus, 1895, *Über den Einfluss der armenischen Sprache auf die gotische*, Indogermanische Forschungen v.2, pp. 168–80, 274

Bühler, Karl, 1895, *Indian Studies III: On the Origin of the Indian Brāhma Alphabet*, Vienna: Sitzungsberichte der kaiserlichen Akademie der Wissenschaften: philosophisch-historische Classe, vol. 132, section 5

Burkhart, Louise M., 1988, "The Solar Christ in Nahuatl Doctrinal Texts of Early Colonial Mexico," *Ethnohistory*, vol. 35, no. 3 (Summer 1988), pp. 234–56

——, 1996, *Holy Wednesday: A Nahua Drama from Early Colonial Mexico*, Philadelphia: University of Pennsylvania Press

——, 2000, "The Native Translator as Critic: A Nahua Playwright's Interpretive Practice," in Robert Blair St. George, ed., *Possible Pasts: Becoming Colonial in Early America*, Albany, NY: Cornell University Press, pp 73–87

Burman, Thomas E., 1998, "Tafsīr and Translation: Traditional Arabic Qur'ān Exegesis and the Latin Qur'āns of Robert of Ketton and Mark of Toledo," *Speculum* 73, pp. 703–32

Cáceres Romero, Adolfo, and Inge Sichra, eds., 1990, *Poésie quechua*, Geneva: Patiño

Cahill, Thomas, 1995, *How the Irish Saved Civilization*, New York: Anchor/ Doubleday

Castenau-L'Estoile, Charlotte, 2000, *Les ouvriers d'une vigne sterile. Les jésuites et la conversion des indiens au Brésil 1580–1620*. Lisbon: Fundação Calouste-Gulbenkian

Chadwick, Nora, 1970, *The Celts*. New York: Penguin Books

Chejne, A.G., 1974, *Muslim Spain: Its History and Culture*. Minneapolis: University of Minnesota Press

Ch'en, Kenneth, 1964, *Buddhism in China: A Historical Survey*, Princeton, NJ: Princeton University Press

Clastres, Hélène, 1975, *La terre sans mal: le prophétisme tupi-guarani*, Paris: Éditions du Seuil. Translated by Jacqueline Grenez Brovender as *The Land-Without-Evil* [1995], Urbana, IL: University of Illinois Press

Cooper, Henry, 2003, *Slavic Scriptures: The Formation of the Church Slavonic Version of the Holy Bible*, Madison, NJ: Fairleigh Dickinson University Press

Corominas, Joan, 1987, *Breve diccionario etimológico de la lengua castellana*, Madrid: Gredos

Cribb, Joseph, 1980, "Kaniṣka's Buddha Coins: The Official Iconography of Śākyamuni and Maitreya," *Journal of the International Association of Buddhist Studies*, pp. 79–88

Crone, Patricia, 2012, *The Nativist Prophets of Early Islamic Iran*, Cambridge and New York: Cambridge University Press

Cumont, Franz, 1896, *Textes et Monuments figures relatifs aux Mystères de Mithra*, I, II, Brussels

Curran, John, 2000, *Pagan City and Christian Capital: Rome in the Fourth Century*, Oxford: Oxford University Press

d'Alverny, Marie-Thérèse, 1946–48, "Deux traductions latines du Coran au moyen âge," *Archives d'histoire doctrinale et littéraire*, pp. 69–113

de Alva, Bartholomé, 1634, *Confessionario Mayor, y Menor en Lengua Mexicana*, Mexico

de Blois, François, 2002, "*Naṣrānī* (Ναζωραῖος) and *ḥanīf* (ἐθνικός): Studies on the Religious Vocabulary of Christianity and Islam," *Bulletin of SOAS*, vol. 65, no. 1, pp. 1–30

de Vincenz, A., 1988–89, "West Slavic Elements in the Literary Language of Kievan Rus'," *Harvard Ukrainian Studies*, vol. 12/13, Proceedings of the International Congress Commemorating the Millennium of Christianity in Rus'-Ukraine, pp. 262–75

Delisle, Jean, and Judith Woodsworth, eds., 2012, *Translators through History*, Amsterdam and Philadelphia: John Benjamins

Dibble, Charles E., 1974, "The Nahuatlization of Christianity," in Munro S. Edmonson, ed., *Sixteenth-Century Mexico: The Work of Sahagún*, pp. 225–33

DIL, 1990, *Dictionary of the Irish Language*, Dublin: Royal Irish Academy (also available electronically as eDIL at http://edil.qub.ac.uk)

Dolan, Autumn, 2005, *The True Patron of Ireland: Saint Brigit and the Rise of Celtic Christianity*, Honors Thesis, Chattanooga: University of Tennessee

Dorfmann-Lazarev, Igor, 2004, *Arméniens et Byzantins à l'époque de Photius: deux débats théologiques après le triomphe de l'orthodoxie*, Louvain: Peeters

Driver, G.R., and Leonard Hodgson, 1925, trans. and eds., *Nestorius: The Bazaar of Heracleides*, Oxford: Clarendon Press

Dulaurier, Édouard, 1859, *Histoire, dogmes, traditions et liturgie de l'église arménienne orientale*, Paris: A. Durand

Durston, Alan, 2007, *Pastoral Quechua*, South Bend, IN: University of Notre Dame Press

Edgerton, Franklin, 2004, *Buddhist Hybrid Sanskrit Grammar and Dictionary*, vol. 2, New Delhi: Munshiram Manoharlal

Ehrman, Bart D., 2005, *Misquoting Jesus*, New York: HarperCollins

Ellingworth, Paul, 2007, "From Martin Luther to the English Revised Version," in Noss 2007, pp. 105–39

Elverskog, Johan, 2010, *Buddhism and Islam on the Silk Road*, Philadelphia: University of Pennsylvania Press

Everett, Daniel, 2009, *Don't Sleep, There are Snakes*, London: Profile

Fedotov, Georgy P., 1946–1966, *The Russian Religious Mind* (vol. 1: *Kievan Christianity*; vol. 2: *The Middle Ages, 13th to 15th centuries*), Cambridge, MA: Harvard University Press

Finegan, Jack, 1992, *The Archeology of the New Testament*, Princeton, NJ: Princeton University Press

Fontaine, Michael, 2015, *Joannes Burmeister: Aulularia and Other Inversions of Plautus*, Leuven: Leuven University Press

Forbes, R.J., 1964, *Studies in Ancient Technology*, vol. 9, Leiden: Brill

Fox, Robin Lane, 1987, *Pagans and Christians*, New York: Knopf

Francis, J. Michael, 2006, "Language and the 'True Conversion' to the Holy Faith: A Document from the Archivium Romanum Societatis Iesu, Rome, Italy, *The Americas*, vol. 62, no. 3, pp. 445–53

Freidel, David, Linda Schele, and Joy Parker, 1995, *Maya Cosmos*, New York: Morrow

Fuchs, Walter, 1930, "Zur technischen Organisation der Übersetzungen buddhistischer Schriften ins Chinesische," *Asia Major*, vol. 6, pp. 84–103

Geiger, Wilhelm, 1916 [1943], *Pāli Literature and Language* (trans. Batakrishna Ghosh), New Delhi: Munshiram Manoharlal

Glass, Andrew, 2000, *A Preliminary Study of Kharoṣṭhī Script Paleography*, M.A. Thesis, University of Washington

González de Pérez, María Stella, 1987, "*Diccionario y gramática chibcha*," Manuscrito anónimo de la Biblioteca Nacional de Colombia, Bogotá: Instituto Caro y Cuervo

——, 1996, "Los sacerdotes muiscas y la paleontología lingüística," *Boletín Museo de Oro*, vol. 40 (January–June), pp. 37–62

Granstrem, Ye. E., 1955, "On the Origin of the Glagolitic Alphabet" *Akademija Nauk SSSR*, TODRL (Trudy Otdela Drevnerusskoj Literatury), vol. 11, pp. 300–13

Green, D.H., 1998, *Language and History in the Early Germanic World*, Cambridge: Cambridge University Press

Gruzinski, Serge, 1985, *La conquête de l'imaginaire*. Paris: Gallimard; [1993] Translated by Eileen Corrigan as *The Conquest of Mexico*, Cambridge: Polity Press

Guasch, Antonio, S.J., 1996, *El idioma guaraní: gramática y antología de prosa y verso*, Asunción: CEPAG

Hamnett, Brian R., 1999, *Concise History of Mexico*. Cambridge: Cambridge University Press

Hanks, William F., 1990, *Referential Practice: Language and Lived Space among the Maya*, Chicago: University of Chicago Press

——, 2010, *Converting Words: Maya in the Age of the Cross*, Berkeley: University of California Press

Harmatta, J., 1994, *History of Civilizations of Central Asia*, vol. 2: *The Development of Sedentary and Nomadic Civilizations: 700 B.C. to A.D. 250*, Paris: UNESCO

Harrison, Paul, 2010, "Experimental Core Samples of Chinese Translations of Two Buddhist *Sūtras* in the Light of Recent Sanskrit Manuscript Discoveries," *Journal of the International Association of Buddhist Studies*, vol. 31, no. 1–2, 2008 (2010), pp. 205–50

Heal, Bridget, 2014, *The Cult of the Virgin Mary in Early Modern Germany: Protestant and Catholic Piety, 1500–1648*, Cambridge: Cambridge University Press

Heather, Peter, 1986, "The Crossing of the Danube and the Gothic Conversion," *Greek, Roman and Byzantine Studies*, vol. 27, no. 3, pp. 289–318

Hen, Yitzhak, 1995, *Culture and Religion in Merovingian Gaul: A.D. 481–751*, Leiden: Brill

Hodgson, Marshall G.S., 1974, *The Venture of Islam*, vol. 3, Chicago: University of Chicago Press

Høgel, Christian, 2010, "An early Anonymous Greek Translation of the Qur'ān: The Fragments from Niketas Byzantios' *Refutatio* and the Anonymous *Abjuratio*," *Collectanea Christiana Orientalia* vol. 7, pp. 65–119

——, 2013, "The Greek Qur'an: Scholarship and Evaluations," *Orientalia Suecana*, vol. 61 (Suppl.), pp. 173–80

Hourani, George F., 1951 (revised John Carswell 1995), *Arab Seafaring*, Princeton, NJ: Princeton University Press

Hulsewé, A.F.P., and M.A.N. Loewe, 1979, *China in Central Asia: The Early Stage 125 BC–AD 23: An Annotated Translation of Chapters 61 and 96 of the History of the Former Han Dynasty*. Leiden: Brill

Huntington, S.L., 1990, "Early Buddhist Art and the Theory of Aniconism," *Art Journal*, vol. 49, no. 4 (Winter), pp. 401–08

Isatchenko, A.V., 1963, "On the Question of the Irish Mission to the Slavs of Pannonia and Moravia," *Questions of Slavic Linguistics*, issue 7, pp. 43–72.

Jackson, Kenneth H., 1953, *Language and History in Early Britain*, Edinburgh: Edinburgh University Press

Jakobson, Roman, 1965, "The Byzantine Mission to the Slavs. Report on the Dumbarton Oaks Symposium of 1964 and Concluding Remarks about Crucial Problems of Cyrillo-Methodian Studies," *Dumbarton Oaks Papers*, xix, pp. 257–65

Jarrott, C. A. L., 1964, "Erasmus' 'In Principio Erat Sermo': A Controversial Translation," *Studies in Philology*, vol. 61, no. 1 (January), pp. 35–40

Johnston, E.H., 1936, *The Buddhacarita or Acts of the Buddha*. Part I: Sanskrit text of cantos I–XIV; Part II: Cantos I to XIV translated from the original Sanskrit supplemented by the Tibetan version, together with an introduction and notes. Lahore. [Reprint 1984] Delhi: Motilal Banarsidass

Jones, A.H.M., 1959, "Were Ancient Heresies National or Social Movements in Disguise?" *Journal of Theological Studies*, vol. 10, pt. 2, (October), pp. 280–98

Jones, J.J., trans., 1949–56, *The Mahāvastu*, 3 vols., London: Luzac

Kamal Hassan, M., and Ghazali bin Basri, 2005, *Encyclopedia of Malaysia*, vol. 10, *Religions and Beliefs*, Singapore: Archipelago Press

Kamen, Henry, 2002, *Spain's Road to Empire*, London: Penguin

Karashima, Seishi, 1992, *The Textual Study of the Chinese Versions of the Saddharmapuṇḍarīkasūtra in the Light of the Sanskrit and Tibetan Versions*. Bibliotheca Indologica et Buddhologica 3. Tokyo: Sankibo Press

Karttunen, Frances, 1990, "Conventions of Polite Speech in Nahuatl," *Estudios de Cultura Nahuatl* vol. 20, pp. 281–96

Knowlton, Timothy W., and Gabrielle Vail, 2010, "Hybrid Cosmologies in Mesoamerica: A Reevaluation of the *Yax Cheel Cab*, a Maya World Tree," *Ethnohistory*, vol. 57, no. 4, pp. 709–39

Konow, Sten, 1929, *Kharoshṭhī Inscriptions with the Exception of Those of Aśoka*. Corpus Inscriptionum Indicarum, Vol. II, Part I. Calcutta: Government of India Central Publication Branch

Krishan, Yuvraj, 1996, *The Buddha Image: Its Origin and Development*, New Delhi: Munshiram Manoharlal

Kruger, G. van W., 1975, *Inleiding tot die studie van Nuwe Testamentiese Grieks*, Stellenbosch, South Africa: T. Wever

Lambert, Pierre-Yves, 1997, *La langue gauloise*, Paris: Éditions Errance

Landa, Diego de, 1566, *Relación de las cosas de Yucatán*, ed. Miguel Rivera, Madrid: Historia 16 [Reprint 1985]

Lee, A.D., 1991, "The Role of Hostages in Roman Diplomacy with Sasanian Persia," *Historia*, vol. 40, no. 3, pp. 366–74

León Portilla, Miguel, 1992, *Literaturas indígenas de México*, Mexico : Editorial MAPFRE

Li, Shaman Hwui, and Samuel Beal, 1914, *The Life of Hiuen-Tsiang*, London: Kegan Paul, Trench and Trübner [reissued by Kessinger Publishing's Rare Reprints, www.kessinger.net]

Liddell, Henry, Robert Scott, Sir Henry Stuart Jones, eds., 1940, *A Greek-English Lexicon*, Oxford at the Clarendon Press

Lietzmann, Hans, 1979, *Mass and Lord's Supper: A Study in the History of the Liturgy*, vol. 1, Leiden: Brill

Lingenthal, Karl Eduard Zachariae von, 1881, *Imperatoris Iustiniani Novellae quae vocantur sive constitutiones quae extra codicem*, Leipzig: Teubner

Liu, Xinru, 1988, *Ancient India and Ancient China: Trade and Religious Exchanges AD 1–600*, Delhi: Oxford University Press

Lockhart, James, 1992, *The Nahuas after the Conquest*, Stanford, CA: Stanford University Press

Lugo, Fray Bernardo de, 1619 [2010] *Gramática en la lengua general del Nuevo Reino, llamada mosca*, Madrid: Bernardino de Guzmán. [Jorge Augusto Gamboa Mendoza, ed., 2010, Bogotá: Biblioteca del Nuevo Reino de Granada]

MacCormick, Sabine, 1993, *Religion in the Andes: Vision and Imagination in Early Colonial Peru*, Princeton, NJ: Princeton University Press

MacCulloch, Diarmaid, 2003, *Reformation: Europe's House Divided 1490–1700*, London: Allen Lane

Mackensen, Lutz, 1966, *Reclams Etymologisches Wörterbuch der deutschen Sprache*, Stuttgart: Philipp Reclam jun.

MacKenzie, D.N., 1971, *A Concise Pahlavi Dictionary*, London, New York, Toronto: Oxford University Press

Mallory, J.P., and D.Q. Adams, 2006, *The Oxford Introduction to Proto-Indo-European and the Proto-Indo-European World*, Oxford and New York: Oxford University Press

Mango, Cyril, 1980, *Byzantium: The Empire of the New Rome*, London: Weidenfeld and Nicholson. References are to the 1994 edition reissued by Phoenix.

Mannheim, Bruce, 1991, *The Language of the Inka since the European Invasion*, Austin: University of Texas Press

——, 1998, "A Nation Surrounded." In Elizabeth Hill Boone and Tom Cummins, eds., *Native Traditions in the Postconquest World*, Washington, D.C.: Dumbarton Oaks, pp. 383–420

Mantilla Ruiz, Luis Carlos, 1986, *Fray Pedro Simón y su vocabulario de americanismos*, Bogotá: Instituto Caro y Cuervo

McManus, Damian, 1983, "A Chronology of the Latin Loan-Words in Early Irish," *Ériu*, vol. 34, pp. 21–71

——, 1984, "On Final Syllables in the Latin Loan-Words in Early Irish," *Ériu*, vol. 35, pp. 137–62

——, 1991, *A Guide to Ogam*, Maynooth: An Sagart

Melià, Bartomeu, 1997, *El guaraní conquistado y reducido*, Asunción: CEPAG

——, 2003, *La lengua guaraní en el Paraguay colonial*, Asunción: CEPAG

Mendieta, Gerónimo de, 1596, *Historia Eclesiástica Indiana*, Mexico: Porrua [Reprint 1980]

Metzger, Bruce, 1945, "St. Jerome's Testimony Concerning the Second Grade of Mithraic Initiation," *American Journal of Philology*, vol. 66, no. 3, pp. 225–33

Meyendorff, John, 1989, *Byzantium and the Rise of Russia*, Crestwood, NY: St. Vladimir's Seminary Press

Miller, Mary, and Karl Taube, eds., 1993, *The Gods and Symbols of Ancient Mexico and the Maya*, London: Thames and Hudson

Moffett, Samuel Hugh, 1998, *A History of Christianity in Asia, Beginnings to 1500*, vol. 1, Maryknoll, NY: Orbis

——, 2005, *A History of Christianity in Asia, 1500–1900*, vol. 2, Maryknoll, NY: Orbis

Monod-Becquelin, Aurore, 1997, *Parlons tzeltal*, Paris and Montréal: L'Harmattan

Montoya, Antonio Ruiz de, 1639, *Tesoro de la lengua Guaraní*, Madrid: Iuan Sanchez [1876 facsimile, Leipzig: B.G. Teubner]

——, 1639, *Conquista espiritual hecha por los religiosos de la Compañía de Jesús en las provincias del Paraguay, Paraná, Uruguay y Tape*, Madrid: Iuan Sanchez [1892 facsimile, Bilbao: Corazón de Jesús]

——, 1640, *Arte y Bocabulario de la lengua Guaraní*, Madrid: Iuan Sanchez

——, 1640, *Catecismo de la lengua Guaraní*, Madrid: Iuan Sanchez [1876 facsimile, Leipzig: B.G. Teubner]

Nagel Beilicke, Federico Beals, 1994, "El aprendizaje del idioma náhuatl entre los franciscanos y los jesuitas en Nueva España," UNAM IIH: *Estudios de Cultura Náhuatl*, vol. 24, pp. 419–41

Nattier, Jan, 1990, "Church Language and Vernacular Language in Central Asian Buddhism," *Numen*, vol. 37, no. 2 (December), pp. 195–219

——, 1991, *Once Upon a Future Time: Studies in a Buddhist Prophecy of Decline*, New Delhi: Jain Publishing

——, 1992, "The Heart Sūtra: A Chinese Apocryphal Text?" *Journal of the International Association of Buddhist Studies*, vol. 15, no. 2, pp. 153–223

Navarro, Eduardo de Almeida, 2004, *Método Moderno de Tupi Antigo*, São Paulo: Global

Neelis, Jason, 2011, *Early Buddhist Transmission and Trade Networks*, Leiden: Brill

Nersessian, Vrej Nerses, 2007, *Armenian Christianity*. In Parry, ed., pp. 23–46

Norman, K.R., 1983, "The Pratyeka-Buddha in Buddhism and Jainism." In P. Denwood and A. Piatigorsky, eds., *Buddhist Studies, Ancient and Modern*, London: Curzon, pp. 92–106

North, Richard, 1997, *Heathen Gods in Old English Literature*, Cambridge: Cambridge University Press

Noss, Philip A., 2007, *A History of Bible Translation*, Rome: Edizioni di storia e letteratura

OED, *Oxford English Dictionary, OED Online*. Oxford: Oxford University Press

Ornsby, Robert, ed., 1865, *The Greek Testament*, Dublin: James Duffy

Ostler, Nicholas, 1994, "Syntactic Typology of Muisca: A Sketch." In Peter Cole, G. Hermon, and M.D. Martin, eds., *Language in the Andes*, Newark, DE: University of Delaware Press, pp. 205–30

——, 1995, "Fray Bernardo de Lugo: Two Sonnets in Muisca." In Duna Troiani, ed., *La "découverte" des langues et des écritures d'Amérique: Amerindia* vols. 19–20, Paris

——, 1999, "Las oraciones y catecismo breve en muisca del MS 2922: historia, texto, terminología." In Sabine Dedenbach-Salazar Sáenz and Lindsey Crickmay, eds., *La Lengua de Cristianización en Latinoamérica: Catequización e instrucción en lenguas amerindias.* (Bonner Amerikanistische Studien, vol. 32), Markt Schwaben: Saurwein, pp. 41–59

——, 2005, *Empires of the Word*, London and New York: HarperCollins

——, 2007, *Ad Infinitum*, London: HarperCollins, and New York: Walker

——, 2010, *The Last Lingua Franca*, London: Penguin, and New York: Walker

Otazú Melgarejo, Angélica, 2006, *Práctica y Semántica en la Evangelización de los Guaraníes del Paraguay (S. XVI-XVIII)*, Asunción: Centro de Estudios Paraguayos "Antonio Guasch"

Parry, Ken, ed., 2007, *The Blackwell Companion to Eastern Christianity*, Chichester: Blackwell Publishing

Piltz, Anders, 1981, *The World of Medieval Learning*, English translation of *Medeltidens lärda värld* (Stockholm: Carmina, 1978) by David Jones. Oxford: Basil Blackwell

Poole, Stafford, 1981, "Church Law on the Ordination of Indians and Castas in New Spain," *Hispanic American Historical Review*, vol. 61, no. 4, pp. 637–80

Prechtel, Martín, 1998, *Secrets of the Talking Jaguar*, New York: Jeremy P. Tarcher/ Putnam

Prieto, Andrés I., 2010, "Reading the Book of Genesis in the New World: José de Acosta and Bernabé Cobo on the Origins of the American Population," *Hispanófila*, vol. 158, pp. 1–19

Rangarajan, L.N., 1992, *Kautilya: The Arthashastra*, New Delhi: Penguin Books

Rapp, Jr., Stephen H., 2007, *Georgian Christianity*. In Parry, ed., pp. 137–55

Reynolds, Gabriel Said, ed., 2008, *The Qur'ān in Its Historical Context*, London and New York: Routledge

Rhys Davids, T. W., 1890, 1894, *The Questions of King Milinda, Translated From Pāli, Parts I, II,* Oxford: Oxford University Press, later reprints Delhi: Motilal Banarsidass

Ricard, Robert, 1966, *The Spiritual Conquest of Mexico: An Essay on the Apostolate and the Evangelizing Methods of the Mendicant Orders in New Spain, 1523–1572* (trans. Lesley Byrd Simpson), Berkeley: University of California Press

Rochette, Bruno, 1997, *Le latin dans le monde grec*, vol. 233, Brussels: Latomus

Rodrigues, Aryon Dall'Igna, 2010, "Tupi, tupinambá, línguas gerais e português do Brasil." In Volker Noll and Wolf Dietrich, eds, 2010, *O português e o tupi no Brasil*, São Paulo: Contexto

Rong, Xinjiang, 2000, "The Migrations and Settlements of the Sogdians in the Northern Dynasties, Sui and Tang," *China Archaeology and Art Digest*, vol. 4, no. 1, pp. 117–63

Runciman, Stephen, 1977, *The Byzantine Theocracy*, Cambridge: Cambridge University Press

Russell, James, 1991–2011, "Christianity i: In Pre-Islamic Persia: Literary Sources." In *Encyclopaedia Iranica*

Russell, James C., 1994, *The Germanization of Early Medieval Christianity*, New York: Oxford University Press

Sabbadini, Remigio, 1900, «Del tradurre i classici in Italia», *Atene e Roma*, vol. 3, pp. 19–20, col. 202–203.

Sachse, Frauke, forthcoming "The Expression of Christian Concepts in Colonial K'iche' Missionary Texts." In Sabine Dedenbach-Salazar Sáenz, ed., Collectanea Instituti Anthropos, *La transmisión de conceptos cristianos a las lenguas amerindias: Estudios sobre textos y contextos en la época colonial*, Sankt Augustin, Germany: Anthropos

Sadakata, Akira, 1996, *Buddhist Cosmology* (trans. Gaynor Sekimori), Tokyo: Kosei

Sadeghi, Behnam, and Mohsen Goudarzi, 2012, "Ṣanʿāʾ 1 and the Origins of the Qurʾān," *Der Islam*, vol. 87, no. 1–2, pp. 1–129

Sahagún, Fray Bernardino de, 1576, *Historia General de las cosas de Nueva España*, Madrid: Alianza [Reprint 1988]

——, 1583 [1993], *Bernardino de Sahagún's Psalmodia Christiana* (trans. and ed., Arthur J. O. Anderson), Salt Lake City: University of Utah Press

Salles-Reese, Verónica, 2010, *From Viracocha to the Virgin of Copacabana: Representation of the Sacred at Lake Titicaca*, Austin, TX: University of Texas Press

Salomon, Richard, 1998, Indian Epigraphy, New York: Oxford University Press

——, 2001, "'Gāndhārī Hybrid Sanskrit': New Sources for the Study of the Sanskritization of Buddhist Literature," *Indo-Iranian Journal*, vol. 44, no. 3, pp. 241–52

——, 2007, "Gāndhārī in the Worlds of India, Iran and Central Asia," *Bulletin of the Asia Institute*, New Series, vol. 21, pp. 179–92

Sarat Chandra Das, ed. (n.d.), "Stupavadana," *Journal and Text of the Buddhist Society of India*, vol. 11, pt. 1, p. 15

Saravia, Facundo Manuel, 2014, "Sermón del Génesis y la cristiandad en lengua chibcha o muisca. Transcripción, análisis y traducción al castellano de un texto doctrinal del siglo xvii." In Yaty Andrea Urquijo Ortiz, Marcela

Hernández Chacón eds., *Portal de lenguas de Colombia: diversidad lingüística y cultural*, Bogotá: Instituto Caro y Cuervo, pp. 65–103

Sarkissian, Karekin, 1975, *The Council of Chalcedon and the Armenian Church*, 2nd ed., New York: Armenian Church Prelacy

Schmidt, Benjamin, 2001, *Innocence Abroad: The Dutch Imagination and the New World, 1570–1670*, Cambridge: Cambridge University Press

Schopen, Gregory, 1985, "The Bodhigarbhālaṅkāralakṣa and Vimaloṣṇīṣa Dhāraṇīs in Indian Inscriptions," *Wiener Zeitschrift für die Kunde Südasiens und Archiv für indische Philosophie*, vol. 29, pp. 119–49

Schwarz, W., 1955, *Principles and Problems of Biblical Translation*, Cambridge: Cambridge University Press

Sen, Tansen, 2002, "The Revival and Failure of Buddhist Translations During the Song Dynasty," *T'oung Pao*, vol. 83, pp. 27–80

Sims-Williams, Nicholas, 2000, "A Bactrian Buddhist Manuscript." In J. Braarvig, ed., *Manuscripts in the Schøyen collection, I: Buddhist manuscripts*. Norway: Hermes Publishing, pp. 275–77. Also at: http://www.indologie.uni-muenchen. de/dokumente/publ_hartmann/exhibition_catalogue.pdf, pp. 72–73

——, 2001, "The Sogdian Ancient Letter II." In M.G. Schmidt and W. Bisang, eds., *Philologica et Linguistica. Historia, Pluralitas, Universitas. Festschrift für Helmut Humbach zum 80. Geburtstag am 4. Dezember 2001*, Trier: Wissenschaftlicher Verlag, pp. 267–80

——, 2012, "Bactrian Historical Inscriptions of the Kushan Period," *The Silk Road*, vol. 10, pp. 76–80

Soper, Alexander Coburn, 1950, *The Art Bulletin*, vol. 32, no. 2 (June), pp. 147–51

Stancliffe, Claire, 1982, "Red, White and Blue Martyrdom." In David Dumville, ed., *Ireland in Early Medieval Europe: Studies in Memory of Kathleen Hughes*, Cambridge: Cambridge University Press, pp. 21–46

Stanzione, Vincent, 2003, *Rituals of Sacrifice*, Albuquerque, NM: University of New Mexico Press

Stark, Rodney, 1996, *The Rise of Christianity*, Princeton, NJ: Princeton University Press

Stokes, Whitley, and John Strachan, 1903, *Thesaurus Palaeohibernicus: A Collection of Old-Irish Glosses Scholia Prose and Verse*, vol. II: *Non-Biblical Glosses and Scholia*. Cambridge: Cambridge University Press

Sullivan, Richard E., 1954, "Early Medieval Missionary Activity: A Comparative Study of Eastern and Western Methods," *Church History*, vol. 23, pp. 28–30

Suny, Ronald Grigor, 1988, *The Making of the Georgian Nation*, Bloomington, IN: Indian University Press and Stanford, CA: Hoover Institution Press

Tachiaos, Anthony-Emil N., 2001, *Cyril and Methodius of Thessalonica: The Acculturation of the Slavs*, Crestwood, NY: St. Vladimir's Seminary Press

Tardif, Adolphe, 1852, "Fragment d'homélie en langue celtique." In: *Bibliothèque de l'école des chartes*, vol. (tome) 13, pp. 193–202

Tarn, W.W., 1951, *The Greeks in Bactria and India*, Cambridge: Cambridge University Press

Taylor, William B., 1987, "The Virgin of Guadalupe in New Spain: An Enquiry into the History of Marian Devotion," *American Ethnologist*, vol. 14, pp. 9–33

Terrien de La Couperie, Albert Étienne, 1886–7, "Did Cyrus Introduce Writing to India?" *Babylonian and Oriental Record*, vol. 1, pp. 58–64

Thackston, W.M., 1999, *Introduction to Syriac*, Bethesda, MD: Ibex

Thakur, Amarnath, 1996, *Buddha and Buddhist Synods in India and Abroad*, New Delhi: Abhinav Publications

Thapar, Romila, 2004, *Early India: From the Origins to AD 1300*, Oakland, CA: University of California Press

Thomson, Francis, 1992, SS. "Cyril and Methodius and a Mythical Western Heresy: Trilinguism," *Analecta Bollandiana*, vol. 110, pp. 67–122

——, 1999, *The Reception of Byzantine Culture in Mediaeval Russia*, Variorum Collected Studies Series, Aldershot, Hants, UK: Ashgate

Tibawi, A.L., 1962, "Is the Qur'an Translatable? Early Muslim Opinion," *The Muslim World*, vol. 52, no. 1, pp. 4–16

Triana y Antorveza, Humberto, 1987, *Las lenguas indígenas en la historia social del Nuevo reino de Granada*. Bogotá: Instituto Caro y Cuervo

Turcan, Robert, 1992, *The Cults of the Roman Empire*, Oxford: Blackwell (Published in French as *Cultes orientaux dans le monde romain*, 1989)

Vaziri, Mostafa, 2012, *Buddhism in Iran: An Anthropological Approach to Traces and Influences*. London: Palgrave Macmillan

Veidlinger, Daniel, 2006, "When a Word is Worth a Thousand Pictures: Mahāyāna Influence on Theravāda Attitudes towards Writing," *Numen*, vol. 53, no. 4, pp. 405–447

Vaissière, Étienne de la, 2006, *Sogdians in China: A Short History and Some New Discoveries*, http://www.silkroadfoundation.org/newsletter/december/new_discoveries.htm

Verma, Archana, 2007, *Cultural and Visual Flux at Early Historical Bagh in Central India*, British Archaeological Reports (December 15)

Vermes, Geza, 2012, *Christian Beginnings*, London: Allen Lane

von Hinüber, Oskar, 1996, *A Handbook of Pāli Literature*, Berlin: de Gruyter

Warder, A.K., 2000, *Indian Buddhism*, New Delhi: Motilal Banarsidass

Watson, G.R., 1969, *The Roman Soldier*, London: Thames and Hudson

White, David Gordon, 1966, *The Alchemical Body: Siddha Traditions in Medieval India*, Chicago: University of Chicago Press

Williams, Paul, 1989, *Mahāyāna Buddhism: the Doctrinal Foundations*, London: Routledge

Ximénez, Francisco, ca. 1710, *Arte de las tres lenguas Kaqchikel, K'iche' y Tz'utujil*, Rosa Helena Chinchilla, ed., Guatemala: Academia de Geografía e Historia de Guatemala [Reprint 1993]

———, 1929, *Historia de la Provincia de San Vicente de Chiapa y Guatemala*, Guatemala: Academia de Geografía e Historia de Guatemala [Reprint 1971]

Xing, Guang, 2013, "Buddhist Impact on Chinese Language," *Journal of Centre for Buddhist Studies, Sri Lanka* (JCBSSL), vol. 10, pp. 155–76

Yapuguay, Nicolás, 1724, (Con intro. de Paulo Restivo.) *Explicaciones de el Catecismo en lengua guaraní. En el pueblo de Santa María la Mayor.*

———, 1727, *Sermones y exemplos en lengua guaraní. En el pueblo de Santa María la Mayor.* (Con intro. de Guillermo Furlong.) Buenos Aires: Guarania [Reprint 1953]

Zabala, Silvio, 1977, *El castellano, ¿lengua obligatoria?*, Mexico City: Centro de Estudios de Historia de México, CONDUMEX

Zajicová, Lenka, 1999, *Algunos aspectos de las reducciones jesuíticas del Paraguay: la organización interna, las artes, las lenguas y la religión.* Acta Universitatis Palackianae Olomucensis, Facultas Philosophica, 74, pp. 145–57

Zakka I Iwas, Patriarch Ignatius, 1983, *The Syrian Orthodox Church of Antioch at a Glance.* sor.cua.edu/Pub/PZakkaı/SOCAtAGlance.html (consulted: January 22, 2014)

Zürcher, Erik, 1972, *The Buddhist Conquest of China*, Leiden: Brill

Zürcher, Erik, Seishi Karashima, and Huanming Qin, 1996, "Vernacular Elements in Medieval Chinese Texts," *Sino-Platonic Papers*, no. 71. Philadelphia: University of Pennsylvania, department of Asian and Middle Eastern Studies, March 1996

Zwartjes, Otto, 2011, *Portuguese Missionary Grammars in Asia, Africa and Brazil, 1550–1800*, Amsterdam/Philadelphia: John Benjamins

Index

A Note on the Author

Nicholas Ostler is the author of *The Last Lingua Franca: English Until the Return of Babel, Ad Infinitum: A Biography of Latin,* and *Empires of the Word: A Language History of the World.* He chairs the Foundation for Endangered Languages (www.ogmios.org), a charity that supports small communities worldwide to better know and use their languages. A British scholar with direct knowledge of two dozen languages living and dead, Ostler has lived in India, the United States, and Japan, but now makes his home in Hungerford, England, just west of London.